COVENANT & CONVERSATION
A WEEKLY READING OF THE JEWISH BIBLE
NUMBERS: THE WILDERNESS YEARS

Other works by the author

Rabbi Jonathan Sacks

COVENANT & CONVERSATION

A Weekly Reading of the Jewish Bible

NUMBERS: THE WILDERNESS YEARS

The Koschitzky Edition

Maggid Books & The Orthodox Union

Covenant & Conversation
Numbers: The Wilderness Years

First Edition, 2017

Maggid Books
An imprint of Koren Publishers Jerusalem Ltd.

POB 8531, New Milford, CT 06776-8531, USA
& POB 4044, Jerusalem 9104001, Israel
www.maggidbooks.com

Cover image: *Balaam and His Ass*, Rembrandt

The Covenant & Conversation online parsha commentary has been generously sponsored by the Maurice Wohl Charitable Foundation.

The publication of this book was made possible through the generous support of *Torah Education in Israel*.

ISBN 978-1-59264-023-2, *hardcover*

A CIP catalogue record for this title is available from the British Library

Printed and bound in the United States

כֹּה אָמַר יְהֹוָה זָכַרְתִּי לָךְ חֶסֶד נְעוּרַיִךְ אַהֲבַת כְּלוּלֹתָיִךְ לֶכְתֵּךְ אַחֲרַי בַּמִּדְבָּר בְּאֶרֶץ לֹא זְרוּעָה:

(ירמיה ב, ב)

This is what the Lord has said,
I remember of you
the devotion of your youth,
your love when you were a bride,
how you followed me in the desert,
through a land not sown

(JER. 2:2)

≈

To Tamar

*Following you
with enduring devotion,
love, and awe*

Jono, Ikey, Kineret, Max, Ellian, Yishai, and Keren

Contents

Numbers: Then and Now

November 1989. The Berlin Wall falls. The Cold War comes to an end. The Soviet Union begins to implode. A young American political scientist, Francis Fukuyama, captures widespread attention with an essay entitled "The End of History."[1] In it he argues that the two great institutions of the modern West, liberal democracy and the market economy, have not only proved stronger than Soviet communism but are about to conquer the world. People are no longer willing to make the sacrifices or endure the privations of war for the sake of nation, class, or creed. John Lennon's vision in his 1971 song "Imagine" – "Nothing to kill or die for / and no religion too / imagine all the people / living life in peace" – is, he claims, about to be realised, a secular equivalent of the Messianic Age.

Within three years, bloody ethnic war had broken out in the former Yugoslavia – first in Bosnia, later in Kosovo – between Muslims, Orthodox Serbs, and Catholic Croats, groups that had lived peaceably together for many decades. A rueful liberal intellectual, Michael Ignatieff,

---

1. Francis Fukuyama, *The End of History and the Last Man* (New York: Avon, 1993).

wrote that the forces of "blood and belonging" had prevailed.[2] In 1993, Harvard political historian Samuel Huntington predicted not the "end of history" but instead a sustained and dangerous "clash of civilizations."[3]

Fast-forward to January 2011. Aided by the new electronic media, a series of mass protests broke out in North Africa and the Middle East, beginning in Tunisia. There were insurgencies in Iraq, Libya, Syria, and Yemen, civil uprisings in Bahrain and Egypt, and mass demonstrations in Algeria, Iran, Lebanon, Jordan, Kuwait, Morocco, Oman, and Sudan. The phenomenon was quickly named the "Arab Spring," in the belief that what had happened in Eastern Europe in 1989 was about to happen in the Middle East as well: a grassroots-led rejection of tyranny in favour of democracy, liberalisation, and human rights.

As I write these words five years later, almost all of that hope has been destroyed as authoritarian regimes still prevail in Egypt and Bahrain, while civil war is tearing Syria, Libya, and Yemen apart at the cost of hundreds of thousands of lives. The twenty-first century has seen swathes of the Middle East, Africa, and Asia descend into a Hobbesian state of nature, a war of "every man against every man" in which life is "solitary, poor, nasty, brutish, and short." What succeeded the Cold War has turned out to be not peace and liberty but rather the old-new barbarism and oppression. Meanwhile, the liberal democratic West seems less sure of itself than it has been for many centuries. Thus do dreams of freedom end in a nightmare of chaos, violence, and fear.

This is why the book of Numbers – in Hebrew, *Bemidbar*, "In the Wilderness" – is a key text for our time. It is among the most searching, self-critical books in all of literature about what Nelson Mandela called "the long walk to freedom." Its message is that there is no shortcut to liberty. Numbers is not an easy book to read, nor is it an optimistic one. It is a sober warning set in the midst of a text – the Hebrew Bible – that remains the West's master narrative of hope.

---

2. Michael Ignatieff, *Blood and Belonging: Journeys into the New Nationalism* (London: Vintage, 1994).
3. Samuel Huntington, *The Clash of Civilizations and the Remaking of World Order* (New York: Simon & Schuster, 1996).

The Mosaic books, especially Exodus and Numbers, are about the journey from slavery to freedom and from oppression to law-governed liberty. On the map, the distance from Egypt to the Promised Land is not far. But the message of Numbers is that it always takes longer than you think. For the journey is not just physical, a walk across the desert. It is psychological, moral, and spiritual. It takes as long as the time needed for human beings to change. That, as we discover in Numbers, can be a very long time indeed.

Political change cannot be brought about by politics alone. It needs human transformation, brought about by rituals, habits of the heart, and a strenuous process of education. It comes along with knowledge borne out of painful experience, preserved for future generations by acts of remembering. It calls not only for high ideals but also a way of life that translates ideals into social interactions. You cannot create a democracy simply by removing a tyrant. As Plato wrote in *The Republic*, democracy is often no more than the prelude to a new tyranny. You cannot arrive at freedom merely by escaping from slavery. It is won only when a nation takes upon itself the responsibilities of self-restraint, courage, and patience. Without that, a journey of a few hundred miles can take forty years. Even then, it has only just begun.

A Bewildering Text

Numbers is a difficult book, the most challenging of the five Mosaic books. It contains an extraordinary range of texts, genres, and subject matters. There are narratives, laws, census lists, itineraries, details of how the tribes encamped and travelled on their journeys and laws about wives suspected of adultery, Nazirites, vows, purifications, sacrifices, and sundry other matters alongside cases that Moses himself had to bring to God for adjudication. There are accounts of battles, rebellions, and collective failures of nerve, and a strange story about a pagan prophet and a talking donkey.

It is not simply that the book contains materials of such different kinds; it is that it mixes them in ways that seem almost random. Stories are interrupted by laws whose proper place would seem to be elsewhere. There are times when Numbers resembles a bricolage of texts pasted together with no overarching structure or theme. Many of its laws, especially those to do with the Sanctuary, read as if they more properly belong to Leviticus, the book of holy places and times. Why place them here, in the context of the Israelites' journey, rather than there, in the sanctity of Sinai where the whole of Leviticus is set? Why break up the narrative flow with legal interjections that seem to have no relevance to the story itself? What is Numbers about? What is its overarching theme?

Other passages come with a sense of déjà vu, because they read like repetitions of stories we have already encountered in the book of Exodus: arguments about food and water and tales of the Israelites, overcome by fear and foreboding, questioning whether they should ever have left Egypt in the first place. Why tell us these stories if they are no more than more of the same?

Then there is the sheer overwhelming negativity of the narratives, forming an almost unbroken sequence of murmuring and complaints. We encounter three of them, immediately following one another, in chapters 11 and 12. First, there is an unspecified complaint. Then comes another in which the mixed multitude, and then the Israelites, bemoan the food they eat. Finally, Moses' own sister and brother criticise him.

No sooner have these ended than we move to the scene that is the turning point of the entire book. Twelve spies are sent on a reconnaissance mission to the land. Ten return with a demoralising report. The land is good, they say, but the people are strong and the cities impregnable. The people despair and say, "Let us appoint a leader and return to Egypt" (Num. 14:4). This is the counterpart of the sin of the Golden Calf in the book of Exodus. On both occasions, God is so angry that He threatens to destroy the people and begin again with Moses. Moses pleads with Him not to do so, this time using the same words God Himself had used – the Thirteen Attributes of Mercy – in the earlier episode. God relents, but nonetheless decrees that no one of that generation, with the sole exceptions of Joshua and Caleb, the two faithful spies, would enter the land. Their children would; they would not.

At this point, one feels that this is as bad as it gets. However, things are about to get worse. Almost immediately comes the rebellion of Korah and his fellow discontents, the most serious of all the challenges to the authority of Moses. Then comes the nadir. After the extended story of

Balaam, the pagan prophet hired to curse Israel who instead blesses them, comes the lowest point of the entire wilderness years. Having protected Israel from the curses of their enemies, God then witnesses the Israelite men engaging in sexual immorality and idolatrous rites with the women of Moab and Midian – a complete breakdown of all that was supposed to characterise the Israelites as "a kingdom of priests and a holy nation" (Ex. 19:6). What hope is there to be rescued from this cumulative tale of failure and faithlessness?

Not only do the people falter, so too does Moses, the one figure we look to as a role model of faith. The man we encounter in Numbers is not the one we met in the book of Exodus. Early on, he gives voice to almost terminal despair in one of the most searing passages in Tanakh: "If this is how You are going to treat me, please go ahead kill me – if I have found favour in Your eyes – and let me not see my own ruin" (Num. 11:15). Moses eventually rallies, but as the narrative proceeds, he seems less and less in control of events. In the episode of the spies, the main burden of leadership is borne by Caleb and Joshua. During the Korah rebellion, Moses seems to overreact; his call that the earth open up and swallow his opponents inflames the situation instead of resolving it. In the next challenge, when the people ask for water after the death of Miriam, Moses and Aaron respond so badly that they are deemed guilty of failure and told they will not enter the Promised Land. Why is Moses of the wilderness so different from Moses of the Exodus?

The book also does strange things with time. The first eleven chapters cover a mere twenty days.[4] There is even a point in chapter 9 when time moves backwards by a month.[5] Later, however, thirty-eight years disappear. At one moment we are little more than a year from Egypt. In the next we are in the fortieth year, with the Israelites nearing their destination. It is also hard to say exactly where the break in time occurs. The obvious place is chapter 26, where a second census introduces us to the new generation that will complete the journey their parents began.

---

4. From "the first day of the second month of the second year" after leaving Egypt (Num. 1:1) to "the twentieth day of the second month of the second year," when the people start journeying from Sinai (10:11).
5. Num. 9:1 is set "in the first month of the second year."

This seems like a new beginning. Yet the temporal leap actually comes earlier, between chapter 20, where we read about the death of Miriam and Aaron, and the next chapter, which describes the Israelites' first battles for the conquest of the land.

What are we to make of these difficulties? In this introduction, I propose seven exegetical principles that allow us to decode much of the mystery of the book and understand why it is structured the way it is.

Principle 1: Journey-from, Journey-to

The first task is to understand the place of Numbers in the Torah's system as a whole. The five books are in rough chronological order. Genesis begins with the creation of the universe, proceeds to the early history of humankind, and moves on to tell the story of Abraham and his immediate descendants. By Exodus, the family has become a people. Exodus to Numbers tell how they were rescued from slavery in Egypt and brought to the brink of the Promised Land. Deuteronomy then recounts the speeches given by Moses in the last month of his life. That is the surface structure. The books are ordered chronologically in temporal sequence. They tell what happened in roughly the order that events occurred.

Beneath this, however, is a chiastic structure, meaning that the books are ordered in the form of mirror-image symmetry – ABCBA – with the apex in the middle rather than at the end:

[A] **Genesis**: Prologue: the pre-history of Israel;
  [B] **Exodus**: Journey from Egypt to Mount Sinai;
    [C] **Leviticus**: At Mount Sinai;
  [B¹] **Numbers**: Journey from Mount Sinai to the banks of the Jordan;
[A¹] **Deuteronomy**: Epilogue – the future of Israel as a nation in its land.

On this reading, the climax of the five books is the long, extended account, covering the whole of Leviticus, the end of Exodus, and the first ten chapters of Numbers. It is about the Israelites at Mount Sinai. There they made a covenant with God, agreeing to become a "kingdom of priests and a holy nation" under divine sovereignty, with the Sanctuary in their midst and a code of ethics built on the idea of holiness.

Within this structure it is immediately clear that Exodus and Numbers have much in common. They are both about journeys. Both tell of distances traversed and battles fought. Both contain stories of complaint about the lack of food and water. Both tell of a series of breakdowns of morale. In Exodus, the people panic as they reach the Red Sea, pursued by the Egyptian chariots. In Numbers, they panic as they envisage the battles that lie ahead, having been told by ten of the twelve spies that they face a land whose cities are fortified and whose inhabitants are giants.

In both books, the people romanticise the past, thinking of Egypt not as a land of oppression but as a place of safety where they had food and security. In both there is a major sin that threatens the entire future of the people: in Exodus, the Golden Calf, in Numbers, the episode of the spies. In both, Moses suffers under the burdens of leadership and is told to delegate. Here are some of the parallels:

Exodus	Numbers
Led by a cloud (13:21)	Led by a cloud (10:11)
Victory over Egypt (14)	Victory over Sihon and Og (21:21–35)
Victory song (15:1–18)	Victory song (21:14–15)
Complaint (15:23–24)	Complaint (11:1)
Manna and quail (16)	Manna and quail (11:4–35)
Complaint about water (17:1–7)	Complaint about water (20:2–13)
Amalek (17:8–16)	Amalek (14:45)
Moses' father-in-law (18:1–12)	Moses' father-in-law (10:29–32)
Leaders to assist Moses (18:14–26)	Leaders to assist Moses (11:16–17)
Rebellion (32:1–8)	Rebellion (14:1; 25:1–3)
Moses intercedes (32:11–13)	Moses intercedes (14:13–19)
Divine judgement (32:34)	Divine judgement (14:26–35; 25:4)

Plague (32:35)	Plague (14:37; 25:8–9)
Sabbath and festivals (23:12–17)	Sabbath and festivals (28–29)
Atonement through priests or Levites (32:26–29)	Atonement through priests or Levites (16:36–50; 25:7–13)
Census (30:11–16)	Census (1–4; 26)

Yet there are also clear differences between the books. In Exodus, the people are not punished for their complaints. In Numbers, they are.[6] The most conspicuous difference is the response of Moses. In Exodus, on each occasion he turns to God, who provides what is needed by way of a miracle. In Numbers, his response is more fraught, ranging from despair to powerlessness. The tone is different. Something has changed.

One difference has to do with the covenant and the Sanctuary. In Numbers, the people are no longer simply a group of escaping slaves. They are now a nation in covenant with God, with a code of laws and the Divine Presence in their midst. The other key difference is in the nature of the journey itself. In Exodus it is a *journey-from*: from Egypt and slavery. It is the story of an escape. In Numbers, it is a *journey-to*: to the land, to conquest and settlement. It is a story of approach and preparation.

These are not just two halves of a single story. Exodus and Numbers represent two different kinds of liberty. In a distinction made famous by Isaiah Berlin, Exodus is about negative freedom, *ḥofesh* in Hebrew. Numbers is about positive freedom, for which the sages coined the word *ḥerut*.[7] Negative freedom is what a slave acquires when he or she is liberated. There is no one to give you orders. Individually, you are free to do what you choose. But a society in which everyone is free to do what they choose is not a free society. It is anarchy. A free society requires codes and disciplines of self-restraint so that my freedom is not

6. One example: In both books, people complain about a lack of meat and in both they are sent quails. In Exodus, no more is said. In Numbers, a plague strikes the people while they are eating the quails.
7. Isaiah Berlin, "Two Concepts of Liberty," in *Four Essays on Liberty* (Oxford: Oxford University Press, 1990).

bought at the cost of yours. It is a society of law-governed liberty. That is why Exodus and Numbers are profoundly different despite their surface similarities. What matters in Exodus is how the people escape from Pharaoh. What matters in Numbers is how they rise to the challenge of self-rule and responsibility.

Principle 2: Technical and Adaptive Challenges

This helps explain why Moses' reactions to the challenges are so different in Numbers from what they were in Exodus. In chapter 11 he comes close to despair. In the episode of the spies, though his prayers sway God, it is Joshua and Caleb who are the key actors vis-à-vis the nation. He loses his calm during the Korah rebellion, and later at Meriva loses his temper with the people, prompting God's verdict that he will not be allowed to lead the Israelites into the Promised Land. At the lowest point in the book, the misconduct of the people at Shittim, it was Pinhas, not Moses, who took decisive action.

Event	Moses' response
People complain about food. (11:4–6)	"I cannot carry all these people by myself; the burden is too heavy for me. If this is how You are going to treat me, please go ahead and kill me – if I have found favour in Your eyes – and let me not see my own ruin." (11:14–15)
Spies' negative report; people demoralised. (13–14)	Moses and Aaron fall on their faces. (14:5)
Israelites seek to make amends by engaging immediately in battle. (14:40)	Moses warns against, but is not listened to; those who fight are defeated. (14:41–45)
Korah rebellion. (16:1–35)	Moses prays for ground to open up and swallow the rebels. This does not end the rebellion; people continue to grumble. (16:28–17:6)

Complaint about water. (20:2–5)	Moses speaks harshly to the people; strikes rock; is denied chance to enter land. (20:7–12)
Shittim: immorality, idolatry, sin of Zimri. (25:1–6)	Averted by Pinhas, not Moses. (25:7–13)

What has changed is not Moses but the specific nature of the leadership task he faced in the two books. A helpful distinction is the one articulated by Ronald Heifetz between *technical* challenges and *adaptive* ones.[8] A technical challenge is one where there is a practical problem and people turn to the leader for a solution. An adaptive challenge is one where the people *are* the problem. It is they who must change. Here the leader cannot solve the problem on his or her own. Leaders must educate the people on the need for change. They must be able to hand the problem back to them, giving them safe space in which to think the problem through and the confidence with which to solve it.

In Exodus, the leadership Moses was called on to show was essentially technical. The people were thirsty; through Moses, God provided water. They were hungry; God sent food. They were trapped between the sea and the approaching Egyptian army; God divided the sea. The people sinned; Moses prayed for forgiveness. No change of character was called for. The people had a problem, they turned to Moses, Moses turned to God, and the problem was solved. The book is about technical challenges and how they were met by miracles.

In Numbers, the challenge was quite different. The people were no longer escaping from Egypt. They were preparing to enter the land. That would involve battles and dangers demanding courage and collective responsibility. No longer would God fight their battles for them. He would give them the strength to fight them for themselves. They now had to become a people that acted, not a people that were acted upon. *They had to adapt, to change.* If they did not, they would no longer *have* a problem. They themselves would *be* the problem.

8. See Ronald Heifetz, *Leadership Without Easy Answers* (Cambridge, MA: Harvard University Press, 1994); Ronald Heifetz and Marty Linsky, *Leadership on the Line* (Boston: Harvard Business Press, 2002).

This transformed the entire relationship between Moses and the people. We see this most clearly in chapter 11 when the people complain about the manna and the lack of meat. Moses is reduced to despair. Yet there was seemingly no reason for him to do so. He had faced the same problem before, in Exodus 16. He did not despair then. Why did he do so now, when he knew that God had sent quail then and could do so again?

It is not that he forgot that earlier episode, nor that he was suffering from sheer exhaustion. It was, rather, that *the people had not changed*, despite the fact that they had received the Torah at Sinai and built the Sanctuary. Those two events should have transformed the people. *The fact that they did not do so meant that Moses could already see that they were not yet ready for the adaptive challenge.* That was why he despaired. He could see in advance that a people who had experienced some of the greatest miracles in history yet still complained about the food lacked the necessary vision and courage to build a nation in the holy land.

Moses never had difficulty in his relationship with God. So long as all that was needed was a heaven-sent miracle, he was on safe ground. But he had profound difficulties in his relationship with the people. He could not get them to adapt. People resist change, especially when they perceive it as a loss. That is why the adaptive challenge is so stressful for leader and people alike. Moses became angry with the people, and they with him.

Principle 3: Time as a Factor in Overcoming the Fear of Freedom

At the heart of the negative emotion that suffuses the central chapters of Numbers is fear, specifically fear of freedom. The Israelites were about to undertake an unprecedented task, to create a new kind of society that would be radically unlike any that existed at that time, a society based on covenant, collective responsibility, and nomocracy – the rule of laws, not men.

Freedom means a loss of security and predictability. It means taking responsibility for your actions in a way a slave does not need to do. It means letting go of passivity and dependence. It means growing up as individuals and as a nation. Throughout their journey from Egypt to Sinai the people did not have to think about freedom. They were fleeing their persecutors. They were focused on survival. But now, as they were leaving Sinai on their way to the land, the full realisation dawned on them of what lay ahead. As a nation, they were about to lose their childhood.

Michael Walzer points out that "there is a kind of bondage in freedom: the bondage of law, obligation, and responsibility." The Israelites could, he says, "become free only insofar as they accepted the discipline of freedom, the obligation to live up to a common standard and to take responsibility for their own actions."[9] Freedom, the Torah candidly acknowledges, is immensely demanding. It is *avoda*, "hard work." It is striking that the Torah uses the same Hebrew word to describe slavery to Pharaoh and servitude to God. There is all the difference in the world between being enslaved to a human ruler and serving the Creator of the universe who made us all in His image, but the difference is not that the one is hard and the other is easy. They are both hard work, but one breaks the spirit, the other lifts and exalts it.

Fearing freedom, the people take refuge in false nostalgia. They say, "We remember the fish we ate without cost in Egypt – also the cucumbers, melons, leeks, onions, and garlic" (Num. 11:5). The sages perceptively understood the meaning of the phrase, "without cost." The cost after all was high: slavery and forced labour. "Without cost" means at no cost in mitzvot, in divine commands and human responsibility.[10] The false nostalgia reaches its bitter climax when, during the Korah rebellion, Datan and Aviram call *Egypt* "a land flowing with milk and honey" (16:13).

In all this, we hear a clear message of political realism. There is no sense in the Torah that the journey to the Promised Land is easy or straightforward, free of doubt or conflict. To the contrary: despite its narratives of bread from heaven, water from a rock, ground that opens up to swallow opponents, talking donkeys, sticks that bud and blossom,

---

9. Michael Walzer, *Exodus and Revolution* (New York: Basic Books, 1985), 53.
10. Rashi to Num. 11:5, quoting *Sifre Zuta*.

and people who turn leprous because of slander, the fundamental message of Numbers is that the road to freedom is longer and harder than anyone anticipated at the outset.

In the end, it took longer than a single generation. That is the key burden of the episode of the spies, the central story of the book. The generation rescued by Moses from oppression in Egypt had grown used to its chains. The people were not yet ready for the "difficult freedom"[11] of battles, military preparedness, and the willingness to take destiny into their own hands. Change must come slowly; revolutions based, as were the French and Russian, on a sudden transformation of human nature are destined to fail.

Evolution, not revolution, is the point of Numbers. It is impossible, writes Moses Maimonides in *Guide for the Perplexed*, to go from one extreme to another in nature, and that includes human nature.[12] And although it took the episode of the spies to condemn Moses' generation to die without reaching the land, Maimonides suggests that this was hinted at almost as soon as the Israelites left Egypt: "When Pharaoh let the people go, God did not lead them on the road through the Philistine country, though that was shorter. For God said, 'If they face war, they might change their minds and return to Egypt'" (Ex. 13:17). When it comes to the human heart, change is slow, slower than can be achieved in a single generation.

But it is not impossible. It takes time – and time is one of Numbers' themes. The two views against which it is set are neatly exemplified in the story of the spies and the immediately following narrative of the *maapilim* (Num. 14:40–45), the people who, having heard of God's anger at the spies, presume the next morning to go straight into battle and begin the conquest. Moses urges them not to go, but they insist and are defeated. The two political ideas to which Numbers is opposed are *never* and *immediately*. *Never* is the counsel of despair and political reaction. *Immediately* is the temptation of political messianism and revolution. Both end in oppression.

---

11. Emmanuel Levinas, *Difficult Freedom* (London: Athlone, 1990). See also Erich Fromm, *The Fear of Freedom* (London: Routledge Classics, 2001).
12. Maimonides, *Guide for the Perplexed*, III:32.

Freedom is the work of generations. It is always an unfinished symphony, a work in progress. If there is one aphorism that sums up Numbers' view of society and its leaders it is R. Tarfon's "It is not for you to complete the work, but neither are you free to desist from it" (Mishna Avot 2:16). Its view of politics is that rarest of combinations: a *pessimism that refuses to let go of hope.*

This is ultimately what makes the Mosaic books rare in the history of political thought. The Torah is among other things a work of philosophy written *not as system but as story*, or more precisely as a series of stories, because only stories operate in the medium of time. Systems do not. Either a system is true or it is false. If it is true, it is true regardless of time. If it is false, it is false regardless of time. But human beings are not like that. What one generation finds impossible, another may find relatively straightforward. It takes one kind of leader, Moses, to liberate slaves, and another, Joshua, to guide the destinies of people born in freedom. The timelessness of philosophy as conceived by Plato in antiquity or Descartes on the threshold of modernity is precisely what makes it inadequate as an account of human beings and the free exercise of choice.

Freedom is a journey across the wilderness that always takes longer than you thought it would, and the route lies midway between the twin temptations of *never* and *immediately*, resistance and revolution.

Principle 4: Rites of Passage and Liminal Space

Once we understand what is involved in adaptive leadership – the transformation of a people through accepting responsibility for their own destiny – we begin to see that not only does it need *time* (a new generation), it also needs a special kind of *place*. Hence the significance of the book's title, *Bemidbar*, "In the Wilderness."[13] In the second essay in this book, I argue that the best way to understand the wilderness is by way of

---

13. In English, the book is known as Numbers, based on the Latin *Numeri* and Greek *Arithmoi*, all of which were derived from the early rabbinic name for the book, as Ḥomesh HaPekudim, "the fifth [of the Torah, that is about] the numberings," i.e., the two censuses detailed in the book, in chapters 1–4 and 26. There is no doubt that this, the succession of the generations, is an important theme – but it is not as important as the theme of the wilderness, the place where the Israelites were transformed.

two concepts developed by the anthropologists Arnold van Gennep and Victor Turner. One is the idea of a *rite of passage* – the transition from one life phase to another. The other, closely related, is *liminal space*, the place that is neither starting point nor destination but the place between. That is what the wilderness was: liminal space in which the Israelites could make the transition from a collection of tribes linked by ancestry and shared fate (in Hebrew, an *am*) to becoming a body politic (*edah*) formed by a covenant with God.

Liminal space plays a significant role in the Torah. It is no accident that the Jewish journey begins with God's command to Abraham to leave his "land ... birthplace and ... father's house" (Gen. 12:1). These three factors – country, culture, and kin – are the primary sources of conformity. We behave as do the people around us. Precisely because God wanted Abraham to be different, it was imperative that he leave and go elsewhere, to a place where he would be seen as *ger vetoshav*, "a foreigner and stranger" (23:4).

It is also no accident that Jacob, who gave the people of the covenant its collective name, had his most intense encounters with God in liminal space: on his outward journey, when he had the vision of a ladder set on earth whose top reached heaven and on whose rungs angels rose and descended (Gen. 28:10–17), and on his return when, alone at night, he wrestled with a mysterious stranger until dawn and was given the name Israel, meaning one who wrestles with God and man and prevails (32:22–32). These, especially the latter, were for him rites of passage, involving a change of identity.

The Israelites were about to undergo one of the most profound rites of passage ever experienced by a people. The historian Eric Voegelin put it well:

> If nothing had happened but a lucky escape from the range of Egyptian power, there only would have been a few more nomadic tribes roaming the border zone between the Fertile Crescent and the desert proper, eking out a meagre living with the aid of part-time agriculture. But the desert was only a station on the way, not the goal; for in the desert the tribes found their God. They entered into a covenant with Him, and thereby became His people....

> When we undertake the exodus and wander into the world, in order to found a new society elsewhere, we discover the world as the Desert. The flight leads nowhere, until we stop in order to find our bearings beyond the world. When the world has become Desert, man is at last in the solitude in which he can hear thunderingly the voice of the spirit that with its urgent whispering has already driven and rescued him from Sheol [the domain of death]. In the Desert God spoke to the leader and his tribes; in the Desert, by listening to the voice, by accepting its offer, and by submitting to its command, they had at last reached life and became the people chosen by God.[14]

The essence of the transition was "to found a new society elsewhere," and to undergo that transformation they had to pass through a space that was literally no-man's-land. There, alone with God, wrestling with Him as did their ancestor Jacob, they had to throw off one identity, a people "crushed, frightened, subservient, despondent,"[15] and acquire another as a free people under the sovereignty of God.

According to van Gennep, there are three stages in a rite of passage. The first is *separation*, a symbolic break with the past. That is what happened when the Israelites left Egypt, the most advanced civilisation of its time. The key moment occurred when the Israelites passed through the divided Red Sea, passing irrevocably from the domain of Pharaoh into the desert. The third stage is *re-incorporation*, re-entering society with a new identity. That is what Moses was preparing the people for in the book of Deuteronomy, a book dedicated to teaching the people about the society they would be called on to make once they entered the land. In between is the *transition*, the point at which the person – here, the people – is remade, reconstituted, reborn.

The word *midbar*, "wilderness," also evokes associations with *davar*, the Word, and *medabber*, the Speaker of the Word. It is there, in no-man's-land, that the Israelites had their most sustained and intense

14. Eric Voegelin, *Israel and Revelation*, vol. 1 of *Order and History* (Baton Rouge: Louisiana State University Press, 1956), 153.
15. Walzer, *Exodus and Revolution*, 47.

encounter with the God who transcends the universe, the austere, invisible God of monotheism, identified neither with the nature familiar to the farmer nor the pinnacle of a hierarchy of power such as is familiar to the dwellers of cities. You have, as it were, to be nowhere to encounter the God of everywhere. In the silence of the desert you hear the voice of God. In the isolation of the desert you find yourself alone with God.

The wilderness was where the Israelites found themselves suspended between a past they could no longer return to and a future they did not yet have the courage to embrace. It was there, in the barren no-man's-land of the desert, that the nation found itself alone with God, with none of the normal distractions of a life rooted in the familiar landscape of home.

Principle 5: Order and Freedom

The fifth principle shaping the structure of Numbers is, in fact, the central drama of the Torah as a whole. In the beginning, God freely created a universe of order. Then He created human beings and gave them the supreme gift that made them "in His image," namely freedom, the ability to obey or break the law. Almost immediately the result was chaos, the breakdown of order. The first command to the first humans led to the first disobedience. The first religious act, in which the first human children, Cain and Abel, offered sacrifices to God, led to the first murder. Within a remarkably short time, the Torah tells us that the world was "filled with violence" (Gen. 6:11) and God "regretted that He had made man on earth" (6:6). To be sure, God could deprive humans of freedom, but without freedom they would cease to be human, to be, as it were, God's "other."

Freedom and order were the essential elements in God's creation of the universe. Can they coexist in the universes human beings create, namely societies? That is the central question of the Torah. It offers us a vivid example of *freedom without order*: the violence of the world before the Flood. Likewise, it shows us an example of *order without freedom*: the Egypt that enslaves the Israelites. Is there a third alternative, a society in which people freely sustain a social order in which there is justice, compassion, respect for human dignity, and reverence for the sanctity of life? That is the challenge of the covenant, most eloquently set out in the speeches of Moses in the book of Deuteronomy.

Numbers is precisely structured to dramatise, in a way unique in Torah, the counterpoint between order and chaos. It is divided into three sections. The first, chapters 1–10, as the Israelites prepare to begin the second half of their journey, is a remarkable portrayal of order within the camp. The tribes are numbered. They are encamped, in precise formation, around the Sanctuary, each with their distinctive banners. The Levites are likewise divided into groups, each with their carefully designated tasks. There is a series of laws designed to maintain the purity of the camp and ward off potential threats to its peace (from husbands who suspect their wives of adultery or non-priests who wish to adopt a priest-like standard of holiness by becoming Nazirites). There is a lengthy account of the offerings brought by the tribes at the inauguration of the Sanctuary, each stated in the same words as if to avoid any favouritism. It is almost as if the Torah were describing the Israelites the way it describes the cosmos in the first chapter of Genesis, everything in its due proportion and proper place.

Then, in chapters 11–25, comes the chaos: dissension in the camp, complaints about the food, and finally Moses' own brother and sister criticising him. The attempt to prepare the people for entry into the land by sending spies ends in disaster. The people panic and rebel. Caleb and Joshua attempt to calm them and fail. Moses prays and saves the people from disaster, but only just. Next comes the story of the Korah rebellion, a tale of the chaos[16] that results when authority – that of Moses and Aaron – is challenged and ceases to command respect. Worse still, in the next episode, when the people need water after the death of Miriam, Moses and Aaron are themselves guilty of disrespect, both towards the people and towards God. Finally, after the story of how the pagan prophet Balaam, hired to curse Israel, was forced by God to bless them, comes the absolute nadir, when the Israelite men bring disaster

---

16. The Korah narrative is deliberately structured to convey a sense of chaos. There are three different factions among the rebels: Levites from Moses' own clan, that of Kehat; Reubenites; and 250 leaders from other tribes – each with their own specific grievance. To them are later added "the assembly," other Israelites outraged at the way Moses has handled the challenge. Biblical scholars who separate the text into different narratives miss the point of the story and its literary function in conveying the sense of chaos, a theme that runs through the central chapters of Numbers.

on themselves by acts of immorality and idolatry, seduced by the local Moabite and Midianite women. Complete chaos reigns in the camp, ended only by an act of violent zealotry on the part of Pinhas.

After this stark contrast between order and chaos comes part 3, chapters 26–36, in which a new beginning is made, starting symbolically with a new census and a new generation. From here on, there are no rebellions. Order prevails. There are provisions for the sacrifices to be brought at their appointed times. The land is apportioned between the tribes. Levitical towns and cities of refuge are designated. Claims such as those of Tzlofhad's daughters (ch. 27) and the heads of their tribe (ch. 36) are resolved peaceably, as is a potential conflict between the rest of the people and the Reubenites and Gadites who wish to settle east of the Jordan. There is an orderly transition from Moses' leadership to his successor Joshua. Battles are fought and won. The long journey is nearing its end, all its stages enumerated and recorded. For all the intervening chaos, order wins in the end.

Principle 6: Narrative and Law

This deliberately heightened contrast between chaos and order is the explanation for the stylistic feature of Numbers that has proved the most puzzling, making it seem at times like a jumble of disconnected parts, the constant juxtaposition of narrative and law. We see this in broad strokes in the following table:

Chapter: content	Subject matter
1–4: Narrative	The taking of a census; the arrangement of the camp.
5–6: Law	Purity of the camp; the wife suspected of adultery; the Nazirite; priestly blessings.
7: Narrative	The leaders of the tribes bring offerings at the dedication of the Tabernacle.
8–10: Law	Lighting of the lamps; inauguration of Levites; Passover in the desert; the trumpets.

10–14: Narrative	The Israelites leave Sinai; the people complain; Miriam and Aaron oppose Moses; the spies.
15: Law	Supplementary offerings; offerings for unintentional sins; the Sabbath-breaker; fringes on garments.
16–17: Narrative	The Korah rebellion.
18–19: Law	Duties of priests and Levites, offerings from priests and Levites; the red heifer.
20–27: Narrative	Miriam dies; the people complain about lack of water; Aaron and Moses punished; Edom denies Israel passage; Aaron dies; Arad; the bronze snake; the journey to Moab; defeat of Sihon and Og; Balak and Balaam; Moab seduces Israel; second census; daughters of Tzlofhad; Joshua to succeed Moses.
28–30: Law	Daily, Sabbath, and festival offerings; vows.
31–34: Narrative	Vengeance on the Midianites; the Transjordan tribes; stages in Israel's journey; boundaries of the land; new leadership; Levitical cities.
35–36: Law	Cities of refuge; murder; intermarriage between tribes.

This mix of law and narrative is a feature of the Torah as a whole, especially in Exodus and Deuteronomy. In neither, though, is the juxtaposition as marked and seemingly random as in the book of Numbers. Why so? *Because the conflicting societal pressures of order and freedom can only be reconciled by law, freely accepted and collectively applied.* Law ensures that my freedom is not bought at the cost of yours. That is the difference between a society in which "everyone did what was right in his own eyes," the biblical description of chaos,[17] and one in which there is an agreed-upon moral code and thus a shared form of order. The narrative of Numbers focuses on the chaos. The legal sections constitute

17. Deut. 12:8; Judges 17:6; 21:25; Prov. 12:15.

in each case a *tikkun*, "repair," or in more biblical terms, a *ge'ula*, "rescue and redemption" of the disorder.

This means that Numbers sets forth in heightened form an important feature of biblical law in general. In her book *What's Divine About Divine Law?* Christine Hayes contrasts two very different conceptions of law, one that it represents the divine *will*, the other that it embodies divine *wisdom*.[18] The first sees it as God's command, the second as God's instructions for human flourishing, given the nature of the universe He created. There is something to be said for each of these conceptions within the broad context of Tanakh as a whole. However, Numbers articulates a quite different approach, seeing law as emerging from the specifics of the nation's history – what happened during the wilderness years, and what must happen in the future when the Israelites enter the land. Here *law is integrally related to narrative*. There is nothing arbitrary about the commands. They are directed against the dysfunctions that emerged as the Israelites journeyed from Sinai to the plains of Moab and which would, if left unchecked, lead to the disintegration of the nation.

Two scholars in different fields understood this connection well. One was the Nobel-prize-winning economist and philosopher Friedrich Hayek. In his book *The Constitution of Liberty*, Hayek argued for the importance of tradition – laws, codes, and customs that emerged in the course of a people's history – in the maintenance of freedom.[19] Coming from a different direction, Robert Cover, the Yale philosopher of law, argued in a famous article, "Nomos and Narrative," that there is often an essential connection between law and the story of how it came to be: "For every constitution there is an epic, for each decalogue a scripture."[20] Law, he argues, creates a "normative universe," a world of right and wrong,

---

18. Christine Hayes, *What's Divine About Divine Law?* (Princeton, NJ: Princeton University Press, 2015).

19. Friedrich Hayek, *The Constitution of Liberty: The Definitive Edition* (Abingdon, UK: Routledge, 2011), ch. 4.

20. In Robert Cover and Martha Minow, *Narrative, Violence, and the Law: The Essays of Robert Cover* (Ann Arbor, MI: University of Michigan, 2010), 109. See also Rémi Brague, *The Law of God: The Philosophical History of an Idea* (Chicago: University of Chicago Press, 2007); Chaya Halberstam, *Law and Truth in Biblical and Rabbinic Literature* (Bloomington: Indiana University Press, 2010).

permitted and forbidden, that defines the social reality in which a community functions and finds meaning. It does this most effectively when
there is a strong connection between its laws and its history. That is what
Numbers is doing when it juxtaposes law and narrative.

In each case, we will find a precise connection between the two. So,
for example, immediately after the episode of the spies come laws about
offerings beginning with the words, "After you enter the land" (Num. 15:1–31),
an assurance that the nation would eventually enter the land despite the
forty-year delay. I show in one of the essays here[21] that there is a precise
connection, verbal and substantive, between the law of tzitzit, fringed
garments, and the failure of the spies to interpret correctly what they saw.
The laws relating to priests (18:1–32) follow the Korah rebellion which
established beyond doubt the right of Aaron and his sons to that office.

The most striking case is that of the ritual of the red heifer. This
seems both unintelligible in its own right and unconnected with the stories it interrupts, but the reverse is the case. The law precedes a notice of
three deaths: the actual deaths of Miriam and Aaron and the announced
death of Moses. These were the three leaders of the Israelites throughout the wilderness years, and there is no more vivid collective reminder
of mortality than that which a people experiences when its leaders die.
The ritual of the red heifer conveys the message that just as the ashes
of death are dissolved in *mayim ḥayim*, the "waters of life," so the death
of individuals is mitigated by the ongoing life of the nation. Mortality
dissolves into the eternity of God and the people of God.

Thus in Numbers, style and substance go hand in hand. Law is the
shape of order, and it coexists with freedom when people understand that
the law is not an arbitrary expression of the divine will. It arises from a
specific history and from the way the community remembers that history.

Principle 7: The Anti-Heroic Narrative

Finally, we miss fundamental aspects of the Torah's project if we fail
to understand that much of it is *a polemic against myth*. This is its real
iconoclasm, and it is not always obvious on the surface.

21. "Law and Narrative: Believing and Seeing."

Read the whole of Genesis, for example, and you will not find a single explicit statement about monotheism or even one denunciation of idolatry – what we would expect if this were a conventional theological document. The monotheism is there, set at the beginning of the book, and it consists in the creation account of Genesis 1:1–2:3. We can only fully understand this text if we understand its context: a plethora of mythic, cosmological accounts from ancient surrounding cultures telling of how things were at the beginning of time, accounts which are universally about clashes between the various elements personified as gods. The serene account of Genesis – "And God said, 'Let there be ...' and there was ... and God saw that it was good" – in which the universe emerges stage by stage harmoniously from a single creative mind, and is seven times pronounced "good," is not a myth but what I call an *anti-myth*. The German nineteenth-century sociologist Max Weber was right to see this as the birth of Western rationality. He saw it as what he called the "disenchantment" – what we would call de-mythologisation – of the world.[22]

Likewise, at the beginning of Exodus, we read of the birth of Moses. This is not simply the story of a birth. As I pointed out in my Haggada,[23] it is a polemic against a well-known myth, what Otto Rank, Freud's most brilliant disciple, called "the myth of the birth of the hero."[24] Rank and Freud noted – though they misinterpreted – one salient fact about it. It is not, as they thought, an example of the myth – told about Sargon, Cyrus, Oedipus, Romulus, and others – but rather, a protest against it. In standard versions of the myth, a ruler receives a warning about a child about to be born to him. The ruler takes steps to kill the child or let him die. The child is saved, often by being placed in a basket and floated down a river, and raised by people of humble birth. Only later does he learn that he has royal blood.

The Moses story is the precise opposite. He is found and raised by royalty – an Egyptian princess, Pharaoh's daughter – and learns that

---

22. See Max Weber, *The Sociology of Religion* (Boston: Beacon Press, 1963); Peter Berger, *The Sacred Canopy* (Garden City, NY: Doubleday, 1967).
23. *Pesaḥ Haggada* (Jerusalem: Maggid, 2013), 19–26.
24. Otto Rank, *The Myth of the Birth of the Hero: A Psychological Exploration of Myth* (Baltimore: Johns Hopkins University Press, 2004).

he is in fact not royalty but a member of what has become, in Egyptian eyes, a pariah people. The point is immeasurably heightened once we realise that the name of the pharaoh, Ramses, means "child of the sun god, Ra," while the child's name, Mose or Moses, is an Egyptian word that means, simply, "child." The Moses story is a subtle and brilliant assault on the concept, central to all polytheistic religions, of a human hierarchy, in which rulers are marked from the outset by royal blood. Moses is the representative of a people every member of whom has been adopted by God, a point made in the first words Moses is commanded to say to Pharaoh: "My child, my firstborn, Israel" (Ex. 4:22).

The book of Numbers is just such an anti-myth, a polemic against one of the world's most widespread myths – recycled today in such stories as *Lord of the Rings, Star Wars,* and the like – of "the journey of the hero."[25] The hero, often reluctantly, undertakes a journey in which he faces a series of trials as a result of which he develops extraordinary strength of character. He then returns, transformed.

The Torah as a whole represents just such a journey, but with three significant differences. First, the journey is undertaken not by an individual as in every other case but by an entire people. Second, the sequence of departure-initiation-return is spread across several centuries, from Joseph to Joshua. Third – and this is the story of Numbers – the people *fail* most of their trials. They are portrayed collectively as an antihero, not a hero. In a complete inversion of the myth, the Torah attributes the people's successes to God and their failures to themselves. Why so?

Here we come to one of the most fundamental features of biblical monotheism. In virtually all ancient cultures, humans battle against implacable and overwhelming forces, external to themselves and indifferent to human suffering. That is the basis of the literary genre of *tragedy.* In modern times myth has been replaced by science, but the scenario remains the same, only this time the forces have to do with economic pressures (Marx), unconscious drives (Freud), natural selection (Darwin), or the human genome.

25. The most famous account is Joseph Campbell's *The Hero with a Thousand Faces* (Princeton, NJ: Princeton University Press, 1972).

Monotheism, as Jack Miles has elegantly shown,[26] internalises the forces that are externalised in myth and science. The real battle lies within – within the human will. What makes humans different from all other life forms thus far known is our capacity to make a distinction between duty and desire, between "I want" and "I ought." Philosophers call this *second-order evaluation*: I know what I desire but I can also ask: Ought I to satisfy this desire?[27] This is the drama played out in almost endless variations in Numbers, from the most rudimentary (wanting to eat meat in chapter 11, sexual gratification in chapter 25) to the most challenging (preferring security-with-slavery to freedom-with-responsibility in the episode of the spies). The message of Numbers is that the human will is weak, but not terminally so. There is no doctrine of original sin in the Torah. Humanity *can* achieve freedom-with-order, but it is hard and needs constantly to be fought for.

Monotheism thus inverts the basic thought structure common to both myth and science.[28] The real conflict to which Torah and the life of faith are addressed is not with external forces but internal ones. On this, Judaism and Freud agree: civilisation is the capacity to defer the gratification of instinct.[29] Curiously and paradoxically, then, by attributing its successes to God and its failures to itself, the Israel of the Bible knows that its fate is in its hands. It knows that the real battle is "in here" rather than "out there." If it is victorious against its destructive and dysfunctional drives it will be victorious against its enemies. Had the people shown courage and faithfulness, the journey to the

---

26. Jack Miles, *God: A Biography* (London: Simon and Schuster, 1996), 397–408.
27. The distinction is usually credited to Harry Frankfurt, *The Importance of What We Care About* (New York: Cambridge University Press, 1968).
28. By this, I do not mean the natural sciences – chemistry, physics, and biology – but rather the human and social sciences insofar as they assume some form of determinism.
29. Sigmund Freud, *Civilization and Its Discontents* (New York: W. W. Norton, 1989). The most famous example of this in recent times is Walter Mischel, *The Marshmallow Test* (London: Bantam Press, 2014). Mischel showed that a four-year-old child's capacity to resist eating a marshmallow for twenty minutes accurately predicted the child's success in later life in virtually every field: academic achievement, career, and marriage. Many of the Torah's laws, especially in relation to food and sexual relations, are a lifelong tutorial in the deferment of instinctual gratification.

Promised Land might have taken only a short time. Instead it took forty years. A people that accepts responsibility for its failures is active, not passive – an agent, not a victim. It has no psychological space for the concept of tragedy.

Since Israel is cast in Numbers in the role of *antihero*, the question arises repeatedly when reading the book: Why, of all peoples on earth, did God choose one that complained, failed, and rebelled constantly? In the words of the famous jingle: "How odd / of God / to choose / the Jews." Only by stepping back from the book and looking at it in the context of Tanakh as a whole do we discover the answer.

In one of the most revisionist utterances in the entire Hebrew Bible, Jeremiah says in the name of God:

> I remember the devotion of your youth,
> how as a bride you loved Me,
> and followed Me through the wilderness,
> through a land not sown. (Jer. 2:2)

This is not Israel the disobedient, the ungrateful, the fainthearted. This is the people who, like Abraham in an earlier age, had the courage – the love – to follow the call of God into an unknown, unsown land. Where, though, in the book of Numbers, with its almost uniformly depressing picture of the people, do we find even a hint of the love Jeremiah was talking about?

The answer lies in a passage that is otherwise almost inexplicable, namely the words of the pagan prophet Balaam, who is hired to curse Israel but instead blesses them three times. Listen to some of the language Balaam uses:

> I see a people dwelling alone, not counting themselves among other nations.... Who can count the dust of Jacob or number the seed of Israel? Let me die the death of the righteous, and let my end be like theirs! (Num. 23:9–10)

> No guilt is seen in Jacob, no sorrow observed in Israel. The Lord their God is with them; the shout of the King is among them. (23:21)

How beautiful are your tents, Jacob, your dwelling places, Israel! ...
May those who bless you be blessed, and those who curse you
be cursed! (24:5, 9)

This *is* the language of love. The entire Balaam story, with its talking donkey who sees the angel Balaam himself cannot see, repeatedly emphasises that the words Balaam uses are not his but God's. Therefore, this
declaration of love is uttered by God – not directly nor through Moses,
not even in the hearing of the Israelites themselves. *This is the obverse
side of the wilderness years,* made explicit only centuries later by prophets such as Jeremiah.

Freedom as an Ongoing Task

In summary, we will understand Numbers if we remember to distinguish
a journey-to from a journey-from, and an adaptive from a technical challenge. We will understand why Moses' reactions are different here from
those in Exodus. Numbers tells us that time is an essential element in
the long walk to freedom, and it may take more than one generation.
The journey is not just a physical one. It is a psychological one, a rite
of passage that requires liminal space: in the case of ancient Israel, the
wilderness. The fundamental tension in the book is between freedom
and order, dramatised in the fugue between narrative and law. Finally,
the journey is a deliberate inversion of myth. There is no human "hero"
in the story, not even Moses. To the contrary, it is a book about responsibility and failure, but it ends in order and hope. Freedom is never less
than *avoda*, hard work, and it must be done by the people. No leader
can do it on their behalf.

What was the result? Jean-Jacques Rousseau has a remarkable
passage in which he describes the Israelites, escaping from Egypt, as
"wretched fugitives" wandering "over the face of the earth without a
single inch of ground to call their own." He continues:

Out of this wandering and servile horde, Moses had the audacity
to create a body politic, a free people; and while they were wandering in the desert without a stone on which to lay their heads,

he gave them that durable set of institutions, proof against time, fortune, and conquerors, which five thousand years have not been able to destroy or even to alter, and which even today still subsists in all its strength.[30]

Numbers and the events it describes represents, quite simply, the greatest tutorial in freedom in history, and its message today is no less powerful. Freedom is not achieved merely by overthrowing tyrants. It is achieved only by a prolonged training in the responsibilities and restraints that freedom requires. "There is nothing more arduous," wrote Alexis de Tocqueville, "than the apprenticeship of liberty." He added, "It is generally established with difficulty in the midst of storms."[31] That is Numbers.

Not only does this apply to parts of the world that have never known freedom; it applies also to those that have known it for centuries. It must be fought for in every generation or it will eventually disappear. As I write these words, I am mindful of the fact that for the past half century, there has been an assumption in the West that liberal democratic politics and market economics are self-sustaining. They are part of a linear, irreversible process that once achieved is never subsequently lost.

Nothing could be further than the truth. A free society is a moral achievement. Without a shared morality, a strong identity based on memory and narrative, without training in character, self-restraint, and the ability to defer the gratification of instinct, civilisation will eventually suffer a decline, as did Athens, Rome, and Italy of the Renaissance. A free society depends on habits of the heart, and without them it declines and falls.

Ultimately, a free society is a spiritual achievement. That is what John F. Kennedy meant when he said in his Inaugural Address that "the rights of man come not from the generosity of the state, but from the hand of God." The great developments in the seventeenth century that laid the foundations for the free societies of the contemporary West – social

30. Jean-Jacques Rousseau, "The Government of Poland," in *Political Writings* (Madison: University of Wisconsin Press, 1986), 163.
31. Alexis de Tocqueville, *Democracy in America*, abr. ed., introduction by Thomas Bender (New York: Vintage Books, 1954), 1:247.

covenant and contract, liberty of conscience and human rights – were articulated by thinkers in active dialogue with the Hebrew Bible: John Milton, Thomas Hobbes, John Locke, and Benedict Spinoza.[32] It is not clear that these ideas are sustainable in the long run without the religious foundations of Tanakh. Freedom is as challenging today as it was in the days of Moses. Numbers remains one of its classic texts.

---

32. See Jeremy Waldron, *God, Locke, and Equality: Christian Foundations in Locke's Political Thought* (Cambridge: Cambridge University Press, 2002), who argues that Locke's thought on equality is inconceivable without its religious foundations. Nicholas Wolterstorff mounts a contemporary argument on similar lines in *Justice: Rights and Wrongs* (Princeton, NJ: Princeton University Press, 2010).

Bemidbar
במדבר

The central theme of the book of Numbers is the second stage of the Israelites' journey, physically from Egypt to the Promised Land, mentally from slavery to freedom. This *parasha* and that of the following week are about the preparations for that journey, the first of which was to take a census. To inherit the land the Israelites would have to fight battles. Hence the census, specifically of men between the ages of twenty and sixty – that is, those eligible to serve in war. The Levites were counted separately because it was not their role to fight but to minister in the Sanctuary.

Instructions were given as to the layout of the camp, which was to be a square with the Sanctuary in the middle. Three tribes were to set up their tents and banners on each side, while the Levites formed an inner square. The order in which they encamped was also the order in which they journeyed.

The duties of the family of Kehat – which also included Moses, Aaron, and Miriam, who had other roles – were spelled out. It was their task to carry the most sacred objects, the Ark, Table, Menora, Altars, curtains, and holy vessels used in the sacrificial service, when the Israelites journeyed. This demanded special care.

The first of the following essays explores the theme of the book as a whole: the fourth act in the Torah's account of the human condition, suspended between order and freedom. The second is about the fact that the founding drama of the Israelites as a nation under the sovereignty of God is enacted *in the wilderness*, what anthropologists call "liminal space." The third looks at the connection between *midbar*, "wilderness," and *davar*, "word." Why did the revelation of God's will have to take place in the desert? The fourth spells out the consequences of the unique fact that the Israelites received the law before the land. The fifth is about the *haftara* and Hosea's revisionary reading of the wilderness years as the honeymoon between Israel and God.

The Human Story: Act 4

How are we to understand the book of Numbers in its entirety? It opens by taking up the story as we left it at the end of Exodus. At that point, the people had left Egypt and journeyed to Mount Sinai. There they received the Torah. There they made the Golden Calf. There they were forgiven after Moses' passionate plea, and there they made the *Mishkan*, the Tabernacle. It was inaugurated "on the first day of the first month in the second year" (Ex. 40:17). The book of Numbers begins one month later, "on the first day of the second month of the second year" (Num. 1:1).[1] After a prolonged stay in the Sinai desert, the people were ready to start the second part of the journey, from the wilderness to the Promised Land.

---

1. Note that for a while in Numbers, time moves backwards. Chapter 9 begins, "The Lord spoke to Moses in the Sinai desert in the first month of the second year after they came out of Egypt." In other words, this takes place some time, possibly as much as a month, before the beginning of the book. This is one source for the principle that "there is no before and after in the Torah" (see Pesaḥim 6b; Rashi to Num. 9:1). Note also that time does not pass at all in the book of Leviticus. This is characteristic of the priestly voice in Torah, which is, in general, meta-historical. The priestly truths, unlike the prophetic ones, are timeless.

But Numbers does not start there. There is a long delay in the narrative. Ten chapters pass until the Israelites actually begin to travel (Num. 10:33). What was detaining them? Or rather, what was slowing down the story? Before we can join the people on their journey, we have to read about a census. Then comes an account of the arrangement of the tribes around the *Ohel Moed*, the Tent of Meeting. There is a long description of the Levites, their families, and respective roles. There are laws about the purity of the camp, restitution, a woman suspected of adultery, and the Nazirite. At inordinate length, we read about the gifts brought by the princes of the tribes at the inauguration of the Tabernacle. Then come further passages describing the final preparations for the journey. Only then does the journey begin. Why the delay? Why this long series of seeming digressions?

One feature of the Mosaic books that has tended to confuse secular Bible scholars for more than two centuries is that they constitute a unique genre. They are not history in the conventional sense, a mere recording of what happened. A prime example is the book of Numbers itself, which passes over in silence almost thirty-eight of the forty years in the wilderness.[2] Events are not recorded in the Torah simply because they happened. They are there because of what they teach us about the human condition under God.

Nor is the Torah a conventional kind of law book. There are substantive similarities between certain biblical laws and other ancient codes such as that of Hammurabi. But there is no similarity in literary form. The Torah moves from law to narrative to law again. It intersperses other kinds of material. In the case of Numbers, this includes census lists, an itinerary, some actual legal cases, battle reports, an Amorite victory song (Num. 21:27–30), and the oracles of a non-Israelite, Balaam. Though the Torah *contains* law codes, it does not look like any other law code.

Secular Bible scholars have therefore sought to understand the text by dismembering it, separating it into (usually) ever-smaller fragments and trying to understand each in isolation. This is wrong: it is

---

2. The only reference is the list of names of places in which the Israelites stopped, in Numbers 33.

precisely how *not* to read a book.[3] You do not understand a symphony by disaggregating its musical themes. It is precisely the way the score holds them together, often in tension and with shifts of mood, that constitutes the symphony as an artistic unity. Likewise with the Torah – with at least this difference: we have nothing to compare it to, not only in ancient religious literature, but among the other books of Tanakh as well.

There is nothing accidental about the mix of law and narrative in the Torah, nor is there anything haphazard about the structure of Numbers as a book. *The Torah reflects the Israelite understanding of God as the unity beneath diversity.* If all you can see is the diversity, not the unity, you do not understand it at all.

The Torah offers a unique contrast to the way of thought we have come to regard as distinctively Western whose origins are in ancient Greece. It does three unusual things. First, it includes philosophy in the narrative mode. It teaches not truth as system but truth as story. Second, it portrays law not as it reflects the will or wisdom of the legislator, but rather as it emerges from history, as if to say: this is what went wrong in the past and this is how to avoid it in the future. Third, it regards history itself as an ongoing commentary on the human condition. The Torah is about *the truths that emerge through time.*

These are among the great differences between ancient Israel and ancient Greece. Ancient Greece sought truth by contemplating nature and reason. The first gave rise to science, the second to philosophy. Ancient Israel found truth in history, in events and what the Torah invites us to learn from them. Science is about nature; Judaism is about *human* nature – and there is a great difference between them.

Nature knows nothing of free will. Scientists often deny that it exists at all. But humanity is constituted by its freedom. We are what we choose to be. No planet chooses to be hospitable to life. No fish chooses to live in water. No peacock chooses to be vain. Humans do choose, and in that fact is born the drama to which the whole Torah is a commentary: *How can freedom coexist with order?* The drama is set on the stage of history, and it plays itself out through four acts, each with multiple scenes.

3.   Clearly, this is a large subject, to be dealt with elsewhere.

The basic shape of the narrative is roughly the same in all four cases. First God creates order. Then people create chaos. Terrible consequences follow. God begins again, sometimes deeply grieved but never losing His faith in the one life form on which He set His image and to which He gave the singular gift that made humanity God-like, namely freedom itself.

Act 1 is told in Genesis 1–11. In this version of the story, the subject is *humanity as a whole*. God creates an ordered universe and fashions human beings from the dust of the earth into which He breathes His own breath. But humans sin – first Adam and Eve, then Cain, then the generation of the Flood. The earth is filled with violence. God brings a flood and begins again, making a covenant with Noah. Humanity still does not learn the lesson. People sin again, this time not by being less than human (i.e., violent), but by seeking to be more than human by making a tower that will "reach heaven" (Gen. 11:4), and by imposing an artificial unity ("one language with uniform words," Gen. 11:1) on human diversity.

So God begins again. Act 2 is told in Genesis 12–50. It is the story of *the covenantal family*: Abraham and Sarah and three generations of their children. The new order is based on family and fidelity, marriage and parenthood, love and trust, and educating children in "the way of the Lord" as it expresses itself in charity and justice (Gen. 18:19). But this too begins to unravel. There is tension between Esau and Jacob, between Jacob's wives Leah and Rachel, and between their children. Ten of Jacob's children sell the eleventh, Joseph, into slavery. This is an offence against freedom, and catastrophe follows – not a flood but a famine, as a result of which Jacob's family goes into exile in Egypt, where the whole extended family is eventually enslaved.

Act 3, set out in the book of Exodus, is about *the Israelites as a nation in covenant with God*. It begins with God rescuing the Israelites from Egypt as He once rescued Noah from the Flood. His covenant with them at Mount Sinai is far more extensive than its two predecessors, God's covenant first with Noah, then with Abraham. It is a blueprint for social order on the basis of law and justice, informed by the people's memories of the way they were treated in Egypt. Their society will be different. They are not to inflict on others what was inflicted on them. To be sure, it does not abolish slavery (that did not happen for three thousand years), nor does it put an end to war (that still has not happened). But it involves the people accepting God as their sovereign. Almost immediately it is badly damaged, when the Israelites make a Golden Calf a mere forty days after the great revelation. God threatens to destroy the entire nation, beginning again with Moses, as He did with Noah and Abraham (Ex. 32:10). Only Moses' passionate plea prevents this from happening. God then institutes a new order.

Act 4 is unprecedentedly long. It is about *a people with the Divine Presence in its midst*. God is no longer simply the distant, majestic Creator of the universe and intervener in history. He is also close, the *Shekhina*, God as immanent as well as transcendent: God-as-neighbour. This story begins at Exodus 35, continues through the whole of the book of Leviticus, and dominates the first ten chapters of Numbers. Its most tangible symbol is the Tabernacle in the centre of the camp. The building of the Tabernacle takes up the last third of Exodus. The Tabernacle itself represented a home for the Divine Presence on earth, and whoever sought to enter it had to be holy and pure. The laws of purity and holiness take up virtually the whole of Leviticus. As Numbers begins, we expect the Israelites to start the journey to the holy land. The first ten chapters are therefore unexpected, and hint at something that only becomes clear later on in the book.

If the Israelites are to become a free people in the land God promised their ancestors, they need to be capable of self-imposed order. Otherwise they will merely repeat the mistakes we have encountered three times already: the violence before the Flood, the divisions within the Abrahamic family, and the making of the Golden Calf. The first ten chapters of Numbers are all about creating a sense of order within the camp.

Hence the census and the detailed disposition of the tribes, and the lengthy account of the Levites, the tribe that mediated between the people and the Divine Presence. Hence, also, in the book's second *parasha*, three laws – about restitution, the *sota* (a woman suspected of adultery), and the Nazirite (a person who forswears wine) – directed at the three forces that always endanger social order: theft, infidelity, and alcohol. In these opening chapters, it is as if God is saying to the Israelites: This is what order looks like. Each person has his or her place within the family, the tribe, and the nation. Everyone has been counted and each person counts. There is an order to the way the tribes are encamped around the Tabernacle, and to the way they proceed when travelling. Preserve and protect this order, for without it you cannot enter the land, fight its battles, and create a society that is both just and free.

Tragically, as Numbers unfolds, we see that the Israelites have not yet internalised this message. They complain about the food. Miriam and Aaron criticise Moses. Then comes the catastrophe: the episode of the spies. The people, demoralised, show that they are not yet ready for freedom. As before in the case of the Golden Calf, there is chaos in the camp. Again God threatens to destroy the nation and begin again with Moses (Num. 14:12). Again only Moses' powerful plea saves the day. God decides once more to begin again, this time with the next generation and a new leader. The book of Deuteronomy is Moses' prelude to Act 5, which takes place in the days of his successor, Joshua.

The Jewish story is a strange one. Time and again the Jewish people has split apart: in the days of the First Temple when the kingdom divided into two, in the late Second Temple period when it splintered into rival groups and sects, and in the modern age, at the beginning of the nineteenth century, when it fragmented into religious and secular in Eastern Europe, Orthodox and others in the West. Those divisions have still not healed.

And so the Jewish people keeps repeating the story told five times in the Torah. God creates order. Humans create chaos. God represents unity. People create disunity. Bad things happen; God and Israel begin again. Will the story never end? One thing is sure. God never gives up. Nor does He cease speaking to us through the timeless words of the Written Torah, translated into time by the ongoing Oral Torah, reminding us that the central human challenge in every age is whether freedom can coexist with order. It can, when humans freely choose to follow God's laws, given universally to humanity after the Flood and in concrete particularity to Israel after the Exodus.

The alternative, ancient and modern, is the rule of power, in which, as Thucydides said, the strong do as they will and the weak suffer as they must. That is not freedom as the Torah understands it, nor is it a recipe for justice and compassion. The Torah is God's call to create a freedom that honours order and a social order that honours human freedom, to respect both what is universal in our shared humanity and what is particular in our historical specificity. The challenge remains, and the stakes become higher every year.

The Space Between

Why "In the Wilderness"? That is a fundamental question when thinking about the biblical story. Recall that Jewish time began with the call of God to Abram to leave his land, his birthplace, and his father's house and travel "to the land I will show you" (Gen. 12:1). Seven times in Genesis, God promises the land to Abraham, once to Isaac, and three times to Jacob. Yet it is a consummation that seems almost endlessly to be delayed.

Abraham does indeed leave his land, his birthplace, and his father's house and arrives in the land of Canaan. It is natural to assume that this is the end of this particular story, but it proves to be only the beginning. No sooner does he arrive than there is a famine in the land and he has to leave and go to Egypt (Gen. 12:10). There is another famine in the days of Isaac, forcing him too to leave, this time to stay among the Philistines in Gerar (Gen. 26:1). Jacob has to leave home not once but twice, once for fear of Esau's violent reprisal for the loss of his blessing, a second time due to famine and the desire to be reunited with his long-lost son Joseph in Egypt. There he dies.

What then has happened to the promise of the land? As if to reassure us, Genesis draws to a close with two confident predictions. Jacob, about to die, tells Joseph, "God shall be with you and *bring you back to the land of your fathers*" (Gen. 48:21). Joseph, before he dies, tells his brothers, "God will surely come to your aid and *bring you up out of this land to the land He promised on oath* to Abraham, Isaac, and Jacob" (Gen. 50:24).

Yet it does not happen – not immediately. As Exodus begins, far from being brought back to the land, the Israelites find themselves enslaved. God calls on Moses to lead the people out, which he does, to the accompaniment of signs and wonders. Yet the return, which should have taken no more than a few weeks, becomes – in the middle of the book of Numbers – extended to forty years, so that the people who left Egypt were not the people who entered the Promised Land, with only two exceptions, Joshua and Caleb. Why the long delay? Why did the road to the holy land have to pass through Egypt, and through forty-two stopping places on the way back? Why is there so much wilderness in space and time in the story of Israel's beginnings?

To understand the answer, it is helpful to turn to the work of two anthropologists, Arnold van Gennep and Victor Turner. A key concept in their work is the idea of *liminal space*, the place that is neither here nor there, neither starting point nor destination, but *the space between*. That is what the wilderness was. It was not Egypt, not Israel, but the no-man's-land between them. Liminal space is important not for what it contains, nor how large it is, but rather, because of what happens there. It is *the place of transformation*.

Arnold van Gennep introduced the term in his classic work, *The Rites of Passage*.[1] In it he argued that societies develop rituals to mark the transition from one state to the next – from childhood to adulthood, for example, or from being single to being married. They involve three stages. The first is *separation*, a symbolic break with the past. The last is *incorporation*, re-entering society with a new identity. Between the two is the crucial stage of *transition* when, having cast off one identity but not yet donned another, people are remade, refashioned, reborn.

Van Gennep used the term *liminal*, from the Latin word for "threshold," to describe this transitional state when you are in a kind of

---

1. Arnold van Gennep, *The Rites of Passage* (Chicago: University of Chicago Press, 1960).

no-man's-land between the old and the new. That is what the *wilderness* signifies for Israel: liminal space between slavery and freedom, past and future, exile and return, Egypt and the Promised Land. *The desert is the space that makes transition and transformation possible.* It is a no-man's-land. It has no settled population, no cities, no civilisational order. There the Israelites, alone with God and with one another, could cast off one identity and assume another. There they could be reborn, no longer slaves to Pharaoh, but instead servants of God, summoned to become "a kingdom of priests and a holy nation" (Ex. 19:6).

This analysis helps us understand certain details of the narrative in the book of Exodus. We now see the significance of the Israelites' daubing of the doorposts with blood (Ex. 12:7). Recall that "liminal" means "threshold," and passing through a door on your way to a new life is often an essential element of transition rituals, a symbolic farewell.

Likewise the division of the Red Sea. The division of one thing into two, through which something or someone passes, is a symbolic enactment of transition, as it was for Abraham in the Covenant between the Pieces (Gen. 15:10–21) when God told him about his children's future exile and enslavement. Abraham divided animals, God divided the sea, but it was the walk between the two halves that signalled the rite of passage, the existential change between one mode of being and another. Both the daubing of the doorpost and the journey through the sea were *separation rituals* – bidding farewell to a past before entering liminal space.

The book of Deuteronomy, on the other hand, is about *incorporation*. It is, essentially, a book of instructions as to how the Israelites should live as a nation in the holy land and as an actor on the stage of history. The central theme of Numbers is the middle stage, *transition*, which involves a journey that is less geographical than existential. Those who left Egypt had to become different kinds of people before they could enter the land. They had to cast off the mindset of slavery and become free.

One of the key messages of Numbers, delivered through an agonising set of stories about complaints, rebellions, and failures of nerve, is to educate us to understand how long and hard a journey that is. In the final analysis, as shown in the story of the spies, it turned out to be too hard, too demanding, to be the work of a single generation. It was not those who left Egypt who found the strength to face freedom without fear, but their children, who were born in the desert and who – unlike their parents – had never developed the mindset of slaves.

Victor Turner adds one significant element to van Gennep's analysis.[2] He draws a distinction between society and *communitas*. Society is always marked by structure and hierarchy. Some have power, some do not. There are classes, castes, ranks, orders, and other gradations of status and honour. *Communitas* is different, and it is this that makes the experience of liminal space vivid and transformative. In the desert, there are no hierarchies. Instead, there is "an intense comradeship and egalitarianism. Secular distinctions of rank and status disappear or are homogenised."[3] People cast together in the no-man's-land of the desert experience the "essential and generic human bond."[4] That is what he means by *communitas*, a rare and special state in which, for a brief but memorable period, everyone is equal.

No sooner have we seen this than we understand one of the critical axes of tension throughout the book. On the one hand, the wilderness was the supreme bonding experience between the people and God. They were close – closer than humans came to God before or since. They ate His manna, "bread from heaven" (Ex. 16:4). They drank, often miraculously, from water He provided. His Sanctuary was in the middle of the camp. His presence was tangible. The people were surrounded by His clouds of glory. The tribes were equidistant from the place of His presence. They had a unique insight into one of the Torah's most revolutionary ideas: *the equal dignity of all under the sovereignty of God.*

But there were limits. The people needed structure. Without it, they were capable of making a Golden Calf. The book of Numbers describes many hierarchies. There were the princes of the tribes who took the census and brought offerings at the inauguration of the Sanctuary. There were the

---

2. Victor Turner, *The Ritual Process: Structure and Anti-Structure* (Chicago: Aldine, 1969); *Dramas, Fields, and Metaphors: Symbolic Action in Human Society* (Ithaca, NY: Cornell University Press, 1974).
3. Turner, *The Ritual Process*, 95.
4. Ibid., 97.

seventy elders who helped Moses with the burden of leadership. There were the Levites who carried the Sanctuary and its sacred objects. There were the priests who officiated at its service, and the high priest, Aaron, Moses' brother. There were the spies, and so on. That is why a recurring theme of Numbers is the nature of, and challenges to, leadership in the context of the intense togetherness – the *communitas* – of the wilderness.

Which then is to prevail, the egalitarianism of community or the hierarchy of society? We hear two quite different approaches in the book. One occurs when Moses gives voice to a pure egalitarianism. Eldad and Medad begin prophesying within the camp, an event that Joshua sees as a threat to Moses' position. "Are you jealous on my account?" says Moses. "Would that all the Lord's people were prophets" (Num. 11:29).

Yet when a similar sentiment is expressed by Korah – "All the congregation are holy and the Lord is in their midst. Why then do you set yourselves above the congregation?" (Num. 16:3) – Moses takes it as a threat to his leadership and crushes the rebellion. There is a significant difference between these two contexts, as we will see. Between them, there is no contradiction. Yet liminal space is where the possibilities and limits of equality are tested.

Evidently there are limits to *communitas* – a society of equals who share responsibility for the fate of the nation as a whole. Yet the tension remains and will do so throughout the whole of the biblical era. We see this most clearly in the deep ambivalence of Tanakh, the Hebrew Bible, about the institution of monarchy. On the one hand stands the statement of Gideon when offered the crown: "I will not rule over you, nor will my son rule over you; the Lord will rule over you" (Judges 8:23). On the other is the closing sentence of the book of Judges: "In those days there was no king in Israel; everyone did what was right in his own eyes" (Judges 21:25).

Ideally, Israel would have no king other than God Himself.[5] Realistically, however, it had to settle for the checks and balances of the division of power between king, priest, and prophet: the king to lead the nation politically and militarily, the priest to connect it to a holiness

---

5. Hence the significance of the line in the *Avinu Malkeinu* prayer: "Our father, our king, we have no other king but You."

that transcends history, and the prophet to criticise priests and kings when they become corrupt. We will encounter this division of powers in the fifth and last of the Mosaic books (Deut. 17). Numbers sets out the problem to which Deuteronomy will provide an answer.

We can, however, now see the significance of the way Numbers begins. Immediately after the census we read of how the twelve tribes were encamped, each equidistant from the Sanctuary. Each tribe was different, but (with the exception of the Levites) all were equal. They ate the same food, they drank the same water. None yet had lands of their own, for the desert has no owners. There was no economic or territorial conflict between them. Each, in chapter 7, brought the same offering at the dedication of the Tabernacle.

Each of these accounts, with their emphasis on equality, fits Turner's description of *communitas*, the ideal state that people experience in liminal space when they have left the past (Egypt) behind but have not yet reached their future destination (the Promised Land). They had not yet begun building a society with all the inequalities to which society gives rise. For the moment, they were together, their tents forming a perfect square with the Sanctuary at its centre.

The poignancy of the book of Numbers lies in the fact that this *communitas* lasted so briefly. The serene mood of its beginning would soon be shattered by quarrel after quarrel, rebellion after rebellion, in a series of disruptions that would cost an entire generation their chance of entering the land.

Yet a positive dimension of that memory remained. The wilderness years were the time when the distance between heaven and earth was never shorter. In those arduous yet memorable years the people went through their rite of passage from slavery to freedom to become a nation unlike any other, forged in fire, formed in covenant, a tiny people that had greatness thrust upon it, sometimes seemingly against its will.

That is why the journey to the Promised Land had to pass through the experience of slavery in Egypt, so that the people would never forget what it feels like to lose their freedom. It is also why it had to pass through the liminal space of the wilderness, so that they could undergo the transformation from a nation of slaves to a people ready to shoulder the responsibilities of freedom.

We now realise that Abraham's journey, continued by his children, was never meant to be a physical one only, from one place to another, from here to there. It was a spiritual and psychological one also, one so profound that it would affect not only those generations but their offspring for all time, inscribed in their memories, engraved on their hearts. Abraham's children were to become the people who learned through their own hard experience that "liberty cannot be established without morality, nor morality without faith."[6]

The wilderness was the liminal space where Israel, "the holy nation," was born.

6. Thomas Bender, introduction to *Democracy in America*, abr. ed., by Alexis de Tocqueville, vol. 1 (New York: Vintage Books, 1954).

Wilderness and Word

T he *parasha* of *Bemidbar*, "In the Wilderness," is usually read immediately prior to Shavuot, the commemoration of the giving of the Torah at Mount Sinai.[1] Accordingly the rabbis strove to find a connection between them. A midrash, for example, states that "the Torah was given in three things: fire, water, and wilderness – wilderness, as it says, 'The Lord spoke to Moses in the wilderness of Sinai.'"[2] There were various suggestions as to what this means. How exactly is Torah essentially connected to the idea of wilderness?

One interpretation is psychological: "Anyone who does not make himself open to all [*hefker*, literally 'ownerless'] like a wilderness cannot acquire wisdom and Torah."[3] To receive the word of God, we must make ourselves open, the way a desert is. We have to engage in active listening. If we bring to the Torah our own presuppositions and preoccupations,

---

1. To be sure, neither the Torah, nor any other book of Tanakh, explicitly connects the two events. For an account of the connection, see my introduction to the *Shavuot Maḥzor* (Jerusalem: Koren, 2016).
2. Numbers Rabba 1:7.
3. Ibid.

we will hear only what we expect to hear. We will never encounter the voice of God, the radically Other, the transformative presence, within the text. We need an open mind and a receptive heart.

Another midrash relates the wilderness to the rabbinic tradition that God offered the Torah to all the nations of the world, but none except Israel wanted to accept it. That is why the Torah was given in open space, in no-man's-land, so that it could be heard by everyone. Had it been given in any specific country, all the other nations except that one could claim that it was not offered to them.[4] Another similar interpretation is that just as fire, water, and wilderness are not things you buy, but are available to all, so the Torah was and is a free gift from God; whoever wishes to avail themselves of it may do so.[5]

However, there is something altogether deeper at stake, and it is suggested by the assonance, the similarity of sound, between *midbar*, "wilderness," and *davar*, "word."[6] There is a connection between the silence and barrenness of the desert and the unique revelation that took place there. Looking back on that event at the end of his life, Moses reminded the people that it was an auditory experience, not a visual one: "Then the Lord spoke to you out of the fire. You heard the sound of words but saw no form; there was only a voice" (Deut. 4:12). This was a radical departure from the history of religion.

Jewish thinkers of the nineteenth and early twentieth centuries were struck by the profound difference between the religion of the Bible and all other religions of the ancient world. God, in Judaism, is invisible. He cannot be seen or visually represented. To attempt to do so – to make an icon or a visible representation of God – is in Judaism a form of idolatry. For every other ancient religion, the gods were eminently visible. They could be seen in the phenomena of nature: the sun, the stars, the sky, the sea, the wind, the rain, the storm. There was no problem of revelation. The gods were everywhere.

---

4. *Mekhilta, Parashat Yitro, BaHodesh* 1.
5. *Midrash Lekaḥ Tov, Parashat Yitro*, 20:2.
6. Noted by, among others, Harold Fisch, *Poetry with a Purpose* (Bloomington: Indiana University Press, 1988), 143.

It was in Israel that a revolutionary idea was born, that God was not in nature but beyond it, for it was He who created nature in the first place:

When I consider Your heavens, the work of Your fingers,
the moon and the stars which You have set in place... (Ps. 8:4)

This was a paradigm-shifting concept.[7] The entire universe, almost infinite in extent, is no more than the work of God's fingers. Everything we can see is not God but merely the work of God. Hence the repeated prohibitions in Judaism against making an image or icon. To Judaism, the idea that God is visible is idolatry. God is beyond the totality of things seen.

How then can He be encountered? In Judaism for the first time, revelation became a problem. When the gods are to be found in nature, they are close. But if God is beyond nature, beyond the universe itself, then He is vast beyond our imagining, and infinitely distant. The answer Judaism gave was radical. God is close, but encountered not in things seen, but in words heard. This is how the historian Heinrich Graetz put it:

The pagan perceives the divine in nature through the medium of the eye, and he becomes conscious of it as something to be looked at. On the other hand, to the Jew who conceives God as being outside of nature and prior to it, the Divine manifests itself through the will and through the medium of the ear. He becomes conscious of it as something to be heeded and listened to. The pagan beholds his god; the Jew hears Him, that is, apprehends His will.[8]

7. "It needs an effort of the imagination to realise the shattering boldness of a contempt for imagery at the time, and in the particular historical setting, of the Hebrews. Everywhere religious fervour... sought plastic and pictorial expression. The Hebrews, however, denied the relevancy of the 'graven image'; the boundless could not be given form, the unqualified could but be offended by a representation.... Every finite reality shrivelled to nothingness before the absolute value which was God" (Henri Frankfort et al., *Before Philosophy: The Intellectual Adventure of Ancient Man* [Harmondsworth: Penguin, 1949], 242). This was, according to Frankfort, a decisive moment in "the emancipation of thought from myth."
8. Heinrich Graetz, "Judaism Can Be Understood Only Through Its History," in *Ideas of Jewish History*, ed. Michael Meyer (New York: Behrman House, 1974), 223.

Other civilisations gave rise to visual cultures, while Judaism is supremely a *culture of the ear* – of words, speech, listening, interpreting, understanding, heeding.

This created, for Jews and Judaism, a distinctive phenomenology, a unique way of experiencing the world. Seeing, said Hans Jonas, is immediate, but hearing requires interpretation. When I hear a dog barking, for example, I hear the bark, not the dog. To know that it was a dog producing the sound, I have to use inference.[9] Sight can be instantaneous; that is what is captured by a photograph. But sound, communication, speaking, and listening are necessarily extended in time. You cannot freeze a sentence.[10] So a culture based on listening rather than seeing encounters God not in timeless moments but in time, which is to say, in history.

Even Sigmund Freud, otherwise hostile to religion, could not avoid being impressed by this idea:

> Among the precepts of Mosaic religion is one that has more significance than is at first obvious. It is the prohibition against making an image of God, which means the compulsion to worship an invisible god…. [This] was bound to exercise a profound influence. For it signified subordinating sense perception to an abstract idea; it was a triumph of spirituality over the senses; more precisely, an instinctual renunciation accompanied by its psychologically necessary consequences…. It was certainly one of the most important stages on the way to becoming human.[11]

A revolution of this magnitude cannot take place under ordinary circumstances. In the great river lowlands where civilisation began (the Tigris-Euphrates and the Nile), the eye is captivated by the shifting scenes of nature; in cities, by the works of man – art and architecture. Only in the emptiness of the wilderness is the eye subordinate to the ear. Only in the silence of the desert can the sound beneath sound be heard:

9. Hans Jonas, "The Nobility of Sight," *Philosophy and Phenomenological Research* 14, no. 4 (1954): 507–519.
10. See Jacques Ellul, *The Humiliation of the Word* (Grand Rapids, MI: Eerdmans, 1985).
11. Sigmund Freud, *Moses and Monotheism* (New York: Vintage, 1939), 144–145.

In Hebrew thought, Book and Desert are contingent upon one another. When God revealed Himself to Moses and charged him with the task of freeing the Hebrews, terms such as "freedom" and "liberty" were not used. The idea of emancipation from bondage is expressed as "going on a three days' journey into the desert, to sacrifice to God our Lord" (Ex. 3:19; 5:3), as if God could not be apprehended without this initial journey into the desert.[12]

Or as Edmond Jabès put it:

The word cannot dwell except in the silence of other words. To speak is, accordingly, to lean on a metaphor of the desert, a space of dust or ashes, where the triumphant word is offered in her unrestricted nudity.[13]

The historian Eric Voegelin saw this as fundamental to the discovery by the Israelites of a completely new form of spirituality:

If nothing had happened but a lucky escape from the range of Egyptian power, there only would have been a few more nomadic tribes roaming the border zone between the Fertile Crescent and the desert proper, eking out a meagre living with the aid of part-time agriculture. But the desert was only a station on the way, not the goal; for in the desert the tribes found their God. They entered into a covenant with Him, and thereby became His people....

When we undertake the exodus and wander into the world, in order to found a new society elsewhere, we discover the world as the Desert. The flight leads nowhere, until we stop in order to find our bearings beyond the world. When the world has become Desert, man is at last in the solitude in which he can hear thunderingly the voice of the spirit that with its urgent whispering

12. Jose Faur, *Golden Doves with Silver Dots* (Bloomington: Indiana University Press, 1986), 4–5.
13. Edmond Jabès, *From the Desert to the Book* (Barrytown, NY: Station Hill Press, 1990), 68.

has already driven and rescued him from Sheol [the domain of death]. In the Desert God spoke to the leader and his tribes; in the Desert, by listening to the voice, by accepting its offer, and by submitting to its command, they had at last reached life and became the people chosen by God.[14]

So there is an intrinsic connection between the desert, *midbar*, and God who reveals Himself in speech, *medabber*. But note also what is unique about the Jewish story. It is not unknown in the history of religion for founders to spend time alone – their "wilderness years" – during which their understanding of their mission takes shape. There are such stories told of the heroes of Buddhism, Christianity, and Islam. What is unique to the Jewish experience is that *this happened to an entire people*. It was not Moses alone but the Israelites as a whole who experienced the wilderness years. This too is essential to the distributed and democratised nature of Jewish spirituality. "The Torah Moses commanded us is the inheritance of [all] the community of Jacob" (Deut. 33:4).

The way to the holy land lies through the wilderness. It was not simply that the more direct route, along the coast, was dangerous: "When Pharaoh let the people go, God did not lead them on the road through the Philistine country, though that was shorter. For God said, 'If they face war, they might change their minds and return to Egypt'" (Ex. 13:17). Rather, the desert was the place where the people would be alone with God. There, undistracted by the sight of natural or man-made beauty, they were hyper-sensitised to sound. They could hear the voice of God, becoming the only people in history to have received a revelation experienced directly by every member of the nation. What they heard was a unique challenge: to take the pain of suffering in Egypt and redirect it into creating a society that would be the opposite of Egypt, not an empire built on power but a society of individuals of equal dignity under the sovereignty of God. To quote Voegelin again:

14. Eric Voegelin, *Israel and Revelation*, vol. 1 of *Order and History* (Baton Rouge: Louisiana State University Press, 1956), 153.

What emerged from the alembic of the Desert was not a people like the Egyptians or Babylonians, the Canaanites or Philistines, the Hittites or Arameans, but a new genus of society, set off from the civilizations of the age by the Divine choice. It was a people that moved on the historical scene while living toward a goal beyond history.[15]

In the silence of the desert, the Israelites heard the Word and became the people of the Word.

15. Ibid., 154.

Law and Land

In the previous essay we looked at one connection between the Torah and the wilderness: in the silence of the desert you can hear the Word. There is, though, another connection that proved fateful on the course of Jewish history, allowing Judaism to survive in a way that has no parallel in the annals of other nations.

What this is becomes immediately apparent if we ask a simple question: What comes first, the law or the land? The answer in general is the land. People settle in a certain territory. They evolve from bands to clans to tribes to larger associations of tribes. They begin to build villages, then towns, then city-states of the kind that first appeared in Mesopotamia where Abraham was born.

So long as groups stay small, they develop a basic structure of cooperation, reciprocity, and trust. If I find food today but you do not, then I will share what I find with you, because I know there will be days when you find food and I do not, and I know you will reciprocate the act of sharing. It is this kind of cooperation that is basic not just to humans but to all social animals. It has been demonstrated by computer simulation as the most effective strategy of group survival and is known as reciprocal altruism.[1]

But there are limits as to how far it can extend. For it to work, I need to know and remember who can be trusted to reciprocate and who cannot. This requires intelligence and memory, and biologists have shown a correlation among social animals between brain size and the optimal size of a group: the larger the brain, the larger the group. This led Oxford anthropologist Robin Dunbar to calculate that for humans the outer limit is around 150. Up to that point we can know everyone in the group. Beyond that, we cannot.[2]

It follows that for relatively small groups – extended families, villages – cooperation can function without the formality of law. Fishermen who operate in the same area, for example, will tend to develop practices that allow each to flourish without one damaging the livelihood of others. The rules are usually implicit rather than explicit; they are "how we do things here." Anyone who breaks the rules will be penalised. Anyone who does so regularly will be excluded from the group – and among social animals, exclusion from the group is a kind of death.

The problem arises when human groups become larger than this, which they did with the domestication of animals and the development of agriculture, the division of labour, and the growth of trade. This led to a new and critical problem. How do you sustain cooperation when the group is too large for people to know one another and thus practise reciprocal altruism? *How do you establish trust between strangers?* That is the problem that had to be solved for civilisation to be born.

It was then that a whole series of breakthroughs emerged: the birth of cities, the invention of writing, formal structures of power (kings, emperors, pharaohs), and the development of law, in such forms as the Sumerian code of Ur-Nammu (c. 2100–2050 BCE) and the Code of Hammurabi (c. 1750 BCE). Law and its enforcement were based on

1. There are many books on this. See, for example, Robert Axelrod, *The Evolution of Cooperation* (New York: Basic Books, 1984); Matt Ridley, *The Origins of Virtue* (New York: Viking, 1997).
2. See Robin Dunbar, *Grooming, Gossip, and the Evolution of Language* (Cambridge, MA: Harvard University Press, 1998).

the edict of the king who ruled over a certain territory, be it as small as a city or as large as an empire. Law was therefore bound to land and to the person who ruled over that stretch of land.

This background is, I believe, essential to an understanding of the basic logic of the Torah. It does not say that monotheism was born with Abraham. To the contrary, according to the Torah it was born with Adam and Eve,[3] that is, *before* there were cities. That is confirmed by the consensus of anthropologists today – that hunter-gatherers tended to have a single deity and social structures that were roughly egalitarian.

Polytheism emerged with the first cities and civilisations (*civis*, the Latin root of terms like *civic* and *civilisation*, means "pertaining to a city") – in the place, and shortly before the time, of Abraham. Also born at the same time were monetary exchange, vast disparities of wealth and power, armies and empires, social hierarchy, the emergence of a literate class, the deification of rulers as demigods with religious as well as civic and military authority, and the birth of slavery, which rarely existed among hunter-gatherers but was already attested to in the Code of Hammurabi.

All of this is alluded to in the Torah, in its assertion that the first city was built by the first murderer, Cain; then in its portrayal of the Tower of Babel; and, most powerfully, in its critique of Egypt in the days of Moses. What was fundamentally wrong from the Torah's perspective is that this kind of civilisation turned some people into gods and most others into slaves. It also turned religion from what it should be – humans serving God – into the opposite, the gods serving humans, specifically rulers, by giving sacred sanction to man-made structures of power and exploitation.

Judaism opposes this entire religious-political configuration, though it recognised that changing it would take time. This is one of the key themes of Numbers – that even when slaves are given freedom, they continue to have the mindset of slaves, which is why the generation that left Egypt was not yet ready to enter the land.

---

3. Adam and Eve represent the first humans not in a biological sense, Homo sapiens, but in a spiritual-psychological sense, *Homo religiosus*.

The fundamentals of the Torah's worldview, though, are clear. All humans are equally in the image of God. Ideally none should rule over any other, though in practice this leads to anarchy (such is the basic theme of the book of Judges). Even when there is a king, he has no legislative powers; God alone is the primary legislator.[4] This is the core meaning of the phrase *Torah min hashamayim*, "Law, or teaching, from heaven." It is also the meaning of the fundamental religious act, *kabbalat ol malkhut shamayim*, "acceptance of the yoke of the kingship of Heaven," fulfilled twice daily by the recitation of the *Shema*. Only God has the authority to frame the rules within which the moral life is to be lived.

All these doctrines were unique in the ancient world; they remain exceptional even today. They are the basis of such Western ideals as human rights, justice-as-fairness, and the moral limits of power. They are this-worldly consequences of belief in a single God who transcends the universe and who in love created humans in His image. They are also what made possible one unique feature of the covenant at Mount Sinai, made with the Israelites in the wilderness, before they had crossed the Jordan and settled in the Promised Land. Everywhere else, first came the land, then the law. Judaism is the one exception. First came the law, and only later – a generation later, as it transpired – came the land. This was made possible because, in Judaism, the source of law is God, not Hammurabi or Pharaoh or any other human being, and because God – Creator of the universe, therefore transcending the universe – is the God of everywhere and everyone.

The fact that the Torah was given *bemidbar*, "in the wilderness," had a dramatic consequence. Everywhere else, if you lost the land, you lost the law. If the Greeks or Romans defeated your country, their rulers were your rulers and their law yours. Even if there was no conquest, merely a personal decision to move elsewhere – if you decide, for example, to leave England and become an Italian citizen – you are no longer subject to English jurisdiction; you are bound by Italian law. Law is bound to land and to the power that prevails in that land.

---

4. Kings may issue temporary edicts for the sake of the common good, as did the Sanhedrin in a later age.

Not so in Judaism. Because the Torah was given in the wilderness before the people entered the land of Israel, the law came before the land. Therefore *even when Jews lost the land, they still had the law. Even when they lost the country, they still had the covenant.* This made Jews a nation unlike any other in history, and allowed them to survive as a nation despite exile and dispersion for a period of almost two thousand years.

Exile was still exile. The loss of the land was a devastating tragedy: "By the waters of Babylon, there we sat and wept as we remembered Zion.... How can we sing the Lord's song in a strange land?" (Ps. 137:1, 4). But Jews survived because the covenant was still in force and God's law was still law. That is what Isaiah meant when in God's name he asked the rhetorical question: "Where is your mother's certificate of divorce with which I sent her away? Or to which of My creditors did I sell you?" (Is. 50:1). Israel was still married to God even though she had been banished from the marital home. She still belonged to God even though she was temporarily in other hands.

Hence the paradox at the heart of Judaism. On the one hand, it has an unbreakable connection to the land of Israel. That is the central theme of the Torah: the promise of and journey to the land. Its laws are about the land. Read the Torah and you will immediately note that it is not a formula for the salvation of the soul or the acquisition of inner peace. It is about welfare and the treatment of employees, war and the conduct of an army, justice and the impartial application of the law, charity and the alleviation of poverty. It is about the construction of a society – and a society needs a land.

Despite the fact that Jews have been scattered across the world, there only ever was one place where they could construct a society according to their own values, namely Israel. Not only is it the holy land; it is impossible to be a holy nation except in the land. *Galut,* "exile," has both a physical and spiritual dimension: if you are not physically at home, you are not fully spiritually at home either.

Yet much of Jewish history has been spent outside that home. The Torah ends with Moses and the people in sight of the Promised Land but tantalisingly not yet there. Much of Jewish history is a story of exiles – to Assyria, then Babylon, then the long series of dispersions and expulsions from the Roman conquest to the birth of the modern State of Israel in 1948. As Isaiah Berlin noted:

> It was once said by the celebrated Russian revolutionary, Alexander Herzen, writing in the mid-nineteenth century, that the Slavs had no history, only geography. The position of the Jews is the reverse of this. They have enjoyed rather too much history and too little geography.[5]

Michael Wyschogrod speaks of the "curious ambivalence to the land in Jewish consciousness":

> On the one hand, it [the land] is an integral part of the election. The same act of election which binds Abraham and his descendants to God also binds the people to its land. These three – God, Israel, and the land – are tied one to the other in an indissoluble unity. But, on the other hand, there is also a curious dispensability to the tie between Israel and the land. Israel becomes a full-fledged people prior to its entry into the land. It remains a people, it does not disappear, after it is severed from the land. It is apparently less dependent on the land than any other people. And yet, the longing for possession of the land and for returning to it when separated from it never leaves the consciousness of the people over millennia. In the small villages of the Russian plain, in Jewish homes, the geography of the holy land was far more vivid than that of the surrounding countryside.[6]

The giving of the Torah in the wilderness is an essential feature of that history. Had the Israelites received the Torah in the land, it would be indissolubly associated with the land. Exile would mean the end

---

5. Isaiah Berlin, *The Power of Ideas* (London: Chatto and Windus, 2000), 143.
6. Michael Wyschogrod, *Abraham's Promise* (Grand Rapids, MI: Eerdmans, 2004), 92.

of the covenant.[7] It would make no more sense to keep Torah while in exile than to obey the laws of Russia while living in Spain. What made the God of Israel different from the gods of antiquity was precisely the fact that He was sovereign of the universe, not a local deity – a Canaanite or Egyptian god. That is why the Jewish people survived dispersion. Only the God of everywhere can be found and worshipped anywhere.

Yet the universal God is also the God who lives in particularity. That is the paradox. God is beyond time, yet He is to be found within particular times – Shabbat, the festivals, the sabbatical and jubilee years. So God is beyond place yet encountered in particular places – the holy land, the holy city, the Temple Mount. God lives *within* the world, not just beyond it; He lives in physical, not just metaphysical, space. No one who has prayed at the Kotel or experienced the quiet of Shabbat in Jerusalem can doubt that there are places and times when we sense a special closeness to God. That is why exile is exile – and why *Eretz Yisrael* is not just a geographical entity or a political fact but a religious and spiritual phenomenon.

The relationship between the Jewish people and the land of Israel is *sui generis*, unique. It does not fit any normal template. The present history of the State of Israel – the only nation among the almost two hundred members of the United Nations whose existence is continually called into question – is the latest chapter in a story that goes back four thousand years. Jews remain the people neither fully lost in exile nor fully at home in their land. Those who believed that the return to Israel would "normalise" the Jewish situation were wrong. The reverse has been the case. What has happened instead is that the Jewish people have been returned to the central drama of Tanakh: the nation that is called on to be something more than just a nation. What this means may well be the central Jewish question of our time.

7. That is in fact the argument of Spinoza in chapter 3 of his *Tractatus Theologico-Politicus*. The Talmud says that this was the claim made by some of the Babylonian exiles to Ezekiel; see Sanhedrin 105a. See also Nahmanides, Commentary to Lev. 18:25.

Hosea Rereads the Wilderness Years

Read Numbers in its entirety and it is hard to avoid the sentiment made famous in William Norman Ewer's jingle: "How odd / of God / to choose / the Jews." God had just brought them out of slavery, set them on the road to freedom, given them bread from heaven and water from a rock, divided the sea for them, and surrounded them with clouds of glory. What did they do in return? They complained.

There are no less than seven rebellions in Numbers. The first was about food (ch. 11). The second was the criticism of Moses by his own brother and sister, Aaron and Miriam (ch. 12). Third was the panic caused by the spies (ch. 13–14). Fourth was the challenge to Moses and Aaron by Korah and his fellow conspirators (ch. 16). Fifth was the protest of the people after Moses had suppressed Korah's revolt (ch. 16–17). Sixth was about water: the occasion when Moses lost his temper and forfeited his chance to enter the land (ch. 20). Seventh was the adultery and subsequent idolatry of the Israelites seduced by the Moabite women (ch. 25).

Not only this – there was the fear of freedom, its battles, and its responsibilities, that led the people into monumental false nostalgia. When they complained about the manna, they said, "We remember the fish we ate without cost in Egypt – also the cucumbers, melons, leeks,

onions, and garlic" (Num. 11:5). After the report of the spies the people
say, "If only we had died in Egypt" (14:2). Most chilling of all are the
words of Korah's companions, Datan and Aviram: "Is it not enough that
you have brought us up out of a land flowing with milk and honey to
kill us in the wilderness?" (16:13). This is a devastating series of failures
and indictments.

In the end – or more precisely in the middle, because the event
is the turning point in the book as a whole – we arrive at the conclusion that the whole generation lacked the courage, the self-restraint, the
ability to focus on the future and act together as a people to enter the
land and shoulder the burden of freedom. The wilderness years were
not the Israelites' finest hour.

Thus far the Torah. But what is striking about Judaism as a whole
is that the Torah is not the sum total of *kitvei kodesh*, sacred Scripture. It
is merely the first and holiest of what are essentially three libraries, the
others being *Nevi'im* and *Ketuvim*, the Prophets and the Writings. One
way of summarising the difference between them is this: The Torah is
God's word *to* human beings. *Nevi'im* represents God's word *through*
human beings. *Ketuvim* are the words of human beings inspired by *ruaḥ
hakodesh*, the "holy spirit," to God.

Tanakh, the Hebrew Bible as a whole, is the work of approximately
a thousand years, from the days of Moses to the last of the prophets.
Nor is it all of equal authority. Only Torah, the Mosaic books, have the
force of law. After Moses, said the rabbis, no prophet has the authority
to innovate by way of primary legislation (Shabbat 104a).

Why then the prophetic books? Because they constitute a commentary on the Torah. Commentary is essential.[1] Without it we simply
would not know what the Torah means for us. Meaning is never a once-
and-for-all phenomenon. It is something that needs to be striven for in
every age. That applies even to secular texts. What do Plato's *Republic* or

---

1. See on this Michael Fishbane, *Biblical Interpretation in Ancient Israel* (Oxford:
    Clarendon Press, 1985), an important and pioneering study of what he calls "inner-
    biblical exegesis." Not least among the implications of this study is that Midrash, the
    primary rabbinic mode of biblical exegesis, is in fact a continuation of the work of
    the prophets.

Aristotle's *Ethics* mean for us? Or Shakespeare's *The Merchant of Venice*?[2] Or for that matter, an event from childhood seared in our memory? As we grow, so does our understanding of the past and its relationship to the present.

That, in essence, is what the great prophets did for Israel. They had a profound, inspired sense of time. Prophets are usually thought of as people who can foretell the future. That may be so, but it is only because they understand the present and the past. Seeing where we are and where we have come from, they know where, unless we change direction, we will find ourselves in a generation's time. Their insight into the past was no less compelling than their warnings about the future.

That is by way of a preface to one of the first literary prophets and one of the most passionate, the eighth-century-BCE figure known as Hosea. His book begins with an astonishing episode. God tells him to marry a prostitute. You will fall in love with her, God implies. She will betray you and cause you immense pain. She will be unfaithful. She will have children and you will not know who their father is. You will have an urge to disown them. You will call one of them "Unloved," and another "Not my people" (Hos. 1:1–9).

Hosea will know on some rational, intellectual level that his wife is causing him pain and that the quicker they separate, the better. But, as Pascal said, "The heart has its reasons of which reason knows nothing."[3] Logic can be powerless against emotion – especially when it comes to love. The fact that she has been unfaithful to you does not stop you loving her, and in the end you will find you cannot disown either her or her children.

There is, though, one thing you can do. You can wait for her to recover her senses and realise that you are the only one who really cared for her. You kept your side of the bargain however often she broke hers. When that happens, you will take her on a second honeymoon

---

2. See Ronald Dworkin, *Law's Empire* (Cambridge, MA: Belknap, 1986), for a fine study of interpretation of legal and other texts. Another key work is Hans-Georg Gadamer, *Truth and Method* (New York: Seabury, 1975).

3. M. R. O'Connell, *Blaise Pascal: Reasons of the Heart* (Grand Rapids, MI: Eerdmans, 1997), xi. He adds, "It is the heart that perceives God, and not the reason. That is what faith is: God perceived by the heart, not by the reason" (p. 169).

and renew your marriage vows. Hosea will learn through his own life experiences what God's relationship with Israel feels like from the perspective of heaven.

In a fascinating passage in the Babylonian Talmud the rabbis speculated as to what led God to make this request of the prophet:

> The Holy One, Blessed Be He, said to Hosea, "Your children have sinned." To this, the prophet should have replied, "[*My* children?] They are *Your* children, the children of Your favoured ones, Abraham, Isaac, and Jacob. Be merciful to them." Not only did he not say this, but he actually said, "Lord of the universe, the whole world is Yours. Exchange them for another nation."
>
> The Holy One, Blessed Be He, said [to Himself], "What shall I do with this old man? I will tell him to go and marry a prostitute and have children by her. Then I will tell him to send her away. If he can, then I too will send Israel away." (Pesaḥim 87a)

This is a fundamental rabbinic insight into the nature of prophecy: *Who is qualified to bring God's word to the Jewish people? Only one who loves the Jewish people.* It is easy to see the prophets as social critics, which they were. They saw the people's faults; they were candid in declaring them. They were the world's first social critics.[4] Their message was often a negative one, foretelling disaster. The Talmud is telling us that such a view is superficial and misses the essential point.

The prophets loved their people. They spoke not out of a desire to criticise but from the depths of solidarity and love. Initially, implies the Talmud, Hosea lacked this love. When God said that the people had sinned, he accepted the verdict and told God to choose another people. This was a fundamental misunderstanding of the role of a prophet. A prophet is entitled to criticise but only out of love for those he critiques. That is why God told him to experience love in his own life. Only then would he understand God's feelings for His people. That is why, in Israel's darkest nights, the prophets always had a message of hope.

---

4. See Michael Walzer, *Interpretation and Social Criticism* (Cambridge, MA: Harvard University Press, 1987).

The significance of Hosea's story here is that part of it forms the *haftara* for *Parashat Bemidbar*. This is the passage in which God talks about His own future second honeymoon with the Israelites:

Therefore I am about to woo her.
I will lead her into the wilderness and speak tenderly to her....
There she will respond as in the days of her youth,
As in the day she came out of Egypt. (Hos. 2:16–17)

Hosea had been given to see by God that the wilderness years were not simply, or even primarily, years of rebellion. They were the first honeymoon between God and His people. They were what we call nowadays *yihud*, the point in the wedding ceremony in which bride and groom are alone together. The making of the covenant at Mount Sinai was a form of marriage, and though there were many domestic quarrels in those first years, on the part of the husband – God Himself – there was never less than love. It may sometimes have been injured, betrayed, and wounded – but it was still love.

The prophets use many metaphors to describe the relationship between God and the people He chose to be His special witnesses on earth. Religious language cannot but be metaphorical – the Infinite cannot be compassed in finite categories. So God is described as artist, creator, king, master, warrior, shepherd, judge, teacher, redeemer, and father, but the loveliest and most intimate is God as husband, with Israel as His bride. Isaiah and Jeremiah both use this language. So, poignantly, does Ezekiel. This, he says, is what God felt when He saw the Israelites in Egypt:

Later I passed by, and when I looked at you and saw that you were old enough for love, I spread the corner of my garment over you and covered your nakedness. I gave you My solemn oath and entered into a covenant with you – declares the Lord God – and you became Mine. (Ezek. 16:8)

But the earliest and supreme poet of faith-as-marriage was Hosea. Reading this *haftara* as we begin the book called "In the Wilderness" completely reframes our image of the wilderness years. Reading it as we usually do, immediately prior to Shavuot, the commemoration of the giving of the Torah, we make another momentous affirmation: that in giving the Torah to Israel, God was not asserting His power, dominance, or lordship over Israel. He was declaring His love.[5] And though the wilderness years were often fraught, they were undergirded by love: God's love for Israel that Israel did not always reciprocate.

The words with which the *haftara* ends are among the most beautiful in the entire religious literature of mankind. Jewish men recite them every weekday morning as they wind the strap of the hand-*tefillin* like a wedding ring around their finger, renewing daily the marriage covenant of Sinai:

> I will betroth you to Me for ever;
> I will betroth you to Me in righteousness and justice, love and compassion;
> I will betroth you to Me in faithfulness,
> And you will know God. (Hos. 2:21–22)

That is what the wilderness years were meant to be, and one day will be again: a time of love, when a people followed God into an unknown future, and faith became a marriage that might be shaken but would never be broken.

---

5. That is what Hosea means when he says, "In that day, declares the Lord, you will call Me 'my husband [*ishi*],' you will no longer call Me 'my master [*baali*]'" (Hos. 2:18). This is a subtle play on words. *Baal*, the name of the Canaanite god, implies power, ownership. The word *ish* refers back to the opening of the Torah, when the first man, seeing the first woman, says, "She shall be called woman [*isha*], because she was taken from man [*ish*]" (Gen. 2:23). This is marriage as love between two individuals who recognise both sameness and otherness. That is the model for love between God and humanity, the other that God created in His image.

Naso
נשא

Continuing the preparations for the Israelites' journey from Sinai to the holy land, *Parashat Naso* contains a melange of subjects whose inner connection is not immediately obvious: the roles of two of the Levitical clans, Gershon and Merari, the census of the Levites as a group, rules about the purity of the camp, the law of the *sota* (the woman suspected of adultery), the Nazirite, and the priestly blessing. The *parasha* concludes with a lengthy and repetitive account of the offerings brought by the tribes at the dedication of the Tabernacle.

The first of the following essays is about the nature of a census in Jewish law and thought. The second looks at a striking feature of the book of Numbers as a whole, its emphasis on the tribes as distinct entities: Why does the Torah focus on this internal division within the nation rather than focusing on the nation as a unified whole? The third explores attitudes within the tradition to the Nazirite, the individual who voluntarily accepted a higher-than-usual standard of personal holiness. The fourth is about the priestly blessings, one of Judaism's oldest liturgies. The fifth advances a theory about the underlying logic of the various aspects of the *parasha* as a whole.

What Counts?

Parashat *Naso* begins with a continuation of the census that gives the entire book its English name, "Numbers," itself based on the old rabbinic name, *Ḥomesh HaPekudim*, the book of "counting" or "numbering." Not only does the book begin with a census, it contains a second one towards the end (ch. 26). The difference between them is one generation. As we will read in the episode of the spies, it was the demoralisation of the people at that point that led to the decree that, with only two exceptions, those who had left Egypt would not enter the Promised Land. It would be their children, born in freedom, who would have that privilege and responsibility.

What is puzzling is the fact that the tradition seems to have two different, seemingly contradictory, attitudes towards the taking of a census. Rashi notes that this is not the first time the people had been counted. Their number ("about six hundred thousand men on foot, besides women and children") had already been given as they prepared to leave Egypt (Ex. 12:37). A more precise calculation had been made when the adult males each gave a half shekel towards the building of the Sanctuary (yielding a total of 603,550; Ex. 38:26). In Numbers, a third and fourth count took place. Why so often? Rashi's answer is simple and moving:

> Because they [the Children of Israel] are dear to Him, God counts them often. He counted them when they were about to leave Egypt. He counted them after the Golden Calf to establish how many were left. And now that He was about to cause His presence to rest on them [with the inauguration of the Sanctuary], He counted them again. (Rashi to Num. 1:1)

For Rashi, the counting of the people was an act of divine love. Yet this is not the impression we receive elsewhere. To the contrary, the Torah sees the taking of a census as profoundly dangerous: "Then God said to Moses, 'When you take a census of the Israelites to count them, each must give to God a ransom for his life at the time he is counted. *Then no plague will come on them* when you number them'" (Ex. 30:11–12).

Without the ransom, the verse implies, a plague may come. Rashi explains that there is a danger of "the evil eye."[1] Centuries later, against the advice of his army commander Joab, King David took a census of the people. There was divine anger, and seventy thousand died. David himself expressed contrition, saying, "I have sinned greatly in what I have done. Now, Lord, I beg You, take away the guilt of Your servant. I have done a very foolish thing."[2] It is hard to reconcile the idea of counting as an act of love with the fact that it involves risk and divine displeasure.

The solution to this seeming contradiction lies in the unusual phrase the Torah uses, here and in the previous *parasha*, to describe the act of counting: *naso* or *se'u et rosh*, literally, "lift the head." There were several other verbs available in classical Hebrew to indicate the act of counting: *limnot, lifkod, lispor, lahshov*. Why, in the books of Exodus and Numbers, does the Torah resort to the strange circumlocution, "lift the heads" of the Israelites?

In the ancient world, and to some extent still today, a census represented the principle that there is power in numbers. Specifi-

---

1. There are many other explanations given by the commentators. The simplest, given by Ibn Ezra and Ḥizkuni, is that a census was usually taken in the ancient world for military purposes, to know the size of the army a nation might deploy. Hence it was an act that reminded people that, in the course of combat, they might die.
2. II Sam. 24:1–17; see also I Chr. 21:1–17.

cally, counting the people was a way of knowing the size of the army a nation could muster. It also determined its capacity to build monumental buildings like the Tower of Babel spoken about in Genesis, or the giant pyramid of Giza, undertaken by Pharaoh Khufu around 2500 BCE, before even the birth of Abraham. In such a world, with the exception of the ruler and the elite, life was cheap. The sages said about the Tower of Babel that if a person fell and died, no one noticed. If a brick fell, they wept.[3] Size meant strength, military or economic. Life was measured in the mass.

The religion of Israel is a principled protest against this view. At this distance in time it is hard fully to appreciate the transformative potential of a single radical idea: that *the human person as such, man or woman, rich or poor, powerful or powerless,* is the image of God and therefore of non-negotiable, unquantifiable value. We are each equally in the image of God, therefore we stand equal in the presence of God. Much of Torah, Jewish history, and the trajectory of Western civilisation – what Martin Luther King Jr. called "the arc of history" – is about the slow translation of this idea into institutions, social structures, and moral codes.

It should now be clear why taking a census is fraught with spiritual risk and why God was angry with King David for doing so. The biblical text says that he told Joab, "Go throughout the tribes of Israel from Dan to Beersheba and enrol the fighting men so that I may know how many there are."[4] Joab instinctively knew that this was wrong and said so, but was overruled. David had fallen into the trap of thinking the way other nations did: that population means power and size equals strength.

David, Israel's second king, laid the foundations of a nation. He waged successful wars, united the tribes, and established Jerusalem as his capital. Shortly after his death, Israel reached its zenith as a power in the Middle East. Under Solomon, through strategic alliances, it became a centre of trade and scholarship. The Temple was built. It must have seemed at the time as if, after many centuries of wandering and war, Israel had become a power to rival any other.

3. *Pirkei DeRabbi Eliezer* 24.
4. II Sam. 24:2; I Chr. 21:2.

It was a short-lived, cruelly-shattered illusion. Almost immediately after Solomon's reign, the kingdom split in two, and from then on, its this-worldly fate was sealed. A history of defeats, exiles, and destructions began, one which has no parallel in the annals of any other nation. The Hebrew Bible is not wrong in seeing the starting point of this decline in the moment at which David acted like any other king and ordered a census of the people.

The numbering of a people is the most potent symbol of mankind-in-the-mass, of a society in which the individual is not valued in and for him- or herself but as part of a totality. That is precisely what Israel was not. God set His special love on a people who never sought to become an empire and never waged war to convert populations to its faith. Israel's strength had nothing to do with numbers. It was and still is tiny both in absolute terms and relative to its surrounding empires.

There is a remarkable demonstration of this in the book of Judges. God tells Gideon to wage war against the Midianites. He assembles a force of 32,000 men. God then says to Gideon: "You have too many men. I cannot deliver Midian into their hands, or Israel would boast against Me, 'My own strength has saved me'" (Judges 7:2). He instructs Gideon to tell the soldiers that whoever wants to leave may leave. Twenty-two thousand do so. He is left with ten thousand men. God tells him that this is still too many. He instructs him to test how the soldiers drink water from the river. Three hundred pass the test by not kneeling down. God tells Gideon to dismiss the rest, "With the three hundred men ... I will save you and give the Midianites into your hands" (Judges 7:1–8).

This idea is fundamental to Judaism. In Greek thought and throughout the European Enlightenment, what mattered were universals. In Judaism, what matter to God are individuals. There is a fine verse in Psalms (147:4) which says that God "counts the number of the stars and *calls them each by name.*" A name is a marker of uniqueness. Collective nouns group things together; proper names distinguish them as individuals. Only what we value do we name. (One of the most chilling acts of dehumanisation in the extermination camps of Nazi Germany was that those who entered were never addressed by their names. Instead they were given, inscribed on their skin, a number.) God gives even the stars their names. All the more so does this apply to human beings, on whom He has set His image. When God calls, He calls our name,[5] to which the reply is simply, *"Hineni,"* "Here I am." God – one and alone – meets us, one and alone, endowing us with a significance that cannot be quantified or measured by a census.

This idea is deeply internalised in Judaism. So when Moses asked God to appoint a successor, he used an unusual phrase, "Lord, God of the spirits of all flesh" (Num. 27:16). The sages interpreted this to mean, "God, You know how different people are from one another. Therefore appoint for them a leader who is able to relate to each according to his character."[6]

The rabbis instituted a blessing to be said on seeing a crowd of 600,000: "Blessed be He … who discerns secrets."[7] This means, says Rashi, that God knows what makes each of us an individual, unique. What makes this blessing so powerful is that most of us, on seeing a crowd of 600,000 people, would lose a sense of individuality. They become a mass, a crowd.[8] That is not how we should see a crowd, imply the sages. We should never forget that each is different, each a universe, each a distinctive fragment of the Divine.

We can now resolve the seeming contradiction between the counting that is a gesture of divine love, and the counting that is fraught with danger. It is the difference between a census commanded by God and one undertaken by a human being who assumes that there is strength in numbers. That is why the Torah does not use any of the normal verbs for counting – *limnot, lifkod, lispor, laḥshov* – and instead uses the circumlocution, "lift the head." This means that those entrusted with the task are commanded to lift the spirits of those they count, making each individual stand tall in the knowledge that he is loved, cherished, held special by God, and not merely a number, a cipher, among the thousands and millions.

---

5. Often twice. See Gen. 22:11; 46:2; Ex. 3:4.
6. *Midrash Tanḥuma, Parashat Pinḥas* 11.
7. Berakhot 58a and Rashi ad loc.
8. See on this Elias Canetti, *Crowds and Power* (New York: Farrar, Straus and Giroux, 1984).

There is a powerful reflection on the Mourner's Kaddish, by the hasidic teacher Rabbi Simha Bunim of Przysucha (Poland, 1765–1827):

> In the ordinary world, when a small unit of a large army is lost, the loss is not felt, and it is not until an entire division is missing that the depletion must be corrected and the army must be reinforced. It is otherwise, however, in the army of God. If only a single Jew is missing, then there is already a lack in the greatness and holiness of God. Therefore, we pray that "His name be magnified and sanctified," that is, that His blessed name may be made complete for what it has lost with the disappearance of the deceased.[9]

That perhaps is why Jews have always been a tiny people. As Moses said, "The Lord did not set His affection on you and choose you because you were more numerous than other peoples, for you were the fewest of all peoples" (Deut. 7:7). The emphasis on the absolute worth of the individual-as-individual, coming more naturally to a small people than to a vast empire, is living testimony to the difference it makes to believe in the One God who endows each of us in our oneness with His image. God "lifts our head" in the most profound way known to humankind, by assuring each of us of His special, enduring, unquantifiable love.

That is the nature of the censuses in the book of Numbers. As the Israelites prepared to become a society with the Divine Presence at its centre, they had to be reminded that they were to become the pioneers of a new social order, whose most famous definition was given by the prophet Zechariah (4:6): "Not by might, nor by strength, but by My spirit, says the Lord."

9. Quoted in Leon Wieseltier, *Kaddish* (London: Picador, 1999), 24.

Tribes

One of the most visible features of Numbers as a book – conspicuously so in *Parashat Naso* – is the great attention it pays to tribes. The book begins with the people being counted according to tribe. Then we read about their positioning in the camp around the Tabernacle by tribe. The order in which they travelled in their journeys through the wilderness was also by tribe. In this *parasha*, at inordinate length we are told of the offerings of each tribe at the dedication of the Tabernacle, despite the fact that each brought exactly the same offering (Num. 7:1–89). Later in the book there is an account of how the land was to be allocated tribe by tribe. The book ends with the second half of the story of the daughters of Tzlofhad, in which the leaders of their tribe bring a case to Moses to ensure that their rights as a tribe are respected.

In no other book of the Torah is there such an emphasis. In Exodus, the story of enslavement, the plagues, and the Exodus is told about the nation as a whole. The division into tribes plays very little part in the narrative. The book *Vayikra* is known in English as Leviticus, that is, matters pertaining to the tribe of Levi, because of their special duties as Levites and priests, but there is no special attention paid to the other tribes. In Deuteronomy, again the emphasis is on the nation as a whole, this time made sharper by its emphasis on a single, centralised Sanctuary "in the place which God chooses," that is, Jerusalem. To give a sense of the disproportion, the word *matteh*, meaning "tribe," appears eighty-nine times in Numbers but not at all in Deuteronomy.[1]

To be sure, in Genesis we read about the origin of the tribes, that is, the twelve sons of Jacob and the various tensions between them. That family history is essential background to the book of Numbers, because it tells us that there was a story of sibling rivalry. Hence the need to be constantly vigilant in making sure that each tribe felt that justice was being done in matters such as the division of the land. Indeed, the Korah rebellion brought to the surface various resentments that had to do with aspects of relationships between the tribes.

That said, the emphasis is, at least on the face of it, odd. We know from the later history of Israel that tribal identities were more a source of division than unity. During the period of the judges, Israel was an amphictyony, that is, a loose federation of tribes. But it was not a system that worked well in the long run. It becomes increasingly frayed as we reach the later chapters of the book. There were occasions on which intertribal war was only narrowly avoided.[2] In the end, there was a certain inevitability about the move, in the days of Samuel, from a federation of tribes to a united nation under the leadership of a king.

Even so, the unification was not very successful – at least not for long. Its most brilliant architect was King David, who united the people by making Jerusalem the capital city, and by initiating plans for the building of the Temple. It was this more than anything else that brought the tribes together, especially to celebrate the pilgrim festivals three times a year. Even so, the sheer brevity of the period of unity is astounding in retrospect. It was Solomon, Israel's third king, who built the Temple, but also he who exposed the political system to stresses and strains that

1. Deuteronomy uses the word *shevet*, not *matteh*, for "tribe." Even so, it appears only eighteen times, compared to the eighty-nine instances of *matteh* and six of *shevet* in Numbers. By contrast, the word *am*, "people," appears thirty-four times in Deuteronomy, but only twelve in Numbers.
2. There was almost war between the other tribes and those of Reuben, Gad, and half of Menashe (Josh. 22). Later there was actual war between the tribe of Benjamin and the others (Judges 20).

reached their climax almost immediately after his death, resulting in the fateful split between the ten northern tribes under Jeroboam and the two southern ones under Solomon's son Rehoboam.

In light of all this, the question remains insistent. Why tell the story this way? Why place the emphasis on tribes? Why was Israel not conceived as a united nation to begin with? To be sure, Jacob had twelve sons. But why segregate them geographically? Why orient the entire book of Numbers along the axis of tribal divisions and distinctions? Why tell us the demographics of the tribes instead of what is surely more significant, the population as a whole? Why not place the emphasis on what became Ezekiel's great hope and vision: "I will make them one nation in the land.... There will be one king over all of them and they will never again be two nations or be divided into two kingdoms" (Ezek. 37:22)?

It seems that the Torah is telling us something compelling and fundamental, relevant not just then but still today. The Torah conceives of politics and identity from the ground up, not from the top down. It is not the ruler, emperor, or king who represents authority and imposes it on the population. To the contrary, the Torah takes us through the slow growth of Israel as an entity – beginning with one couple, Abraham and Sarah, who become a family, then an extended family, then a tribe, then a series of tribes. They are forged into a nation negatively by the experience of oppression in Egypt, positively by redemption and by the covenant they made with God at Mount Sinai. But those early structures – family, clan, tribe – remain important in the body politic, not just at the beginning but throughout.

One of the best accounts of the emergence of political society as the Torah conceives it was given by the sixteenth-century political theorist Jean Bodin. Societies began initially, he says,

> from the love that was betwixt man and wife: from them to have flowed the mutual love betwixt parents and their children: then the love of brothers and sisters one towards another: and after them the friendship between cousins and other kinsmen: and last of all the love and good will, which is betwixt men joined in alliance: which had all at length grown cold, and been utterly

> extinguished, had it not been nourished, maintained and kept by
> societies, communities, corporations and colleges: the union of
> whom have for a long time maintained many people, without any
> Commonwealth or sovereign power over them.[3]

This is an extremely important point – the slow growth of society from
basic human groups to an ever-wider radius of concern – and it has often
been forgotten in modern times.

Not everything social is political. Not everything we do together
as a nation is because of governments, laws, courts, and the potential
use of force. Societies are usually held together by a whole series of
institutions larger than the individual but smaller than the state: families,
communities, neighbourhoods, charities, voluntary associations, neighbourhood groups, and the like. Edmund Burke called them the "little
platoons." Alexis de Tocqueville called them "associations." Nowadays
they are usually called mediating structures, or third-sector organisations,
and together they constitute civil society. What makes them important
is that they are based not on transactions of wealth (the market) or
power (the state) but on a sense of identity, belonging, loyalty, collective responsibility, and trust.

You can see the difference this makes by comparing the four revolutions that created the modern world: the English (1640s), American
(1776), French (1789), and Russian (1917). England and America had
strong civil societies. They had a rich range of congregations, communities, fellowships, charities, and the like. The French and Russian
revolutionaries were, by contrast, essentially distrustful of civil society,
believing that as little as possible should intervene between the individual and the state. That is one of the reasons why England and America,
despite their internal wars, remained essentially free societies, while
France during the reign of revolutionary terror and Russia under com-
munist rule became totalitarian states. *To be free, something must stand
between the individual and the state.* That is why the book of Numbers,

---

3. Jean Bodin, *The Six Bookes of a Commonweale*, trans. Richard Knolles (London:
    Adam Islip, 1606). See Jonathan Sacks, *The Politics of Hope* (London: Jonathan Cape,
    1997), 55–65.

charting the final stages of the journey to the Promised Land, speaks about families, clans, and tribes.

The Torah is not anti-political. It recognises the need for a state, which in biblical times essentially meant a king. A sense of collective nationhood needs a degree of centralisation. That is why, as a tribal federation during the era of the judges, Israel became increasingly dysfunctional. Eventually the people came to Samuel and requested a king. This was important militarily; only a nation united under a recognised leader could effectively defend itself against its enemies. It was important religiously as well. There had to be a central sanctuary where the nation as a nation could come together, giving thanks to God for the past and offering collective prayer for the future. But the Hebrew Bible, more than any other document from ancient times, is sceptical about the scope of politics. It knows, with Lord Acton, that power tends to corrupt and absolute power corrupts absolutely. It also shares the scepticism of Oliver Goldsmith: "How small of all that human hearts endure, That part which laws or kings can cause or cure!"[4]

A free society cannot be built on centralised institutions alone. The Torah is predicated on devolved responsibility. Each person is party to the covenant. Parents are responsible for the education of their children. Every family is charged with including in its festival celebrations widows, orphans, strangers, and servants. Every tribe (except the Levites), and every family within the tribe, is to have its share in the land. Every town should have its local judges. Education, welfare, the provision of charity, and the alleviation of poverty are done best locally, where people know one another and come to one another's aid. The book of Ruth gives us a vivid picture of how this worked during the era of the judges.

We are tribal animals. That is where we gain our identity and sense of belonging. It is the focus of our loyalty and the source of our pride. In a recent book, *Tribe*, subtitled *On Homecoming and Belonging*, Sebastian Junger draws our attention to some strange phenomena.[5] In America, many of the early English settlers chose to live with Native Americans,

4. *The Traveller* (London: J. Newberry, 1765), 22.
5. Sebastian Junger, *Tribe: On Homecoming and Belonging* (London: Fourth Estate, 2016).

but there was almost no movement in the opposite direction. In London, people who lived through the Blitz, when the city was under nightly attack, speak of that time with nostalgia. Suicide and depression rates often *fall* in countries at war or at times of natural disaster. In recent years, while the number of American soldiers killed in combat has fallen, rates of post-traumatic stress disorder have risen.

All these things, argues Junger, have to do with our deep instinctual need to belong to a group. "The earliest and most basic definition of community – of tribe – would be the group of people that you would both help feed and help defend." He adds, "A society that doesn't offer its members the chance to act selflessly in these ways isn't a society in any tribal sense of the word; it's just a political entity that, lacking enemies, will probably fall apart on its own."[6] That is what the early English settlers were drawn to when they encountered Native Americans: their strong tribes. That, he says, is why rates of post-traumatic stress disorder have risen: soldiers fail to find, when they return to contemporary American society, the intense camaraderie they had with their fellow combatants in the unit in which they served. The exception, he says, is Israel, "arguably the only modern country that retains a sufficient sense of community to mitigate the effects of combat on a mass scale."[7]

Tribes have received bad press in the modern world. The European Enlightenment was a response to a century of tribal wars between Catholics and Protestants following the Reformation. Its answer was universalism: a world of universal humanity based not on religion but on the power of reason and observation in the form of philosophy and science. Its supreme expression was the last movement of Beethoven's Ninth Symphony, with its words from Schiller's "Ode to Joy": *Alle Menschen werden Brüder*, "All men shall become brothers." For Enlightenment intellectuals, everything tribal was primitive. It was one of the great moments in the history of the West. But it failed, not because its dream was anything less than noble, but because it ignored human nature.

The nineteenth century witnessed the return of the repressed. Tribal identities returned to Europe in three forms: the nation, the race,

6. Ibid., 109–110.
7. Ibid., 96.

and the socioeconomic class. In the twentieth century, worship of the nation led to two world wars; worship of the race led to the Holocaust; and worship of the class led to the Soviet Union, Stalin, the Gulag, and the KGB. That is what happens when you try to eliminate the tribe.

Following the Second World War and the Holocaust, another attempt was made by the West to abolish tribes. This time the solution was not universalism but individualism. There would be no more consecration of marriage, family, and community, and no universal moral principles except one, the right of the individual to choose to live as he or she wishes so long as others are not harmed. Tribalism would be confined to soccer matches or baseball games. This too will fail, and it has already begun to do so.

Already in 1975, Harold Isaacs, a professor of political science at MIT, warned that the tribes were returning. They never really went away. This fact was "well known to great masses of people for a long time but not to generations of elite, humanistic scholars and strivers for human perfectibility: namely that our tribal separatenesses are here to stay." The good news is that "these diversities are the wealth of humanity." The bad news is that "with all the beauty goes all the blood." Tribes are the primal source of identity, but they are also a source of conflict, violence, and war.[8]

Hence the wisdom of the Torah, so profoundly different from the Enlightenment universalism of the eighteenth century and the radical individualism of the contemporary West. *The Torah is about a form of ethics and politics that goes with the grain of human nature.* So it begins, in Genesis, with the most basic forms of relationship: husbands and wives, parents and children, and siblings and their rivalries. In Exodus, Leviticus, and Numbers, it turns to the nation, formed negatively by slavery in Egypt, positively by the covenant at Sinai. But it preserves the tribes as fundamental social units, just as America did when it formed itself as a federation of states.[9] Indeed, the early motto of America was *E pluribus unum*, "Out of the many, one."

---

8. Harold Isaacs, *Idols of the Tribe* (Cambridge, MA: Harvard University Press, 1989), 216.
9. There were originally thirteen states, exactly as in biblical Israel, the twelve landed tribes plus the tribe of Levi. Though Jacob had twelve sons, he gave a double portion to Joseph, whose two sons, Ephraim and Menashe, became tribes in their own right.

This is a difficult balance to maintain, based as it is on sustaining diversity within a framework of overarching unity, and it can easily split apart, as biblical Israel did after the death of Solomon and as America might have done over the issue of slavery. Yet despite the fact that the northern kingdom with its ten tribes was defeated, Jews and Judaism have shown a repeated tendency to divide into other tribes: Ashkenazim and Sephardim, hasidim and *mitnagdim,* and the myriad *edot* and ethnicities that make up the contemporary State of Israel.

The bad news is that this leads to internal strife. The good news is that Jews, "the fewest of all peoples" (Deut. 7:7), continue to be one of the most diverse groups on the face of the planet, yet capable nonetheless of coming together at times of crisis to help and defend one another as well as to provide relief and assistance to any other nation suffering from humanitarian disaster.

We are not one thing. We have multiple identities, as members of this family, that neighbourhood, this congregation, that religious faith, this ethnicity, that nation, and ultimately the human family itself, brothers and sisters under the parenthood of God. The insistence on one identity to the exclusion of all others is the mark of a potentially totalitarian regime. Hence the insistence of the book of Numbers on the continuing significance of the twelve tribes even when Israel is one nation under the One God.

Sages and Saints

Parashat Naso contains the law of the Nazirite – the individual who undertook to observe special rules of holiness and abstinence: not to drink wine or other intoxicants (including anything made from grapes), not to have his hair cut, and not to defile himself by contact with the dead (Num. 6:1–21). Such a state was usually undertaken for a limited period; the standard length was thirty days. There were exceptions, most famously Samson and Samuel who, because of the miraculous nature of their birth, were consecrated before their birth as Nazirites for life.[1]

What the Torah does not make clear, though, is why a person might wish to undertake this form of abstinence, and even whether it was commendable, or merely permissible, to do so. On the one hand the Torah calls the Nazirite "holy to God" (Num. 6:8). On the other, it requires him, at the end of the period of his vow, to bring a sin offering (Num. 6:13–14).

---

1. Judges 13:1–7; I Sam. 1:11. The Talmud distinguishes these kinds of cases from the standard vow for a fixed period. The most famous Nazirite of modern times was Rabbi David Cohen (1887–1972), a disciple of Rabbi Kook and father of the chief rabbi of Haifa, Rabbi She'ar-Yashuv Cohen (1927–2016).

This led to an ongoing disagreement between the rabbis in Mishnaic, Talmudic, and medieval times. According to R. Elazar, and later to Nahmanides, the Nazirite is praiseworthy. He has voluntarily undertaken a higher level of holiness. The prophet Amos (2:11) said, "I raised up some of your sons for prophets, and your young men for Nazirites," suggesting that the Nazirite, like the prophet, is a person especially close to God. The reason he had to bring a sin offering was that he was now returning to ordinary life. His sin lay in *ceasing to be* a Nazirite.

R. Eliezer HaKappar and Shmuel held the opposite opinion. For them the sin lay in *becoming* a Nazirite in the first place and thereby denying himself some of the pleasures of the world God created and declared good. R. Eliezer added: "From this we may infer that if one who denies himself the enjoyment of wine is called a sinner, all the more so one who denies himself the enjoyment of other pleasures of life."[2]

Clearly the argument is not merely textual. It is substantive. It is about asceticism, the life of self-denial. Almost every religion knows the phenomenon of people who, in pursuit of spiritual purity, withdraw from the pleasures and temptations of the world. They live in caves, retreats, hermitages, monasteries. The Qumran sect known to us through the Dead Sea Scrolls may have been such a movement.

In the Middle Ages there were Jews who adopted similar kinds of self-denial – among them the Hasidei Ashkenaz, the Pietists of Northern Europe, as well as many Jews in Islamic lands. In retrospect it is hard not to see in these patterns of behaviour at least some influence from the non-Jewish environment. The Hasidei Ashkenaz who flourished during the time of the Crusades lived among self-mortifying Christians. Their southern counterparts may have been familiar with Sufism, the mystical movement in Islam.

The ambivalence of Jews towards the life of self-denial may therefore lie in the suspicion that it entered Judaism from the outside. There were ascetic movements in the first centuries of the Common Era in both the West (Greece) and the East (Iran) that saw the physical world as a place of corruption and strife. They were, in fact, dualists, holding that the true God was not the creator of the universe. The physical world

2. Taanit 11a; Nedarim 10a.

was the work of a lesser, and evil, deity. Therefore God – the true God – is not to be found in the physical world and its enjoyments but rather in disengagement from them.

The two best-known movements to hold this view were Gnosticism in the West and Manichaeism in the East. So at least some of the negative evaluation of the Nazirite may have been driven by a desire to discourage Jews from imitating non-Jewish practices. Judaism strongly believes that God is to be found in the midst of the physical world that He created that is, in the first chapter of Genesis, seven times pronounced "good." It believes not in renouncing pleasure but in sanctifying it.

What is much more puzzling is the position of Maimonides, who holds *both* views, positive and negative, in the same book, his law code the *Mishneh Torah*. In *Hilkhot Deot*, he adopts the negative position of R. Eliezer HaKappar:

> A person may say: "Desire, honour, and the like are bad paths to follow and remove a person from the world; therefore I will completely separate myself from them and go to the other extreme." As a result, he does not eat meat or drink wine or take a wife or live in a decent house or wear decent clothing.... This too is bad, and it is forbidden to choose this way.[3]

Yet in *Hilkhot Nezirut* he rules in accordance with the positive evaluation of R. Elazar: "Whoever vows to God [to become a Nazirite] by way of holiness, does well and is praiseworthy.... Indeed Scripture considers him the equal of a prophet."[4] How does any writer come to adopt contradictory positions in a single book, let alone one as resolutely logical as Maimonides?

The answer lies in a remarkable insight of Maimonides into the nature of the moral life as understood by Judaism. What Maimonides saw is that there is not a single model of the virtuous life. He identifies two, calling them respectively the way of the saint (*ḥasid*) and the way of the sage (*ḥakham*).

---

3. Maimonides, *Mishneh Torah, Hilkhot Deot* 3:1.
4. Maimonides, *Mishneh Torah, Hilkhot Nezirut* 10:14.

The saint is a person of extremes. Maimonides defines *ḥesed* as extreme behaviour – good behaviour, to be sure, but conduct in excess of what strict justice requires.[5] So, for example, "If one avoids haughtiness to the utmost extent and becomes exceedingly humble, he is termed a saint [*ḥasid*]."[6]

The sage is a different kind of person altogether. He or she follows the "golden mean," the "middle way," the way of moderation and balance. He or she avoids the extremes of cowardice on the one hand, recklessness on the other, and thus acquires the virtue of courage. He or she avoids miserliness in one direction, prodigality in the other, and instead chooses the middle way of generosity. The sage knows the twin dangers of too much and too little, excess and deficiency. He or she weighs the conflicting pressures and avoids the extremes.

These are not just two types of person but *two ways of understanding the moral life itself*. Is the aim of the moral life to achieve personal perfection? Or is it to create gracious relationships and a decent, just, compassionate society? The intuitive answer of most people would be to say: both. What makes Maimonides so acute a thinker is that he realises that you cannot have both – that they are in fact different enterprises.

A saint may give all his money away to the poor. But what about the members of the saint's own family? They may suffer because of his extreme self-denial. A saint may refuse to fight in battle. But what about the saint's country and its defence? A saint may forgive all crimes committed against him. But what then about the rule of law, and justice? Saints are supremely virtuous people, considered as individuals. Yet *you cannot build a society out of saints alone*. Indeed, saints are not really interested in society. They have chosen a different, lonely, self-segregating path. I know no moral philosopher who makes this point as clearly as Maimonides – not Plato or Aristotle, not Descartes or Kant.[7]

---

5. Maimonides, *Guide for the Perplexed*, III:52.
6. Maimonides, *Mishneh Torah, Hilkhot Deot* 1:5.
7. However, see J. O. Urmson's famous article, "Saints and Heroes," in *Essays in Moral Philosophy*, ed. A. Melden (Seattle: University of Washington Press, 1958). See also P. F. Strawson, "Social Morality and Individual Ideal," *Philosophy* 36, no. 136 (Jan. 1961): 1–17.

It was this deep insight that led Maimonides to his seemingly contradictory evaluations of the Nazirite. The Nazirite has chosen, at least for a period, to adopt a life of extreme self-denial. He is a saint, a *ḥasid*. He has adopted the path of personal perfection. That is noble, commendable, and exemplary. That is why Maimonides calls him "praiseworthy" and "the equal of a prophet."

But it is not the way of the sage – and *you need sages if you seek to perfect society.* The sage is not an extremist – because he or she realises that there are other people at stake. There are the members of one's own family as well as the others within one's community. There are colleagues at work. There is a country to defend and a society to help build. The sage knows he or she cannot leave all these commitments behind to pursue a life of solitary virtue.[8] In a strange way, saintliness is a form of self-indulgence. We are called on by God to live in the world, not escape from it; in society not seclusion; to strive to create a balance among the conflicting pressures on us, not to focus on some while neglecting the others.

Hence, while from a personal perspective the Nazirite is a saint, from a societal perspective he is, at least figuratively, a "sinner" who has to bring an atonement offering.

Maimonides lived the life he preached. We know from his writings that he longed for seclusion. There were years when he worked day and night to write his *Commentary to the Mishna,* and later the *Mishneh Torah.* Yet he also recognised his responsibilities to his family and to the community. In his famous letter to his would-be translator Ibn Tibbon,[9] he gives him an account of his typical day and week – in which he had to carry a double burden as a world-renowned physician and an internationally sought halakhist and sage. He worked to exhaustion. There were times when he was almost too busy to study from one week to the next.

8. There were sages who believed that in an ideal world, tasks such as earning a living or having children could be "done by others" (see Berakhot 35a for the view of R. Shimon b. Yoḥai; Yevamot 63b for that of Ben Azzai). These are elitist attitudes that have surfaced in Judaism from time to time but which are criticised by the Talmud.

9. See Rabbi Yitzhak Sheilat, *Letters of Maimonides* [Hebrew] (Jerusalem: Miskal, 1987–88), 2:530–554.

Maimonides was a sage who longed to be a saint, but knew he could not be, if he was to honour his responsibilities to his people. That is a profound and moving judgement and is praiseworthy. Indeed Scripture considers him the equal of a prophet – one that still has the power to inspire today.

The Priestly Blessings

I n 1979, in Ketef Hinnom, a group of archaeologists under the direction of Gabriel Barkay was exploring an ancient burial site southwest of the Old City of Jerusalem in the area now occupied by the Menachem Begin Heritage Center. At first, the caverns and burial chambers seemed to be bereft of objects of interest, but a persistent thirteen-year-old boy helping the team discovered that beneath the floor of one of the caves was a hidden chamber. There the group found almost one thousand ancient artefacts, including two tiny silver scrolls no more than an inch long.

They were so fragile that it took three years to work out a way of unrolling them without causing them to disintegrate. Eventually the scrolls turned out to be *kameyot*, amulets, containing, among other passages, a section from *Parashat Naso*: the priestly blessings. Scientifically dated to the early sixth century BCE, they come from the time of the prophet Jeremiah, just prior to the destruction of the First Temple, built by King Solomon. So ancient are they, that they are written not in the Hebrew alphabet as we recognise it today, which dates from the Babylonian exile, but rather in the ancient paleo-Hebrew script, a direct descendant of the first alphabet known to humankind. Older by far than the most ancient of biblical texts known hitherto, the Dead Sea Scrolls, the amulets can be seen today in the Israel Museum, testimony to the ancient connection of Jews to the land and the continuity of Jewish faith itself.

There is something almost poetic in the fact that it should have been this text that survived. It is among the oldest of our prayers, yet we still recite it daily.[1] It was used by the priests in the Temple. It is said today by the priests in the reader's repetition of the *Amida*, in Israel every day, in most of the Diaspora only on festivals. It is used by parents when they bless their children on Friday night. It is often said to the bride and groom under the *ḥuppa*. It is among the shortest of blessings, a mere fifteen words long, but marked by beauty and simplicity. Here is how the Torah sets them out:

> The Lord said to Moses, "Tell Aaron and his sons: This is how you are to bless the Israelites. Say to them:
> The Lord bless you and protect you;
> the Lord make His face shine upon you and be gracious to you;
> the Lord turn His face towards you and give you peace.
> So they will put My name on the Israelites, and I will bless them."
> (Num. 6:22–27)

The literary structure is precise. In the original Hebrew, the first line has three words, the second, five, and the third, seven (these prime numbers have special significance throughout the Mosaic books: three-, five-, and seven-fold repetitions always signify a keyword). Equally precisely, the first has fifteen (3 × 5) letters, the second twenty (4 × 5), and the third, twenty-five (5 × 5).

What is the meaning of the blessings?

The Lord bless you and protect you: Blessing in the Mosaic books always means material blessing. Against the idea basic to many other faith systems – which embrace poverty, asceticism, or other forms of self-denial – in Judaism the world as God's creation is fundamentally

---

1. At the beginning of the morning prayers and during the reader's repetition of the morning *Amida*. Many say it at night as part of the bedtime recitation of the *Shema*.

good. Religion is neither other-worldly nor anti-worldly. It is precisely in the physical world that God's blessings are to be found.

But material blessings can sometimes dull our sensitivities towards God. The great irony is that when we have most to thank God for, often we thank Him least. We tend to remember God in times of crisis rather than in eras of prosperity and peace:

> Be careful that you do not forget the Lord your God.... Otherwise, when you eat and are satisfied, when you build fine houses and settle down, and when your herds and flocks grow large and your silver and gold increase and all you have is multiplied, then your heart will become proud and you will forget the Lord your God, who brought you out of Egypt, out of the land of slavery.... You may say to yourself, "My power and the strength of my hands have produced this wealth for me." (Deut. 8:11–17)

This more than any other factor has led to the decline and fall of civilisations. In the early, pioneering years they are lifted by a collective vision and energy. Then as people become affluent they begin to lose the very qualities that made earlier generations great. They become less motivated by ideals than by the pursuit of pleasure. They think less of others, more of themselves. They begin to be deaf and blind to those in need. They become *decadent*. What happens to nations happens also to individuals and families.[2] Hence the first blessing. "May the Lord protect you," means: May He protect you from the blessing turning into a curse.

The Lord make His face shine upon you and be gracious to you: The word "grace" has such strong Christian associations that we sometimes forget its centrality to Judaism. What is grace?

Judaism is a religion of intellect: of study, questioning, ideas, argument, and the life of the mind. The historian Paul Johnson described rabbinic Judaism as an "ancient and highly efficient social machine for the production of intellectuals."[3] Yet the book of Proverbs says: "Let

2. The Jewish-American singer Neil Sedaka, who achieved great success in the 1960s, in 1975 wrote a song on this theme called "The Hungry Years."
3. *A History of the Jews* (New York: Harper and Row, 1988), 340–341.

kindness and truth not leave you. Bind them around your throat, inscribe them on the tablet of your heart. Then you will find *grace and good intellect* in the eyes of the Lord and man" (Prov. 3:3–4). Grace (*ḥen*) takes precedence over good intellect (*sekhel tov*).

In *Kaddish DeRabbanan*, the prayer we say after studying a rabbinic text, we pray for spiritual leaders who have "grace, lovingkindness, and compassion." Once again the power of intellect is secondary to the personal qualities of sensitivity and graciousness. Grace is that quality which sees the best in others and seeks the best for others. It is a combination of gentleness and generosity.

The second priestly blessing is: May God "make His face shine on you," meaning, may His presence be evident in you. May He leave a visible trace of His Being on the face you show to others. How is that presence to be recognised? Not in severity, remoteness, or austerity but in the gentle smile that speaks to what Lincoln called "the better angels of our nature." That is grace.

The Lord turn His face towards you and give you peace: To make peace in the world we must be at peace with ourselves. To be at peace with ourselves we must know that we are unconditionally valued. That does not often happen. People value us for what we can give them. That is conditional value, what the sages called "love that is dependent on a cause" (Mishna Avot 5:16). God values us unconditionally. We are here because He wanted us to be. Our very existence testifies to His love. Unlike others, God never gives up on us. He rejects no one. He never loses faith, however many times we fail. When we fall, He lifts us. He believes in us more than we believe in ourselves.

You are in a crowd. In the distance you see someone you recognise. This person is well known. You met him once, briefly. Did you make an impression on him? Does he remember you? Does he know who you are? Briefly your eyes touch. From the distance, he smiles at you. Yes, he remembers you, he knows who you are, he is pleased you are here, and by his eye contact and his smile he communicates these things to you. You are relieved, lifted. You are at peace with yourself. You are not merely an anonymous face in a crowd. Your basic worth has in some way been affirmed. That, in human terms, is the meaning of "May the Lord turn His face towards you and give you peace."

We speak of "seeking recognition." It is a telling phrase. More even than power or wealth or success or fame, we long for what we believe these things will give us: standing in the eyes of others, respect, esteem, honour, worth. We can dedicate a lifetime to this search, but it is not a good one. People do not confer respect for the right reasons. They follow politicians who pander to their worst instincts. They feel the charisma of pure power. They flatter the wealthy. They are like moths to the flame of fame.

The recognition that counts is our reflection in the eyes of God. He loves us for what we are and what we could become. He loves the good in us, not the successful or persuasive or charismatic. He ignores the image we try to project because He knows us from within. His is the voice within us that says, "With Me, you do not have to pretend. I know you. I knew you before you were born. I know you because I made you, and I made you because I need you – or more precisely, because the world needs you. There is a task only you can do. Now, therefore, be strong and do it. You need not seek praise, nor shall you be deflected by criticism, for I will be with you every step of the way. When you feel most alone, that is when I will be closest." That is, metaphorically, *making eye contact with God*. It is the meaning of the third blessing: "May the Lord turn His face towards you and give you peace."

There is also a profound message in the concluding sentence: "So they will put My name on the Israelites, and I will bless them."

In the ancient world, magi, oracles, and religious virtuosi were held to have the power of blessing. They were able to invoke supernatural forces. This is the meaning of what Balak, king of Moab, says to the pagan prophet Balaam:

> A people has come out of Egypt; they cover the face of the land and have settled next to me. Now come and put a curse on these people, because they are too powerful for me. Perhaps then I will be able to defeat them and drive them out of the country. For I know that *those you bless are blessed, and those you curse are cursed.* (Num. 22:5–6)

The biblical story of Balaam is a satire on this idea. Balaam's contemporaries, and perhaps he himself, believed that blessing or curse lay within the power of the holy person. Nothing more arouses the ridicule of the Bible than self-importance. Balaam is made to see that his own donkey has greater powers of spiritual insight than he does. It is not the person who has power over God; it is God who has the power to reveal Himself to the person – and if He so chooses, He can give it to a donkey rather than to an esteemed religious figure. Holiness is not – though it is often confused with – self-importance. True holiness is *transparency to the Divine.*

This is the meaning of the verse, "So they will put My name on the Israelites, and I will bless them." In themselves, the priests have no power. They are intermediaries, channels through which God's blessing flows.

An ancient midrash says:

> The House of Israel said to the Holy One, Blessed Be He, "Lord of the universe, You order the priests to bless us? We need only Your blessing. Look down from Your holy habitation and bless Your people." The Holy One, Blessed Be He, replied to them, "Though I ordered the priests to bless you, I will stand together with them and bless you."[4]

It is not the priests who bless the people. Rather, it is through them that God blesses the people.

Finally, why was it the priests who were chosen to be vehicles of God's blessing? One reason is self-evident. The entire being of the priests was within the precincts of the holy. They were the intermediaries between the people and God. But there is another reason offered by the commentators. Apparently prosaic, it has nonetheless profound wisdom.

The priests had no share in the land. Unlike the rest of the Israelites, they had no fields or farms, no businesses, no source of income through the work of their hands. Instead, they were dependent on the gifts of the people. The Israelites gave them a portion of the harvest called *teruma.* They received other statutory gifts. So when the Israelites prospered as a whole, the priests benefited. They had a direct interest in the prosperity of the nation. More than anyone else, the priests were

4. *Midrash Tanḥuma, Parashat Naso* 15.

dependent on the welfare of others. They were able to bless the people with a full heart, because if others were favoured, so too would they be.

This may seem like an appeal to self-interest precisely where it does not belong, in the sphere of the holy, the sacrosanct, the Temple. Yet the genius of Judaism is that it is not predicated on superhuman virtue. It is not addressed to angels or saints, but to human beings in all our fallibility. Though its ideals are surpassingly high, its psychology is realistic throughout.

It was Adam Smith in his masterwork, *The Wealth of Nations*, who pointed out that self-interest, when properly channelled, led to the welfare of all. Smith himself sensed that there was something religious about this, and he gave it a quasi-religious name. He called it "the invisible hand," which was as near as he could come to speaking about divine providence – the mysterious yet benign way in which, though each of us may be concerned about our own narrow welfare, we are part of something larger than ourselves, in ways we cannot always understand. Our separate strands are part of a larger pattern.

The great Spanish poet and philosopher Judah Halevi noted that almost all our prayers are in the plural. We do not pray that God should give *me* something; we pray that he should give *us* something. "Bless us, O our Father, all of us together." There is a spirit of community written into the liturgy. We do not ask our God to listen to the prayers of individuals but to those of the Jewish people as a whole. When Moses prayed on behalf of the people, he was answered. When he prayed for himself – to be allowed to enter the Promised Land – he was not.

Halevi adds that there is nothing mystical in this idea. He explains it with the following analogy. Imagine, he says, trying to defend your house against enemies. There are two ways of doing so. One is to build a wall around the house. The other is to join with neighbours and build a wall around the town. The former is more expensive and offers less protection. To act *with* others *for* everyone is easier and more secure.[5]

So, he says, with prayer: If we pray *by* ourselves *for* ourselves, then we rely on our own merits, about which we can never be certain. But when we pray together with the whole community, we combine

5.   Judah Halevi, *The Kuzari*, III:19.

our merits with theirs. Prayer is like a protective wall, and praying together is more powerful and effective. We do not need superhuman piety – merely enlightened self-interest – to realise that our destinies are interconnected. When we are blessed, we are blessed together. Prayer is *community made articulate*, when we delete the first-person singular and substitute the first-person plural.

Protection, grace, peace – these are God's blessings, communicated by the priests. We are what we pray for. If you seek to understand a people, look at its prayers. The Jewish people did not ask for wealth or power. They did not hunger after empire. They had no desire to conquer or convert the world. They asked for protection, the right to live true to themselves without fear; for grace, the ability to be an agent for good in others; and peace, that fullness of being in which each of us brings our individual gifts to the common good. That is all our ancestors prayed for, and it is still all we need.

Pursuing Peace

What is the logic of *Parashat Naso*? It seems, on the face of it, to be a heterogeneous collection of utterly unrelated items. First there is the account of the Levitical families of Gershon and Merari and their tasks in carrying parts of the Tabernacle when the Israelites journeyed. Then, after two brief laws about removing unclean people from the camp and about restitution, there comes the strange ordeal of the *sota*, the woman suspected by her husband of adultery. Next comes the law of the Nazirite, who, as we saw earlier, voluntarily and usually for a fixed period took upon himself special holiness restrictions, among them the renunciation of wine and grape products, haircuts, and defilement by contact with a dead body.

This is followed, again seemingly with no connection, by one of the oldest prayers in the world still in continuous use, the priestly blessings. Then, with almost inexplicable repetitiousness, comes the account of the gifts brought by the princes of each tribe at the dedication of the Tabernacle, a series of long paragraphs repeated no less than twelve times, despite the fact that each prince brought an identical offering.

Why does the Torah spend so much time describing an event that could have been stated far more briefly by naming the princes and then simply telling us generically that each brought a silver dish, a silver basin, and so on? The rabbis made the assumption that every word of the Torah is meaningful. It tells us something we need to know, and does so in the fewest possible words. So the repetitiousness of this particular passage cries out for explanation.

The question that overshadows all others, though, is: What is the logic of this apparently disconnected series? The answer we will find time and again in Numbers, more than in any other book of the Torah, lies in *the close connection between law and narrative*. Law in Judaism is not random, arbitrary. It is not there simply because God wills it. The Torah wants us to understand why the law is as it is, and it does so by telling a story – a story about events in the past that did not turn out as they should have, and to which law is the antidote, the remedy, the *tikkun*. So it is here.

In the previous essay we spoke about the priestly blessings, with their concluding line, "The Lord turn His face towards you and give you peace" (Num. 6:26). It is no accident that the concluding word of this highly structured blessing is *shalom*, translated here as "peace." However, the translation is not precise. In English, peace means the absence of war, freedom from disturbance, calm, tranquillity, restfulness, and the like. In Hebrew, *shalom* means more than that.

In a long analysis, the fifteenth-century Spanish Jewish commentator Rabbi Isaac Arama explains that *shalom* does not mean merely the absence of strife. It means completeness, perfection, the harmonious working of a complex system, integrated diversity, a state in which everything is in its proper place and all is at one with the physical and ethical laws governing the universe: "Peace is the thread of grace issuing from Him, may He be exalted, stringing together all beings, supernal, intermediate, and lower. It underlies and sustains the reality and unique existence of each."[1]

Similarly, Isaac Abrabanel writes, "That is why God is called 'Peace,' because it is He who binds the world together and orders all things according to their particular character and posture. For when things are in their proper order, peace will reign" (commentary to Mishna Avot 2:12).

1. Isaac Arama, *Akedat Yitzhak*, ch. 74.

This is a concept of peace heavily dependent on the vision of Genesis 1, in which God brings order out of *tohu vavohu*, chaos, creating a world in which each object and life form has its place. Peace exists where each element in the system is valued as a vital part of the system as a whole and where there is no discord between them.

In this vein, the nineteenth-century commentator Rabbi Samson Raphael Hirsch (Germany, 1808–1888) explained the conclusion of the story of creation in Genesis 1. Six times, God sees what He has made and pronounces it "good." On the seventh occasion, we read, "God saw all that He had made, and behold it was *very good*" (Gen. 1:31). What is the difference between "good" and "very good"? "Good," said Hirsch, means good in itself. "Very good" means good in its totality. It is a reference to the harmony of the universe despite its complexity (commentary to Gen. 1:31).

That is the theological background to the biblical concept of *shalom*. Whereas the ancient myths of all other cultures saw reality in terms of the clash of primal forces, Judaism saw God as the-Unity-that-creates-diversity. *Shalom* is the harmonious coexistence of otherwise conflicting individuals, tribes, and nations, each with their distinctive nature and unique contribution to the totality of humankind. *Shalom* is thus not uniformity but *integrated diversity*.

The philosopher Joseph Albo (Spain, 1380–1444) saw conflict at the heart of physical/metaphysical existence. Everything that exists is a composite of different elements, each of which seeks to overcome the others. Thus, the need to establish peace is a constant requirement of physical being:

> Each opposing element seeks to overcome and vanquish the other, and once it has overcome the other, it will not rest until it has absolutely destroyed it and wiped it out of existence, and the composite object will thus cease to exist.... Conciliation between these two opposing elements is called peace, and on its account being is sustained, and the composite entity can continue to exist.[2]

2. Joseph Albo, *Sefer HaIkkarim* III, ch. 51. For an essay on this theme, see Aviezer Ravitsky, "Peace," in *Contemporary Jewish Religious Thought*, ed. Arthur A. Cohen and Paul Mendes-Flohr (New York: Scribners, 1987), 685–702.

The various provisions of *Parashat Naso* are all about bringing peace where there is actual or potential conflict within families or communities. The most obvious case is that of the *sota*, the woman suspected by her husband of adultery – a situation fraught with danger of violence and abuse. What struck the sages most forcibly about the ritual of the *sota* is the fact that it involved obliterating the name of God, something strictly forbidden under other circumstances. The officiating priest recited a curse including God's name, wrote it on a parchment scroll, and then dissolved the writing into specially prepared water. The sages inferred from this that God was willing to renounce His own honour, allowing His name to be effaced "in order to make peace between husband and wife" by clearing an innocent woman from suspicion.[3] Though the ordeal was eventually abolished by Rabban Yoḥanan b. Zakkai after the destruction of the Second Temple, the law served as a reminder as to how important domestic peace is in the Jewish scale of values.

The passage relating to the Levitical families of Gershon and Merari signals that they were given a role of honour in transporting items of the Tabernacle during the people's journeys through the wilderness. Evidently they were satisfied with this honour, unlike the family of Kehat, detailed at the end of the previous *parasha*, one of whose number, Korah, eventually instigated a rebellion against Moses and Aaron.

Likewise, the long account of the offerings of the princes of the twelve tribes is a dramatic way of indicating that each was considered important enough to merit its own passage in the Torah. People will do destructive things if they feel slighted and not given their due role and recognition. Again the case of Korah and his allies is proof of this. By giving the Levitical families and the princes of the tribes their share of honour and attention, the Torah is telling us how important it is to preserve the harmony of the nation by honouring all.

The case of the Nazirite is in some ways the most interesting. There is an internal conflict within Judaism: on the one hand, there is a strong emphasis on the equal dignity of everyone in the eyes of God; on the other, there exists a religious elite in the form of the tribe of Levi in general and the *kohanim*, the priests, in particular. It seems that the law

3.   Sifre, *Parashat Naso* 42.

of the Nazirite was a way of opening up the possibility to non-priests of a special sanctity close to, though not precisely identical with, that of the priests themselves. This too is a way of avoiding the damaging resentments that can occur when people find themselves excluded by birth from certain forms of status within the community.

If this analysis is correct, then a single theme binds the laws and narrative of this *parasha*: the theme of making special efforts to preserve or restore peace between people. Peace is easily damaged and hard to repair. Much of the rest of the book of Numbers is a set of variations on the theme of internal dissension and strife. So has Jewish history been as a whole.

The fact that these laws are stated *before* the narratives of conflict that dominate many of the later chapters of Numbers is an instance of the principle that "God creates the cure before the disease."[4] *Parashat Naso* tells us that we have to go the extra mile in bringing peace between husband and wife, between leaders of the community, and among lay-people who aspire to a more-than-usual state of sanctity. We have to make sure that all the tribes who participate in a ceremony such as the inauguration of the Tabernacle get equal attention, even if it means repeating the description twelve times.

Shalom has such a rich meaning in Hebrew – harmony between conflicting elements, each of which has its distinctive part to play in the integrated diversity of the whole. Thus the laws that illustrate the pursuit of peace are clustered together at the beginning of Numbers, the book that more than any other in the Torah documents the conflicts and self-inflicted injuries of the Israelites in the wilderness.

The Jewish solution is not strong government, central control, and the imposition of uniformity. To the contrary, it is valuing diversity as the way to achieve *shlemut*, "wholeness, perfection," and thus *shalom* as calibrated harmony between the various elements, each with its role, each in its place.

It is no accident that the priestly blessings end – as do the vast majority of Jewish prayers – with a prayer for peace. Peace, said the rabbis, is one of the names of God Himself, and Maimonides writes that

4. *Midrash Lekaḥ Tov*, Exodus 3:1.

the whole Torah was given to make peace in the world.[5] *Parashat Naso* is a series of practical lessons in how to ensure, as far as possible, that everyone feels recognised and respected, and that suspicion is defused and dissolved.

We have to work for peace, not just pray for it.

---

5. Maimonides, *Mishneh Torah, Hilkhot Ḥanukka* 4:14.

Behaalotekha
בְּהַעֲלֹתְךָ

Parashat Behaalotekha begins with the final preparations for the Israelites' journey from the Sinai desert to the Promised Land. There are instructions for Aaron, the high priest, to tend to the light of the Menora, and for consecrating the Levites into their special role as guardians of the sacred. Before setting out, the Israelites celebrate Passover, one year after the Exodus itself, and provisions are made for those who are unable to celebrate it at its proper time to do so a month later. Details are given about the cloud that signals when to encamp and when to move on. Moses is commanded to make two silver trumpets to summon the people.

The narrative now changes tone. The Israelites set out after their long stay in the Sinai desert, but almost immediately there are problems, protests, and complaints. Moses suffers his deepest emotional crisis. He prays to God to die. God tells him to gather seventy elders who will help him with the burdens of leadership. In the last scene of the *parasha*, Moses' own sister and brother speak against him. Miriam is punished. Moses, here described as the humblest of men, prays on her behalf. After a week's wait for Miriam to be healed, the people move on.

In the first essay we look at an unusual feature of the text as it appears in a Torah scroll: a passage is separated from the rest by two brackets, leading the rabbis to say that this brief section is a book in itself. What does this mean? The second essay is about two ways of characterising Jewish identity. The third and fourth are about Moses' despair. Why here and not before? And how is this related to the specific kind of leader Moses is? The fifth is about the role of the seventy elders in lifting Moses' depression. The sixth is about Miriam's complaint. What was it, and why was she punished for it?

The Book Between the Books

There is a small detail in *Parashat Behaalotekha* which, if properly understood, sheds considerable light on the structure of Jewish spirituality. A two-sentence paragraph appears at the end of chapter 10, roughly halfway through the *parasha*:

> When the Ark was to set out, Moses would say: Advance, O Lord! May Your enemies be scattered, and may Your foes flee before You! And when it halted, he would say: Return, O Lord, You who are Israel's myriads of thousands! (Num. 10:35–36)

The meaning of the passage is this: The Israelites were about to begin the second half of their journey through the wilderness. They travelled, tribe by tribe, in the order specified earlier in the book, with the Ark, symbolising the Divine Presence, in their midst. So at the beginning and end of each stage on the way, Moses would remind the people that they were not alone, nor were they defenceless. God was with them, giving them strength in battle and security in their resting places. We still say these verses in the synagogue when we take the *sefer Torah* out of the ark, and when we replace it.

What makes this passage unusual is that, as written in the Torah scroll, it is separated from the rest of the text by two inverted Hebrew letters, each a *nun*. The rabbis rightly surmised that they form a set of brackets, parentheses, separating this one paragraph from the words that precede and follow it. Some rabbis went so far as to say that this shows that *these two sentences are a book in its own right.* In other words, Numbers is not one book but three.[1] I want to explore the meaning of this idea. In what sense does this one paragraph divide the entire book of Numbers into a before-and-after, and what does it add of its own?

If we look at the beginning of *Parashat Behaalotekha*, we see that it focuses on an aspect of the service of Aaron the high priest:

> The Lord said to Moses, "Speak to Aaron and say to him, 'When you set up the lamps, see that all seven light up the area in front of the lampstand.'" Aaron did so; he set up the lamps so that they faced forwards on the lampstand, just as the Lord commanded Moses. (Num. 8:1–3)

This simple daily ritual epitomised the role of the priest. *A priest engages in rites that in essence never change.* One symbol of this was the Menora, the lampstand, tended each day so that a *ner tamid*, an everlasting light, burnt in the Sanctuary as a sign of the presence of the eternal God. Priestly rituals followed a daily, weekly, monthly, and yearly cycle that never changed. Barring tragedies such as the destruction of the Temple, they could be calculated in advance until the end of time.

On the phrase "Aaron did so... *just as the Lord commanded Moses*" – Rashi comments, "This is stated *in order to praise Aaron*, that he did so [i.e., followed Moses' instructions] without making any change."[2] On the face of it, this is a very odd comment. Do we need to be told every occasion on which a priest – or anyone else, for that matter – did what

---

1. Soferim 6:1, Genesis Rabba 64:8. As to why the text is inserted here, R. Shimon b. Gamliel's view is that it "separates between two punishments" (Shabbat 116a). In this essay I offer another interpretation.
2. Rashi is quoting a midrash, Sifre ad loc.

God commanded? Is that an occasion for praise? It is and ought to be the norm. Only the exceptions are newsworthy.

In fact, though, Rashi is alluding to an earlier drama: the inauguration of the Tabernacle at which two of Aaron's sons, Nadav and Avihu, offered up "strange fire that had not been commanded," and they died (Lev. 10:1–2). I have argued elsewhere[3] that what Nadav and Avihu were doing is what they had seen Moses do at moments of great spiritual intensity, namely acting on his own initiative. What they failed to understand was that he was a prophet; they were priests. A prophet responds to the unique circumstances of the here-and-now. A priest – who lives in the shadow of the Eternal – inhabits eternity. The essence of priestly service is to do what you are commanded "without making any change" (Deut. 28:14). What the Torah is saying about Aaron at this point is that he understood his role. He was Aaron, not Moses; a priest not a prophet; he epitomised *that which does not change.*

Contrast this with what we see in the second half of *Parashat Behaalotekha,* where the focus is not on Aaron but on Moses. No sooner do the people begin the journey than they begin to complain – we are not told what about – at Taberah. Next, at *Kivrot HaTaava,* they complain about the food in such a way as to induce in Moses a temporary breakdown. Then in the next chapter, Moses' own sister and brother, Miriam and Aaron, complain about his behaviour. There is nothing relaxing, regular, or predictable about the life of a prophet. He or she lives in the turbulence of time. The prophet has to be alert to every danger, internal and external, physical and spiritual, to the people. Today is different from yesterday, and tomorrow will be different again. There is only one thing predictable about the future, namely that it will be unpredictable.

The prophets of Israel were radically unlike their counterparts in other cultures. Every religion has had its oracles, soothsayers, stargazers, necromancers, diviners, and foretellers of the future, just as now we have economists, meteorologists, pundits, and futurologists. All of these are people who supply an answer to the question, "What is going to happen?" The prophets of Israel did not believe you could predict

3. *Covenant and Conversation: Leviticus – The Book of Holiness* (Jerusalem: Maggid, 2015), 149–152.

anything with certainty in the human domain because what is going to happen depends on us. We face an open future, because we are free. We, with God, are co-authors of the script, which has not been written in advance. Therefore the prophets did not predict. They warned. They said, in effect, "This will happen *unless* ...." They summoned the people to *teshuva*, to repentance and return. There is no evil decree that cannot be averted. That is the difference between Aeschylus and Isaiah, or between Sophocles and Jeremiah. It is the difference between Greek tragedy and Jewish hope.

So the two halves of *Parashat Behaalotekha* focus respectively on Aaron the priest and Moses the prophet. Despite the fact that they were brothers, they could not be less alike. Their roles, sensibilities, and responsibilities, their very ways of experiencing and interacting with the world, were altogether different.

Now consider the structure of the three central books of the Torah: Exodus, Leviticus, and Numbers. The outer sections – the first nineteen chapters of Exodus and the last twenty-five of Numbers – are full of incidents. The Israelites leave Egypt and travel through the desert. There are dangers, battles, and miracles on the way. There are human complaints, divine anger, and crises that call for strong leadership of the people and daring intercession with God. Events transpire. The text is predominantly narrative. We are in the presence of history. This is the world of the prophet. Here the dominant figure is Moses.

However, within this outer wrapping are fifty-nine chapters – the last part of Exodus, the whole of Leviticus, and the first ten chapters of Numbers – in which almost nothing happens. The Israelites do not travel. They stay in the Sinai desert. Time slows to a standstill. At the end of Exodus we read, "So the Tabernacle was set up on the first day of the first month in the second year" (Ex. 40:17). Scores of chapters later, in *Parashat Behaalotekha*, we read, "The Lord spoke to Moses in the desert of Sinai in the first new moon of the second year after the Exodus from the land of Egypt" (Num. 9:1). *For more than half of the Torah's inner three books, the Israelites hardly move in time or space.* It is as if they are suspended in a realm beyond both, in a place (the desert) that is no place, and in a time that seems to defy time. That is the world of the Tabernacle and the Temple, the home of God as He is not in history but in eternity.

This is the universe of *kedusha*, holiness, in which the dominant figures are Aaron, the high priest, and his descendants.

These are the two faces of Judaism. There are aspects of Judaism that never change, wherever and whenever we are. The laws of purity and impurity, permitted and forbidden, sacred and secular – these have barely changed through the centuries. And though many of them are no longer operative, because there is no Temple and its service, they remain part of the Jewish law still studied in yeshivas and houses of study throughout the world. This is where we encounter the holiness, the otherness, of God as He exists beyond time and space, infinite and eternal.

But there are aspects of Judaism that are deeply enmeshed in time and place, above all in the fate of the Jewish people as a nation in its land or as a people scattered and dispersed throughout the world. Most of the books in Tanakh – some historical, others prophetic – are about this dimension. They tell a story about the faithfulness or faithlessness of the people to their covenant with God. There is nothing metaphysical or other-worldly about this story. It is about politics and economics, battles won or lost, about Israel as a nation in a world of nations, and about its ability or otherwise to stay true to its founding principles as a covenanted people through the whitewater rapids of history.

Judaism lives in the creative tension between these two essential elements of its being. If Israel was only a people of eternity, it would never have had an impact on history. Jews would have been a priestly sect like the one known to us from the Dead Sea Scrolls, or like monks and mystics of other faiths, holy and harmless, secluded and serene, in touch with the ethereal music of the spheres but not the substance of everyday life.

If, on the other hand, Jews had been only a people of history, they would have ceased to exist after the Babylonian conquest, or if they had survived that half-century of exile they would certainly have disappeared in the almost two-thousand-year exile after the failed revolts against Rome. They would have been like the Jebusites and Perizzites, at best a brief footnote in the history of a long-vanished past.

We now return to where we began, the two verses each flanked by an inverted *nun*: "When the Ark was to set out, Moses would say: 'Advance, O Lord! May Your enemies be scattered, and may Your foes flee before You!' And when it halted, he would say: 'Return, O Lord,

You who are Israel's myriads of thousands!'" This passage is set at the dividing line between the timelessness of the Israelites at Sinai and the time-bound nature of their journey towards the Promised Land. It is symbolised by the radical difference between Aaron the priest, daily tending the everlasting light in a ritual that never changed, and Moses the leader and prophet who faced the uncertainty of constant change.

See how precisely the inserted passage – the book between the books – sums up Jewish history in a mere two verses. There are times when Jews halt and encamp, when time itself seems to stop and the people feel close to eternity as they did, long ago, in their prolonged stay in the desert of Sinai. And there are moments when the cloud shifts, the trumpet sounds, and the people know it is time to move on. History beckons. Destiny calls. For God exists within, not just beyond, time and space and we have to engage in the world as it is, even as we aspire to the world as it ought to be.

These are the two books of Jewish life: the Judaism-of-eternity and the Judaism-of-history. Nowhere is the line between them clearer than it is in *Parashat Behaalotekha*, as the long stay at Sinai comes to an end and the people have to gather their belongings and travel on. It is precisely here, at the juncture between the two, that the two verses each flanked by an inverted *nun* appear.

So this brief and simple paragraph is indeed a kind of book between the books, the interlude between two movements of the symphony, the adagio of the stay and the allegro of the journey. What it tells us is simply this: that whether setting out or halting, the Ark must always be there at the heart of Jewish life, reminding us that God is to be found both in eternity and history, stasis and change, beyond time and within time, joining His fate to ours, the God of both priest and prophet, who gives us the patience to rest and the courage to move on.

Camp and Congregation

The *parasha* of *Behaalotekha* speaks about the silver trumpets – clarions – Moses was commanded to make:

> The Lord spoke to Moses, saying, "Make two trumpets of silver; make them of hammered work. They shall serve you to summon the congregation [*edah*] and cause the camps [*maḥanot*] to journey." (Num. 10:1–2)

This apparently simple passage became a springboard for one of the most profound meditations of the late Rabbi Joseph Soloveitchik. It appears in the course of his great essay *Kol Dodi Dofek* on the Jewish approach to suffering.[1]

There are, says Rabbi Soloveitchik, two ways in which people become a group – a community, society, or nation. The first is when they

---

1. Rabbi Joseph B. Soloveitchik, *Kol Dodi Dofek: Listen, My Beloved Knocks*, trans. David Z. Gordon (Jersey City, NJ: Ktav, 2006). A translation also appears in Bernhard H. Rosenberg (ed.), *Theological and Halakhic Reflections on the Holocaust* (Hoboken, NJ: Ktav, 1992).

face a common enemy. They band together for mutual protection, knowing that only by so doing can they survive. This phenomenon extends far beyond Homo sapiens. Animals too come together in herds or flocks to defend themselves against predators. Such a group is a *maḥaneh* – a camp, a defensive formation.

There is a quite different form of association. People can come together because they share a vision, an aspiration, a set of ideals. This is the meaning of *edah*, congregation. *Edah* is related to the word *ed*, witness. *Edot* (as opposed to *ḥukkim* and *mishpatim*) are the commands that testify to Jewish belief – as Shabbat testifies to creation, Passover to the divine involvement in history, and so on. An *edah* is not a defensive formation but a creative one. People join to do together what none of them could achieve alone. A society built around a shared project, a vision of the common good, is not a *maḥaneh* but an *edah* – not a camp but a congregation.

These are, says Rabbi Soloveitchik, not just two types of group, but in the most profound sense, two different ways of existing and relating to the world. A camp is brought into being by what happens to it from the outside. A congregation comes into existence by internal decision. The former is reactive, the latter proactive. The first is a response to what has happened to the group in the past. The second represents what the group seeks to achieve in the future. Whereas camps exist even in the animal kingdom, congregations are uniquely human. They flow from the human ability to think, speak, communicate, envision a society different from any that has existed in the past, and to collaborate to bring it about.

Jews are a people in *both* of these two quite different ways. Our ancestors became a *maḥaneh* in Egypt, forged together in the crucible of slavery and suffering. They were different. They were not Egyptians. They were *Hebrews* – a word which probably means "on the other side," "an outsider." Ever since, Jews have known that we are thrown together by circumstance. We share a history all too often written in tears. Rabbi Soloveitchik calls this the *covenant of fate* (*brit goral*).

This is not a purely negative phenomenon. It gives rise to a powerful sense that we are part of a single story – that what we have in common is stronger than the things that separate us:

Our fate does not distinguish between aristocrats and common folk, between rich and poor, between a prince garbed in the royal purple and the pauper begging from door to door, between the pietist and the assimilationist. Even though we speak a plethora of languages, even though we are inhabitants of different lands ... we still share the same fate. If the Jew in the hovel is beaten, then the security of the Jew in the palace is endangered. "Do not think that you, of all the Jews, will escape with your life by being in the king's palace" (Est. 4:13).[2]

It leads also to a sense of *shared suffering*. When we pray for the recovery of a sick person, we do so "among all the sick of Israel." When we comfort a mourner, we do so "among all the other mourners of Zion and Jerusalem." We weep together. We celebrate together. This in turn leads to *shared responsibility*: "All Israel are sureties for one another."[3] And this leads to *collective action* in the field of welfare, charity, and deeds of loving kindness. As Maimonides puts it:

All Israelites and those who have attached themselves to them are to one another like brothers, as it is said, "You are children of the Lord your God" (Deut. 14:1). If brother shows no compassion to brother, who then will? To whom shall the poor of Israel raise their eyes? To the heathens who hate and persecute them? Their eyes are therefore lifted to their brothers.[4]

All these are dimensions of the covenant of fate, born in the experience of slavery in Egypt. But there is an additional element of Jewish identity. Soloveitchik calls this the *covenant of destiny* (*brit ye'ud*) – entered into at Mount Sinai. This defines the people Israel not as the object of persecution but the subject of a unique vocation, to become "a kingdom of priests and a holy nation" (Ex. 19:6).

2. In Rosenberg, *Theological and Halakhic Reflections*, 84.
3. Sanhedrin 27b; Shevuot 39a.
4. Maimonides, *Mishneh Torah, Hilkhot Matanot LeEvyonim* 10:2.

Under this covenant, the Jewish people was defined not by what others do to it but by the task it has undertaken, the role it has chosen to play in history. The Israelites did not choose to become slaves in Egypt. That was a fate thrust upon them by someone else. They did, however, choose to become God's people at Sinai when they said, "We will do and obey" (Ex. 24:7). Destiny, call, vocation, purpose, task: these create not a *maḥaneh* but an *edah*, not a *camp* but a *congregation*.

No one defined the Jewish destiny more simply or nobly than the prophet Isaiah, who said in the name of God:

> "You are My witnesses [*edai*]," declares the Lord,
> "and My servant whom I have chosen....
> I have revealed and saved and proclaimed –
> I, and not some foreign god among you.
> You are My witnesses [*edai*]," declares the Lord, "that I am God."
> (Is. 43:10–12)

The word *edai*, "My witnesses," is from the same root as *edah*, "congregation." Our task as a people of destiny is to bear witness to the presence of God – through the way we lead our lives (Torah) and the path we chart as a people across the centuries (history).

G. K. Chesterton once wrote that "America is the only nation in the world that is founded on a creed."[5] Chesterton was notoriously anti-Semitic, and this evidently prevented him from recalling that the reason America was founded on a creed was that its founders, Puritans all, were steeped in the Hebrew Bible (or as they called it, the Old Testament). They took as their model the covenant made between God and the Israelites at Sinai, and it was this that linked nationhood and the idea of a specific task or mission. Herman Melville gave this one of its classic expressions in his 1849 novel, *White-Jacket*:

> We Americans are the peculiar, chosen people – the Israel of our time; we bear the ark of the liberties of the world.... God has

---

5. G. K. Chesterton, *What I Saw in America* (New York: Dodd, Mead and Company, 1922), 7.

predestined, mankind expects, great things from our race; and great things we feel in our souls. The rest of the nations must soon be in our rear. We are pioneers of the world; the advance-guard, sent on through the wilderness of untried things, to break a new path in the New World that is ours.[6]

It is the concept of covenant that gives Jewish (and American) identity this strange dual character. Nations are usually forged through long historical experience, through what happens to them – rather than what they consciously set themselves to do. They fall into the category of *maḥaneh*. Religions, on the other hand, are defined in terms of beliefs and a sense of mission. Each is constituted as an *edah*. What is unique about Judaism is the way it brings together these separate and quite distinct ideas. *There are nations that contain many religions and there are religions that are spread over many nations, but only in the case of Judaism do religion and nation coincide.*

This has had remarkable consequences. For almost two thousand years Jews were scattered throughout the world, yet they saw themselves and were seen by others as a nation – the world's first global nation. It was a nation held together not by geographical proximity or any other of the normal accompaniments of nationhood. Jews did not speak the same vernacular. Rashi spoke French, Maimonides Arabic. Rashi lived in a Christian culture, Maimonides in a Muslim one. Nor was their fate the same. While the Jews of Spain were enjoying their Golden Age, the Jews of northern Europe were being massacred in the Crusades. In the fifteenth century, when the Jews of Spain were being persecuted and expelled, those of Poland were enjoying a rare spring of tolerance. What held Jews together during these centuries was shared faith.

In the trauma that accompanied European Emancipation and the subsequent rise of racial anti-Semitism, many Jews lost that faith. Yet the events of the past century – persecution, pogroms, and the Holocaust, followed by the birth of the State of Israel and the constant fight it has had to survive against war and terror – tended to bind Jews together

---

6. *White-Jacket* (Oxford: Oxford University Press, 2000), 153. See Jonathan Sacks, "The Universal Story," in *Pesaḥ Haggada* (Jerusalem: Maggid, 2013), 75–84.

in a covenant of fate in the face of the hostility of the world. So when Jews were divided by fate they were united by faith, and when they were divided by faith they were united again by fate. Such is the irony, or the providential nature, of Jewish history.

Judaism in the past two centuries has fissured and fractured into different *edot*: Orthodox and Reform, religious and secular, and the many subdivisions that continue to atomise Jewish life into non-communicating sects and subcultures. Yet in times of crisis we are still capable of heeding the call of collective responsibility, knowing as we do that Jewish fate tends to be indivisible. No Jew, to paraphrase John Donne, is an island, entire of him- or herself. We are joined by the gossamer strands of collective memory, and these can sometimes lead us back to a sense of shared destiny.

The duality was given its first expression in *Parashat Behaalotekha*, with the command: "Make two trumpets of silver; make them of hammered work. They shall serve you to summon the congregation [*edah*], and cause the camps [*maḥanot*] to journey." Sometimes the clarion call speaks to our sense of faith. We are God's people, His emissaries and ambassadors, charged with making His presence real in the world by healing deeds and holy lives. At other times the trumpet that sounds and summons us is the call of fate: Jewish lives endangered in Israel or the Diaspora by the unremitting hostility of those who call themselves children of Abraham yet claim that they, not we, are his true heirs.

Whichever sound the silver instruments make, they call on that duality that makes Jews and Judaism inseparable. However deep the divisions between us, we remain one family in fate and faith. When the trumpet sounds, it sounds for us.

The Adaptive Challenge

Many of the events in Numbers seem to have a déjà vu quality about them. We have met them already in Exodus. In both books, the people complain about the water and the food. In both they are guilty of false nostalgia, and in both they express regret at ever having left Egypt. Yet there is a striking and thoroughly perplexing difference between Moses' responses in the two books.

In Exodus, Moses speaks to God, God tells him what to do, and he does it. In Numbers, by contrast, Moses seems to suffer from strong, almost despairing emotion, as if he is exhausted by the ingratitude and fractiousness of the people and the constant strain of striving to keep the peace between them and God. This *parasha* contains the most extreme and unnerving example.

This is what the people say: "If only we had meat to eat! We remember the fish we ate in Egypt at no cost – also the cucumbers, melons, leeks, onions, and garlic. But now we have lost our appetite; we never see anything but this manna!" (Num. 11:5).

Moses had faced a very similar complaint before. In Exodus, the people had said: "If only we had died by the Lord's hand in Egypt! There we sat around pots of meat and ate all the food we wanted, but you have brought us out into this desert to starve this entire assembly to death" (Ex. 16:3). On that occasion God told Moses to tell the people that He would rain down for them "bread from heaven" (Ex. 16:4), and so it happened. On this occasion, however, Moses reacts in such a way that we can only call it a breakdown. It is the lowest emotional ebb of his entire career as a leader. These are his words to God:

> Why have You brought this trouble on Your servant? What have I done to displease You that you put the burden of all these people on me? Did I conceive all these people? Did I give them birth?...
> I cannot carry all these people by myself; the burden is too heavy for me. If this is how You are going to treat me, please go ahead and kill me – if I have found favour in Your eyes – and let me not see my own ruin. (Num. 11:11–15)

This is undeniably strange. Usually, when leaders face repeated challenges, they grow stronger each time. They learn how to respond and how to cope. They develop resilience, a thick skin. They formulate survival strategies. Why then does Moses seem to do the opposite, not only here but often throughout the book of Numbers?

In the chapters that follow, Moses seems to lack the unshakable determination he had in Exodus. At times, as in the episode of the spies (Num. 13–14), or later, in the episode of Zimri (Num. 25:1–15), he seems surprisingly passive, leaving it to others to fight the battle. At other times, as when he brought water from the rock (Num. 20:1–13), he seems to lose control and becomes angry, something a leader should not do. Something has changed, but what? Why the breakdown, the burnout, and the despair?

A fascinating insight is provided by the innovative work of Prof. Ronald Heifetz, co-founder and director of the Center for Public Leadership at the John F. Kennedy School of Government, Harvard University.[1]

---

1. Ronald Heifetz, *Leadership Without Easy Answers* (Cambridge, MA: Harvard University Press, 1994); Ronald Heifetz and Marty Linsky, *Leadership on the Line* (Boston: Harvard Business Press, 2002); Ronald Heifetz, Marty Linsky, and Alexander Grashow, *The Practice of Adaptive Leadership: Tools and Tactics*

Heifetz makes a fundamental distinction between *technical* challenges and *adaptive* challenges. A technical challenge is one where you have a problem and someone else has the solution. You are ill, you go to the doctor, he or she diagnoses your condition and prescribes a pill. All you have to do is follow the instructions.

Adaptive challenges are different. They arise when *we* are part of the problem. You are ill, you go to the doctor, and the doctor tells you: I can give you a pill, but the truth is that you are going to have to change your lifestyle. You are overweight, out of shape, you sleep too little and are exposed to too much stress. Pills will not help you until you change the way you live.

Adaptive leadership is called for when the world is changing, when circumstances are no longer what they were, when what once worked works no more. There is no quick fix, no pill, no simple following of instructions. *We* have to change. The leader cannot do it for us.

The fundamental difference between the books of Exodus and Numbers is that in Exodus, Moses is called on to exercise technical leadership. The Israelites had problems and it was his task to ask God to provide the solutions. The Israelites were enslaved, so God sent signs and wonders, ten plagues, and the Israelites went free. They needed to escape from Pharaoh's chariots; God told Moses to lift his staff and divide the sea. The people were hungry, so God sent manna from heaven. They were thirsty, so God sent water from a rock. When they had a problem, the leader, Moses, together with God, provided the solution. The people did not have to exert themselves at all.

In the book of Numbers, however, the task was quite different. The Israelites had completed the first part of their journey. They had left Egypt, reached Sinai, and made a covenant with God. Now they were on their way to the Promised Land. What Moses now had to do was to help the people transform themselves from liberated slaves to people willing to undertake the responsibilities of freedom. Instead of providing *technical* leadership, he had to provide *adaptive* leadership. He had to get the people to change, to face challenges, to develop courage and

for Changing Your Organization and the World (Boston: Harvard Business Press, 2009).

stamina, to be able to cope with the privations of the wilderness, to learn to do things for themselves while trusting in God, instead of relying on God to do things for them.

It is precisely because Moses understood this that he was so devastated when he saw that the people *had not changed at all*. They were still complaining about the food, almost exactly as they had before the revelation at Mount Sinai, before their covenant with God, before they themselves had built the Sanctuary, their first creative endeavour together. In a sense they had become even worse. In Exodus they had complained about the total lack of food. The unleavened bread they had brought with them from Egypt had been consumed and they had nothing to eat at all. In Numbers they had the manna from heaven. They were simply complaining that it was boring. This was not just a failure to grow. It was regressive behaviour.

Moses had to teach the people to adapt, but he sensed – rightly, as it transpires – that this was beyond them. Their strength had become atrophied by years of slavery. They were psychologically passive, dependent. They had lost the capacity for self-motivated action. As we eventually discover, it would take a new generation, born in freedom, to develop the strengths needed for self-governance, the precondition of freedom.

Adaptive leadership is intensely difficult. People resist change. They erect barriers against it. One is denial. A second is anger. A third is blame. That is why adaptive leadership is emotionally draining in the extreme. Many of the great adaptive leaders – among them Lincoln, Gandhi, John F. and Robert Kennedy, Martin Luther King Jr., Anwar Sadat, and Yitzhak Rabin – were assassinated. Their greatness was posthumous. Only in retrospect were they seen by their own people as heroes. At the time, they were seen by many as a threat to the status quo, to all that is comfortingly familiar.

Moses, with the insight of the greatest of the prophets, intuitively saw all this. Hence his despair and wish to die. It is far easier to be a technical leader than an adaptive one. It is easy to leave it to God, hard to realise that God is calling us to responsibility, to become His partners in the work of redemption.

Of course, the Torah does not leave it there. In Judaism, despair never has the last word. God comforts Moses, tells him to recruit seventy elders to share the burden of leadership with him, and gives him the strength to carry on. Adaptive leadership is, for Judaism, the highest form of leadership. That is what the prophets did. Without relieving people of their responsibility, they gave them a vision and a hope. They spoke difficult, challenging truths, and they did so with a passion that still has the power to inspire the better angels of our nature.

With devastating honesty – never more so than in its account of Moses' temporary breakdown – the Torah tells us that adaptive leadership is not easy, and that those who exercise it will face anger and criticism. They may come to feel that they have failed. But they have not. Moses remains the greatest leader the Jewish people has ever known, the man who almost single-handedly shaped the Israelites into a nation that never gave up or gave way to despair.

The difficulty of adaptive leadership is powerfully hinted at in God's words to Moses' successor, Joshua: "Be strong and courageous, for you will lead these people to inherit the land I swore to their ancestors to give them. Only be strong and *very* courageous to keep and obey all the law My servant Moses gave you" (Josh. 1:6–7).

The first sentence speaks about *military* leadership. Joshua was to lead the people in their conquest of the land. The second verse speaks about *spiritual* leadership. Joshua was to ensure that he and the people kept faith with the covenant they had made with God. The first, says the verse, demands courage, but the second demands *exceptional* courage.

Change always does. To fight an enemy is hard, to fight with yourself harder still. To help people find the strength to change – that is the greatest leadership challenge of all.

Is a Leader a Nursing Father?

In the previous essay, we looked at Moses' emotional collapse after the people complained about the food. I suggested that the difference between Moses' reaction in Numbers and in Exodus had to do with the distinction between technical and adaptive leadership challenges. A technical challenge is one where the people have a problem and the leader provides the solution. An adaptive one is where the people themselves are part of the problem and the solution requires that the people change.[1] People resist change, especially when it involves jettisoning habits of the past. It can feel like a loss, almost a bereavement, and they can react with a mixture of resistance, denial, anger, sadness, and nostalgia – a desire to be back where they once were. These things are emotionally draining, especially for the leader, and they are all documented with great accuracy in the various crises described in Numbers.

In this and the following essay I want to stay with this episode of Moses' breakdown, because it is so powerful, emotive, and challenging. For a moment, the greatest of all Jewish heroes of faith loses faith – not,

---

1. Essential here are the writings of Ronald Heifetz, cited in the previous essay.

to be sure, in God, but in himself and his role. In this essay I ask a single, simple question: Was Moses himself part of the problem?

The question is prompted by – and an answer intimated in – Moses' own words at the beginning of the outburst that ended with him asking God to "please go ahead and kill me" (Num. 11:15). This is how he begins:

> Why have You brought this trouble on Your servant? What have I done to displease You that You put the burden of all these people on me? *Did I conceive all these people? Did I give them birth? Why do You tell me to carry them in my arms, as a nurse carries an infant,* to the land You promised on oath to their ancestors? (Num. 11:11–12)

Inevitably, when we read Moses' anguished plea, our attention focuses on his wish to die. But this is not the most interesting part of his speech. Moses was not the only Jewish leader to pray to die. So did Elijah. So did Jeremiah. So did Jonah.[2] Spiritual leadership is difficult. Unlike politicians, prophets tell the people what they least want to hear. This is one of the most stressful tasks anyone can undertake. Jeremiah is eloquent on the subject: "I am ridiculed all day long; everyone mocks me…. The word of the Lord has brought me insult and reproach all day long" (Jer. 20:7–8). Moses was not the only prophet to find his mission almost unbearable.

What is singular here is his statement that God had told him to carry the people in his arms "as a nurse carries an infant." But God had never used those words or even remotely implied such a thing. He had asked Moses to lead but did not tell him how to lead. He told Moses what to do, but never discussed with him his leadership style.

It seems that the Torah is here hinting that *the way Moses conceived the role of leader was itself part of the problem.* "Did I conceive all these people? Did I give them birth? Why do You tell me to carry them in my arms?" This is the language of the leader-as-parent, the "great man" theory of leadership.

---

2. See, on Elijah, I Kings 19:3–4; on Jeremiah, Jer. 20:7–18; on Jonah, Jonah 4:1–3.

Sigmund Freud was deeply absorbed by this issue. He argued that crowds become dangerous when a certain kind of leader comes to power.[3] Such a leader, often highly charismatic, resolves the tensions within the group by seeming to promise solutions to all their problems. He is strong. He is persuasive. He is clear. He offers a simple analysis of why the people are suffering. He identifies enemies, focuses energies, and makes the people feel whole, complete, part of something great. "Leave it to me," he seems to say. "All you have to do is follow and obey."

Moses was not a typical charismatic leader. He said of himself, "I am not a man of words" (Ex. 4:10). He was not particularly close to the people. Aaron was. Perhaps Miriam was also. Caleb had the power to calm the people, at least temporarily. Moses had neither the gift nor the desire to sway crowds, resolve complexity, attract a mass following, or win popularity. That was not the kind of leader the Israelites needed, which is why God chose Moses, an awkward, angular man but one with a strong sense of justice and a passion for liberty.

But Moses, especially here, seems to have felt that *the leader must do it all.* He must be the people's father, mother, and nursemaid. He must be the doer, the problem-solver, omniscient and omnipotent. If something needs to be done it is for the leader to do it.[4] He says, for example, "Where can I get meat for all these people? They keep wailing to me, 'Give us meat to eat!'" (Num. 11:13). But this was either God's problem or the people's. It was not Moses'.

The trouble is that if the leader is a parent, then the followers remain children. They are totally dependent on him. They do not develop skills of their own. They do not acquire a sense of responsibility or the

3. See Sigmund Freud, *Totem and Taboo* (New York: Norton, 1952) and *Moses and Monotheism*, part III (New York: Vintage, 1967). See also Mark Edmundson, *The Death of Sigmund Freud: The Legacy of His Last Days* (New York: Bloomsbury, 2007), who argues that this is why Freud spent the last year of his life writing the third part of *Moses and Monotheism*, as a warning of the danger of the craving for strong leadership.

4. Note that Joseph, in Genesis, is this kind of leader. That is how he is described in three different roles, as head servant in Potiphar's house, as chief assistant to the warden in prison, and as viceroy of Egypt (Gen. 39, 41). It is highly significant that this kind of leadership is portrayed as effective in an Egyptian context but not in an Israelite one.

self-confidence that comes from exercising it. It was this dependency that led to the sin of the Golden Calf (Ex. 32). Moses had been absent up the mountain for a long time and the people did not know what had happened to him. They panicked and made a Golden Calf. This is one of the reasons why God told Moses to gather a team of seventy elders to share the burden with him. He was saying: Do not even try to do it all yourself.

The "great man" theory of leadership haunts Jewish history like a recurring nightmare. In the days of Samuel, the people believed their problems would be solved if they appointed a king "like all the other nations" (I Sam. 8:5). In vain, Samuel warned them that this would only make their problems worse. Saul, their first king, looked the part, handsome, upright, "a head taller than anyone else" (I Sam. 9:2), but he lacked strength of character. David, their second, committed adultery. Solomon, their third, blessed with wisdom, was seduced by his wives into folly. The kingdom split. Only a few subsequent kings were equal to the moral and spiritual challenge of combining faith in God with a politics of realism and civic virtue.

During the Second Temple period, the success of the Macca-bees was dramatic but short-lived. The Hasmonean kings themselves became Hellenised. The office of high priest became politicised. No one could contain the growing rifts within the nation. Having defeated the Greeks, the nation fell to the Romans. Sixty years later, R. Akiva identified Bar Kokhba as another "great man" in the mould of Judah the Maccabee,[5] and the result was the worst tragedy in Jewish history until the Holocaust.

Judaism is about diffused responsibility, making each individual count, building a cohesive nation on the basis of a shared vision, edu-cating people to their full potential, and valuing honest argument and the dignity of dissent. That is the kind of culture the rabbis inculcated during the centuries of dispersion. It is how the pioneers built the land and State of Israel in modern times. It is the vision Moses articulated in the last month of his life in the book of Deuteronomy.

---

5. He believed that he was the Messiah. See Maimonides, *Mishneh Torah, Hilkhot Melakhim* 11:3.

It is precisely this kind of leadership that was needed for the adaptive challenge that lay ahead. It took a strong leader – Moses – to lead the people out of slavery. But it took a quite different kind of figure – Joshua – to allow the people to develop their own strengths. The rabbis said that "the face of Moses was like the sun; the face of Joshua was like the moon" (Bava Batra 75a). This is precisely what made Joshua the right leader for the new generation. The sun dazzles almost blindingly, but moonlight allows even the flame of a candle to burn brightly. Joshua left space for the people to fill and thereby grow.

Perhaps this was what God was hinting to Moses when He told him to take seventy elders to stand with him in the Tent of Meeting, and "I will come down and speak with you there, and I will take some of the spirit that is on you and put it on them" (Num. 11:16–17). He was telling Moses that his task was not to solve the crisis of the people's demand for meat. His task was to inspire others with his spirit – delegating, empowering, guiding, and encouraging. God was telling Moses that great leaders do not create followers; they create leaders. They share their inspiration. They give of their spirit to others. They do not see the people they lead as children who need a father-mother-nursemaid, but as adults who need to be educated to take individual and collective responsibility for their own future.

People become what their leader gives them the space to become. When that space is large, they grow into greatness.

The Seventy Elders

When Moses reached the end of his despairing speech to God – "If this is how You are going to treat me, please go ahead and kill me" (Num. 11:15) – God replied, calmly and simply:

> Gather for Me seventy of Israel's elders, ones you know to be elders and leaders of the people. Bring them to the Tent of Meeting, and let them stand there with you. I will come down and speak to you there, and I will emanate some of the spirit that is on you and put it on them. They will share the burden of the people with you so that you will not have to carry it alone. (Num. 11:16–17)

Clearly, Moses felt alone. He had just said, "I cannot carry all these people by myself" (Num. 11:14). It was perhaps not by coincidence that Moses' burnout occurred immediately after we read, at the end of the previous chapter, of his father-in-law Yitro's departure (10:30). Something very similar happened later in *Parashat Ḥukkat* (Num. 20). First we read of the death of Miriam. Then immediately there follows the scene in which the people ask for water and Moses loses his temper and strikes the rock, the act that costs him the chance to lead the people across the Jordan into the Promised Land.

It seems that in their different ways, Yitro and Miriam were essential emotional supports for Moses. When they were there, he coped. When they were not, he lost his poise. Leaders need soulmates, people who lift their spirits and give them the strength to carry on. No one can lead alone.[1]

Yet there are real puzzles here when it comes to understanding God's response. In what way would the appointment of elders address the internal crisis Moses was undergoing? His problem was that he did not see how he could provide the people with meat. Would seventy elders help solve this problem? Clearly not. Either meat would appear by a miracle or it would not appear at all.

Did he need them to share the burdens of leadership? The answer again is no. Already, not long before, on the advice of Yitro, he had created an infrastructure of delegation. Yitro had said:

> What you are doing is not good. You and these people who come to you will only wear yourselves out. The work is too heavy for you. You cannot handle it alone. Listen now to me and I will give you advice, and may God be with you. You must be the people's representative before God and bring their disputes to Him. Teach them the decrees and laws, and show them the way to live and the duties they are to perform. But select capable men from all the people – men who fear God, trustworthy men who hate dishonest gain – and appoint them as officials over thousands, hundreds, fifties, and tens. (Ex. 18:17–21)

Moses acted on the suggestion. He therefore already had assistants, deputies, a leadership class. In what way would this new appointment of seventy elders make a difference?

---

1. The two places in the Torah where the words *lo tov*, "not good," appear are both about being alone. At the dawn of history, God says, "It is not good for man to be alone" (Gen. 2:18). And when Yitro comes and sees Moses leading alone, he says, "What you are doing is not good" (Ex. 18:17).

Besides which, why the emphasis in God's reply on *spirit*: "I will emanate some of the spirit that is on you and put it on them"? In what way did the elders need to share Moses' prophetic spirit in order to help him? Being a prophet does not help someone carry out the burdens of leadership. It helps only in knowing what guidance to give the people – and for this, one prophet, Moses, was sufficient. To put it more precisely, either the seventy elders would deliver the same message as Moses or they would not. If they did, they would be superfluous. If they did not, they would undermine his authority – precisely what Joshua feared when two others, Eldad and Medad, caught his spirit and started prophesying in the camp (Num. 11:28).

Aware of the multiple difficulties in the text, Nahmanides offers the following interpretation:

> Moses thought that if they had many leaders, they would appease their wrath by speaking to their hearts when the people started complaining. Or it is possible that when the elders prophesied, and the spirit was on them, the people would know that the elders were established as prophets and would not all gather around Moses but would ask for their desires from them as well. (Commentary to Num. 11:14)

The seventy would be able to calm the people down or diffuse some of the wrath that currently had only Moses as its target. Both suggestions are insightful, but neither is without difficulty. The first – that the elders would become peacemakers among the people – did not call for a new leadership cadre. Moses already had the heads of thousands, hundreds, fifties, and tens. The second – that their presence would diffuse the people's anger by giving them many people to complain to – is equally hard to understand. We recall that when the people had one other person to turn to with their concerns (Aaron), this led to the making of the Golden Calf. Why did God not "emanate the spirit" that was on Moses and place it on Aaron at that time? It would have prevented the single greatest catastrophe in the wilderness years.

Besides this, we do not find that the seventy elders actually *did* anything. There is no indication in the chapter that they did. The text

(Num. 11:25) even says, "When the spirit rested on them, they prophesied, but they did not do so again."[2] How then did this once-and-never-to-be-repeated flow of the prophetic spirit make a difference? The more we reflect on the passage, the more the difficulties multiply.

Yet something happened. Moses' despair disappeared. His attitude was transformed. Immediately thereafter, it is as if a new Moses stands before us, untroubled by even the most serious challenges to his leadership. When two of the elders, Eldad and Medad, prophesied not in the Tent of Meeting but in the camp, Joshua sensed a threat to Moses' authority and said, "Moses, my lord, stop them!" (Num. 11:28). Moses replied, with surpassing generosity of spirit, "Are you jealous for my sake? Would that all the Lord's people were prophets and that the Lord would put His spirit on them" (11:29).

In the next chapter, when *his own brother and sister,* Aaron and Miriam, complained about him, he did and said nothing – "Now the man Moses was very humble, more so than anyone else on the face of the earth" (Num. 12:3). Indeed, when God became angry at Miriam, Moses prayed on her behalf. The despair had gone. The crisis had passed. These two challenges were far more serious than the request of the people for meat, yet Moses met them with confidence and equanimity. Something had taken place as a result of the presence of the seventy elders, and he had been transformed. What was it?

The answer, it seems to me, is this. The people had complained about the food before (Ex. 16). Since then, however, they had been through what should have been utterly transformative experiences. They had heard the voice of God at Mount Sinai. They had made a covenant with Him. They had been through the trauma of the Golden Calf. They had built the Tabernacle. The Divine Presence was in their midst. They had accepted the mission of becoming "a kingdom of priests and a holy nation" (Ex. 19:6).

Hence Moses' despair when, once again, they complained about the food. It was *as if nothing had changed.* If these epic events that had never happened to a nation before and would never do so again had not changed them, what would?

2. This is the plain sense according to most commentators, though the *Targum* reads it as "they did not cease [prophesying]."

Moses' despair is thus all too understandable. He could see failure staring him in the face. Nothing, it seemed, could transform this people from a petulant rabble to one equal to the unique ethical-spiritual destiny to which they had been called. Perhaps God, from the perspective of eternity, could see some positive outcome in the future. Moses, as a human being, could not. "I would rather die," he was saying, "than spend the rest of my life labouring in vain."

There can come a time in the life of any transformative leader when the sun of hope is eclipsed by the clouds of doubt – not about God, but about people, above all about oneself. Am I really making a difference? Am I deceiving myself when I think I can change the world? I have tried, I have given the very best of my energies and inspiration, yet nothing seems to alter the depressing reality of human frailty and lack of vision. I have given the people the word of God Himself, yet they still complain, thinking only about the discomforts of today, not the vast possibilities of tomorrow. Such despair can occur to the very greatest – and Moses *was* the very greatest. Therefore God gave him the greatest gift of all.

God let Moses see the influence he had on others. For a brief moment, God took "the spirit that is on you and put it on them" so that Moses could see the difference he had made to one group, the seventy elders. He needed nothing more. He did not need their help. He did not need them to continue to prophesy. All he needed was a glimpse of how his spirit had communicated itself to them. Then he knew he had made a difference.

Little could he have known that he – who encountered little in his lifetime but complaints, challenges, and rebellions – would have so decisive an influence that the People of Israel thirty-three centuries later would still be studying and living by the words he transmitted. He had helped forge an identity that would prove more tenacious than any other in the history of mankind.

He could not know these things; he did not *need* to know these things. All he needed was to see that seventy elders had internalised his spirit and made his message their own. Then he knew that his life was not in vain. He had disciples. His vision was not his alone. He had planted it in others. Others, too, would continue his work after his lifetime. That was enough for him, as it must be for us. Once Moses knew this, he could face the future with equanimity.

Understood thus, there is a message in Moses' crisis for all of us. I remember when my late father died and we – my mother and brothers and I – were sitting *shiva*. Time and again people would come and tell us of kindnesses he had done for them, in some cases more than fifty years before. Many people who have sat *shiva* have had similar experiences.

How moving, I thought, and at the same time, how sad that my father was not there to hear their words. What comfort it would have brought him to know that despite the many hardships he faced, the good he did was not forgotten. How tragic that we so often keep our sense of gratitude to ourselves, saying it aloud only when the person to whom we feel indebted has left this life, and we are comforting his or her mourners.

But that is the human condition. We never fully know how much we have given others – how much the kind word, the thoughtful deed, the comforting gesture changes lives and is never forgotten. In this respect, if in no other, we are like Moses. He too was human. He had no privileged access into other people's minds. Without a miracle, he could not have known the influence he had on those closest to him. All the evidence seemed to suggest otherwise. The people, en masse, were still ungrateful, querulous, quick to criticise and complain. But for a moment, God gave Moses a glimpse of how his spirit had entered the seventy elders and lifted them, however briefly, to the level of prophetic vision.

God performed this miracle for no other person. But the glimpse it afforded ought to serve to comfort us all. The good we do lives after us. It is the greatest thing that does. We may leave a legacy of wealth, power, even fame, but these are questionable benefits and sometimes harm rather than help those we leave them to. Our true legacy is the trace of our influence for good. We may never see it, but it is there. That is the greatest blessing of leadership. It alone is the antidote to despair, the solid ground of hope.

Miriam's Error

Parashat *Behaalotekha* ends with one of the more cryptic episodes in the Torah. It begins with these words: "Miriam and Aaron began to talk against Moses because of his Cushite wife, for he had married a Cushite" (Num. 12:1). This gives us a rough idea of what was happening. Moses' brother and sister were critical of Moses, and it was about his wife.

The next sentence, however, throws us into confusion. "Has the Lord spoken only through Moses?" they asked. "Has he not also spoken through us?" (Num. 12:2). What did this have to do with his wife? We are then told that "Moses was very humble, more so than anyone else on the face of the earth" (12:3). Again this seems to be a nonsequitur. Then God summons all three of them and tells them to come to the Tent of Meeting. There He expresses His anger, and says that Moses is unique. The Divine Presence then departs, leaving Miriam's skin leprous. Moses prays on her behalf one of the shortest prayers in Tanakh, a mere five words: "Please God, heal her now" (12:13). God refuses to remove the punishment, saying to Moses, "If her father had spit in her face, would she not have been in disgrace for seven days?" (12:14). But He does mitigate it, limiting the disfigurement to a week. Then the Israelites move on.

The questions are obvious:

1. Who was the Cushite or Ethiopian woman Moses had married? We have only been told that Moses had one wife, Tzippora, daughter of Yitro, the Midianite priest. There is no reference to Moses having a second wife, let alone an Ethiopian one.
2. What have the two reported complaints to do with one another? There seems to be no connection between Moses' wife and his siblings' remark, "Has the Lord spoken only through Moses?"
3. Why was only Miriam punished? The text says that Aaron too was guilty.
4. What has any of this to do with Moses' humility?
5. Why is this episode here at all? It seems to have no connection with what preceded it, the complaint of the people about the food.
6. Whatever happened, it seems to have had lasting significance, since Moses refers to it almost forty years later, in the book of Deuteronomy (24:9): "Remember what the Lord your God did to Miriam along the way after you came out of Egypt." What was it that the people were supposed to remember and why?

Mindful of all these problems, the sages reconstructed the event, filling in the details and turning it into a fascinating story about Moses' family life. It began, they say, with the events reported in the previous chapter, when God caused Moses' spirit to rest on the seventy elders he had chosen, together with Eldad and Medad. A midrash tells us that Miriam said, in effect: I am sorry for their wives, because if the elders have been filled with Moses' spirit, they are likely to do what Moses has done, namely discontinue marital relations.[1] Evidently, he had ceased to have any intimate relationship with his wife Tzippora, described here as a "Cushite woman" not as a reference to her ethnic origin but rather to her physical appearance as a person of dark skin.

Miriam was critical of this, saying that God had spoken not just to Moses but to her and Aaron also, yet they had not discontinued

---

1. See Ex. 19:10 for the need for purification prior to receiving divine revelation.

marital relations with their spouses. Moses heard about this complaint but did nothing. That is what the text means when it says that he was a very humble man, meaning that he was unmoved by this ad hominem attack. The rabbis in general connected the skin condition known as *tzaraat* with the sin of *lashon hara*, speaking slightingly of others. That is why Miriam was punished.

Evidently, from the nature of the complaint, it was she who had initiated it – not out of malice, to be sure, but out of sympathy with the wives of the elders – which is why she, not Aaron, was punished.[2] He was deemed guilty only of listening to *lashon hara* and not protesting it.[3] So great is the sin of evil speech that Moses warned against it in Deuteronomy, telling the people, "Remember what the Lord your God did to Miriam." Evidently the episode was still in people's memories, so they knew to what he was referring.

A midrash dramatises the point. Miriam was punished, it says, despite the fact that that she made the complaint not in the presence of Moses, despite the fact that she was, at least in age, his senior, and despite her intention not being a negative one. Miriam simply intended to ensure that people inspired by *ruah hakodesh*, the "holy spirit," should not neglect their spouses. The entire episode, implies the midrash, is there to teach us how even a casual remark, made privately and without malicious intent, can still count as *lashon hara*, and still have potentially negative consequences.

Stepping back and seeing the passage in the wider context of the Torah narrative, we immediately see something consequential. One of the fundamental themes of Genesis is sibling rivalry. It appears, with variations, five times: in the stories of Cain and Abel, Isaac and Ishmael, Jacob and Esau, Joseph and his brothers, and the two sisters Leah and Rachel. Until now we had no reason to associate this theme with life after the Exodus. Miriam and Aaron, Moses' siblings, had been until

2. Note that the verb is in the feminine singular, "she spoke," not in the plural as we would expect if both Miriam and Aaron spoke against Moses.
3. The sages said that *lashon hara* harms three people: the person who says it, the one who hears it, and the one about whom it is said (Arakhin 15b). Aaron fell into the second category.

now admirably free of rivalry. Miriam had watched over her brother's fate as a baby. Aaron had shared with Moses the burden of leadership from the outset of his mission. Neither had uttered a word of criticism, still less of envy, until now.

Yet *lashon hara* is contagious and seems to exist in almost every human grouping.[4] There is a fascinating indication of this in the previous chapter. Before we hear about the people's complaints about the food, we read: "And the people were as murmurers, speaking evil in the ears of the Lord; and when the Lord heard it, His anger was kindled" (Num. 11:1).

What is striking about this episode is that the Torah gives us no indication of what the people were complaining about. Usually we are told exactly what the issue was – but not here. The Torah seems to be implying that they complained because that is what they had become accustomed to doing, even when they had nothing specific to complain about. When that happens, the whole mood of the group is badly affected. People find fault where there is none. And the result eventually is that it can affect even the best, even two people as generous-spirited as Moses' own brother and sister.

We are social animals. We are affected by those around us. Consciously or unconsciously, we conform to the norms of the group. Social phenomena are contagious. Recent research has shown that if your friends are overweight, you are more likely to be overweight.[5] An

---

4. See Robin Dunbar, *Grooming, Gossip, and the Evolution of Language* (Cambridge, MA: Harvard University Press, 1998). Dunbar argues that language is an essential part of human bonding and group formation, and that it is used to establish reciprocity and trust. In a sense, then, gossip plays a large part in the ability of groups to act cooperatively and altruistically – but this is specifically in relation to supplying the group with factual information about individuals within the group. Idle gossip, on the other hand, and specifically if it denigrates individuals, is destructive of the group. That is why *lashon hara* is so dangerous and why the sages were right to dramatise its effects. For an excellent modern study of *lashon hara* in Jewish law and thought, see Daniel Feldman, *False Facts and True Rumors: Lashon HaRa in Contemporary Culture* (Jerusalem: Maggid, 2016).

5. Nicholas A. Christakis and James H. Fowler, "The Spread of Obesity in a Large Social Network over 32 Years," *New England Journal of Medicine* 357, no. 4 (2007): 370–379.

entire way of speaking – lifting your voice at the end of a sentence as if asking a question, using "like" in every sentence and so on – spread from the San Fernando Valley in southern California (hence the name "Valleyspeak") through almost the whole English-speaking world. And so on. Already in the twelfth century, Maimonides had codified social contagion as an axiom of Jewish law.[6]

The Torah – as understood by the sages in the light of Jewish history from the days of Moses to their own – attaches huge significance to the tone of conversation within a society as a whole, within communities, and even within families. It may sound extreme to say so but *freedom depends on civility*, on people speaking courteously of and to one another.[7]

In any group, where the predominant tone is one of complaint, criticism, envy, backbiting, cynicism, and mutual suspicion, not only is the group itself weakened; a profound disempowerment also takes place. Free people do not blame others for their misfortune. They accept and practise responsibility. They assume that if something bad has happened, they must work together to put it right. When criticism is necessary, and it often is, they do so constructively, without animus, and with respect for the person concerned as well as the good of the group as a whole.

The prophets of Israel were not Pollyannas, naïve optimists, blind to the evils and injustices of the world. They were deeply critical of the failings of their generation, sometimes to the point of near despair. But they spoke out of loyalty and love. Even the most critical of them never left the people without hope. Their belief that society and people could change testifies to their deep faith in humankind, and in their people. Speech does not have to be positive to be *lashon tov*, good speech. But it does have to be constructive, creative, positive in intent. And the lead has to be given by the leaders. That is why God was angry with Miriam and Aaron. If leaders speak like this, how can one blame the people for doing likewise?

One can understand Miriam and Aaron's concerns about Moses. They did not know what it meant to be the unique individual that Moses

6. Maimonides, *Mishneh Torah, Hilkhot Deot* 6:1.
7. See Os Guinness, *The Case for Civility* (New York: HarperOne, 2008).

was. One can sympathise with Miriam's concern if she believed, as the midrash suggests, that Moses' wife (and perhaps his children also) suffered from a lack of attention. That is one of the burdens of leadership in general – all the more so in the case of one who felt the need to be perpetually ready for a communication from God Himself.

Moreover, Miriam was expressing her concern for the wives of Moses' newly inspired leadership group, in case they too suffered husbandly neglect. Her motives were honourable. Miriam was never less than a heroic and compassionate human being. Yet because others less noble might derive the wrong lesson from her behaviour, she was stigmatised for seven days by an unsightly skin condition that Moses recalled many years later to remind the people how dangerous it is to "judge the judges" and heap unjustified criticism on leaders.

Never give way to sibling rivalry. Never speak badly of others. Never underestimate the damaging effect of words. These are the lessons from the story of Miriam in *Parashat Behaalotekha*, and they remain intensely valid today.

Shelaḥ
שלח

Parashat Shelaḥ tells the story of the spies sent by Moses to survey the land. Ten return with an ambivalent and fearful report: the land is good but the people are giants and their cities impregnable. Two, Joshua and Caleb, argue to the contrary – but their confidence is ignored and the people, fearful and demoralised, say, "Let us appoint a leader and go back to Egypt" (Num. 14:4).

God, angry, threatens to destroy the people and start again with Moses. Moses intercedes and succeeds in averting this fate, but God insists that the people will be punished by having to spend forty years in the desert. Their children, not they, will enter the land. There then follows a series of laws about sacrifices, challa, and forgiveness for sins committed inadvertently. This legal section is interrupted by a brief narrative about a Shabbat-breaker. The *parasha* ends with the law about tzitzit, fringes on the corners of garments, a text recited daily as the third paragraph of the *Shema*.

The first of the following essays asks: Of what were the spies afraid? The second explores the role of time in political transformation. The third suggests a deep connection between the story of the spies and the law of tzitzit. The fourth asks what made Joshua and Caleb different from the other ten spies who were overcome by fear. The fifth focuses on a comment by Rashi about the significance of defensive walls. The sixth looks at the command of tzitzit and the two different ways in which it has come to be fulfilled, by an inner and an outer garment.

Fear of Freedom

The episode of the spies was one of the most tragic in the entire Torah. Who sent them and to what end is not entirely clear. In *Parashat Shelaḥ*, the text says that it was God who told Moses to do so (Num. 13:1–2). In Deuteronomy (1:22), Moses says that it was the people who made the request. Either way, the result was disaster. An entire generation was deprived of the chance to enter the Promised Land. The entry itself was delayed by forty years. According to the sages, it cast its shadow long into the future.[1]

Moses told the spies to go and see the land and bring back a report about it: Are the people many or few, strong or weak? What is the land itself like? Are the cities open or fortified? Is the soil fertile? They were also tasked with bringing back some of its fruit. The spies returned with a positive report about the land itself: "It is indeed flowing with milk and honey, and this is its fruit" (Num. 13:27). There then followed one

---

1. On the phrase, "the people wept that night" (Num. 14:1), the Talmud says that God vowed, "I will make this a day of weeping throughout the generations." That day was Tisha B'Av, on which, in later centuries, the First and Second Temples were destroyed (Taanit 29a; Sota 35a).

of the most famous buts in Jewish history: "But – the people who live there are powerful, and the cities are fortified and very large. We even saw descendants of Anak ['the giant'] there" (13:28).

Sensing that their words were demoralising the people, Caleb, one of the spies, interrupted with a message of reassurance: "We should go up and take possession of the land, for we can certainly do it." Undeterred, the other spies insisted: "We cannot attack those people; they are stronger than we are.... All the people we saw there are of great size.... We seemed like grasshoppers in our own eyes, and so we were in their eyes" (Num. 13:30–33). The next day, the people, persuaded that the challenge was completely beyond them, expressed regret that they had ever embarked on the Exodus and said, "Let us appoint a leader and go back to Egypt" (14:4).

Thus far the narrative. However, it is monumentally difficult to understand. It was this that led the Lubavitcher Rebbe, Rabbi Menachem Mendel Schneerson, to give a radically revisionary interpretation of the episode.[2] He asked the obvious questions. How could ten of the spies come back with a defeatist report? They had seen with their own eyes how God had sent a series of plagues that brought Egypt, the strongest and longest-lived of all the empires of the ancient world, to its knees. They had seen the Egyptian army with its cutting-edge military technology, the horse-drawn chariot, drown in the sea while the Israelites passed through it on dry land. Egypt was far stronger than the Canaanites, Perizzites, Jebusites, and other minor kingdoms that they would have to confront in conquering the land. Nor was this an ancient memory. It had happened not much more than a year before.

What is more, they were entirely wrong about the people of the land. We discover this from the book of Joshua, in the passage read as the *haftara* to *Parashat Shelaḥ*. When, a generation later, Joshua sent spies to Jericho, the woman who sheltered them, Rahab, described for them what her people felt when they heard that that the Israelites were on their way:

---

2. A translation can be found in Rabbi Menachem M. Schneerson, *Torah Studies*, adapted by Jonathan Sacks (London: Lubavitch Foundation, 1986), 239–245.

I know that the Lord has given this land to you and that a great fear of you has fallen on us, so that all who live in this country are melting in fear because of you. We have heard how the Lord dried up the water of the Red Sea for you when you came out of Egypt.... *When we heard of it, our hearts melted and everyone's courage failed because of you,* for the Lord your God is God in heaven above and on the earth below. (Josh. 2:9–11)

The people of Jericho were not giants. They were as fearful of the Israelites as the Israelites were of them. Nor was this something that was disclosed only later. The Israelites of Moses' day had already sung in the Song at the Sea:

> The peoples have heard; they tremble;
> pangs have seized the inhabitants of Philistia.
> Now are the chiefs of Edom dismayed;
> trembling seizes the leaders of Moab;
> all the inhabitants of Canaan have melted away.
> Terror and dread fall upon them;
> because of the greatness of Your arm, they are still as a stone.
> (Ex. 15:14–16)

How was it that they forgot what, not long before, they knew?

What is more, continued the Rebbe, the spies were not people plucked at random from among the population. The Torah states that they were "all of them men who were heads of the People of Israel." They were leaders. They were not people given lightly to fear. The questions are straightforward, but the answer the Rebbe gave was utterly unexpected. *The spies were not afraid of failure,* he said. *They were afraid of success.*

What was their situation then? They were eating manna from heaven. They were drinking water from a miraculous well. They were surrounded by Clouds of Glory. They were camped around the Sanctuary. They were in continuous contact with the *Shekhina.* Never had a people lived so close to God.

What would be their situation if they entered the land? They would have to fight battles, maintain an army, create an economy, farm the land, worry about whether there would be enough rain to produce a crop, and all the other thousand distractions that come from living in the world. What would happen to their closeness to God? They would be preoccupied with mundane and material pursuits. Here they could spend their entire lives learning Torah, lit by the radiance of the Divine. There they would be one more nation in a world of nations with the same kind of economic, social, and political problems that every nation has to deal with.

The spies were not afraid of failure. They were afraid of success. Their mistake was the mistake of very holy men. They wanted to spend their lives in the closest possible proximity to God. What they did not understand was that God seeks, in the midrashic phrase, "a dwelling in the lower worlds."[3] One of the great differences between Judaism and other religions is that while others seek to lift people to heaven, Judaism seeks to bring heaven down to earth.

Much of Torah is about things not conventionally seen as religious at all: labour relations, agriculture, welfare provisions, loans and debts, land ownership, and so on. It is not difficult to have an intense religious experience in the desert, or in a monastic retreat, or in an ashram. Most religions have holy places and holy people who live far removed from the stresses and strains of everyday life. There was one such Jewish sect in Qumran, known to us through the Dead Sea Scrolls, and there were certainly others. About this there is nothing unusual at all.

But that is not the Jewish project, the Jewish mission. God wanted the Israelites to create a model society where human beings were not treated as slaves, where rulers were not worshipped as demigods, where human dignity was respected, where law was impartially administered to rich and poor alike, where no one was destitute, no one was abandoned to isolation, no one was above the law, and no realm of life was a morality-free zone. That requires a society, and a society needs a land. It requires an economy, an army, fields and flocks, labour and enterprise. All these, in Judaism, become ways of bringing the *Shekhina* into the shared spaces of our collective life.

3.   See *Midrash Tanḥuma, Parashat Naso* 16.

The spies did not doubt that Israel could win its battles with the inhabitants of the land. Their concern was not physical but spiritual. They did not want to leave the wilderness. They did not want to become just another nation among the nations of the earth. They did not want to lose their unique relationship with God in the reverberating silence of the desert, far removed from civilisation and its discontents. This was the mistake of deeply religious men – but it was a mistake.

Clearly this is not the plain sense of the narrative, but we should not dismiss it on that account. It is, as it were, a psychoanalytical reading of the unconscious mindset of the spies. They did not want to let go of the intimacy and innocence of the time-out-of-time and place-out-of-place that was the experience of the wilderness. Ultimately the spies feared freedom and its responsibilities.

But Torah is about the responsibilities of freedom. Judaism is not a religion of monastic retreat from the world. It is a religion of engagement with the world. *God chose Israel to make His presence visible in the world. Therefore Israel must live in the world.* The Jewish people were not without their desert-dwellers and ascetics. The Talmud speaks of R. Shimon b. Yoḥai living for thirteen years in a cave. When he emerged, he could not bear to see people engaged in such earthly pursuits as ploughing a field (Shabbat 33b). He held that engagement with the world was fundamentally incompatible with the heights of spirituality (Berakhot 35b). But the mainstream held otherwise.[4] It maintained that "Torah study without an occupation will in the end fail and lead to sin" (Mishna Avot 2:2).

Maimonides speaks of people who live as hermits in the desert to escape the corruptions of society.[5] But these were the exceptions, not the rule. It is not the destiny of Israel to live outside time and space as the world's recluses. Far from being the supreme height of faith, such a fear of freedom and its responsibilities is, according to the Lubavitcher Rebbe, the sin of the spies.

They did not want to contaminate Judaism by bringing it into contact with the real world. They sought the eternal dependency of God's

---

4. Berakhot 35b cites the view of R. Ishmael as evaluated by Abaye.
5. Maimonides, *Mishneh Torah, Hilkhot Deot* 6:1; *Shemoneh Perakim*, ch. 4.

protection and the endless embrace of His all-encompassing love. There is something noble about this desire, but also something profoundly irresponsible. The spies demoralised the people and provoked the anger of God. The Jewish project – the Torah as the constitution of the Jewish nation under the sovereignty of God – is about building a society in the land of Israel that so honours human dignity and freedom that it will one day lead the world to say, "Surely this great nation is a wise and understanding people" (Deut. 4:6).

The Jewish task is not to fear the real world but to enter and transform it, healing some of its wounds and bringing to places often shrouded in darkness fragments of divine light.

Time as a Factor in Politics

In the previous essay we encountered the Lubavitcher Rebbe's revisionary reading of the episode of the spies. His argument was that they did not fear failure. They feared success. They wanted to stay in the wilderness, as pious individuals have done throughout history: in ashrams, monasteries, retreats of various kinds, cloistered spaces where you can be close to God but at the expense of being removed from the world. That might be the wish of very holy individuals, as we noted in our discussion of the Nazirite. But as a formula for the nation as a whole, it was a fundamental misunderstanding of their mission, which was and is to create a model society that would be an inspiration to others.

The simpler reading, closest to the plain sense of the text, is that the people were not yet ready to assume the burdens and responsibilities of fighting a series of battles, establishing a functioning society with an economy, welfare system, courts and the administration of the law, and all else that goes with freedom, independence, and nationhood.

This was Maimonides' view, and he saw it prefigured in the verse with which the Exodus begins:

When Pharaoh let the people go, God did not lead them on the road through the Philistine country, though that was shorter. For God said, "If they face war, they might change their minds and return to Egypt." So God led the people around by the desert road towards the Red Sea. (Ex. 13:17)

Maimonides comments:

Here God led the people about, away from the direct route He had originally intended, because He feared that they might encounter hardships too great for their present strength. So He took them by a different route in order to achieve His original object.

Yet despite the detour, what God feared came to pass. The people had second thoughts. They regretted ever leaving. "They said to each other, 'Let us appoint a leader and go back to Egypt'" (Num. 14:4).

Maimonides adds that this is why the entry into the land was delayed for a generation – so that it could be undertaken by those who had been born in the desert:

It is a well-known fact that travelling in the wilderness without physical comforts such as bathing produces courage, while the opposite produces faintheartedness. Besides this, another generation rose during the wanderings that had not been accustomed to degradation and slavery.[1]

This is an unusual position, because *Maimonides does not mention the spies at all*. It was, he implies, a given of the state of the people at the time and of the constraints of human nature. People cannot change overnight. It takes time to move from slavery to the responsibilities of freedom. It can take an entire generation, sometimes longer still. This is a radical suggestion because it implies that the negative report of the spies was only the precipitating factor, not the underlying cause. Nor was the divine verdict, that the people would be condemned to spend forty years in

1. Maimonides, *Guide for the Perplexed*, III:32.

the wilderness, a *punishment* as such. It was a consequence of human nature. People long deprived of their freedom grow used to their chains.

There is a moving moment in the film *The Shawshank Redemption* in which one of the prisoners, Brooks Hatlen, achieves his release from prison where he has spent almost half a century, from 1905 to 1954. He had become the prison librarian; he is a gentle soul who has adopted a stray bird that he hides under his jacket at mealtime and feeds. The prospect of going back into the real world terrifies him, and he almost commits a crime in prison so as not to have to leave. Eventually his release comes, but the world has changed beyond recognition. He cannot get used to the cars, the rush, the unfamiliar face of a world he has not seen for so long. Above all, he is simply unused to making decisions and having the liberty to do simple things without asking permission. Eventually he commits suicide. He had become so deeply institutionalised that he could not handle a world of choice and responsibility.

That is an extreme case, but the Torah itself contemplates the possibility that people who have been enslaved for a prolonged period may lose the appetite for living another way. This is intimated not in a narrative section of the Torah but in a legal one. The law code in Exodus that follows the Ten Commandments states that a Hebrew slave is to be set free after six years of service. It then adds:

> But if the servant declares, "I love my master and my wife and children and *I do not want to go free*," then his master must take him before the judges. He shall take him to the door or the doorpost and pierce his ear with an awl. Then he will be his servant for life. (Ex. 21:5–6)

Rabban Yoḥanan b. Zakkai rightly saw the act of piercing the slave's ear as a stigmatisation ceremony:

> The ear that heard God saying at Sinai, "The Israelites are My slaves. They are My slaves because I brought them out of Egypt. I am the Lord your God" (Lev. 25:55) but nevertheless preferred subjection to men rather than to God, deserves to be pierced. (Y. Kiddushin 1:2)

The fact remains, however, that some prefer servitude to the responsibilities of freedom. As Rousseau famously said in the opening sentence of *The Social Contract*: "Man was born free, and he is everywhere in chains."[2]

Writing as a refugee from Nazi Germany in America in 1941, Erich Fromm wrote:

> We have been compelled to recognize that millions in Germany were as eager to surrender their freedom as their fathers were to fight for it; that instead of wanting freedom, they sought for ways of escape from it; the other millions were indifferent and did not believe the defense of freedom to be worth fighting and dying for.[3]

This abdication of freedom is a constant in human history. The chronicles of humanity are filled with this willingness to hand the burden of responsibility over to a strong leader who promises a return to national greatness or a revolutionary vanguard that declares itself harbinger of a new utopia; it also tells of people simply acceding without protest to a military or religious dictatorship. As Michael Walzer puts it, the "childish and irresponsible slave or subject is free in ways the republican citizen" can never be. And there is, as he says, "a kind of bondage in freedom: the bondage of law, obligation, and responsibility."[4] The word for "slave" (of Pharaoh) and for "servant" (of God) is the same in biblical Hebrew: *eved*. Freedom, like slavery, is *avoda*, "hard work."

It takes more than a few days or weeks to turn a population of slaves into a nation capable of handling the responsibilities of freedom. In the case of the Israelites it needed a generation born in liberty, hardened by the experience of the desert, untrammelled by habits of servitude. Freedom takes time, and there are no shortcuts.

That is why time plays such a major role in Judaism. *Liberty is the work of more than one generation.* It took thousands of years to abolish slavery. It took centuries, wars, and trauma to create the ideas formulated

---

2. Jean-Jacques Rousseau, *The Social Contract*, trans. Maurice Cranston (Harmondsworth: Penguin Classics, 1968), 49.
3. Erich Fromm, *Escape from Freedom* (New York: Holt, 1994), 3.
4. Michael Walzer, *Exodus and Revolution* (New York: Basic Books, 1985), 53.

in the seventeenth century that stand as the basis of the free societies of the West: social covenant and contract, the moral limits of human power, the doctrine of toleration, the idea of liberty of conscience, and the notion of "inalienable" human rights. The forty years of wandering in the wilderness were the prefiguration of a much larger, longer journey that would eventuate in a society that sanctifies human life as the gift of God and the human person as the image of God.

Time is fundamental to the Jewish view of politics and progress. That is why, in the Torah, Moses repeatedly tells the adults to educate their children, to tell them the story of the past, to "remember." It is why the covenant itself is extended through time by being handed on from one generation to the next. It is why the story of the Israelites is told at such length in Tanakh; the time span covered by the Hebrew Bible is *a thousand years* from the days of Moses to the last of the prophets. It is why God acts in and through history.

Unlike Christianity or Islam, there is in Judaism no concept of a sudden transformation of the human condition, no one moment or single generation in which everything significant is fully disclosed. Why, asks Maimonides, did God not simply give the Israelites in the desert the strength or self-confidence they needed to cross the Jordan and enter the land? His answer: Because it would have meant saying goodbye to human freedom, choice, and responsibility.[5]

Even God Himself, implies Maimonides, has to work with the grain of human nature and its all-too-slow pace of change. Not because God *cannot* change people; of course He can. He created them; He could recreate them. The reason is that God *chooses* not to. He practises what the Safed kabbalists called *tzimtzum*, self-limitation. He wants human beings to construct a society of freedom – and how could He do that if, in order to bring it about, He had to deprive them of the very freedom He wanted them to exercise and honour? There are some things a parent may not do for a child if he or she wants the child to become an adult. There are some things even God must choose not to do for His people if He wants them to grow to moral and political maturity.

5. Maimonides, *Guide for the Perplexed*, III:32.

I call this Jewish sense of the need for time, the *chronological* imagination, as opposed to the Greek *logical* imagination. Logic lacks the dimension of time. It is essentially timeless. That is why philosophers tend to be either rigidly conservative (Plato did not want poets in his Republic; they threatened to disturb the social order) or profoundly revolutionary (Rousseau, Marx). The current social order is either right or wrong. If it is right, we should not change it. If it is wrong, we should overthrow it. The fact that change takes time, even many generations, is not an idea easy to square with philosophy (even those philosophers, like Hegel and Marx, who factored in time, did so mechanically, speaking about "historical inevitability" rather than the unpredictable exercise of freedom).

The two revolutions inspired by the Hebrew Bible – the English in the 1640s and the American in 1776 – led to an enhancement of human rights. The two revolutions inspired by secular philosophy – the French in 1789 and the Russian in 1917 – led to reigns of terror or totalitarianism. The austere logic of philosophy cannot cope with the unpredictability of the human heart and the sheer difficulty of getting people to internalise the disciplines of self-restraint necessary to a free society. On this, the Hebrew Bible could not be more honest.

One of the odd facts about Western civilisation in recent centuries is that the people who have been most eloquent about tradition – Edmund Burke, T. S. Eliot, Michael Oakeshott – have been deeply conservative, defenders of the status quo. Yet there is no reason why a tradition should be conservative. We can hand on to our children not only our past but also our unrealised ideals. We can want them to go beyond us, to travel further on the road to freedom than we were able to do. That, for example, is how the Seder service on Passover begins: "This year, slaves, next year, free; this year here, next year in Israel." A tradition can be evolutionary without being revolutionary. It can look forwards as well as back.

That is the lesson of the spies. Despite the divine anger, the people were not condemned to permanent exile. They simply had to face the fact that their children would achieve what they themselves were not ready for.

People still forget this. There have been wars in the twenty-first century – in Afghanistan and Iraq, for example – that were undertaken in the name of democracy and freedom. Yet that is the work not of war, but of education, society-building, and the slow acceptance of responsibility. It takes generations. Sometimes it never happens at all. The people – like the Israelites, demoralised by the spies' report – lose heart and want to go back to the predictable past, not the unseen, hazardous, demanding future. That is why, historically, free societies are so rare. The democracy in Athens, instituted by Solon in the sixth century BCE, lasted only two centuries. By the time we reach Plato, in the fourth century BCE, disillusion had set in to the point where he saw democracy as merely the prelude to tyranny.

Liberty takes time and demands patience. It needs years of struggle without giving up hope. Emmanuel Levinas spoke about "difficult freedom" – and freedom *is* difficult, always. The story of the spies tells us that those who left Egypt were not yet ready for it. That was their tragedy. But their children would be. That was their consolation.

Law and Narrative: Believing and Seeing

P*arashat Shelaḥ* begins with the story of the spies. It ends with the laws of tzitzit: the fringes with their cord of blue to be placed on the corners of garments so the people will "remember all the commands of the Lord and keep them" (Num. 15:39) – the passage that became, in Temple times and still today, the third paragraph of the *Shema*.

On the face of it there is no connection between the two whatsoever. They belong to different literary genres. One was a historical incident, the other a timeless law. One concerned the fate of the nation, the other has to do with individual dress. Their dissonance is part of what gives the fourth book of the Torah its uneven feel and its puzzling structure. Why interrupt a historical narrative with seemingly unrelated paragraphs of legislation? However, close reading reveals that the two are not unrelated at all. They are deeply connected. They are a key instance of "intertextuality" – the interrelationship between two texts that shed light on one another. Their juxtaposition is there to tell us something profound about both the narrative and the law.

How does the Torah signal intertextuality? Often it does so by using the same word or words in two passages. A classic example is the phrase *haker na*, "please recognise," used in both Genesis 37 and 38 to link the story of Joseph's brothers and the bloodstained cloak they show their father, with that of Tamar and her father-in-law Judah.[1] Biblical critics who regarded chapter 38 as a later interpolation into the story of Joseph were tone-deaf to this use of language to connect the two episodes so as to give us an insight into the moral growth of Judah's character.

Something similar happens in the *parasha* of *Shelaḥ*. It begins with an account of what has become known traditionally as the story of the "spies." However, the narrative never uses the standard Hebrew word, based on the root *r-g-l*, that means "spy." When Joseph's brothers came before him in Egypt to buy food and failed to recognise him, he accused them of being *meraglim*, spies (Gen. 42). The word appears seven times in that chapter – a significant number often used to indicate a keyword. When Moses, in Deuteronomy, recalls the episode, he too uses the verb *leragel* (Deut. 1:24). When Joshua sends spies to Jericho, the Bible calls them *meraglim* (Josh. 2:1). The other verb used to connote the act of spying is *laḥpor*, also meaning, "to explore," "search out," "look carefully at" (Deut. 1:22; Josh. 2:2–3).

We would expect one or other of these terms to be used in our passage. In fact, neither is. Instead the word used is *latur*, which means not "to spy" but rather "to see," "explore." In the main narrative (the description of the spies and their return) it is used seven times.[2] In the next chapter, which relates the punishment of those involved, it appears five times.[3] These significant repetitions of a relatively rare verb are clearly intended to draw our attention to the word. *It is precisely this verb that the Torah uses in the law of tzitzit* to explain what the fringes are intended to prevent: "It shall be for you as a fringe, and you shall see it and remember all the commands of the Lord and keep them and not be led astray [*velo taturu*] after your heart and eyes, which have led you to immorality" (Num. 15:39).

---

1. Gen. 37:32; 38:25. These are the only two places in Tanakh where the phrase appears. For the significance of the connection, see Genesis Rabba 84:19; David Daube, *Studies in Biblical Law* (Cambridge: Cambridge University Press, 1947); Robert Alter, *The Art of Biblical Narrative* (London: George Allen and Unwin), 1981.
2. Num. 13:2, 16, 17, 21, 25, 32 (twice).
3. Num. 14:6, 7, 34, 36, 38.

The verbal connection is usually missed in translation, since "to spy" and "to be led astray" are (in English) two quite different things. In Hebrew, however, the echo is unmistakable – *veyaturu* in the case of the spies, *velo taturu* in the case of tzitzit. Bear in mind that the Torah was originally written to be read out loud in public. It still is. It is an auditory phenomenon. Listening to the text, one cannot but hear the echo of the narrative of the spies in the law of fringes, and this is not accidental but essential. The law was designed *precisely to avoid the error that occurred in the case of the spies.* The fringes on the corner of the garments are there so that in the future, people will not do what the spies did.

There is a second verbal connection. The word *ure'item*, "and you shall see," appears only three times in the Torah, two of them in this *parasha.* The first occurs in Moses' briefing of the spies: "*And you shall see the land, what it is*" (Num. 13:18). The second is in the command of the tzitzit: "*And you shall see it and remember all of God's commands*" (15:39).

There is a third connection, the verb *z-n-h*, meaning "to commit fornication," "to prostitute oneself." This appears both in God's description of the people after the report of the spies and in the reasoning behind the tzitzit. The King James translation preserves this better than modern versions that take refuge in circumlocution. About the generation of the spies, God says: "But as for you, your carcasses, they shall fall in this wilderness. And your children shall wander in the wilderness forty years, and bear your *whoredoms*, until your carcasses be wasted in the wilderness" (Num. 14:32–33). About the tzitzit, God says: "And it shall be for you as a fringe, that you may look upon it, and remember all the commandments of the Lord, and do them; and that you seek not after your own heart and eyes, after which you use to go *a-whoring*" (Num. 15:39).

What the first two connections – *t-u-r* and *ure'item* – have in common is that they are verbs of seeing. What is at stake is visual perception, the testimony of our eyes.

Often in these essays I have pointed out how non-visual, even anti-visual, a culture ancient Israel was – not completely, to be sure, but far more so than any other ancient civilisation. This was because in Judaism God cannot be seen. He is beyond the universe. He is not visible. Making a visual representation of God is the paradigm case of idolatry. Judaism is radically aniconic. We do not see God; we hear

Him. Knowing, in Judaism, is not modelled on the metaphor of sight but rather of sound. The supreme act of faith is *Shema*, meaning, "to listen," "to hear."

This is what the Torah wishes us to understand about the mission of the spies. It was fraught with danger because it was about seeing. The Torah is consistently sceptical about knowledge based on appearances.

One of the ways it signals this is its set of variations on the theme of clothes in Genesis. Almost always they are used to deceive. Jacob wears Esau's clothes to take his blessing. Tamar dresses as a prostitute to deceive Judah. The brothers daub Joseph's richly embroidered robe in blood to convince their father that he has been eaten by a wild animal. Potiphar's wife uses Joseph's abandoned cloak as evidence for a false charge of rape. Joseph, dressed in the robes of an Egyptian viceroy, is not recognised by his brothers. The first time clothes appear in the biblical narrative sets the tone for all the others. The first man and woman eat the forbidden fruit, realise that they are naked, feel ashamed, and make themselves coverings of fig leaves. It is thus with a shock of recognition that we discover that the Hebrew word for garment, *beged*, also means "betrayal." Clothes deceive. People are not what they appear to be.

The assumption in all visually based cultures is that sight is the most reliable form of knowledge. If you are in doubt about something, go and see. However, one of the achievements of social psychology has been to show that seeing is not a cognitively neutral activity. It is not a simple matter of the impact of sense impressions on the tabula rasa of the brain as if the mind were a kind of camera. To the contrary, our impressions and perceptions are largely shaped by what we pay attention to and what we expect to see.

In one well-known test, students were given a description of a guest lecturer before he entered the room. One group was told that he was intelligent, skilful, industrious, warm, determined, practical, and cautious. A second group was given the same list of traits, with one difference: the word "cold" was substituted for the word "warm." After the lecture, students were asked to give their impressions of the speaker. The "cold" group found him to be more unsociable, self-centred, irritable, humourless, and ruthless than did the "warm" group, despite the fact that they had heard the same talk from the same person.[4]

Likewise, we make judgements of character on the basis of physical appearance. One survey, for example, showed that tall college graduates (six-foot-two and over) received average starting salaries 12.4 per cent higher than those under six feet.[5] The individuals elected as president of the United States during the twentieth century were almost invariably taller than their opponents.[6] Three thousand years ago the Torah noted this fact and how misleading it can be. The first man chosen to be king of Israel, Saul, was "a head taller than anyone else" (I Sam. 9:2). However, he proved to be a man of weak character – physically tall, morally small. When Saul failed and God sent Samuel to anoint a son of Jesse in his place, the prophet was impressed by Eliav, but God told him, "Take no account of it if he is handsome and tall; I reject him. The Lord does not see as man sees. Men judge by appearances, but the Lord judges by the heart" (I Sam. 16:6–7). Appearances mislead.

Psychologists also speak of a phenomenon known as confirmation bias, which means that we have a tendency to notice facts that confirm our pre-existing attitudes and disregard those that challenge or disconfirm them.[7] Optimists and pessimists, radicals and reactionaries, religious believers and atheists tend to find that what happens, or what is discovered, proves that they were right all along. We select for attention the evidence that supports our prior convictions. We see what we expect to see. That is the central theme of the story of the spies.

Rabbi Menachem Mendel of Kotzk pointed out that the spies made a statement that was highly emotive but completely unwarranted. They said: "We were in our eyes like grasshoppers, and so we were in their eyes" (Num. 13:33). They were entitled to say the first half of the sentence. It accurately described how they felt. But they were not entitled

---

4. H. H. Kelley, "The Warm-Cold Variable in First Impressions of Persons," *Journal of Personality* 18 (1950): 431–439.
5. Robert Roy Britt, "Taller People Earn More Money," *Live Science*, July 11, 2009.
6. Gregg R. Murray, "It's Weird: Candidate Height Matters in Elections," *Psychology Today*, October 30, 2012.
7. See, for example, Raymond Nickerson, "Confirmation Bias: A Ubiquitous Phenomenon in Many Guises," *Review of General Psychology* 2, no. 2 (1998): 175–220.

to say the second half. They had no idea how they appeared in the eyes of the inhabitants of the land. They merely inferred it and they were wrong. They assumed that others saw them as they saw themselves. They projected their sense of inadequacy onto the external world, with the result that they misinterpreted what they saw. Instead of ordinary people, they saw giants. Instead of towns, they saw impregnable fortresses. They were afraid. The confirmation bias meant that they paid selective attention to phenomena that gave them reasons to be afraid. But their perception was not in the world but in the mind.

Long before the birth of psychology, the Torah signalled that there is no such thing as the "innocent eye." We do not simply see what is there. We select and interpret what is there. We notice some things but not others. We make inferences on the basis of pre-judgements. But we are for the most part unaware of this. The result is that we believe what we see or what we think we see. In truth, however, we often see what we believe, that is, what we expect to see. The Torah conveys this with elegance and brevity – by using the one word, *latur*, that means both "to see" and "to be led astray."

That is the logic behind the command of tzitzit. Tzitzit, with its cord of blue reminding us of heaven, and God, and faith, helps us liberate ourselves from our anxieties. It lets us see what is actually there, not what we fear is there. The law of tzitzit states, "You shall see it and remember all of God's commands … and not be led astray [*velo taturu*] after your heart and eyes, which have led you to immorality." The order of the nouns – first heart, then eyes – is strange. We would have expected the Torah to say, "after your eyes and heart."[8] Indeed, as Rashi says in his commentary at this point, "The eye sees, the heart desires, and the body commits the sin." It should by now be clear, however, that the Torah is making a different point. The heart determines what the eye sees. Those with faint hearts see a world filled with danger. Those with strong hearts see the same world, but it is not filled with danger. It contains risks, but that does not make them dismayed. That is what Joshua and Caleb said: "God is with us; do not be afraid of them" (Num. 14:9).

8. In actual fact, the New English Bible does just that, translating the verse, "And not go your own wanton ways, led astray by your own eyes and hearts."

In the deepest sense, tzitzit is an antidote to the sin of the spies. They saw, but misinterpreted what they saw, because they doubted their ability to overcome their opponents. They attributed to objective reality what was in fact, subjective self-doubt. Had that been rare, the Torah would not have legislated against it. It is, however, one of the most common and fateful errors of humankind.

Tzitzit is more than an outward sign of Jewish identity. On the surface it is, as the Torah says, a way of remembering the commandments. It is a reminder to keep the law. But it is significantly more than this. It is a call from God to see the world through Jewish eyes. Faith is not seeing the world as we would like it to be. Nor is it a matter of blaming the world for not being as we would like it to be. Faith is the courage to see the world precisely as it is while refusing to be intimidated by it.

The spies were otherwise good people who failed to separate their perceptions from their fears. They carried with them a confirmation bias. They saw, but misinterpreted what they saw. That mistake cost an entire generation the chance to enter the Promised Land. Seeing is not always a form of knowing. Sometimes you have to listen, not just look. And sometimes, when looking, you need to remind yourself that you are not alone, or helpless, or friendless in the world.

That is the function of the tzitzit, with its thread of the blue of heaven. When we know that God is with us, we can face reality without self-deceit or self-defeat. Not by accident is the command of tzitzit, which is about seeing, the third paragraph of the prayer *Shema* which is about listening or hearing ("Hear O Israel"). The perennial lesson God taught after the episode of the spies is: first we must hear with our heart before we can learn to see with our eyes.

What Made Joshua and Caleb Different?

Ten of the twelve spies came back with a defeatist and demoralising report. The people are strong. The cities are well fortified. There are giants there. It is a "land that devours its inhabitants." We are not up to the task. Compared to the locals, we are like grasshoppers (Num. 13:31–32).

They were, as it happens, completely wrong. But that made little difference under the circumstances. They had fulfilled their mission and delivered their report and who could gainsay them? Two of the twelve, however, did: Joshua and Caleb. Caleb stilled the people initially, saying, "We should go up and take possession of the land, for we can certainly do it" (Num. 13:30). Then as the people spoke about appointing a new leader and going back to Egypt, the two of them stood and addressed the crowd:

> If the Lord is pleased with us, He will lead us into that land, a land flowing with milk and honey, and will give it to us. Only do not rebel against the Lord. And do not be afraid of the people of the land, because we will devour them. Their protection is gone, but the Lord is with us. Do not be afraid of them. (Num. 14:8–9)

This took courage of a high order. First, they knew they were a minority: two against ten. What did they know that the others did not? Second, the crowd was in a dangerous state. The people had been weeping. They were already saying, "If only we had died in Egypt." They were angry with Moses and Aaron, who themselves had fallen prostrate rather than confront the people. Caleb and Joshua were on the verge of being stoned by the mob (Num. 14:1–10). What gift, what strength of character, did they have that the other ten spies – themselves princes, chieftains, leaders – did not?

Stanford University psychologist Carol Dweck has written a fascinating book, *Mindset*,[1] on why some people fulfil their potential while others do not. Her interest, she says, was aroused when she observed the behaviour of ten-year-old children when given puzzles to solve. Some, when the puzzles became difficult, thrived. They relished the challenge, even when it proved too hard for them. Others became anxious. When the puzzles became hard, they were easily discouraged.

She wanted to understand why. What makes the difference between people who enjoy being tested and those who do not? What makes some people grow through adversity while others become demoralised? Her research drove her to the conclusion that it is a matter of mindset. Some see their abilities as given and unalterable. We just are gifted or ordinary, and there is not much we can do about it. She calls this the "fixed" mindset. Others believe that we grow through our efforts. When they fail, they do not define this as failure but as a learning experience. She calls this the "growth" mindset.

Those with a fixed mindset tend to avoid difficult challenges because they fear failure. They think it will expose them as inadequate. So they are reluctant to take risks. They play it safe. People with the growth mindset react differently. "They do not just *seek* challenge, they thrive on it. The bigger the challenge, the more they stretch." When do people with the fixed mindset thrive? "When things are safely within their grasp. If things get too challenging … they lose interest."[2]

---

1. Carol Dweck, *Mindset: The New Psychology of Success* (New York: Ballantine Books, 2007).
2. Ibid., 21–22.

Parents can do great damage to their children, she says, when they tell them they are gifted, clever, or talented. This encourages the child to believe that he or she has a fixed quantum of ability. This discourages them from taking risks. Such children say things like, "I often feel that my parents won't value me if I'm not as successful as they would like." The result is that they tend to stay away from challenges they fear they may fail. They become risk-averse.

Parents who want to help their children, she says, should praise them not for their ability but for their effort, for their willingness to try hard even if they fail. Dweck quotes a great basketball coach who used to say to his players, "You may be outscored, but *you will never lose*."[3] If they gave of their best, they might not win the game but they would gain and grow. They would be winners in the long run. The fixed mindset lives with the constant fear of failure. The growth mindset does not think in terms of failing at all.

Applying this logic to the spies, we see something fascinating. The Torah describes them in these words: "All were men [of standing]; they were heads of the Israelites" (Num. 13:3). They were people with reputations to guard. Others had high expectations of them. They were princes, leaders, men of renown. If Dweck is right, people laden with expectations tend to be risk-averse. They do not want to be seen to fail. That may be why they came back and said, in effect: We cannot win against the Canaanites. Therefore we should not even try.

Now consider the two exceptions, Caleb and Joshua. Caleb came from the tribe of Judah, and Judah, we learn in the book of Genesis, was the first *baal teshuva*.[4] Early in life he had been the one who proposed selling Joseph into slavery. But he matured. He was taught a lesson by his daughter-in-law, Tamar. He confessed, "She is more righteous than I am" (Gen. 38:26). That experience changed his life. Later, when the viceroy of Egypt (Joseph, not yet recognised by the brothers) threatened to hold Benjamin as a prisoner, Judah offered to spend his life as a slave so that his brother could go free. Judah is the clearest example in Genesis

---

3. Ibid., 210.
4. See Jonathan Sacks, *Covenant and Conversation: Genesis – The Book of Beginnings* (Jerusalem: Maggid, 2009), 311–314.

of someone who *takes adversity as a learning experience* rather than as failure. In Dweck's terminology, he had a growth mindset. Evidently he handed on this trait to his descendants, Caleb among them.

As for Joshua, the text tells us, specifically in the story of the spies, that Moses *had changed his name*. Originally he was called Hoshea, but Moses added a letter to his name (Num. 13:16). *A change of name always implies a change of character or calling.* Abram became Abraham. Jacob became Israel. When our name changes, says Maimonides, it is as if we or someone else were saying, "You are not the same person as you were before."[5] Anyone who has experienced a name change has been inducted into a growth mindset.

People with the growth mindset do not fear failure. They relish challenges. They know that if they fail, they will try again until they succeed. It cannot be coincidence that the two people among the spies who had the growth mindset were also the two who were unafraid of the risks and trials of conquering the land. Nor can it be accidental that the ten others, all of whom carried the burden of people's expectations (as leaders, princes, men of high rank), were reluctant to do so.

If this analysis is correct, the story of the spies holds a significant message for us. God does not ask us never to fail. He asks of us that we give of our best. He lifts us when we fall and forgives us when we fail. All He asks in return is that we acknowledge our failures. This gives us the courage to take risks. That is what Joshua and Caleb knew, one through his name change, the other through the experience of his ancestor Judah.

Hence the paradoxical but deeply liberating truth: Fear of failure causes us to fail. It is the willingness to fail that allows us to succeed.

5.   Maimonides, *Mishneh Torah, Hilkhot Teshuva* 2:4.

Without Walls

There is a sentence in Rashi's commentary to *Parashat Shelaḥ* that, if taken seriously, has the power to transform Jewish life. The context is the story of the spies. Moses charged them with various tasks. They are to see whether the inhabitants are few or many, weak or strong; what the soil is like; whether there are trees; and so on. One specific question was about the cities. Are they open? Or are they fortified, surrounded by walls?

The spies came back and in the course of their report, they said: "The people living in the land are powerful, and the cities are fortified and very large. We even saw descendants of the giant there" (Num. 13:28). Note the sequence. The first and third remarks are about the people. The middle one is about the cities. It is an odd sequence.

Recalling the event forty years later, Moses states that the people said: "Our brothers took away our courage by telling us that they saw there a race that was larger and taller than we, with great cities fortified to the skies, as well as children of the giants" (Deut. 1:28). Note the same sequence: first the people, then the cities, then the people again.

The general sense in both accounts is that the spies said: The people are strong and so are the cities. Hence their conclusion: We cannot win.

We should not even try. However, Rashi, quoting *Midrash Tanḥuma*, makes the following comment: "Moses gave the spies a sign. If the cities are open, unwalled, this is a sign that the people are strong since they rely on their strength," and do not need the protection of high walls. If however the cities are fortified, walled, "this is a sign that the people are weak" (Rashi to Num. 13:18). *Instead of a direct correlation between the strength of the walls and the people, there is an inverse relationship.* The higher the walls, the more fearful the people.

So indeed it proved, judging by the later story of the spies sent by Joshua to Jericho and read as the *haftara* for *Parashat Shelaḥ*. This was a walled city. Yet, as Rahab tells the spies, the people of Jericho were terrified of the Israelites (Josh. 2:8–11). Walls are a sign of weakness, not strength.

There were times in Jewish history when Jews were unafraid of the challenge posed by the wider culture. The prophets knew that idolatry was false, and they made fun of it.[1] They were certainly not threatened by it. Moses was convinced that the nations would recognise the power of Judaism as a way of life. "This is your wisdom and understanding in the eyes of the nations," he said (Deut. 4:6). "They will hear all these rules and say: 'This great nation is certainly a wise and understanding people.'" Isaiah foresaw the day when "many peoples will come and say, 'Come, let us go up to the mountain of the Lord, to the Temple of the God of Jacob. He will teach us His ways, so that we may walk in His paths.' The law will go out from Zion, the word of the Lord from Jerusalem" (Is. 2:3).

In the language of this *parasha* and Rashi's commentary to it, they were strong in their faith. Therefore they did not have to shelter behind high walls. Their world, their city, was open. They were not afraid.

At some point, that changed. We find, most notably in the nineteenth century, a turning inward within the strongholds of Jewish learning. Secular studies were discouraged, then banned. The faith that was once intellectually fearless became intellectually fearful. It built high walls.

Perhaps it was inevitable. In retrospect there were multiple reasons for the failure of Jews to meet the challenges of post-Enlightenment Europe. First they were, in John Murray Cuddihy's phrase, "latecomers

---

1. See Is. 44:6–22 for a fine example.

to modernity."[2] Unlike Christians, they had not been prepared for it through the long centuries from the Reformation (1517) onward.

The emergence of Jews into the supposedly neutral societies of Europe was both dramatic and traumatic. It came suddenly in the nineteenth century. For the first time in the history of the Diaspora, Jews were being offered a place in the mainstream of society. But the promise came at a price. They were expected to integrate, adopting the manners and mores of the surrounding culture. It spelled the end of the ghetto.[3]

In itself, this was good news. The ghetto condemned them to being – as Max Weber put it – a "pariah people."[4] But it led to crisis. Until Emancipation, Jewish life had been a totality, infusing every aspect of existence with a distinctively Jewish flavour – dress, food, the Yiddish language, the *Beit Din* which resolved internal disputes, and the rich literatures, sacred and secular, which Jews had accumulated.

Now they were being asked to fit their faith into essentially Protestant dimensions, a "religion" confined largely to private life. A measure of how radical a demand this was is the fact that before the nineteenth century there was no word for "Judaism." There was Torah, there were Jews, and there was Jewish life. The question was: Could Jews become Europeans in culture, while remaining Jews in faith and practice? Could they – as nineteenth-century Jews themselves put it – be "people in the street, and Jews at home"? It meant a break with eighteen centuries of semi-autonomy and self-sufficiency.

What was infinitely worse was that, beneath the veneer of tolerance, many European societies remained ferociously hostile to Jews. The countries – France, Germany, and Austria, in particular – that most loudly proclaimed their liberalism gave birth to the most virulent, persistent anti-Semitism, no longer based on religion as it had been in the Middle Ages, but rather on race. This was the beginning of a descent into hell, for one can change one's religion but not one's race. Jews found

2. John Murray Cuddihy, *The Ordeal of Civility: Freud, Marx, Lévi-Strauss, and the Jewish Struggle with Modernity* (New York: Basic Books, 1974).
3. See Jacob Katz, *Out of the Ghetto: The Social Background of Jewish Emancipation, 1770–1870* (New York: Schocken, 1978).
4. Max Weber, *Ancient Judaism*, trans. and ed. Hans H. Gerth and Don Martindale (New York: Free Press, 1967).

that however hard they tried to integrate they were regarded with fear and loathing as outsiders.

Within decades, European Jewry had been shattered into fragments. Some converted. Many assimilated, abandoning most elements of Jewish life. A few – most notably Rabbi Samson Raphael Hirsch – managed the delicate balancing act. Jews could be culturally European (Hirsch himself loved German poetry) while remaining uncompromising in their religious practice. The synthesis came to be known as *Torah im derekh eretz*, "Torah combined with [secular] culture."[5]

The entire story, viewed in retrospect, was tragic. By the end of the nineteenth century, far-seeing Jews, some religious, some secular, had already reached the conclusion that European Emancipation had failed and that there was no place for Jews in Europe. That was when Zionism was born. A half-century later, the Holocaust had taken place. To some extent Jewish life today is still scarred by those events.

But that was then, not now. Today[6] Jews enjoy a situation they have never experienced before in all the almost four thousand years of their history: sovereignty and independence in Israel, freedom and equality in the Diaspora. Jews have their own land and state. Nor do they have to hide their identity to purchase their "entrance ticket" to Western culture. Jews proved themselves masters and shapers of that culture, contributing to the world an astonishing proportion of shapers of the modern mind. A distinguished Catholic intellectual, William Rees-Mogg, wrote: "One of the gifts of Jewish culture to Christianity is that it has taught Christians to think like Jews. Any modern man who has not learned to think as though he were a Jew can hardly be said to have learned to think at all."[7]

Yet today the world of tradition is for the most part as closed as it was a century ago. Jewish piety, in the main, lives behind high walls and imagines that this constitutes strength. They forget the Midrash and Rashi. This is not strength. It is weakness.

---

5. I have told the story in detail in Jonathan Sacks, *Arguments for the Sake of Heaven* (Northvale, NJ: Jason Aaronson, 1991).
6. These words were written in 2016.
7. William Rees-Mogg, *The Reigning Error* (London: Hamilton, 1974), 11.

The result is that there are still all too few Jewish works that address the central challenges of modernity: the sceptical-scientific outlook, Darwinian biology, deterministic neuroscience, biblical scholarship, the rise of individualism, and the ethical challenges of the twenty-first century. Jews have recovered national sovereignty after a lapse of two thousand years, yet there is far too little written about what would constitute a Jewish political philosophy for our time and what a Jewish and democratic state of Israel would look like were it to seek to be a living embodiment of biblical ideals. There are almost no books written by religious Jews that answer the fundamental questions young people have about faith.

Religious Jews for the most part have not engaged with the wider conversation of humankind. Jews have re-entered history as a nation among nations. They have achieved little less than greatness as a "start-up nation," embracing and enhancing the latest information technology. Yet paradoxically there has been little of the intellectual conviction of Moses or the passionate universalism of Isaiah. This is not the fault of Judaism but of us, and it is based on the same mistake that was made by the spies: the belief that living behind high walls is a sign of strength. To the contrary, it is a sign of weakness – not, as it was then, physical weakness, but spiritual and intellectual weakness.

There were exceptions, among them two outstanding figures, Rabbi Abraham Isaac Kook and Rabbi Ben-Zion Uziel, both of whom encouraged engagement with the wider world of humankind. Rabbi Kook wrote:

> The Holy One, Blessed Be He, dealt charitably with His world by not putting all the talents in one place, not in any one man or in any one nation, not in any one country, not in one generation or in one world; but the talents are scattered.... The store of the special treasure of the world is laid up in Israel. But in order, in a general sense, to unite the world with them, certain talents have to be absent from Israel so that they may be completed by the rest of the world and the princes of the nations.[8]

8. Rabbi Abraham Isaac Kook, *Lights* [Hebrew] (Jerusalem: Degel, 1920), 152, par. 2.

Other nations, in other words, have made their own distinguished contributions to human culture, and Jews should be open to them. He added:

> Narrowness of sympathy, which causes one to see in everything outside the boundary of one particular people, even if that people is the People of Israel, only ugliness and impurity, is one of the most terrible sources of darkness, and causes general destruction to every good spiritual construction, to whose light every refined soul looks forwards.[9]

In a similar vein, Rabbi Uziel wrote:

> Each country and each nation which respects itself does not and cannot be satisfied with its narrow boundaries and limited domains; rather, they desire to bring in all that is good and beautiful, that is helpful and glorious to their national [cultural] treasure. And they wish to give the maximum flow of their own blessings to the treasury of humanity as a whole. [Each self-respecting nation desires] to establish a link of love and friendship among all nations, for the enrichment of the human storehouse of intellectual and ethical ideas and for the uncovering of the secrets of nature. Happy is the country and happy the nation that can give itself an accounting of what it has taken in from others; and more importantly, of what it has given of its own to the repository of all humanity. Woe unto that country and nation that encloses itself in its own four cubits [i.e., its own private confines] and limits itself to its own narrow boundaries, lacking anything of its own to contribute [to humanity] and lacking the tools to receive [cultural contributions] from others.[10]

I have quoted these sources at length because there are so few counterparts today. This is a great mistake. It may be that much secular scholarship today in both the arts and the sciences is hostile to Jewish values,

9. Rabbi Abraham Isaac Kook, manuscript, *Ancient Anthology* [Hebrew], 128.
10. Rabbi Ben-Zion Uziel, *Meditations of Uziel* [Hebrew] (Jerusalem: 1953), 2:127.

but to be fearful of it and hide oneself away from it is to commit the intellectual equivalent of the sin of the spies. *If we truly believe that the God of creation is also the God of revelation, then in principle there can be no contradiction between scientific truth and the truth of Torah.* To demonstrate this is one of the great tasks of Jewry in our time.

It is easy to hide behind high walls and imagine you are strong. It remains, however, a form of self-deception. In the seventeenth century, John Milton, a man whose thought and work were dominated by the Hebrew Bible, wrote:

> I cannot praise a fugitive and cloistered virtue, unexercised and unbreathed, that never sallies out and sees her adversary, but slinks out of the race where that immortal garland is to be run for, not without dust and heat.[11]

A century earlier, Rabbi Judah Loewe of Prague (also known as the Maharal, 1525–1609) wrote about having the courage to confront views that challenge your own:

> Do not say to your opponent: "Speak not, close your mouth." If that happens, there will take place no purification of religion.... This is the opposite of what some people think, namely, that when you prevent someone from speaking against religion, that strengthens religion. That is not so, because curbing the words of an opponent in religious matters is nothing but the curbing and enfeebling of religion itself.[12]

Faith does not hide behind high walls.

11. John Milton, *Areopagitica, and Other Political Writings* (Indianapolis: Liberty Fund, 1999), 17.
12. Rabbi Judah Loewe (Maharal), *Be'er HaGola* 7:7.

Fringe Phenomena

Parashat Shelaḥ ends with one of the great commands of Judaism – tzitzit, the fringes we wear on the corner of our garments, as a perennial reminder of our identity as Jews and our obligation to keep the Torah's commands:

> God spoke to Moses, telling him to speak to the Israelites and instruct them to make for themselves fringes on the corners of their garments for all generations. Let them attach a cord of blue to the fringe at each corner. It shall be for you as a fringe, and you shall see it and remember all the commands of the Lord and keep them and not be led astray after your heart and eyes, which have led you to immorality. You will thus remember and keep all My commandments and be holy to your God. (Num. 15:37–40)

So central is this command that it became the third paragraph of the *Shema*, the supreme declaration of Jewish faith. I once heard the following commentary from my teacher, Rabbi Dr. Nachum Rabinovitch.[1]

---

1. The talk is reproduced in Zvi Kaplan, ed., *Speaker for Zion* [Hebrew] (Jerusalem: Mizrachi-Hapoel Mizrachi, n.d.), 217–218.

He began by pointing out some of the strange features of the command. On the one hand, the sages said that the command of tzitzit is equal to all the other commands together, as it is said: "You shall see it and remember *all the commands of the Lord* and keep them." It is thus of fundamental significance.

On the other hand, it is not absolutely obligatory. It is possible to avoid the command of fringes altogether by never wearing a garment of four or more corners. Maimonides rules: "Even though one is not obligated to acquire a [four-cornered] robe and wrap oneself in it in order to [fulfil the command of] tzitzit, it is not fitting for a pious individual to exempt himself from this command."[2] In other words, it is important and praiseworthy but not categorical. It is conditional: *if* you have such a garment, *then* you must put fringes on it. Why so? Surely it should be obligatory, in the way that *tefillin* (phylacteries) are.

There is another unusual phenomenon. In the course of time, the custom has evolved to fulfil the command in two quite different ways: the first, in the form of a *tallit* (robe, shawl) which is worn *over* our other clothes, specifically while we pray; the second in the form of an *under*garment, worn *beneath* our outer clothing throughout the day.

Not only do we keep the one command in two different ways. We also make different blessings over the two forms. Over the *tallit*, we say, "who has sanctified us with His commandments, and commanded us *to wrap ourselves* in a fringed garment." Over the undergarment, we say, "who has sanctified us with His commandments, and commanded us *concerning the precept* of the fringed garment." Why is one command split into two in this way?

Rabbi Rabinovitch gave this answer: There are two kinds of clothing. There are the clothes we wear to project an image. A king, a judge, a soldier all wear clothing that conceals the individual and instead proclaims a role, an office, a rank. As such, clothes, especially uniforms, can be misleading.[3] A king dressed as a beggar will not (or would not, before television) be recognised as royalty. A beggar dressed as a king may find himself honoured. A policeman dressed as a policeman carries with him

2. Maimonides, *Mishneh Torah, Hilkhot Tzitzit* 3:11.
3. As we saw in the chapter titled "Law and Narrative."

a certain authority, an aura of power, even though he may feel nervous and insecure. Clothes disguise. They are like a mask. They hide the person beneath. Such are the clothes we wear in public when we want to create a certain impression.

But there are other clothes we wear when we are alone that may convey more powerfully than anything else the kind of person we really are: the artist in his studio, the writer at his desk, the gardener tending the roses. They are not dressed to create an impression. To the contrary, these people dress as they do because of what they are, not because of what they wish to seem.

The two kinds of tzitzit represent these different forms of dress. When we engage in prayer, we sense in our heart how unworthy we may be of the high demands God has made of us. We feel the need to come before God as something more than just ourselves. We wrap ourselves in the robe, the *tallit*, the great symbol of the Jewish people at prayer. We conceal our individuality – in the language of the blessing over the *tallit*, we "*wrap ourselves* in a fringed garment." It is as if we were saying to God: I may only be a beggar, but I am wearing a royal robe, the robe of Your people Israel who prayed to You throughout the centuries, to whom You showed a special love and took as Your own. The *tallit* hides the person we are and represents the person we would like to be, because in prayer we ask God to judge us, not for what we are, but for what we wish to be.

The deeper symbolism of tzitzit, however, is that it represents the commandments as a whole ("you shall see it and remember all the commands of the Lord") – and these become part of what and who we are only when we accept them without coercion, of our own free will. That is why the command of tzitzit is not categorical. We do not *have* to keep it. We are not obligated to buy a four-cornered garment. When we do so, it is because we *choose* to do so. We obligate ourselves. That is why opting to wear tzitzit symbolises the free acceptance of all the duties of Jewish life.

This is the most inward, intimate, intensely personal aspect of faith whereby in our innermost soul we dedicate ourselves to God and His commands. There is nothing public about this. It is not for outer show. It is who we are when we are alone, not trying to impress anyone, not wishing to seem what we are not. This is the command of tzitzit as undergarment, beneath, not on top of, our clothing. Over this we make a different blessing. We do not talk about "*wrapping ourselves* in a fringed garment," because this form of fringes is not for outward show. We are not trying to hide ourselves beneath a uniform. Instead, we are expressing our innermost commitment to God's word and call to us. Over this we say the blessing, "who has... commanded us concerning the *precept* of the fringed garment" because what matters is not the mask but the reality, not what we wish to seem but what we really are.

In this striking way, tzitzit represents the dual nature of Judaism. On the one hand it is a way of life that is public, communal, shared with others across the world and through the ages. We keep Shabbat, celebrate the festivals, observe the dietary laws and the laws of family purity in a way that has hardly varied for many centuries. That is the public face of Judaism – the *tallit* we wear, the cloak woven out of the 613 threads, each a command.

But there is also our inner life as people of faith. There are things we can say to God that we can say to no one else. He knows our thoughts, hopes, fears, better than we know them ourselves. We speak to Him in the privacy of the soul, and He listens. That internal conversation – the opening of our heart to Him who brought us into existence in love – is not for public show. Like the fringed undergarment, it stays hidden. But it is no less real an aspect of Jewish spirituality. The two types of fringed garment represent the two dimensions of the life of faith – the outer persona and the inner person, the image we present to the world and the face we show only to God.

Koraḥ
קרח

The rebellion of Korah that dominates this *parasha* was the most devastating challenge to Moses' leadership. As Nahmanides points out, it could only have happened after the sin of the spies and the subsequent condemnation of the generation who left Egypt, told that they would not live to enter the land. Building on their unrest and shattered hopes, Korah assembled a heterogeneous group of malcontents – some from his own tribe, some from that of Reuben, yet others who had leadership positions elsewhere – and challenged the leadership of Moses and Aaron.

The rebellion failed – ended by the ground opening and swallowing the chief rebels – yet the complaints of the people continued. They ended only when Aaron's rod, alone among the rods for each tribe, budded, blossomed, and brought forth almonds, a paradigm of peaceful conflict resolution. The *parasha* ends with a legal section detailing the duties of the priests and Levites and the offerings to be given to them by the rest of the people.

The Korah revolt was the most fraught and devastating assault on Moses and Aaron's leadership. For that reason, most of the essays are focused on it and the way it was understood within the rabbinic tradition. The first explains how Korah misunderstood the nature of spiritual leadership, thinking it to be a matter of status rather than service. The second looks at how rabbinic Midrash understood the revolt. The third examines the rabbinic understanding of argument in general. The fourth looks at the psychology of Moses' response to the crisis. The fifth contrasts Moses' reaction here to his very different response to the prophecy of Eldad and Medad. The sixth asks whether Korah was right or wrong to say, "All the congregation are holy."

Servant Leadership

The Korah rebellion, the most serious of the many challenges to Moses' leadership, was a complex affair. As the commentators point out, there was not one party to the rebellion but three, each with its own grievance.

First, there was Korah himself. The genealogy given in the opening verse of the *parasha* – "Korah, son of Yitzhar, son of Kehat, son of Levi" – suggested to the sages the nature of his discontent:

> My father was one of four brothers... Amram was the firstborn. Of his sons, Aaron was awarded the priesthood and Moses was given kingship. Who is worthy of receiving the next honour if not the second [brother, Yitzhar]? I, Yitzhar's son, should have been made prince of the clan, but instead Moses appointed Elizaphan, son of Uziel [the fourth and youngest brother]. Should the youngest of father's brothers be greater than I? I will dispute with him and undo whatever he does.[1]

1. Numbers Rabba 18:2.

Korah was aggrieved that he had been passed over when leaders were appointed for the various clans. In Numbers 3:30 we read that "the leader of the families of the clans of Kehat was Elizaphan, son of Uziel." Elizaphan was the youngest of the four sons of Kehat. Korah was the son of Yitzhar, the second eldest of the brothers. Having already felt slighted that his father's elder brother, Amram, had provided the Israelites with their two supreme leaders, Moses and Aaron, this further rejection was the final insult. He felt humiliated, and was determined to bring Moses and Aaron down.

Frustrated ambition lay behind the involvement of two other groups as well, the Reubenites and the 250 "leaders" from the other tribes. Here is the analysis of Rabbi Meir Loeb ben Yechiel Michel, Malbim (Romania, 1809–1879):

> The grievance [of Datan and Aviram and On ben Pelet] lay in the fact that they belonged to the tribe of Reuben who, as the firstborn son of Jacob, was entitled to the highest offices of spiritual and political leadership. Instead, they complained, the priesthood and divine service had been given to the tribe of Levi and leadership of the tribes to Judah and Joseph.
>
> Similarly, the 250 men contended that, as "princes of the assembly, famous in the congregation, men of renown," they should have been accorded the priesthood. They were against conferring a hereditary title on a tribe, but asserted that individual prestige and distinction should be considered. Ibn Ezra suggests that these 250 rebels were in fact firstborns who considered that the priesthood was their natural prerogative. (Commentary to Num. 16:1)

Reuben was Jacob's firstborn, yet his tribe was systematically passed over when it came to leadership roles, leaving its members with a sense of grievance. In the case of the firstborn of other tribes and families, there was a different resentment, namely that after the sin of the Golden Calf the office of priesthood had been taken from the firstborn and passed to the priests of the tribe of Levi.

In short, each of the three groups was motivated by malice and envy towards the two men, Moses and Aaron, who seemed to have arrogated leadership to themselves and their tribe. The complaints were different and could not all be satisfied. Indeed, had any of them been acceded to they would merely have generated new complaints in turn. What united them – as happens so often in the strange bedfellow alliances between disaffected groups – was less a shared vision of the future than discontent about the present.

The precise details of the narrative are complex, but one thing is luminously clear – the accusation the rebels made against Moses and Aaron:

> They came as a group to oppose Moses and Aaron and said to them, "You have gone too far! All the congregation are holy and the Lord is in their midst. Why then do you *set yourselves above* [*titnasu*] the Lord's assembly?" (Num. 16:3)

Two of the rebels, Datan and Aviram, went further: "Is it not enough that you have brought us up out of a land flowing with milk and honey to kill us in the wilderness? And now you also want *to lord it* [*tistarer*] over us?" (Num. 16:13). On the face of it, there was compelling logic to their claim. God had called on all Israel to become "a kingdom of priests and a holy nation" (Ex. 19:6), meaning a kingdom each of whose members is a priest, a nation all of whose citizens are holy. Why then should there be a cadre of priests and one high priest?

The military hero Gideon said, in the later era of the judges, "I will not rule over you, nor will my son rule over you. The Lord will rule over you" (Judges 8:23). Why then should there be a single life-appointed Moses-type leader? Why should it not be like the days of the judges, charismatic figures who led the people through a particular crisis and then went back to their previous anonymity, as Caleb did during the lifetime of Moses? Surely the people needed no other leader than God Himself.

Later still, Samuel warned the people of the dangers of appointing a king.

He will take your sons and make them serve with his chariots and horses, and they will run in front of his chariots.... He will take the best of your fields and vineyards and olive groves.... When that day comes, you will cry out for relief from the king you have chosen, but the Lord will not answer you in that day. (I Sam. 8:11–18)

This is the biblical anticipation of Lord Acton's famous remark that all power tends to corrupt. Why then give individuals the power Moses and Aaron in their different ways seemed to have?

What did the rebels get wrong? The answer lies in Korah's claim that Moses and Aaron were setting themselves "above" the people, and in Datan and Aviram's remark that Moses was "lording it." The rebels saw leadership in terms of status. A leader is one higher than the rest: the alpha male, the top dog, the ruler, commander, superior, controller, the one before whom people prostrate themselves and to whom others defer. That is what leaders are in hierarchical societies.

But that is not what leadership is in the Torah, and we have had many hints of it already. Of Moses it says that he "was very humble, more so than anyone else on the face of the earth" (Num. 12:3). Of Aaron and the priests, in their capacity as those who blessed the people, it says, "So they will put My name on the Israelites, and I will bless them" (Num. 6:27). In other words, the priests were mere vehicles through which the divine force flowed. *Neither priest nor prophet had personal power or authority.* They were transmitters of a word not their own. The prophet spoke the word of God for *this* time. The priest spoke the word of God for *all* time. But neither was author of the word. That is why humility was not an accident of their personalities but the essence of their role.

Even the slightest hint that they were exercising their own authority, speaking their own word, or doing their own deed immediately invalidated them. That, in fact, is what sealed the fate of Moses and Aaron later, when the people complained and they said, "Listen, you rebels, shall *we* bring you water out of this rock?" (Num. 20:10). There are many interpretations of what went wrong on that occasion but one, undeniably, is that they attributed the action to themselves rather than God (Ḥizkuni [Hezekiah ben Manoah; France, thirteenth century] to Num. 20:10).

Even a king in Jewish law – the office that *is* about honour and status – is commanded to be humble. He is to carry a Torah scroll with him and read it all the days of his life "so that he may learn to revere the Lord his God and follow carefully all the words of this law and these decrees and *not consider himself better* than his fellow Israelites."[2]

In Judaism, a leader is not one who holds himself higher than those he or she leads. That is a moral failing, not a mark of stature. The absence of hierarchy does not mean the absence of leadership. A leader is one who coordinates, giving structure and shape to the enterprise, making sure that everyone is following the same script, travelling in the same direction, acting as an ensemble rather than a collection of prima donnas.

A leader must have a vision and communicate it. At times he has to impose discipline. Without leadership even the most glittering array of talents produces not music but noise. That is not unknown in Jewish life, then and now. "In those days there was no king in Israel; everyone did what was right in his own eyes" (Judges 17:6; 21:25). That is what happens when there is no leadership.

The Torah, and Tanakh as a whole, has a memorable way of putting this. Moses' highest honour is that he is called *eved Hashem*, "the servant of God." He is called this once on his death (Deut. 34:5) and no less than eighteen times in Tanakh as a whole. God calls Abraham, and later Caleb, "My servant" (Gen. 26:24; Num. 14:24). Joshua is twice called "the servant of God" (Josh. 24:29; Judges 2:8). In Judaism, a leader is a servant and to lead is to serve. Anything else is not leadership as Judaism understands it.

Note that we are *all* God's servants. The Torah says so: "To Me the Israelites are servants; they are My servants whom I brought out of Egypt" (Lev. 25:55). So it is not that Moses was a different kind of being than we are all called on to be. It is that he epitomised it to the utmost degree. *The less there is of self in one who serves God, the more there is of God.* Moses was the supreme exemplar of R. Yoḥanan's principle, that "where you find humility, there you find greatness."[3]

2. Deut. 17:19–20. Also see Maimonides' *Mishneh Torah, Hilkhot Melakhim* 2:6.
3. *Midrash Lekaḥ Tov, Ekev*, 15a.

This principle turned out to be fateful to the history of Israel because of one specific event. Towards the end of the reign of King Solomon, the people grew restless at the burden he had placed on them, in part because of the building of the Temple. When the king died, the people formed a delegation – led by an ambitious would-be leader, Jeroboam – to Solomon's son Rehoboam. They had a simple and specific demand: "Your father put a heavy yoke on us, but now lighten the harsh labour and the heavy yoke he put on us, and we will serve you" (I Kings 12:4). Rehoboam told them to come back in three days' time and he would give them an answer. He then went to the elders who had been his father's counsellors. "What would you advise me to say?" he asked (12:6). Their answer is fascinating: "If today you will be a servant [eved] to these people and serve them [vaavad'tem] and give them a favourable answer, they will always be your servants [avadim]" (12:7).

The task of a king, they said, is to *serve* the people, not to impose burdens on them. It was wise advice. Unfortunately, Rehoboam – young, impetuous – ignored it. Instead he asked his friends, with whom he had grown up. Their advice was the opposite. In effect, they said: Show them who is boss. Tell them, "My little finger is thicker than my father's waist. My father laid on you a heavy yoke; I will make it even heavier. My father scourged you with whips; I will scourge you with scorpions" (I Kings 12:10–11).

Rehoboam did so. The result was predictable. The majority of the people followed Jeroboam. The kingdom split in two. It was the beginning of the end of the first commonwealth. Authoritarian leadership – in which the leader sets himself above and lords it over the people – has never been acceptable in Israel.

There is an important concept popularised by Robert K. Greenleaf (1904-1990),[4] namely "servant leadership." His view, inspired by a Hermann Hesse novel with Buddhist undertones, was that a leader is the servant of those he leads. Judaism has its own and somewhat different version of servant leadership, namely that the leader is the servant of God, not of the people; but neither is he their master. Only God is that. The leader is not "above" the people: he and they are equal. Rather, he is

---

4. Robert K. Greenleaf, *Servant Leadership* (New York: Paulist Press, 2002).

their teacher, guide, advocate, and defender. His task is to remind them endlessly of their vocation and inspire them to be true to it.

In Judaism, leadership is not about popularity: "If a scholar is loved by the people of his town, it is not because he is gifted but because he fails to rebuke them in matters of heaven" (Ketubbot 105b). Nor is a true leader eager for the job. Almost without exception, the great leaders of Tanakh were reluctant to assume the mantle of leadership. Rabban Gamliel summed it up when he said to two sages he wanted to appoint to office: "Do you imagine I am offering you rulership? I am offering you *avdut*, the chance to serve" (Horayot 10a–b).

A true leader is a servant, not a master. He does not seek to set himself above others or lord it over them. Leadership as power, dominance, mastery, or rule has no place in Judaism. To the contrary, the greatest achievement of a leader is to have served God and helped others to do so. That is what Moses understood, and what Korah and his fellow rebels did not.

A Cloak Entirely Blue

Midrash is the ancient rabbinic way of understanding a biblical text. It is not a simple, literal interpretation. For this, the rabbis had as different phrase, *peshuto shel mikra*, the "plain sense" of a verse or phrase. They believed the plain sense is important and underlies everything else.[1] But it is not everything. There is much in Torah that is deeper, subtler, than the plain sense. For that they turned to Midrash.

In Midrash the rabbis explored the apparent inconsistencies and contradictions in the text. Sometimes they spelled out what the Torah leaves unsaid. The Torah can be very cryptic. All sorts of details are missing. The rabbis used Midrash in two ways: first to tease out details of the law (*midrash halakha*), second to fill in the gaps in the narrative (*midrash aggada*). By interpreting and re-interpreting the Torah, they were continuing the work already begun by Israel's prophets.[2]

---

1. "Scripture does not depart from its plain meaning" (Shabbat 63a). As Wallace Stevens memorably put it: "After the leaves have fallen, we return / To a plain sense of things" ("The Plain Sense of Things").
2. See Michael Fishbane's important book, *Biblical Interpretation in Ancient Israel* (Oxford: Clarendon Press, 1985).

In particular, Midrash is the bridge across the abyss of time between biblical and post-biblical Judaism. *Peshat,* the plain sense, asks, "What did the text mean *then*?" Midrash asks the question, "What does the text mean *now*?" *Peshat* asks, "What did it mean for our ancestors?" Midrash asks, "What does it mean for us?" If God is beyond time then His word must have meaning for all time, including the present. Midrash is built on this faith.[3]

This is by way of introduction to a famous midrash at the beginning of *Parashat Koraḥ*. Rashi cites it in his commentary. It takes as its starting point a simple question. The story of the Korah rebellion begins with the words, "And Korah took" (Num. 16:1). What did he take? The verb requires but does not have an object. Rashi begins by stating what he believes is the plain sense. It means, "And Korah *took himself to one side*." He separated himself from the rest of the community. He readied himself for an argument. He prepared to start a revolt.

However, Rashi begins his commentary to the story of Korah by telling us that "this passage is well explained in *Midrash Tanḥuma,*" and having explained the plain sense of the opening words, he turns to the Midrash. This is what it says:

> He took a cloak that was made entirely of blue wool, and dressed his fellow rebels in similar cloaks. They came and stood before Moses and asked him, "Does a cloak made entirely of blue wool require tzitzit, or is it exempt?" He replied, "It does require them." They began laughing at him, saying, "Is it possible that one thread of blue wool exempts an entire garment made of other material, yet a cloak made entirely of threads of blue wool does not exempt itself?"[4]

The midrash, in other words, answers the question, "What did Korah take?" by saying that he took a blue cloak, knowing that he could use it

---

3. A faith, we might add, radically different from that presupposed by much of academic biblical scholarship since Spinoza, but that is a subject for another time and a different book.
4. *Midrash Tanḥuma, Koraḥ* 2.

to ridicule Moses in public. He was clever enough to know two things: first, that even a blue cloak requires tzitzit, a set of fringes that contain a thread of blue; second, that it is difficult, perhaps impossible, to explain this convincingly to a large and sceptical public. Korah had mastered the art of hitting below the belt by asking an impossible question (the classic secular example is, "When did you stop beating your wife?"). Whichever way you answer, there is no way of avoiding embarrassment. Korah knew that when Moses gave the correct answer, he could be made to seem absurd. Korah could then claim that this showed he was making up all the laws he claimed to have received from God. God could not have issued so ridiculous a command.

Thus far the Midrash. How are we to understand it? Clearly, it is not the plain sense of the text. Neither Korah nor any of his fellow rebels mentioned tzitzit, or any other Jewish law for that matter. Their complaints were quite different. Moses had acted high-handedly. He had appointed his brother as high priest, an act they could portray as nepotism. He had failed in his central mission of bringing the people to the Promised Land. Because of the episode of the spies, the people now knew that they would not live to cross the Jordan. Their complaints had nothing to do with a cloak of blue and the laws of tzitzit. So what is the Midrash telling us?

The first answer is that it is doing what Midrash does. It is asking not "What did the Torah mean then?" but "What does the Torah mean now?" Living after the destruction of the Second Temple, the rabbis were not faced with would-be usurpers wanting to be leaders of the Jewish people. The age of kings and high priests was over. What they faced were what they called *minim*, "sectarians," some of whom argued that that the Torah was not "from heaven" (Mishna Sanhedrin 10:1), and that – apart from the Ten Commandments that the people heard directly from God – the laws were made by Moses himself and were therefore not binding.[5] We do not know exactly who these sectarians were, but we have strong evidence that this is the kind of claim they made. The rabbis were therefore making the Korah story directly relevant to their time.

---

5. Berakhot 12a as explained by Rashi ad loc.

But that is not all they were doing. The second thing they were doing was engaging in *a close reading of the text*. Listen to it carefully and we immediately note several significant problems. We have already mentioned one. The story begins by saying, "And Korah took," but it does not say what he took. Rashi's reading, that he "took himself," is based on an ancient *Targum*, but can hardly be said to be the obvious sense of the text.

Then there is the accusation that the rebels seem to have levelled against Moses, but which is not mentioned in the text. At one point, Moses says: "By this you shall know that it was the Lord who sent me to do all these things, that *they were not of my own devising*" (Num. 16:28). Moses is countering the suggestion that in his capacity as leader, he had taken certain decisions himself and falsely attributed them to God. What were these decisions? Next, there is the problem that arises many times in the book of Numbers, namely, what is the logic of the Torah's sequence of subjects and chapters? Narrative is consistently interrupted by law – and by laws that seem to have no connection with the narrative. Immediately prior to the story of Korah we read of the command of tzitzit – to place fringes with a cord of blue at the corners of our garments. What is the connection between this and the story of Korah?

The brilliant suggestion of the sages is that each question answers the other. What did Korah take? He took a blue garment and asked Moses whether it still needed tzitzit. Moses replied that it did. Korah was thus able to ridicule Moses' account of the command. What, after all, is tzitzit for? The blue thread reminds us of the sky, heaven, and the Throne of Glory. If so, a garment made entirely of blue does this far better than one that merely has fringes with a single thread of blue. The illogicality of the law shows that it was not divine. It must have been made up by Moses. That is why, defending himself, Moses was forced to find a way of showing that what he had done was "not of his own devising." Though none of this is explicit in the Torah, it can be inferred from the juxtaposition of the laws of tzitzit and the story of Korah.

The Midrash is doing more than answering the questions and filling in the gaps. It is telling us something fundamental about the Jewish project itself. There is a perennial temptation in Jewish life to say that we do not need law, halakha, to achieve our religious ideals. There are commands for which a reason is given, and tzitzit is one. It is not a *ḥok*, a "statute," a command without explicit purpose. It is, rather, one of the *edot*, a "testimony," whose purpose is to remind us of certain truths, historical or spiritual. For any command with a given purpose, it can always be claimed that what is sacred is the end, not the means, the purpose but not the specific way of attaining it. Korah's argument is that there are other ways of remembering Heaven than by attaching a blue fringe to the corners of our clothes. Another is to make a garment entirely of blue – surely a far more visible, eye-catching symbol.

Korah's argument is logical but not rational. What he forgot is that the essence of the command *is* the means, not the end. It is precisely by doing things God's way that we achieve personal transformation. The apprentice who is impatient with the instructions of the master will never grow, never become a master himself. Apprenticeship is a matter of doing things we do not fully understand until we have undergone the discipline of subordinating ourselves to the instructions of an expert. That is the meaning of mitzva, command. It is our apprenticeship to the Master of the universe. In telling us this, the Midrash is teaching us something deep not only about the nature of a mitzva, a commandment, but also about leadership itself. *Korah could never be a leader because he was incapable of being a follower.* He did not understand what it is to obey. Such a person will never get others to obey. That is Midrash as a close reading of the text.

The third thing the Midrash is doing is theology. Judaism is a set of strong beliefs. This particular midrash tells a remarkable story about leadership, holiness, and the Jewish people. It takes as its starting point Korah's opening words to Moses and Aaron: "You have gone too far! *All the congregation are holy* and the Lord is in their midst. Why then do you set yourselves above the Lord's assembly?" (Num. 16:3). The inescapable question we find ourselves asking is: Was Korah right or wrong in saying this? Are all the community holy?

The Midrash does not answer this directly but does so implicitly. It tells us that Korah based his challenge on the law of tzitzit. If we turn to that law, we immediately see the strength of the point he was making. The law says this:

> Speak to the Israelites and instruct them to make for themselves
> fringes on the corners of their garments for all generations. Let
> them attach a cord of blue to the fringe on each corner. It shall
> be for you as a fringe, and you shall see it and remember all the
> commands of the Lord.... You will thus remember and keep all
> My commandments *and be holy to your God.* (Num. 15:38–40)

By linking Korah's remarks to the immediately preceding law of the
tzitzit, the Midrash is suggesting that Korah's claim was an exceptionally strong one. He did not make up the idea that "all the congregation
are holy." Moses himself had just said so. It was part of the logic of tzitzit.

In the light of archaeological research, we can put the point more
strongly still. Egyptian and Mesopotamian paintings and sculptures
from the first and second millennia BCE show garments with tassels.[6]
Rock engravings at Timna dating from the thirteenth century BCE show
Midianites or Bedouin wearing fringed cloaks.[7] The wearers were often
nobles. *Tekhelet,* the specific blue of the tzitzit, is associated with holiness and royalty. The robe of the ephod worn by Aaron the high priest
was entirely made of *tekhelet* (Ex. 28:31). The Ark was wrapped in cloth
of *tekhelet* (Num. 4:6–7). When in the book of Esther we read of Mor-
dekhai going out in "royal robes," they included *tekhelet* (Est. 8:15).

In other words, Korah was making a very strong case indeed. The
very fact that *all* the men were commanded to wear tzitzit with its thread
of royal blue, the colour associated with royalty and Aaron's priestly
robe, meant that they were indeed all holy, all noble, and all worthy to
be priests. Had not God Himself summoned Israel to be "a kingdom of
priests and a holy nation" (Ex. 19:6), meaning a kingdom all of whose
members are priests, and a nation each of whom is holy? And since
God Himself had said, even before the Exodus, "My child, My firstborn,
Israel" (Ex. 4:22), it followed that every Israelite, as the firstborn of the
King of kings, was a member of a royal family.

6. Stephen Bertman, "Tasselled Garments in the Ancient East Mediterranean," *Biblical Archaeologist* 24 (1961): 119–128.
7. Beno Rothenberg, *Timna: Valley of the Biblical Copper Mines* (London: Thames and Hudson, 1972), 123–124.

Korah could not have said this until now. Each of these statements could be taken as merely metaphorical, not literal. But now that Moses had told the entire people to wear garments with fringes of royal and priestly blue, this was no longer metaphor. Garments, official dress, uniforms, worn in obedience to a royal command, are not symbols or fancy dress; they are incontrovertible statements of status and rank. Korah's challenge, once we locate it in the context of tzitzit, becomes immeasurably more powerful.

In fact, the Midrash takes Korah's statement and dignifies it. It is no longer a piece of crude populism. It has become a piece of sublime theology. It is not just that Korah and his followers were wearing blue robes. They were making the statement that *the Jewish people itself is a robe entirely blue*. Every strand of the nation is royal, holy, priestly. *It therefore needs no further thread*, meaning, *it needs no additional leader*. If we understand the midrash in its true depth we realise that Korah was not simply saying that Moses had made a mistake in the command of tzitzit. It was the same mistake he had made in creating a priesthood and a high priest for the Jewish people. *The people did not need a priesthood because it already was a priesthood.* By telling the entire people to wear fringes with a strand of royal blue on their clothes, God was summoning them all to become "a kingdom of priests." God was calling not just Aaron and his sons but the entire nation to become leaders. He wanted them to be the human equivalent of a garment every thread of which is blue.

Instead of weakening Korah's argument, the Midrash strengthens it. What then was Korah's mistake? *Saying that a robe that is entirely blue does not need tzitzit. Saying that a congregation of leaders does not need a leader.* The truth is otherwise. A people, every one of whom is holy, still needs a leader, just as a garment, every thread of which is blue, still needs a fringe. A garment that is entirely blue but which lacks tzitzit is simply a blue garment. It has no special sanctity. A blue cloak is still only a cloak. A blue scarf is just a scarf. The function of the tzitzit is not to diminish the significance of the garment but to endow it with a special and recognisable character.

Rabbi Abraham Isaac Kook put this beautifully. In his book *Arpelei Tohar*,[8] he wrote that the role of the mitzvot in relation to a culture

8. *Arpelei Tohar* (Jerusalem: Mossad HaRav Kook, 1983), 6.

is the same as that of tzitzit in relation to a garment. It is the part that reveals the holiness of the whole. It defines it, as a frame defines a painting, or as a prologue and epilogue define a story. It is not the tzitzit that is holy, but the garment. However, without the tzitzit we would never be aware of the holiness of the garment. It would be potential, not actual; latent, not manifest.

An orchestra of virtuosi still needs a conductor. An ensemble of brilliant actors still needs a director. A team of superstars still needs a captain. Indeed, the more prodigiously gifted the individuals, the more they need a leader – not one who is necessarily better than they are, certainly not one who "sets himself above" them, but one who can orchestrate their various talents, thinks more of the team than the stars, who, to paraphrase Matthew Arnold, "sees life steadily and sees it whole,"[9] who can, from time to time, stand outside the group and see the distant dangers and the far-off destination, who can unite people as Aaron could, and who can inspire with his vision as Moses did.

We see, therefore, how one simple midrash helps us rescue a text from its pastness, from a sad, squalid quarrel thousands of years ago, letting us read it with the closest possible attention to the text as a whole, and showing us the real nature of Korah's error. He was not wrong to say that all the people were holy. He was wrong to say that holy people do not need leaders – they do. He was even more wrong to say in public that people do not need leaders while privately seeking to be a leader himself. His populism was disingenuous.

Korah did, though, have one virtue. He saw that the Jewish people should aspire to be a "cloak that is entirely blue." He died for his sins, but his sons survived, and many centuries later their descendants sang psalms in the Temple – a whole series of psalms bear their name.[10] If ambition had not corrupted him, Korah might have been a genuine leader. For he saw a real and moving truth, that if a people dedicates itself to God it can become a robe every strand of which is royal blue.

9. "To a Friend."
10. See Psalms 42, 44–49, 84–88.

Argument for the Sake of Heaven

T he Korah rebellion was not just the worst of many in the wilderness years. It was also different in kind. It was not about a problem the Israelites had encountered – a lack of food or water or a way through the sea or the prospect of having to fight a battle against giants. It was an ad hominem attack, a direct assault on Moses and Aaron. Korah and his fellow rebels in essence accused Moses of nepotism, of failure, and above all of being a fraud – of attributing to God decisions and laws that Moses had devised himself for his own ends. So grave was the attack that it became, for the sages, a paradigm of the worst kind of disagreement:

> Every argument for the sake of Heaven will in the end be of permanent value, but every argument not for the sake of Heaven will not endure. Which is an argument for the sake of Heaven? The argument between Hillel and Shammai. Which is an argument not for the sake of Heaven? The argument of Korah and his company. (Mishna Avot 5:17)

Menahem Meiri (Catalonia, 1249–1306) explains this teaching in the following terms:

> *The argument between Hillel and Shammai*: In their debates, one of
> them would render a decision and the other would argue against
> it, out of a desire to discover the truth, not out of cantankerous-
> ness or a wish to prevail over his fellow. That is why when he
> was right, the words of the person who disagreed, endured. An
> argument not for the sake of Heaven was that of Korah and his
> company, for they came to undermine Moses, our master, may
> he rest in peace, and his position, out of envy and contentious-
> ness and ambition for victory.[1]

The sages were drawing a fundamental distinction between two kinds of
conflict: *argument for the sake of truth* and *argument for the sake of victory*.

The passage must be read this way, because of the glaring dis-
crepancy between what the rebels said and what they sought. What
they said was that the people did not need leaders. They were all holy.
They had all heard the word of God. There should be no distinction
of rank, no hierarchy of holiness, within Israel. "Why then do you set
yourselves above the Lord's assembly?" (Num. 16:3). Yet from Moses'
reply, it is clear that he had heard something altogether different behind
their words:

> Moses also said to Korah, "Now listen, you Levites! Is it not
> enough for you that the God of Israel has separated you from
> the rest of the Israelite community and brought you near Him-
> self to do the work at the Lord's Tabernacle and to stand before
> the community and minister to them? He has brought you and
> all your fellow Levites near Himself, but now you are trying to
> get the priesthood too." (Num. 16:8–10)

It was not that they wanted a community without leaders. It is, rather,
that they wanted to be the leaders. The rebels' rhetoric had nothing to
do with the pursuit of truth and everything to do with the pursuit of
honour, status, and (as they saw it) power. They wanted not to learn but
to win. They sought not verity but victory.

---

1. Meiri, *Beit HaBeḥira* ad loc.

We can trace the impact of this in terms of the sequence of events that followed. First, Moses proposed a simple test. Let the rebels bring an offering of incense the next day and God would show whether He accepted or rejected their offering. This is a rational response. Moses had done what God had commanded him. Korah and his fellows disputed this, saying or suggesting that Moses had acted on his own accord. Since what was at issue was what God wanted, let God decide. It was a controlled experiment, an empirical test. God would let the people know, in an unambiguous way, who was right. It would establish, once and for all, the truth.

But Moses did not stop there, as he would have done if truth were the only issue involved. As we saw in the quote above, Moses tried to argue Korah out of his dissent, not by addressing his argument but by speaking to the resentment that lay behind it. He told him that he had been given a position of honour. He may not have been a priest but he was a Levite, and the Levites had special sacred status not shared by the other tribes. He was telling him to be satisfied with the honour he had and not let his ambition overreach itself.

He then turned to Datan and Aviram, the Reubenites. Given the chance, he would have said something different to them since the source of their discontent was different from that of Korah. But they refused to meet with him altogether – another sign that they were not interested in the truth. They had rebelled out of a profound sense of slight that the tribe of Reuben, Jacob's firstborn son, seemed to have been left out altogether from the allocation of honours.

At this point, the confrontation became yet more intense. For the one and only time in his life, Moses staked his leadership on the occurrence of a miracle:

> Then Moses said, "By this you shall know that it was the Lord who sent me to do all these things, that they were not of my own devising: If these men die a natural death and suffer the fate of all mankind, then the Lord has not sent me. But if the Lord brings about something totally new, and the earth opens its mouth and swallows them, with everything that belongs to them, and they go down alive into the grave, then you will know that these men have treated the Lord with contempt." (Num. 16:28–30)

He was immediately answered. No sooner had he finished than "the ground under them split apart and the earth opened its mouth and swallowed them" (Num. 16:32). The rebels "went down alive into the grave" (16:33). One cannot imagine a more dramatic vindication. God had shown, beyond possibility of doubt, that Moses was right and the rebels wrong. *Yet this did not end the argument.* That is what is extraordinary. Far from being apologetic and repentant, the people returned the next morning still complaining – this time, not about who should lead whom but about the way Moses had chosen to end the dispute: "The next day the whole Israelite community grumbled against Moses and Aaron. 'You have killed the Lord's people,' they said" (17:6).

You may be right, they implied, and Korah may have been wrong. But is this a way to win an argument? To cause your opponents to be swallowed up alive? This time, God suggested an entirely different way of resolving the dispute. He told Moses to have each of the tribes take a staff and write their name on it, and place them in the Tent of Meeting. On the staff of the tribe of Levi, he should write the name of Aaron. One of the staffs would sprout, and that would signal whom God had chosen. The tribes did so, and the next morning they returned to find that Aaron's staff had budded, blossomed, and produced almonds. That, finally, ended the argument (Num. 17:16–24).

What resolved the dispute, in other words, was not a show of power but something altogether different. We cannot be sure, because the text does not spell this out, but the fact that Aaron's rod produced almond blossoms seems to have had rich symbolism. In the Near East, the almond is the first tree to blossom, its white flowers signalling the end of winter and the emergence of new life. In his first prophetic vision, Jeremiah saw a branch of an almond tree (*shaked*) and was told by God that this was a sign that He, God, was "watching" (*shoked*) to see that His word was fulfilled (Jer. 1:11–12).[2] The almond flowers recalled the gold flowers on the Menora (Ex. 25:31; 37:17), lit daily by Aaron in the Sanctuary. The Hebrew word *tzitz*, used here to mean "blossom," recalls the *tzitz*, the "frontlet" of pure gold worn as part of Aaron's headdress,

2. See L. Yarden, *The Tree of Light* (London: East and West Library, 1971), 40–42.

on which were inscribed the words "Holy to the Lord" (Ex. 28:36).[3] The sprouting almond branch was therefore more than a sign. It was a multi-faceted symbol of life, light, holiness, and the watchful presence of God.

One could almost say that the almond branch symbolised the priestly will to life as against the rebels' will to power.[4] The priest does not *rule* the people; he *blesses* them. He is the conduit through which God's life-giving energies flow.[5] He connects the nation to the Divine Presence. What makes a spiritual leader is not ambition but humility, as we noted in an earlier essay.[6] Moses answered Korah in Korah's terms, by a show of force. God answered in a quite different way, showing that leadership is not self-assertion but self-effacement.

What the entire episode shows is the destructive nature of argument not for the sake of Heaven – that is, argument for the sake of victory. In such a conflict, what is at stake is not truth but power, and the result is that both sides suffer. If you win, I lose. *But if I win, I also lose, because in diminishing you, I diminish myself.* Even a Moses is brought low, laying himself open to the charge that "you have killed the Lord's people." Argument for the sake of power is a lose-lose scenario.

The opposite is the case when the argument is for the sake of truth. If I win, I win. *But if I lose I also win – because being defeated by the truth is the only form of defeat that is also a victory.* There is a magnificent passage in the Talmud that gives expression to this idea:

> Shimon the Imsonite – others state, Nehemiah the Imsonite – used to interpret every *et* in the Torah, but when he came to the verse, "You shall fear [*et*] the Lord your God," he retracted. His

---

3. There may also be a hint of a connection with the tzitzit, the fringes with their thread of blue, that according to the Midrash was the occasion for the Korah revolt (see the previous essay).
4. On the contemporary relevance of this, see Jonathan Sacks, *Not in God's Name* (New York: Schocken, 2015), 252–268.
5. The phrase that comes to mind is Dylan Thomas' "The force that through the green fuse drives the flower" (from the poem by the same name). Just as life flows through the tree to produce flowers and fruit, so a divine life force flows through the priest to produce blessings among the people.
6. "Servant Leadership."

disciples said to him: "Master, what is to become of all the *etin* you have interpreted?" He replied, "Just as I received reward for the exposition, so I will receive reward for the retraction." (Kiddushin 57a)

Shimon, a contemporary of R. Akiva, held that no word in the Torah is superfluous. What then of the word *et*, whose only function is to indicate the object of a verb, but which has no meaning in and of itself? Shimon's answer was simple. In each case, *et* came to *include* something not explicitly stated in the text. He used this principle successfully in a long series of interpretations – until he came to the command, "You shall fear [*et*] the Lord your God" (Deut. 10:13). Here, he suddenly realised, the principle broke down. What else could one include in this verse? To place the fear of something else alongside the fear of God was surely blasphemy.

Like a true scientist, Shimon realised that a single counter-example refutes a rule. Not only did he admit defeat in this case, but drew the logical conclusion that if the rule was refuted, he would have to retract all other interpretations based on it. In effect, he jettisoned his entire life's work. As it happens, his decision was premature.[7] R. Akiva later solved the problem. *You shall fear* [et] *the Lord your God*, he said, includes scholars (Kiddushin 57a). "The reverence one should have for one's teachers should be like the reverence one has for God Himself" (Pesaḥim 108a).

Here, almost two thousand years ago, is the first articulation of a principle made famous in the twentieth century by the late Sir Karl Popper in his work on scientific methodology, *Conjectures and Refutations*.[8] A scientific theory, Popper argued, can never be conclusively verified. However many times the sun has risen in the morning, it is always possible that tomorrow it will not. But a scientific theory can be conclusively refuted. Therefore it is refutation that advances scientific knowledge – or

---

7. There is an interesting modern parallel. Albert Einstein came to doubt some of his own theories, including the existence of gravitational waves. He had proposed them in 1917; twenty years later he wrote a paper retracting his theory, but it was not published. The original theory was empirically confirmed in 2016.
8. Karl Popper, *Conjectures and Refutations* (New York: Routledge Classics, 2002).

as Shimon the Imsonite put it: "Just as I received reward for the exposition, so I will receive reward for the retraction." *To be defeated by the
truth is the only defeat that is also a victory.*

In another famous passage, the Talmud explains why Jewish law
usually follows the view of the School of Hillel as against their opponents, the School of Shammai:

> [The law is in accord with the School of Hillel] because they were
> kindly and modest, because they studied not only their own rul-
> ings but also those of the School of Shammai, and because they
> taught the words of the School of Shammai before their own.
> (Eiruvin 13b)

They sought truth, not victory. That is why they listened to the views of
their opponents, and indeed taught them before they taught their own
traditions. In the eloquent words of a contemporary scientist, Timothy
Ferris:

> All who genuinely seek to learn, whether atheist or believer, sci-
> entist or mystic, are united in having not *a* faith, but faith itself.
> Its token is reverence, its habit to respect the eloquence of silence.
> For God's hand may be a human hand, if you reach out in loving
> kindness, and God's voice your voice, if you but speak the truth.[9]

Judaism has sometimes been called a "culture of argument."[10] It is the
only religious literature known to me whose key texts – the Hebrew
Bible, Midrash, Mishna, Talmud, the codes of Jewish law, and the com-
pendia of biblical interpretation – are *anthologies of arguments.* That is the
glory of Judaism. The Divine Presence is to be found not in this voice
as against that, but in the totality of the conversation.[11]

---

9. Timothy Ferris, *The Whole Shebang* (London: Weidenfeld & Nicolson, 1997), 312.
10. David Dishon, *The Culture of Argument in Judaism* [Hebrew] (Jerusalem: Schocken,
    1984).
11. I have written more extensively on this in Jonathan Sacks, *Future Tense* (London:
    Hodder and Stoughton, 2009), 181–206.

In an argument for the sake of victory, both sides lose. In an argument for the sake of truth, both sides win, for each is willing to listen to the views of its opponents, and is thereby enlarged. In argument as the collaborative pursuit of truth, the participants use reason, logic, shared texts, and shared reverence for texts. They do not use ad hominem arguments, abuse, contempt, or disingenuous appeals to emotion. Each is willing, if refuted, to say, "I was wrong." There is no triumphalism in victory, no anger or anguish in defeat.

The story of Korah remains the classic example of how argument can be dishonoured. The Schools of Hillel and Shammai remind us that there is another way. "Argument for the sake of Heaven" is one of Judaism's noblest ideals – conflict resolution by honouring both sides and employing humility in the pursuit of truth.

Not Taking It Personally

One of the most instructive ways of reading the Korah story is to track Moses' reactions. His was an almost impossible situation. He had already suffered a number of crises, most significantly the episode of the spies that had condemned an entire generation to die in the wilderness. Now his own personal authority was on the line. The Korah revolt was not a complaint about the food or water or the impossibility of defeating the people of the land. The challenge was to Moses himself, and it was coming from several directions, some implicit, others explicit.

As the commentators note, Korah seems to have accused him of nepotism in appointing his own brother as high priest and of elevating Aaron's family exclusively to the priesthood. The Reubenites, Datan and Aviram, accuse him, simply and starkly, of failing in his own mission. He had not brought the people, as he promised, to a land flowing with milk and honey. To the contrary, he had taken them out of a fertile country "to kill us in the wilderness" (Num. 16:13). The 250 leaders from the other tribes had their own complaints. As for the people as a whole, they were restless. For the most part, the text does not focus on them. Were they for or against the rebels? It is not clear. But what is clear is that they did not come to Moses and Aaron's defence.

Moses' first response was to fall facedown (Num. 16:4). Rashi says this was in near despair. He had already prayed to God to forgive the people three times. He did not know how he could succeed a fourth time. Rashbam says he fell in prayer. Saadia Gaon and Ibn Ezra say he did so to receive prophetic guidance from God.

Immediately thereafter, he stood, composed. He told the rebels that God would deliver the verdict the next day. They should bring censers, fire, and incense, and God would show whose He favoured. This was a shrewd move. By deferring the test to the next day, he gave the rebels a chance to think again and back down. By choosing the test he did, he was warning the rebels of the risk they were taking. Whenever the Korah rebellion took place – either immediately after the inauguration of the Sanctuary or later, after the episode of the spies – the people could still vividly recall what had happened to Aaron's two sons, Nadav and Avihu, when they offered up incense and fire "that had not been commanded" (Lev. 10:1–2): they died. Once Moses had proposed this test, Korah and his fellows knew that they were risking their lives.

The third thing he did was to speak to Korah directly. He knew that not all the rebels shared the same discontent. He knew also that their apparent egalitarianism – "all the congregation are holy" (Num. 16:3) – was a complete sham. He knew exactly what Korah wanted. He wanted Aaron's position as high priest. Korah was Moses and Aaron's cousin and felt that the second leadership role, the high priesthood, should have gone to him. Moses now reasoned with him firmly: "Is it not enough for you that the God of Israel has separated you from the rest of the Israelite community.… He has brought you and all your fellow Levites near Himself, but now you are trying to get the priesthood too" (16:9–10). He was telling Korah that he was going a step too far.

So far, Moses' responses were considered and calm. Now, though, something breaks. He attempts to meet with Datan and Aviram, the Reubenites.[1] They refuse the meeting, and send a deeply wounding message. With blatant disregard for the truth, they accuse Moses of

---

1. There is a rabbinic tradition, cited in Rashi's commentary to Ex. 2:14, that they were the ones to challenge Moses' behaviour even when he was a young man in Egypt. There seems to be a qualitative difference between their behaviour and that

taking them "out of a land flowing with milk and honey to kill us in the wilderness." Next they accuse him of self-aggrandisement: "And now you also want to lord it over us" (Num. 16:13). Finally they say: "Do you think you can gouge out these men's eyes and blind them?" (16:14) – meaning, "Do you think you can deceive us?" or "Do you think you can intimidate us?"[2] These are savage attacks, and they are, for Moses, the final straw. We sense all the accumulated pain that has been building up over the previous chapters explode. To be accused of failure is one thing; to be accused of seeking your own aggrandisement is another; to be accused of seeking to intimidate or deceive your opponents is something else again. To Moses, it is unbearable. He responds in ways that are troubling. He says to God: "Do not accept their offering. I have not taken so much as a donkey from them, nor have I wronged any of them" (Num. 16:15).

There are problems with this response.[3] First, no one had yet said that he had "taken a donkey" from them or harmed them. Second, Moses, as Israel's leader, had always prayed on behalf of the people, even for his sister Miriam when she was struck with leprosy for speaking badly about him. Abraham had prayed for the people of Sodom even though he knew that most of them were wicked. It is an extraordinary thing to pray to God *not* to accept someone's offering. Sforno explains his behaviour by saying that there is a rule that offences against other people are only atoned for when they have forgiven you. "I," Moses was saying to

of Korah and the other rebels. The others had reasons for their resentments. Datan and Aviram go far beyond reasonable behaviour.

2. *Targum Yonatan* interprets this remark as referring to the inhabitants of the land of Canaan. Datan and Aviram were saying, "Even were the inhabitants to be struck blind, we still could not defeat them in battle." See Alshikh ad loc.

3. Note that Jewish tradition focuses on this specific moment in the Korah story, by pairing the *parasha* with a *haftara* taken from the book of Samuel, in which the prophet, having anointed Saul as king, says to the people: "Here I stand. Testify against me in the presence of the Lord and His anointed. Whose ox have I taken? Whose donkey have I taken? Whom have I cheated? Whom have I oppressed? From whose hand have I accepted a bribe to make me shut my eyes? If I have done any of these things, I will make it right" (I Sam. 12:2–3). Samuel is experiencing the same emotion as Moses: the shame and humiliation of feeling accused for something one did not do, after a lifetime of self-sacrificing service to others.

God, "refuse to forgive them."[4] But this too was odd. The challenge at that stage was to restore order, not to deal with ultimate questions of forgiveness and retribution.

God then threatened to punish the whole congregation. Moses and Aaron interceded on their behalf. God told Moses to separate the community from the rebels so that they would not be caught up in the punishment, which Moses did. But then he heightened the drama, saying:

> By this you shall know that it was the Lord who sent me to do all these things, that they were not of my own devising: If these men die a natural death and suffer the fate of all mankind, then the Lord has not sent me. But if the Lord brings about something totally new, and the earth opens its mouth and swallows them, with everything that belongs to them, and they go down alive into the grave, then you will know that these men have treated the Lord with contempt. (Num. 16:28–30)

This was the only time Moses asked God to punish someone, and the only time he in effect forced God to perform a miracle. God immediately did as Moses asked, and we would expect this to end the rebellion. But, as we saw in the previous essay, it did not.[5] Far from ending it, it made it worse. The next day the people gathered in collective complaint

---

4. Sforno to Num. 16:15. He quotes a striking parallel in the case of Jeremiah: "Listen to me, Lord; hear what my accusers are saying! Should good be repaid with evil? Yet they have dug a pit for me. Remember that I stood before You and spoke on their behalf to turn Your wrath away from them.... But You, Lord, know all their plots to kill me. Do not forgive their crimes or blot out their sins from Your sight. Let them be overthrown before You; deal with them in the time of Your anger" (Jer. 18:19–23). Not everything, especially in the absence of remorse, contrition, and apology, is forgivable.

5. There is, in fact, an almost exact parallel in the famous case of Elijah challenging the prophets of Baal to a confrontation at Mount Carmel (I Kings 18). The Baal prophets are discredited. God answers Elijah's prayer. The people present are convinced. They shout, "The Lord, He is God" (18:39). Yet Queen Jezebel is unmoved and issues a warrant for his arrest. Elijah, forced to flee and hide, suffers a breakdown and prays to die (19:1–5).

against the way Moses had put down the rebellion: "You have killed the Lord's people" (Num. 17:6).

A crowd gathered around Moses and Aaron as if to attack them. God then began smiting the people with a plague. Moses told Aaron to make atonement, and eventually the plague stopped. But 14,700 people had died. Not until a quite different demonstration took place – Moses taking twelve rods representing the twelve tribes, and Aaron's budding and blossoming and bearing fruit – did the rebellion finally end.

How are we to understand Moses' behaviour? It is possible that he thought a dramatic event like the ground opening up would re-establish order, much as smashing the tablets did after the sin of the Golden Calf. Maimonides rules that, though it is forbidden ever to get angry, it is sometimes permitted to *look as if* you are angry in order restore discipline.[6]

It may be that he felt compelled to demonstrate his innocence of the charges made against him. There is a rule – derived by the sages from Hannah, Samuel's mother – that one suspected of a wrong he or she has not committed must clear his or her name.[7] Moses had been accused of doing certain things – appointing his brother high priest, sending the spies, even making up laws he had pronounced in the name of God. He himself said, "By this you shall know that it was the Lord who sent me to do all these things, *that they were not of my own devising.*" So one can find justifications for what he did. Yet it is hard to avoid the conclusion that challenging God to make the earth swallow his opponents was a mistake. It failed to restore order. It made him look authoritarian. It focused attention on the dispute rather than refocusing on God, the future, and the mission.

It looks, in fact, very much as if Moses was taking the attack on his leadership personally. It is hard to do otherwise, especially as it was meant personally. But to respond to an ad hominem attack in this way is always a mistake. It means that you have allowed your opponents to

---

6. Maimonides, *Mishneh Torah, Hilkhot Deot* 2:3.
7. Berakhot 31b. Eli the priest, seeing Hannah praying silently, thought she was drunk. She told him she was a woman of "sorrowful spirit" who had been "pouring out her soul" in prayer to God (I Sam. 1).

frame the terms of the dispute. The Harvard leadership scholar, Ronald Heifetz, argues that a leader must always distinguish between *role* and *self*. A role is a position we hold. The self is who we are. Leadership is a role. It is not an identity. Therefore *a leader should never take an attack on his or her leadership personally*:

> You want to respond when you are attacked…. You want to leap into the fray when you are mischaracterized…. When people attack you personally, the reflexive reaction is to take it personally…. But being criticized by people you care about is almost always a part of exercising leadership…. When you take personal attacks personally, you unwittingly conspire in one of the common ways you can be taken out of action – you make yourself the issue.[8]

Moses was not the issue. The issues were real and substantive. There were the repercussions of the sin of the Golden Calf. There was the crushing sense of loss after the episode of the spies. At such moments, a leader will be attacked. He will be blamed personally. He will bear the brunt of people's anger. It then becomes exceptionally important to separate the issues from the personalities. Moses had surely taken the right course of action in proposing the test of the incense offering. That would have resolved the question of the priesthood. As for the resentments of the rebels, there was nothing Moses could do.

Moses' subsequent behaviour, however, prolonged and intensified the conflict. It is hard not to see this as the first sign of the failing that would eventually cost Moses his chance to lead the people into the land. When, almost forty years later, he said to the people who complained about the lack of water, "Listen, you rebels, shall *we* bring you water out of this rock?" (Num. 20:10), he showed the same tendency to personalise the issue. It never was about "we" – Moses and Aaron. It was about God.

The Torah is devastatingly honest about Moses, as it is about all its heroes. Humans are only human. Even the greatest make mistakes.

---

8. Ronald Heifetz and Marty Linsky, *Leadership on the Line* (Boston: Harvard Business Press, 2002), 130, 190–191.

In the case of Moses, his supreme strength was also his weakness. His anger at injustice singled him out as a leader in the first place. But he allowed himself to be provoked to anger by the people he led, and it was this, according to Maimonides,[9] that eventually caused him to forfeit his chance of entering the land of Israel.

Heifetz writes: "Receiving anger … is a sacred task…. Taking the heat with grace communicates respect for the pains of change."[10] After the episode of the spies, Moses faced an almost impossible task. How do you lead a people when they know they will not reach their destination in their lifetime?

In the end, what stilled the rebellion was the sight of Aaron's rod, a piece of dry wood coming to life again, bearing flowers and fruit. Perhaps this was not just about Aaron but about the Israelites themselves. Having thought of themselves as condemned to die in the desert, they now realised that they too had borne fruit – their children – and they would complete the journey their parents had begun. That, in the end, was their consolation.

Of all the challenges of leadership, not taking criticism personally and staying calm when the people you lead are angry with you may be the hardest of all. That may be why the Torah says what it does about Moses, the greatest leader who ever lived. It is a warning for future generations. If at times you are pained by people's anger, take comfort. So was Moses. But remember the price Moses paid, and stay calm.

Though it may seem otherwise, the anger you face has nothing to do with you as a person and everything to do with what you stand for and represent. Depersonalising attacks is the best way to deal with them. People get angry when leaders cannot magically make harsh reality disappear. Leaders in such circumstances are called on to accept that anger with grace. That truly is a sacred task.

---

9. Maimonides, *Shemoneh Perakim*, ch. 4.
10. *Leadership on the Line*, 142, 146.

Power and Influence

In this essay, we explore one aspect of the Korah rebellion, namely the seeming inconsistency between Moses' reaction here and in the episode, just a few chapters earlier, of Eldad and Medad. Moses, on that occasion, had reached the lowest point in his own emotional struggle with the burdens of leadership. The people had complained about the food. Moses was devastated that they had not matured after the transformative experiences, first of the revelation of God at Mount Sinai, then of the construction of the Tabernacle and the knowledge that the Divine Presence was visibly in their midst. So low were his spirits that he prayed to God to allow him to die rather than carry on (Num. 11:4–15).

God told him to choose seventy elders to share with him the burden of leadership. Evidently Moses had chosen six from each tribe, making seventy-two. Lots were cast as to which two should be left out, and they fell on Eldad and Medad, who remained in the camp while Moses and the seventy went to the Tent. When God caused Moses' spirit to rest on them, it rested also on Eldad and Medad, who started prophesying. We then read:

The youth ran and told Moses, "Eldad and Medad are prophesying in the camp." Joshua son of Nun, who had been Moses' servant since his youth, spoke up and said, "Moses, my lord, stop them!" But Moses replied, "Are you jealous for my sake? Would that all the Lord's people were prophets and that the Lord would put His spirit on them!" (Num. 11:27–29).

There is something magnificently generous about this response. Moses, anguished just a little while earlier, is now calm and untroubled. He does not see any threat whatsoever. To the contrary, he expresses the wish that everyone could wear the mantle of prophecy and experience God's spirit as he did. And that is the end of the episode.

His response to the challenge represented by Korah, Datan and Aviram, and the 250 "princes of the congregation," was quite different. First – as the prophet Elijah was later to do with the prophets of Baal at Mount Carmel – he proposed a test. Let all those who challenged him and Aaron offer incense and see whose offering is accepted. This was immediately confrontational.

Then, as we saw in the previous essay, he went further. He asked God not to accept any offering from Datan and Aviram, the most objectionable of the rebels. Then he invoked a miracle to prove the authenticity of his mission:

> If these men die a natural death and suffer the fate of all mankind, then the Lord has not sent me. But if the Lord brings about something totally new, and the earth opens its mouth and swallows them, with everything that belongs to them, and they go down alive into the grave, then you will know that these men have treated the Lord with contempt. (Num. 16:29-30)

In effect, Moses used his power to eliminate the opposition.

What was the difference between Eldad and Medad on the one hand and Korah and his co-conspirators on the other? Why was Moses prepared to say, "Would that all the Lord's people were prophets," while rejecting Korah's claim that "all the congregation are holy and the Lord is with them"? Why was the first, but not the second, a legitimate sentiment? Was Moses simply being inconsistent? Hardly. There is a distinction to be made between the two episodes that made the latter but not the former a challenge that Moses had to take seriously and stop in its tracks. What is it?

The sages, in one of their profound methodological observations, said that "The words of the Torah may be poor in one place but rich in another."[1] By this they meant that if we seek to understand a perplexing passage, we may need to look elsewhere in the Torah for the clue. A similar idea is expressed in the last of R. Ishmael's thirteen rules of biblical interpretation: "Where there are two passages which contradict each other, the meaning can be determined only when a third passage is found which reconciles them."[2]

In this case, the answer is to be found later in the book of Numbers, when Moses asked God to choose the next leader of the Israelites. God told him to take Joshua and appoint him as his successor:

> So the Lord said to Moses, "Take for yourself Joshua, son of Nun, a man of spirit, and lay your hand [*vesamakhta et yadekha*] on him. Make him stand before Eleazar the priest and the entire assembly and you shall command him in their presence. Give him some of your splendour [*venatatekha mehodekha*] so that the whole Israelite community will obey him." (Num. 27:18–20)

Moses was commanded to perform two acts over and above presenting Joshua to the priest and people. First he was to "lay his hand" on Joshua. Then he was to give him "some of [his] splendour." What is the significance of these two gestures? How did they differ from one another? Which of them constituted induction into office? The sages, in Midrash Rabba, added a commentary which at first sight only deepens the mystery: "'Lay your hand on him' – this is like lighting one light from another. 'Give him some of your splendour' – this is like pouring

---

1. Y. Rosh HaShana 3:5. See also Rabbi Meir Simha HaKohen of Dvinsk, *Meshekh Hokhma* to Deut. 12:13; 29:24.
2. The *baraita* of R. Ishmael is part of the introduction to Sifra, the halakhic Midrash to the book of Leviticus. It is included in the daily morning prayers.

from one vessel to another."[3] It is this statement that will enable us to decode the mystery.

There are two forms or dimensions of leadership. One is *power*, the other, *influence*. Often we assume the two are intimately related. After all, those who have power often have influence, and those who have influence have a certain kind of power. In fact, however, the two operate by quite different logics.

We can see this by a simple thought experiment. Imagine you have total power, and then you decide to share it with nine others. You now have one-tenth of the power with which you began. Imagine, by contrast, that you have a certain measure of influence, and now you share it with nine others. How much do you have left? Not less. In fact, more. Initially there was only one of you; now there are ten. Your influence has spread. Power operates by division, influence by multiplication. *With power, the more we share, the less we have. With influence, the more we share, the more we have.*

So deep is the difference that the Torah allocates them to two distinct leadership roles: *king* and *prophet*. Kings had power. They could levy taxes, conscript people to serve in the army, and decide when and against whom to wage war. They could impose non-judicial punishments to preserve social order. Hobbes famously called kingship a "Leviathan" and defined it in terms of power. The very nature of the social contract, he argued, was the transfer of power from individuals to a central authority. Without this, there could be no government, no defence of a country, and no safeguard against lawlessness and anarchy.

Prophets, by contrast, had no power at all. They commanded no armies. They levied no taxes. They spoke God's word, but had no means of enforcing it. All they had was influence – but what influence! To this day, Elijah's fight against corruption, Amos' call to social justice, Isaiah's vision of the End of Days are still capable of moving us by the sheer force of their inspiration. Who, today, is swayed by the lives of Ahab or Jehoshaphat or Jehu? When a king dies, his power ends. When a prophet dies, his influence begins.

---

3. Numbers Rabba 21:15.

Moses occupied two leadership roles, not one. On the one hand, though monarchy was not yet in existence, he had the power and was the functional equivalent of a king.[4] He led the Israelites out of Egypt, commanded them in battle, appointed leaders, judges, and elders, and directed the conduct of the people. He had power.

But Moses was also a prophet, the greatest and most authoritative of all. He was supremely a man of vision. He heard and spoke the word of God. As God Himself said of him: "When there is a prophet among you, I, the Lord, reveal Myself to him in visions, I speak to him in dreams. Not so My servant Moses; he is faithful in all My house. With him I speak face to face, clearly and not in dark speeches" (Num. 12:6–8). The epitaph the Torah gives him is: "No other prophet has risen in Israel like Moses, whom the Lord knew face-to-face" (Deut. 34:10).

The mystery of Moses' double investiture of Joshua is now solved. First, he was told to give Joshua his authority as a *prophet*. The very phrase used by the Torah – *vesamakhta et yadekha*, "lay your hand" on him – is still used today to describe rabbinic ordination, *semikha*, meaning, the "laying on of hands" by master to disciple. Second, he was commanded to give Joshua the power of kingship, which the Torah calls "splendour" (perhaps "majesty" would be a better translation). The nature of this role as head of state and commander of the army is made quite clear in the text. God says to Moses: "Give him some of your splendour so that the whole Israelite community will obey him.... At his command, he and the entire community of the Israelites will go out [to battle], and at his command they will come in" (Num. 27:18–21). This is the language not of influence but of power.

The meaning of the midrash, too, is now clear and elegantly precise. The transfer of influence ("Lay your hand on him") is "like lighting one light from another." When we take a candle to light another candle, the light of the first is not diminished. Likewise, when we share our influence with others, we do not have less than before. Instead, the sum total of light is increased. Power, however, is different. It is like

---

4. Maimonides, *Mishneh Torah, Hilkhot Beit HaBeḥira* 6:11 rules that Moses had the halakhic status of a king. The rule that one who rebels against the king forfeits his life is derived from the case of Joshua; see Josh. 1:18, Sanhedrin 49a.

"pouring from one vessel to another." The more we pour into the second, the less is left in the first. Power is a zero-sum game. The more we give away, the less we have.

This, then, is the solution to the mystery of why, when Joshua feared that Eldad and Medad (who "prophesied within the camp") were threatening Moses' authority, Moses replied, "Would that all the Lord's people were prophets." Joshua had confused influence with power. Eldad and Medad neither sought nor gained power. Instead, for a while, they were given a share of the prophetic "spirit" that was on Moses. They participated in his influence. That is never a threat to prophetic authority. To the contrary, the more widely it is shared, the more there is.

Power, however, is precisely what Korah and his followers sought – and in the case of power, rivalry *is* a threat to authority. "There is one leader for a generation," said the sages, "not two" (Sanhedrin 8a). Or, as they put it elsewhere, "Can two kings share a single crown?" (Ḥullin 60b). There are many forms of government – monarchy, oligarchy, and democracy – but what they have in common is the concentration of power within a single body, whether person, group, or institution (such as a parliament). Without this monopoly of the legitimate use of coercive force, there is no such thing as government. That is why in Jewish law "a king is not allowed to renounce the honour due to him" (Kiddushin 32b).

Moses' request that Korah and his followers be swallowed up by the ground was, from this perspective, neither anger nor fear. It was based on the simple realisation that whereas prophecy can be shared, kingship cannot. If there are two or more competing sources of power within a single domain, there is no leadership. Had Moses not taken decisive action against Korah, he would have fatally compromised the office with which he had been charged.

Rarely do we see more clearly the stark difference between influence and power than in these two episodes: Eldad and Medad on the one hand, Korah and his fellow rebels on the other. The latter represented a conflict that had to be resolved. Either Moses or Korah would emerge the victor; they could not both win. The former did not represent a conflict at all. Knowledge, inspiration, vision – these are things that can be shared without loss. Those who share them with others add to the spiritual wealth of a community without losing anything of their own. Hence the wonderful prophecy of Joel that at the End of Days, "I will pour out My spirit on all people. Your sons and daughters will prophesy, your old men will dream dreams, your young men will see visions" (Joel 2:28). Moses' wish that "all the Lord's people will be prophets"[5] will be realised.

To paraphrase Shakespeare, the influence we have lives after us; the power is oft interred with our bones. Much of Judaism is an extended essay on the supremacy of prophets over kings, right over might, instruction over coercion, influence over power. For only a small fraction of our history have Jews had power, but at all times they have had an influence over the civilisation of the West.

People still contend for power. Perhaps they always will. That is the essence of politics. The Torah does not negate the significance of power. Without it, Jews as a nation would lack sovereignty, and thus the ability to carry out the central program of the Torah, namely the construction of a society on the principles of law, justice, righteousness, and compassion. But if only humanity were to realise how narrow are the limits of power if we genuinely believe in freedom. It is one thing to force people to behave in a certain way; it is quite another to teach them to see the world differently so that, of their own accord, they act in that way. The use of power diminishes others; the exercise of influence enlarges them. That is one of Judaism's most humanising truths. Not all of us have power, but we are all capable of being an influence for good.

5.   See also Maimonides, *Mishneh Torah, Hilkhot Melakhim* 12:5.

The Egalitarian Impulse in Judaism

Was Korah right or wrong when he said, "All the congregation are holy and the Lord is in their midst" (Num. 16:3)? He may have been insincere, disingenuous, and manipulative. But was he speaking the truth? That is a not unimportant question. To what extent is Judaism egalitarian?

Even to ask the question is, in some circles, to risk ridicule. Did Judaism not have its hierarchies? There were Levites and priests and a high priest. There were kings and royal courts. These were not open to everyone. Specifically, they were not open to women. And they were dynastic. They were prerogatives of birth. The priesthood was limited to male descendants of Aaron. The kings, at least in principle, were descendants of David.[1] At least one of these hierarchies, that of the Levites and the priesthood, had already been instituted before the Korah rebellion. Indeed that was one of the events that provoked the rebellion.

---

1. This rule was systematically broken twice, first when the northern ten tribes seceded after the death of King Solomon, second when kingship was resumed after the victory of the Maccabees against the Seleucids. The Hasmonean kings were not descendants of David.

So it seems clear that he was wrong. Yet Moses never challenged that particular statement. So – was he wrong, and if so, how?

Nahmanides suggests that Korah was not arguing for egalitarianism in the modern sense of the word. Rather, he was protesting the transfer of priestly and Levitical duties to the tribe of Levi after the sin of the Golden Calf.[2] Until then, that role had gone to the firstborn males in each family and tribe, in memory of the time when God "passed over" the houses of the Israelites during the tenth plague, the killing of the firstborn. Korah was saying not that everyone was equally holy, but rather that the original plan – in which the firstborn were consecrated as holy – was fairer than the system that replaced it. At least that had been a structure in which each family and tribe could feel equal. They were all represented in the service of the Sanctuary. Now all that had gone to just one tribe. That, Korah argued, was incompatible with the spirit of Judaism. Had God not commanded, "Speak to *the whole congregation of Israel* and say to them: Be holy because I, the Lord your God, am holy" (Lev. 19:1–2)? That is democratised holiness, distributed throughout the people, the holiness that allows each family and tribe to feel equidistant from God. In transferring priestly functions to a single tribe, Moses was in danger of creating a dynastic elite set apart from the rest of the population.

Yeshayahu Leibowitz argued for a different interpretation.[3] Korah said, "All the congregation *are* holy." He was basing himself on Moses' own words in the command of tzitzit: "You will thus remember and keep all My commandments and *be* holy to your God" (Num. 15:40). But there is a difference, said Leibowitz, between "*are* holy" and "*be* holy." One is a statement of fact, the other is a command. Think of a class of children whose teacher has told all of them, "Be good." It would not follow that all of them *are* good. They are all commanded, but not everyone obeys. Korah was making an elementary mistake in confusing a fact and a command.

2. See Num. 3:9–45; 8:13–20.
3. Y. Leibowitz, *Notes to the Weekly Torah Readings* [Hebrew] (Jerusalem: Akademon, 1988), 96–98.

There is a third possibility, that the mistake Korah made was in saying "all the congregation *are* holy [*kulam kedoshim*]" instead of "all the congregation *is* holy [*kulah kedosha*]." In Judaism, holiness is collective, not individual. A *davar shebikedusha*, a holy act, like saying the *Kedusha* in the reader's repetition of the *Amida*, requires a quorum of ten adult males, the minimum halakhic definition of a community. In fact, this very rule was derived by the sages from the episode of the spies, ten of whom brought a negative report of the land – the event that, according to Nahmanides, led to the Korah rebellion. In this view Korah made the mistake of thinking that what applies to a community as a whole applies to each of its members – which clearly is not the case. The community is holy but that does not mean that everyone within it has the same level of holiness.

On each of these interpretations Korah was wrong. But in an earlier essay, "A Cloak Entirely Blue," I argued that in fact Korah was right. His mistake lay not in saying that all the congregation were holy. His mistakes lay in his assertions – first, that a group of people of equal dignity do not need a leader; second, that leaders "set themselves above" those they lead; third, that there was no need to change the structures of holiness after the sin of the Golden Calf. But his opening sentence articulated an important and fundamental truth.

Judaism was the world's first attempt to create a society of equal dignity under the sovereignty of God. It was the inspiration behind the statement in the American Declaration of Independence that "we hold these truths to be self-evident, that all men are created equal [and] that they are endowed by their Creator with certain unalienable rights." Far from being self-evident, this statement would have been regarded as absurd by the ancient Greeks. Plato believed that that society was divided into three classes – rulers, soldiers, and the masses – who were as different as gold, silver, and brass.[4] Aristotle believed that some people are born to be free, others to be slaves.

To be sure, Korah's egalitarianism was not the twenty-first-century variety. We should not be anachronistic in attributing to people in the

---

4. Plato, *The Republic*, 415a.

past concepts that did not exist in the past.[5] But he was right in thinking that a profound impulse towards egalitarianism exists at the heart
of Judaism.

This has three sources. The first and most famous is the statement
in the first chapter of the Torah that God created human beings in His
image and likeness. The sages of the Mishna were unequivocal in their
understanding of this idea:

> It was for this reason that man was created singly, to teach you
> that anyone who destroys a life is considered by Scripture to have
> destroyed an entire world, and anyone who saves a life is as if he
> saved an entire world. And also, to promote peace among the
> creations, that no man would say to his friend, "My ancestors
> are greater than yours." And also, so that heretics will not say,
> "There are many rulers up in heaven." And also, to express the
> grandeur of the Holy One, Blessed Be He: For a man strikes
> many coins from the same die, and all the coins are alike. But
> the supreme King of kings, the Holy One, Blessed Be He, strikes
> every man from the die of the first man, and yet no man is quite
> like his friend. Therefore, every person must say, "For my sake
> the world was created." (Mishna Sanhedrin 4:5)

This is a remarkable theological statement. It tells us, first, that we are
each of infinite value: "an entire world." Second, we each have the same
ancestry; we are all children of Adam and Eve. No one is entitled to say,
"My ancestors are greater than yours." Third, difference does not make
a difference. Even someone not in my image – whose colour, culture,
caste, or class are unlike mine – is still in God's image. *This, rather than
any secular philosophy, is the basis for the ideas of equality, liberty, and
justice in the West.*[6]

---

5. That is one reason why the Torah does not attempt to abolish slavery despite the
   fact that it surely believes slavery to be inconsistent with human dignity. See on this
   Rabbi N. L. Rabinovitch, *Pathways in Their Hearts* [Hebrew] (Jerusalem: Maaliyot,
   2015), 38–45.
6. See Nicholas Wolterstorff, *Justice: Rights and Wrongs* (Princeton: Princeton University Press, 2008); Jeremy Waldron, *God, Locke, and Equality* (New York: Cambridge

Then there was the covenant at Sinai. The concept of covenant was well known in the ancient Near East. Many such treaties have been preserved. Two things were unique to the covenant at Mount Sinai. The first was that God was one of the partners. The idea that a god, let alone *the* God, might bind Himself with a moral bond to a people was unknown, almost inconceivable. The second was that the other partners were the people as a whole. All other ancient covenants were between rulers: emperors, pharaohs, heads of state. Time and again the Torah emphasises that the entire people, collectively and individually, gave their assent.[7] Equally the sages went out of their way to suggest that God offered the covenant to the women before the men.[8] Here, according to tradition, women were enfranchised in the most significant decision in Jewish history. When it came to the revelation itself, all the people heard the voice of God. At that moment, Moses had no privileged position. They were all equally recipients of revelation; equally voices in the collective assent; and equally bound by the covenant and its collective responsibility.

The third factor behind the Korah rebellion, I suggest, is the point made by Victor Turner about liminal space – in this case, the wilderness. As we noted earlier, he argued that in liminal space, no-man's-land, there is *community* rather than *society*. The normal structures of hierarchy do not apply. There is intense bonding. Leadership is respected but only so long as people feel that the leader has their interests at heart, that he knows what he is doing, and that he is minimising the risks to the group. So the fact that in the middle of the journey, the holy task of ministering to God was taken from the firstborn of each tribe and handed over to a single tribe was bound to be more inflammatory than had that decision been made before setting out or at a later stage after the conquest of the land.

Korah, in other words, had fundamental principles – humans as the image of God, the entire people as partners to the covenant, and

University Press, 2002); Nick Spencer, *Freedom and Order: History, Politics and the English Bible* (London: Hodder and Stoughton, 2011).

7. Ex. 19:8; 24:3, 7.
8. *Mekhilta, Parashat Yitro, BaḤodesh* 2 and Exodus Rabba, *Parashat Yitro*, 28:2.

priestly functions distributed throughout all the tribes – on his side, as well as time and place. He was right to suggest that there is a basic egalitarianism at the foundations of Judaism.[9] His mistakes lay elsewhere.[10]

Stepping back from the Korah revolt and looking at Tanakh and Jewish history as a whole, we see that *hierarchy was introduced into Judaism only in response to crisis*. The restriction of priesthood to the sons of Aaron, and of secondary holiness to the Levites, only happened according to the Torah because of the sin of the Golden Calf. Had that not happened, sacred duties would have stayed the prerogative of the firstborn of all the tribes. Monarchy was only introduced after the breakdown of law and order in the last days of the judges.[11] Despite the fact that the Torah contains a command to appoint a king, still God said that in seeking a king the people were "rejecting" Him (I Sam. 8:7). It can be argued that neither monarchy nor the special status of the tribe of Levi and the family of Aaron were part of the original plan.[12] They were responses to human weakness and failure.

Only thus can we understand the direction taken by Judaism in the long period between the return of Ezra and the destruction of the Second Temple. What emerged was, by historical standards, an extraordinarily egalitarian structure, based not on kings and priests but on Torah study and the dignity of *Knesset Yisrael*, the congregation of Israel as a whole. In place of sacrifices offered by priests came prayer offered by everyone. In place of rule by kings came governance by "the townsfolk" or "the notables" (*tuvei ha'ir*) – not quite representative democracy but a move in that direction nonetheless.

---

9. See Joshua Berman, *Created Equal* (New York: Oxford University Press, 2008). This was taken for granted by many of the Christian revolutionaries in the Middle Ages. Famously, John Ball, leader of the Peasants' Revolt (1381) said, "When Adam delved and Eve span, who was then the gentleman?" The concept of a "priesthood of all believers" was one of the fundamental elements of the Protestant revolt against the Catholic Church.
10. As noted above.
11. See I Sam. 8.
12. On monarchy, see in particular Rabbenu Baḥya and Abrabanel to Deut. 17:15. Of course, not everyone agreed. According to Maimonides, monarchy was part of the divine plan from the outset.

Above all, though, came the belief that status was conferred by scholarship, Torah study. On this, the rabbis' remarks were forceful and unambiguous:

> With three crowns was Israel crowned.... The crown of priest-hood was bestowed on Aaron and his descendants. The crown of kingship was conferred on David and his successors. But the crown of Torah is for all Israel. Whoever wishes, let him come and take it.... A Torah scholar of illegitimate birth takes prec-edence over an ignorant high priest.[13]

Alongside statements like these went the creation of the world's first system of community-funded, universal education (Bava Batra 21a).

Significantly, the rabbis traced their descent not from kings or priests – the two dynastic roles in Judaism – but to the prophets: "Moses received the Torah from Sinai and handed it on to Joshua, who handed it on to the elders, the elders to the prophets, and the prophets to the men of the Great Assembly" (Mishna Avot 1:1). Prophecy was not a dynasty. It was available to anyone of the right character, dedication, and spiritu-ality. The rabbis also understood that since knowledge is power, and the distribution of power is the central concern of politics, the distribution of knowledge is the single greatest issue affecting the structure of soci-ety. It was not on the streets or behind the barricades but in the house of study that the rabbis achieved the revolutionary ideal of a society of equal dignity under the sovereignty of God.

Korah and his fellow rebels were wrong in their attempt to seize power, wrong in their challenge to Moses and Aaron, and wrong in their failure to understand the task of leadership in the wilderness years. They were not good men. But in one respect they were right. All the congre-gation were holy and the Lord was in their midst. It took more than a thousand years, and several tragedies, before this could become a live-able ideal. But it remains the greatest-ever vision of a society under the sovereignty of God.

---

13. Maimonides, *Mishneh Torah, Hilkhot Talmud Torah* 3:1–2.

Ḥukkat

חוקת

Ḥukkat begins with the law of the red heifer, judged by the sages to be the most incomprehensible in the Torah. It became a classic example of a ḥok, a "statute," often understood as a law that has no reason, or at least none we can understand.

The text then shifts from law to narrative. After the death of Miriam the people find themselves without water. They complain to Moses and Aaron, who turn to God. They then respond to the people in a way that seems to suggest anger. They are judged to have acted wrongly, and both are told they will not enter the land. Aaron dies.

The people complain again and are attacked by venomous snakes. Moses, at God's command, places a brass serpent on a pole, so that all who look up to it will be healed. The people sing a song about a miraculous well that gave them water. Moses then leads the people into successful battles against Sihon and Og.

In the essays in this section, the first looks at one of the recurring themes in Numbers, the close connection between law and ritual, in this case between the law of the red heifer and the story that follows, about Miriam, Aaron, and Moses. The second examines the approach of one of the early masters of rabbinic Judaism, Yoḥanan b. Zakkai, to the red heifer. The third offers a new approach to "statutes" in terms of contemporary neuroscience. The fourth looks at the famous episode in which Moses struck the rock, for which he was sentenced not to enter the land. Was this a punishment, or something else? The fifth looks at an alternative way of understanding the episode. The sixth examines a strange rabbinic interpretation of a fragment of a song that appears towards the end of the parasha, about "the book of the Wars of the Lord."

Statute and Story

The rabbis found the law of the red heifer with which *Parashat Ḥukkat* opens hard to understand. Without going into detail, they found it odd that a ritual that purified the impure also made the pure impure.[1] It seemed to cleanse and defile at the same time. It was, they said, a law that even King Solomon, wisest of men, found unfathomable.[2] Rabban Yoḥanan b. Zakkai, one of the deepest of rabbinic thinkers, had to make up a fanciful story about it to ward off the ridicule it evoked in his Roman contemporaries.[3] I hope that after this and the following two essays it will seem less obscure. But what is really odd is: What is the law doing *here*?

Surely this law belongs elsewhere. It is about a ritual of purification for one who had come into contact with the dead and now sought to enter the precincts of the Sanctuary. Its place should be in the book of

---

1. *Midrash Lekaḥ Tov*, 119b.
2. *Pitron Torah, Ḥukkat*, 174, which interprets Eccl. 7:23, "All this have I tested by wisdom: I said, 'I will be wise,' but it was far from me," as relating to Solomon's inability to understand the law of the red heifer.
3. See the next essay.

Leviticus, which deals with purification rituals. It does not obviously belong in the book of Numbers, which deals with the second half of the Israelites' journey through the wilderness. We have just read about a serious revolt against Moses' leadership. We are about to read a story in which Moses and Aaron are rebuked by God for failing to believe in Him. These are stories of high drama. Why are they interrupted by a law about purification by sprinkling a mixture of the ashes of a heifer, hyssop, cedar wood, scarlet thread, and water? What has this to do with Moses, his anger and anguish? This is not a minor matter but a major one because it touches on the compositional logic of the Torah as a whole. Why is it written this way?

The Torah is a unique book, written in a strange, seemingly disjointed way. There is nothing like it anywhere else in the Hebrew Bible. There is nothing quite like it in the religious literature of humankind. What is odd is the way it mixes genres. It contains all sorts of texts. Numbers alone includes two censuses, lists of names, a heterogeneous collection of laws, battle accounts, legal disputes, travel itineraries, oracles from a non-Jewish prophet, fragments of songs, and much else, in no apparent order. Above all, it mixes law and narrative.

Law and narrative are two different things that do not naturally belong together. The ancient world had law codes: those, for example, of Urukagina, Ur-Nammu, Eshnunna, and Hammurabi, dating from the time of Abraham or before. It also had its stories and myths, tales of the fights between the gods and human beings – some of them not unlike the stories of Genesis, most notably the Flood. But these were two different literatures that did not overlap – not then, and not now. You would not expect to find a history of the United States in a book about American law, or a complete guide to English legislation in a book of British history. Once in a while, on campus, there might be an interdisciplinary seminar between members of the law and history faculties, but that would only serve to highlight the differences between the disciplines.

This, sadly, has led many generations of Bible scholars to the conclusion that what we have in the Torah is a composite work, a palimpsest or patchwork quilt of different documents, and the best way to understand it is to disaggregate the fragments, reading each one separately, so that they can be seen to be the work of different schools with different agendas, in different places at different times. This, I believe, is a monumental failure of understanding, a "map of misreading."[4] The Mosaic books constitute a tightly organised and integrated text weaving together multiple voices and perspectives into a unity that is the literary correlate of the unity of God in His relationship to the diversity of humankind and the frequent disunity of His adopted children, the Israelites.

What does it mean to call the Five Books of Moses, with all their internal variety, *Torah*? The word itself means "law," but it also means "teaching," "instruction," "guidance." The verb *y-r-h* from which it derives also means "to shoot an arrow," "to aim at a target." Clearly, we have here a concept larger than "law" in a narrow, legalistic sense, for which the Mosaic books have other words, among them *ḥok, mishpat, edut, din,* and *mitzva. Torah* does sometimes have a narrow meaning, roughly, "the procedure to be followed in such-and-such a case." But in its more general sense, it seems to mean guidance as it emerges not only from laws but also from history. *"Torah" in this broad sense is about the counterpoint, the creative tension, between law and life, between the world as it ought to be and the world as it is.*

Torah tells us that law is not merely a set of rules whose only logic is that they are the will of God. Judaism is not a matter of blind obedience. Astonishingly, despite the fact that the Torah is full of commands – 613 of them, according to tradition – there is no word in biblical Hebrew that means "to obey."[5] Law, in Judaism, is rooted in history and cosmology. It reflects something other and larger than the law itself. Many of the laws have as their explanation some such phrase as "because you were slaves in Egypt," as if to say: You know what it feels like to suffer injustice or oppression. Therefore do not inflict these things on others.

4. The phrase is borrowed from Harold Bloom, *A Map of Misreading* (New York: Oxford University Press, 2003). This, together with his *The Anxiety of Influence* (New York: Oxford University Press, 1973), argues that misreading a text is not accidental. It has deep psychological roots. That is certainly the case for Western readings of the Hebrew Bible, especially from the Enlightenment onward.
5. The word used by the Torah is *shema*, which means many other things as well as "to obey."

The central law of the Noahide covenant, "He who sheds the blood of man, by man shall his blood be shed" (Gen. 9:6), emerged directly from the violence that led to the Flood, making God regret that He had created man in the first place. Law is a way of putting right what we know, from our or our ancestors' experience, to have been wrong. *Judaism exists in the cognitive dissonance between the order God creates and the chaos we create. Law is the path that leads us back from chaos to order, from discord to harmony, from death to life.*

That is why the Torah is constructed as a counterpoint between law and narrative, between statute and story. God wants us to understand not only *what* to do, but *why*. He wants us not merely to obey but also to reflect on and internalise the lessons of history, the experiences of our ancestors, the story of our people that tells us where we came from and what we learned on the way.

Rarely is this set out more subtly and powerfully than in the *parasha* of Ḥukkat. Something extraordinary happens between the previous *parasha* and this one. It is not stated explicitly in the text and it takes us a while to realise that it has happened. *Almost forty years have passed.* In chapter 18 we read the final stages of the Korah revolt, in the second year of the journey, and now suddenly we are near the end. There is nothing in the text to signal the leap in time, but the characters have aged. Almost an entire generation has died.

Until this point we have had a reasonable grasp of time. In the book of Exodus, epic events succeed one another at a breathless pace: oppression, slavery, plagues, escape, the sound of Pharaoh's chariots in the distance, the division of the sea, the journey into the wilderness, and the divine voice at Sinai. Then time slows almost to a stop. From the end of Exodus to the ninth chapter of Numbers, no time passes at all. Then the journey begins again, but as soon as it does so, it threatens to fall apart in a welter of complaints, despair, and the simmering resentments that surface in the Korah revolt.

Then without warning, the story leaps forwards thirty-eight years. We are now nearing the end not only of the journey but of the generation of those who left Egypt. They proved unequal to the challenge of fighting battles and building a society in the Promised Land. This is, by any standards, a devastating moment. For almost four decades the people who left Egypt have lived with the knowledge that they would not reach their destination. They would die before they set foot in the land flowing with milk and honey.

The first sign we have of the passage of time is so simple that we almost miss it. Miriam dies (Num. 20:1). She was the one who set the story of the Exodus in motion as she watched over baby Moses floating in a basket down the Nile. Just as she was there at the beginning of the beginning, so her death marks the beginning of the end of the story of that generation.

The Torah then adds a detail. Suddenly there was no water (Num. 20:2). This simple fact – one we have come across before[6] but not one that provoked any major crisis – will in the end prove to be the beginning of the end for Aaron and Moses also. Uncharacteristically, they lose their temper with the people – "Listen, you rebels" (Num. 20:10). For this they are condemned not to enter the Promised Land. Aaron dies, and the people mourn. Moses too knows that his days are numbered. He will not live to cross the Jordan. He will die in sight of the land but without setting foot on it.

Parashat Ḥukkat is thus about mortality. It is about the death of an entire generation, symbolised in the fate of its three leaders. It is about the discovery of a painful truth, most famously expressed by R. Tarfon in the Mishna: *It is not for you to complete the task, but neither are you free to desist from it* (Mishna Avot 2:16). The great challenges of humanity are too large to be completed in a single generation. The kind of leadership needed to lead a people out of slavery is not the same as that needed to lead them across the Jordan into the responsibilities of freedom. It takes a long time for people to change. We rarely live to see the full consequences of the changes we have lived through. That is the human condition, and this *parasha* tells us that even Moses, Aaron, and Miriam, for all their greatness, were also only human. But this can be a bitter truth. Ecclesiastes is an entire book driven by the fear that our lives are no more than *hevel*, a "fleeting breath."[7]

---

6. Ex. 15:22; 17:1.
7. I have written about this at length in my introduction to the *Koren Sukkot Maḥzor* (Jerusalem: Koren, 2015).

That is why the narrative of *Parashat Ḥukkat*, which speaks about the death of the leaders of the wilderness generation, is preceded by the law of the red heifer, whose entire purpose is to purify those who have come into contact with death. The whole passage exemplifies one of the axioms of Judaism that "God provides the cure before the disease" (Megilla 13b).

The symbolism of the red heifer is simple. The red heifer itself represents life in its most primal form. Firstly it is an animal – and an animal lives without consciousness of death. Secondly it is red, symbolising blood, which for the Torah represents life itself. Thirdly it is an animal "on which a yoke has not yet come" (Num. 19:2). Its life has never been constrained by being domesticated, used. This is life at its most vigorous and elemental.

The heifer is killed and burned and reduced to ash in the most dramatic possible enactment of death. The ashes are then mixed with those of burnt cedar wood, hyssop, and crimson thread (part of the purification ritual of the *metzora* or "leper" as well; see Lev. 14 – evidently these three elements had a particular power, physical or symbolic, to absorb and thus remove impurity). They are then dissolved in "living water" to be sprinkled over the person who has been contaminated by contact with, or proximity to, a human corpse. The phrase "living water" is an explicit metaphor. Water is the source of all life, plant, animal, and human. In the desert, or more generally in the Middle East, you feel this with a peculiar vividness. Hence it became the symbol of God-who-is-life. Jeremiah says of his generation, "They have forsaken the Lord, the fountain of living water" (Jer. 17:13). We now understand the symbolic significance of the fact that when Miriam died, the flow of water to the Israelites ceased. As long as she was alive, there was water, i.e., life. Her death marked the beginning of the end of Moses' generation, and the sign of this was the drying up of the well that had served the people until then.

We die, but life goes on – that is the symbolic statement of the red heifer rite. All that lives eventually turns to dust and ash, but life continues to flow like a never-ending stream. Significantly, the Hebrew word for "inheritance," *naḥala*, is related to the word for a stream or spring, *naḥal*. Heraclitus said that no one bathes in the same river twice. The water that was once here is gone. It has flowed into the sea, evaporated into cloud, and fallen again as rain. But the stream continues to flow in the same course, between the same banks. There is death, yes, but there is also continuity. We are not always privileged to complete the task, but others will take it on and move a little closer to fulfilment. So long as there is a covenant between the dead, the living, and those not yet born, mortality is redeemed from tragedy. The dead live on in us, as we will live on in our children or in those whose lives we touch. As dust dissolves in living water, so death dissolves in the stream of life itself.

Far from being unintelligible, the law of the red heifer is a powerful statement about life and death, grief and consolation, the ephemeral and the eternal. And far from being disconnected with the narrative that follows, it is intimately related to it, and the two are commentaries on one another. Together they form a fugue. Before we are exposed to the death of Miriam and Aaron and the decree of death against Moses, the Torah provides us with a profound metaphysical comfort. They died, but what they lived for did not die. The water ceased, but after an interval, it returned. We are destined to mourn the death of those close to us, but eventually we reconnect with (the water of) life.

Law informs the narrative, and the narrative explains the law. We need both, just as we need the analytical left hemisphere and the integrating right hemisphere of the brain. We now also have a deeper understanding of the word that gives the *parasha* its name: *ḥok*, usually translated as "statute" or "decree." In actual fact, *ḥok* is a word that brings together two concepts of law. There are *scientific* laws, which explain the "isness" of the world, and there are *moral* laws, which prescribe the "oughtness" of the world.[8] The singular meaning of *ḥok* is that it brings both concepts together. There are laws we ought to keep because they honour the structure of reality.

The most significant feature of the structure of human reality is death. To be human is to be mortal. The law of the red heifer honours the fact of death. It does not try to deny it. Death is real; grief is inevitable; bereavement is the most painful of all human experiences. But God is life. God is to us as water is to the desert ("God, you are my God; I search

8. Jer. 31:34–35 speaks of "the laws [*ḥukkot*] of the moon and the stars," or what we would nowadays call laws of science.

for You, my soul thirsts for You, my body yearns for You, as a parched and thirsty land that has no water"; Ps. 63:2). The red heifer comforts us for the loss of Miriam, Aaron, and Moses, and for the existence of death itself. The touch of God, like the sprinkled drops of the waters of purification, heals our loss and brings us back to life.

Yoḥanan b. Zakkai and the Red Heifer

Parashat Ḥukkat opens with a concept that gives it its name: "This is the statute of [*ḥukkat*] the Torah" (Num. 19:2). The root *ḥ-k-k* means "engraved," as if on tablets of stone, and it carries the sense of "permanent," "indelible," "foundational." *Ḥukkim*, statutes, constitute a specific category of biblical law. Traditionally they refer to the commands that seem to have no obvious reason – either in terms of social justice (*mishpatim*) or historical memory (*edot*). They include such laws as the prohibition against eating meat and milk together, wearing clothes of mixed wool and linen (*shaatnez*), and sowing a field with two kinds of grain (*kilayim*).

The law of the red heifer with which the *parasha* begins was regarded as the statute par excellence, the supreme example of a law that has no obvious rationale. It is based on the idea that death defiles, and that therefore someone who had come into contact with or been in close proximity to a dead body had to undergo the elaborate purification rites, taking seven days, before he or she could enter the precincts of the Tabernacle or, in a later age, the Temple.

The sages knew that the *ḥukkim* seemed to defy any analysis in terms of social utility. They said that these were laws about which "Satan and the nations of the world made fun" (Rashi to Num. 19:2). They looked irrational, even superstitious.

There is a famous passage in the rabbinic literature in which Rabban Yoḥanan b. Zakkai was challenged by a Roman who claimed that the law of the red heifer was just that: a combination of sorcery and superstition. He regarded it as absurd that a red heifer should be killed and burned and its ashes mixed with water and various other substances and sprinkled on those who had been defiled, at the end of which they were declared clean.

Yoḥanan b. Zakkai gave him an artful reply. He asked the Roman whether he believed that people could be possessed by an evil spirit. The Roman said yes. What do you do in such circumstances? Yoḥanan asked. The Roman replied: We perform an exorcism. We light a fire, bring roots, make smoke, sprinkle water on the affected person, and the spirit flees. (Many ancient cultures believed in demonic possession and had rituals of exorcism.) Well, said Yoḥanan, you have answered your own question. The red heifer ceremony is a form of exorcism for one possessed by an unclean spirit. We perform it and the spirit flees. The Roman left, satisfied.

What makes the passage fascinating is that it does not end there. Rabban Yoḥanan's students, who had witnessed the encounter, challenged the master as soon as the Roman had left. "You drove him away with a mere straw of an answer," they said, "But *what will you answer us?*" In effect, they were saying to Yoḥanan: You may have given an answer that satisfied a Roman who believes in evil spirits and exorcism. But we do not. We know perfectly well that the red heifer was not a form of exorcism. What then is the logic of the ceremony in terms of Judaism itself?

Yoḥanan's reply was breathtaking in its radicalism: "By your life, the dead body does not defile and the waters of the red heifer do not purify. Rather, God says: I have ordained a decree, I have issued a statute, and you have no permission to transgress My decree."[1] This is a fascinating exchange. Evidently, Yoḥanan empowered his students to challenge him, even after a successful defence of Jewish practice in the context of a Roman culture that found many aspects of Judaism hard

---

1. *Midrash Tanḥuma, Parashat Ḥukkat* 26; Numbers Rabba 19:8.

to understand.[2] He and they both recognised the legitimacy of asking "Why?" questions about Judaism.

This is not coincidental. A careful examination of the early rabbinic literature reveals that Rabban Yoḥanan b. Zakkai, who lived in the first century and witnessed the destruction of the Temple, was one of the pioneers of the search for *taamei hamitzvot*, "reasons for the commands."[3] Several famous explanations are attributed to him. For example, he explained why the Torah is stricter in the case of a thief, who takes other people's property surreptitiously, than it is towards the robber who takes openly: the thief has to pay double, while the robber has only to restore what he took. The reason, he said, is that the thief honours the servant more than the master, while the robber puts them on the same level (Bava Kamma 79b). The robber does not care who sees him, whereas the thief is careful not to be seen by other people but is not bothered by the fact that God always sees. The robber has committed an offence against someone's property. The thief has committed an offence against God as well.

What then did Rabban Yoḥanan mean when he said, "The dead body does not defile and the waters do not purify"? Was he simply saying that the law is indeed irrational, that it has no logic, and that all we can do is obey? Some people did think this about the *ḥukkim*.[4] I suspect, however, that he was saying something quite different.

What I believe Rabban Yoḥanan was doing was making a sharp distinction – made in our time by philosopher John Rawls[5] – between two kinds of rules: *regulatory* and *constitutive*. Regulatory rules, as their name implies, regulate something that exists independently of the rules. There were employers and employees before there was employment law.

---

2. Not all. There were many aspects of Judaism, especially its austere monotheism, that appealed to many Romans, and there appear to have been many half-converts to Judaism in the first centuries BCE and CE. Many of these eventually gravitated to Pauline Christianity.

3. See E. E. Urbach, *The Sages: Their Concepts and Beliefs* (Jerusalem: Magnes Press, 1975), 365–399.

4. See the following essay.

5. John Rawls, "Two Concepts of Rules," *The Philosophical Review* 64, no. 1 (1955): 3–32. See also J. R. Searle, *Speech Acts* (London: Cambridge University Press, 1969).

A practice exists and then come laws to ensure fairness, justice, and so on. In Judaism, *mishpatim*, social legislation, is of this kind.

Constitutive laws *create* a practice. The laws of chess create the game called chess. Without the laws there is no game. Rabban Yoḥanan was saying that the laws of purity are like this. They are not like medicine because impurity is not like disease. Disease existed long before there were healers, doctors, diagnoses, and cures. But purity and impurity did not exist before the laws were given. Here the laws are constitutive, not regulatory. Before they were given, death did not defile and the waters did not purify. The laws created a new reality, but that does not mean that they are irrational or incomprehensible.

To the contrary, despite their obscurity and complexity, Judaism's laws of purity have a simple underlying logic. They exist because of the extreme paradox of the Sanctuary – the Tabernacle in the wilderness and later the Temple in Jerusalem. I have argued elsewhere[6] that the command to build a Sanctuary was God's response to Moses' prayer, after the sin of the Golden Calf, that God should be close to the people.

The Sanctuary became the place dedicated to the *Shekhina*, the Divine Presence. What was paradoxical about it was that it was the home in space and time of God who is beyond space and time. God is infinite, while we and the Temple are finite. God is eternal, while we are mortal. Hence the radical insistence in Jewish law that the boundaries between human and Divine must never become blurred. What is common to all forms of impurity is that they have to do with *mortality*, with the fact that we are embodied beings in a physical world, exposed to the "thousand natural shocks that flesh is heir to." To enter sacred space, where we feel close to infinity and eternity, we must divest ourselves of any consciousness of mortality, disease, and decay. Hence the supreme source of impurity is death: contact with or proximity to a dead body. That is what the rite of the red heifer was about.

Rabban Yoḥanan was telling his students not that the ritual was irrational but that the purity it brought and the impurity it removed were not features of the physical world that you could detect independently of

6. See Jonathan Sacks, *Covenant and Conversation: Leviticus – The Book of Holiness* (Jerusalem: Maggid, 2015), 1–49.

the law. You cannot take an X-ray or an MRI scan or any other empirical test to see whether a person or object is pure or impure. *These categories exist only within the world created by the law.* The law did so for a reason, but not the kind of reason that someone standing outside the system can understand.

The reason for the law is that the Torah sought to embed within Jewish consciousness an idea that may seem obvious now but in its time was nothing less than revolutionary: *Death defiles. God is to be found in life.* Do not associate death with sanctity. To the contrary, contact with death debars you from contact with God. King David was debarred from building the Temple because he had been a soldier and had killed in the course of war (I Chr. 22:8). Holy people – priests, and all the more so the high priest – had restrictions limiting their contact with or proximity to a dead body (Lev. 21). Judaism was conspicuous among the religions of the ancient world in not praying to dead ancestors.[7] In most other religions, heaven is life after death. In Judaism we seek heaven in life before death. Again and again that note sounds in the Hebrew Bible: "It is not the dead who praise the Lord" (Ps. 115:17); "Will the dust praise You? Will it proclaim Your faithfulness?" (Ps. 30:9); "Among the dead no one proclaims Your name. Who praises You from the grave?" (Ps. 6:5). These are radical statements. God lives in life. To come close to God you must cleanse yourself of any contact with death.

This much was doubtless clear to Yoḥanan's students. But he was telling them something else as well: Do not think the connection between the law and the reason for the law is always direct, palpable, and immediate. He had taught his students to search for *taamei hamitzvot*, the reasons for the commands. But now he was teaching them something no less fundamental: the *limits* of reason. The human mind must learn humility. We cannot understand everything at once. There are elements of existence that, at any given time, are opaque to reason. Wisdom, if it is truly to be wise, must respect its own boundaries.

Strangely, it was a self-confessed agnostic, Friedrich Hayek, one of the great liberal thinkers of the twentieth century, who at the end of his life came to the same conclusion. He called his last book *The Fatal*

---

7. See Mary Douglas, *Leviticus as Literature* (New York: Oxford University Press, 1999).

Conceit.[8] In it he argued that the great failures of the modern world – socialism, communism, and other attempts at social engineering – came about because of the "fatal conceit" that we can plan human destiny in advance by the application of rationality: science, technology, bureaucracy, utilitarianism, and so on.

We cannot. All social engineering is subject to the "law of unintended consequences." Things go wrong. They do not turn out as we planned. A programme devised to eliminate poverty is discovered, a generation later, to have made poverty worse, not better.[9] A revolution undertaken in the name of freedom results in a new form of tyranny. The saddest words in history are: it seemed like a good idea at the time. Meanwhile, outcomes that were entirely *unintended* turn out to be benign. That is what Adam Smith discovered about the economics of the free market. A large number of individuals pursuing their own interests create a process that enhances the common good. No one intended this. It just happened. Smith himself – in a strikingly religious phrase – called this the "invisible hand."[10]

What we need, said Hayek, is a series of rules – "Thou shalt nots" – that we obey because they are rules, and because societies that have observed these rules have survived. We may never fully understand why and how they contribute to survival. They just do. They are our greatest protection against the fatal conceit of rationality when applied, not to nature, but to human beings and their interactions.

The Talmud anticipated Hayek. It understood that there are certain commands to which, if you state their reason, people will say: I can achieve that end, that outcome, without obeying the command. The Talmud gives one of the most powerful examples in all of history. The Torah forbids a king to accumulate three things – wealth, wives, and horses – because they will "lead his heart astray" (Deut. 17:16–17). King Solomon, wisest of men, broke all three rules, confident that his heart would not be led astray. That was his "fatal conceit," and it proved disastrous to the history of Israel (Sanhedrin 21b).

8. London: Routledge, 1988.
9. This was the insight of Charles Murray, *Losing Ground* (New York: Basic Books, 1984).
10. Adam Smith, *The Wealth of Nations* (1776).

Hayek was no irrationalist. Nor, nineteen centuries earlier, was Rabban Yoḥanan b. Zakkai. What they taught was similar to the famous theorem proved by Godel: that for any system there are truths unprovable within the system. Logic has limits. Reason has boundaries. *Ḥukkim* are laws directed not at immediate results but at shaping the sensibility of a nation in the long run.[11] They are about training a nation to respect limits and to cherish life.

Yoḥanan b. Zakkai did not advocate a life of blind obedience. He taught his disciples to search for reasons for the commandments. But he also taught them to respect what they could not immediately understand. Sometimes a law that seems unfathomable to one generation becomes lucidly self-evident to the next. That is what has happened in the case of many of the *ḥukkim*. As we will see in the next essay, many of them have to do with respect for the integrity of the environment. Only recently has concern for the environment alerted us to the importance of that respect, which lies at the core of the Torah's laws against crossbreeding and the mixture of species. The ritual of the red heifer is directed against one of the most powerful and dangerous of all human drives: the death instinct, which has often been consecrated by religions that value heaven more than earth. The logic of biblical law, opaque for centuries, has become clear in ways we could not have anticipated.

The concept of a *ḥok* tells us not to reject what we do not yet comprehend. There are aspects of life that call for faith in a wisdom greater than ours. We must strive to understand what we can, but we must also have the humility to make space in our lives for that which we cannot.

---

11. See the next essay.

Neuroscience and Ritual

I n his study of the science of human nature, *The Social Animal,* New York Times columnist David Brooks writes:

> We are living in the middle of the revolution in consciousness. Over the past few years, geneticists, neuroscientists, psychologists, sociologists, economists, anthropologists, and others have made great strides in understanding the building blocks of human flourishing. And a core finding of their work is that we are not primarily products of our conscious thinking. We are primarily the products of thinking that happens below the level of awareness.[1]

Too much takes place in the mind for us to be fully aware of it. Timothy Wilson of the University of Virginia estimates that the human mind can absorb eleven million pieces of information at any given moment. We are conscious of only a tiny fraction of this. Most of what is going on mentally lies below the threshold of awareness.

---

1. David Brooks, *The Social Animal: The Hidden Sources of Love, Character, and Achievement* (New York: Random House, 2011), x.

One result of the new neuroscience is that we are becoming aware of the hugely significant part played by emotion in decision-making. The French Enlightenment emphasised the role of reason, and regarded emotion as a distraction and distortion. We now know scientifically how wrong this is.

Antonio Damasio, in his *Descartes' Error*, tells the story of a man who, as the result of a tumour, suffered damage to the frontal lobes of his brain. He had a high IQ, was well informed, and had an excellent memory. But after surgery to remove the tumour, his life went into free-fall. He was unable to organise his time. He made bad investments that cost him his savings. He divorced his wife, married a second time, and rapidly divorced again. He could still reason perfectly but had lost the ability to feel emotion. As a result, he was unable to make sensible choices.[2]

Another man with a similar injury found it impossible to make decisions at all. At the end of one session, Damasio suggested two possible dates for their next meeting. The man then took out a notebook, began listing the pros and cons of each, talked about possible weather conditions, potential conflicts with other engagements, and so on for half an hour, until Damasio finally interrupted him, and made the decision for him. The man immediately said, "That's fine," and went away.

It is less reason than emotion that lies behind our choices, and it takes emotional intelligence to make good choices. The problem is that much of our emotional life lies beneath the surface of the conscious mind. This discovery allows us a new insight into the otherwise puzzling phenomenon of *ḥukkim*, the "statutes" of Judaism, laws that seem to make no sense in terms of rationality.

These include laws like the prohibition of sowing mixed seeds together (*kilayim*), wearing cloth of mixed wool and linen (*shaatnez*), and eating milk and meat together. A key example is the law of the red heifer with which *Parashat Ḥukkat* begins, described as the *ḥok* par excellence: "This is *the* statute of the Torah" (Num. 19:2). Jewish thinkers through the ages have developed different theories about the nature and purpose of these laws. Broadly speaking, there are four approaches.

2.   Antonio R. Damasio, *Descartes' Error: Emotion, Reason, and the Human Brain* (New York: Avon Books, 1995).

First is the view expressed in the Midrash by R. Abba b. Eliashiv[3] that *ḥukkim* bring us to life in the World to Come. They exist, in other words, to give us spiritual reward. Rabbi Saadia Gaon in his philosophical treatise on Judaism, *The Book of Beliefs and Opinions* (written in 933),[4] distinguishes two kinds of commandments, *sikhliyot*, commands of reason, and *shimiyot*, commands of "hearing and obeying." Commands of the first kind we might have arrived at ourselves because they have obvious human benefits. Those of the second kind, which include statutes, we know only through revelation, and they were given to us by God so that we could receive reward for our obedience.

The second view, found in the Midrash in the name of R. Ḥama b. R. Ḥanina, is that *ḥukkim* are an antidote to the "evil inclination."[5] They are, as it were, an ongoing tutorial in impulse control. The fact that we may not have milk after meat, or eat certain kinds of food, or use certain types of cloth, means that we are constantly practising self-restraint in the pursuit of desire. The commands were given, said Rav, "to refine human character."[6] Every civilisation, said Freud, depends on "coercion and the renunciation of instinct."[7] The very fact that we do not understand a particular law means that when we obey it we are acknowledging an authority higher than ourselves, and this strengthens our capacity for self-control. In this view, *ḥukkim* are an important element in the development of character.

In both of these views, there is no particular significance as to the content of the commands. The Torah bans one thing but it could have banned another. The details make no difference to our reward or to the renunciation of desire. Maimonides strongly objected to this approach. His proof was a verse from Deuteronomy (4:6): "Safeguard and keep [these statutes], for this is your wisdom and understanding in the eyes of the nations. They will hear all these statutes and say, 'This

3. Leviticus Rabba 35:6.
4. Saadia Gaon, *The Book of Beliefs and Opinions* (*Sefer Emunot VeDeot*), book 3, trans. Samuel Rosenblatt (New Haven, CT: Yale University Press, 1948).
5. Numbers Rabba 35:5.
6. Genesis Rabba 44:1.
7. Sigmund Freud, *The Future of an Illusion* (London: Hogarth Press: Institute of Psychoanalysis, 1928), 7. He gives a similar account in *Civilization and Its Discontents*.

great nation is certainly a wise and understanding people."' How, asked Maimonides, could statutes evoke the admiration of the nations if they were essentially irrational? His own theory, discussed in *Guide for the Perplexed*, is that *ḥukkim* are Judaism's defence against idolatry.[8] Many of the practices banned by the Torah were key features of idolatrous rites and cultures.

The fourth view, set out in the thirteenth century by Nahmanides and in the nineteenth by Samson Raphael Hirsch, is that the *ḥukkim* are laws that teach respect for the integrity of the created world.[9] Nature, the Torah is telling us, has its own laws, domains, and boundaries, the crossing of which is an offence against the divinely appointed order. So we do not combine animal (wool) and vegetable (linen) textiles, or mix animal life (milk) and animal death (meat). Behind these and other such commands is the idea that God is the creator of bio-diversity rather than hybrid uniformity. As for the red heifer, Hirsch says that the ritual exists to cleanse humans from depression brought about by reminders of human mortality.[10]

Contemporary neuroscience, however, suggests a fifth approach. Recall Damasio's conclusion that much of our behaviour is driven by instincts that lie beneath conscious awareness and the rational, reflective part of the brain, the prefrontal cortex. The question then arises: How, if our instincts are largely unconscious, can we change them? The short answer is ritual. *Ritual is behaviour that bypasses the prefrontal cortex.* It is action based not on a rational decision that this is how we should act. Rather, it is behaviour that follows a precise set of rules, a fixed choreography. Doing certain acts repeatedly, we form new "habits of the heart" that work at an unconscious level to form new patterns of instinctual behaviour.

---

8. Maimonides, *Guide for the Perplexed*, III:29–31. Maimonides gives his explanation for the law of the red heifer in *Guide for the Perplexed*, III:47.
9. Nahmanides' view is set out in his commentary to Lev. 19:19. Hirsch's appears in the eleventh of the *Nineteen Letters of Ben Uziel*, trans. Bernard Drachman (New York: Funk & Wagnalls, 1899).
10. See Hirsch's commentary to Num. 19.

Virtually all great artists, writers, and composers practise rituals.[11] So do chess masters and outstanding sports stars.[12] Repeated behaviour creates new neural pathways. It reconfigures our character so that there are certain things we do and feel differently. We are no longer the people we once were. We have engraved into our instincts, the way certain strokes are engraved in the minds of tennis champions or moves in the minds of chess masters, automatic responses to circumstance. Prayer engenders gratitude. Daily charitable giving makes us generous. The "Thou shalt nots" of religion teach us self-control. Ritual changes the world by changing us.

This would not have surprised Aristotle or Maimonides because that is how they believed virtue is acquired, by constantly repeating virtuous acts. "Habit becomes second nature," as the medieval thinkers put it.[13] "The heart follows the deed," says *Sefer HaḤinnukh*.[14] Though they lacked the neuroscience, philosophers and sages knew this through experience and observation. The mistake – Descartes' error – was born at the start of the Enlightenment, one of the great ages of rationalism. We now know, however, that we are not rational animals. Daniel Kahneman won the Nobel Prize in economics for inventing, together with Amos Tversky, the field of behavioural economics, which shows that even when we make economic choices we do so on the basis of irrational instincts.[15] The entire model on which much of modern thought is based – the so-called "rational actor" – fails to get to grips with the emotional side of human character, which can sometimes be very destructive indeed.

Today the principle of the *Sefer HaḤinnukh*, that the heart follows the deed, has been reinvented as "fake it until you feel it." Brain scans have shown that when people hold a pencil sideways in their mouth, forcing them to smile, they show the same pattern of brain activity as people who are happy. It follows that if you want to change the way you feel, you can do so by repeatedly performing the act associated with a particular

---

11. See Mason Currey, *Daily Rituals: How Artists Work* (New York: Knopf, 2013).
12. See Daniel Coyle, *The Talent Code* (New York: Bantam, 2009).
13. See, for example, Abrabanel's commentary to Ex. 32.
14. *Sefer HaḤinnukh*, command 16.
15. See Daniel Kahneman, *Thinking, Fast and Slow* (London: Penguin, 2012).

emotion. Ritual allows us to reconfigure the brain, transforming our emotional life and allowing us to control our more destructive instincts.

We know for example – Jared Diamond has chronicled this in his book *Collapse*[16] – that wherever humans have settled throughout history they have left behind them a trail of environmental disaster, wiping out whole species of animals and birds, destroying forests, damaging the soil by over-farming, and so on. So the prohibitions against sowing mixed seeds, mixing meat and milk or wool and linen, and so on, create an *instinctual respect for the integrity of nature*. They establish boundaries. They set limits. They inculcate the feeling that we may not do to our animal and plant environment everything we wish. Some things are forbidden – like the fruit of the tree in the middle of the Garden of Eden. The whole Eden story, set at the dawn of human history, is a parable whose message we can understand today better than any previous generation: without a sense of limits, we will destroy our ecology and discover that we have lost paradise.

As for the ritual of the red heifer, it is directed at the most destructive irrational instinct of all: what Sigmund Freud called *Thanatos*, the death instinct. He described it as something "more primitive, more elementary, more instinctual than the pleasure principle which it overrides."[17] In *Civilization and Its Discontents*, he wrote that "a portion of the [death] instinct is diverted towards the external world and comes to light as an instinct of aggressiveness," which he saw as "the greatest impediment to civilization."[18]

The red heifer ritual told all those who saw it or underwent it that *the holy is to be found in life, not death*. Anyone who had been in contact with a dead body needed purification before entering the Temple. Priests, whose life was lived in the precincts of the holy, had to avoid, as far as possible, contact with or close proximity to a corpse. Judaism has, from the beginning, refused to consecrate death. It was almost certainly to

---

16. Jared Diamond, *Collapse: How Societies Choose to Fail or Succeed* (London: Penguin, 2011).
17. Sigmund Freud, "Beyond the Pleasure Principle," in *On Metapsychology* (Harmondsworth: Penguin, 1984), 294.
18. Freud, *Civilization and Its Discontents*, 78, 81.

avoid the tomb of Moses becoming a holy site that the Torah says, "To this day, no one knows where his grave is" (Deut. 34:6). God and the holy are to be found in life, not death.

What recent neuroscience has made eminently clear is that changes of attitude, when they are associated with deep emotion, cannot be achieved by reason or conscious deliberation alone. Freud was right to suggest that the death instinct is powerful and largely unconscious, yet under certain conditions it can be utterly devastating in what it leads people to do.

The Hebrew word *ḥok*, as we saw, comes from the verb meaning, "to engrave." Just as a statute is carved into stone, so a behavioural habit is carved deeply into our unconscious mind and alters our instinctual responses. The result is a personality trained to see death and holiness as two utterly opposed states – just as meat (death) and milk (life) are.

Ḥukkim are Judaism's way of reconfiguring the limbic system, the emotional brain, by way of acts that bypass the prefrontal cortex, the rational brain. Contemporary neuroscience has shown us how this works, and why. Rationality, vitally important in its own right, is only half the story of why we do what we do. The "rational actor" model that dominated Western thought in recent centuries turns out to be radically inadequate to understanding some of humanity's most self-destructive tendencies. The Torah's ancient wisdom may help us confront the instinct to violence and death that still lurks beneath the surface of the conscious mind.

Did Moses Sin?

I t is one of the most perplexing and disturbing passages in the Torah. Moses, the faithful shepherd, who had led the Israelites for forty years, was told that he would not live to cross the Jordan and enter the Promised Land.

No one has cast a longer shadow over the history of the Jewish people than Moses – the man who confronted Pharaoh, announced the plagues, brought the people out of Egypt, led them through the sea and desert, and suffered their serial ingratitudes. He brought the word of God to the people, and prayed for the people to God. Jacob was given the name Israel, meaning one who "wrestle[s] with God and with men and prevail[s]" (Gen. 32:29). More even than Jacob, the phrase epitomises Moses, whose passion for justice and hyper-receptivity to the voice of God made him the greatest Jewish leader of all time. Yet he was not destined to enter the land to which he had spent his entire time as a leader travelling towards. Why?

The biblical text is both lucidly clear and deeply obscure. The facts are not in doubt. Almost forty years had passed since the Exodus. Most of the generation who remembered Egypt had died. So too had

Miriam, Moses' sister. The people had arrived at Kadesh in the Zin desert, and they were now close to their destination. In their new encampment, however, they found themselves without water. They complained.

> Why have you brought the assembly of the Lord into this wilderness for us and our livestock to die? Why did you take us up from Egypt to bring us to this vile place, where nothing grows, not corn or figs, not vines or pomegranates? There is not even any water to drink. (Num. 20:4–5)

The tone of voice, the petulance, is all too familiar. The Israelites had hardly deviated from it throughout. Yet suddenly we experience not déjà vu, but tragedy:

> Moses and Aaron went from the presence of the congregation to the entrance of the Tent of Meeting and fell on their faces. The glory of the Lord appeared to them.
>
> The Lord spoke to Moses and said, "Take the staff, and then with Aaron your brother assemble all the community and, in front of them all, speak to the rock and it will yield water. You shall bring forth for them water from the rock, for them and their livestock to drink."
>
> Moses took the staff from before the Lord, as He had commanded him. Then he and Aaron gathered the assembly together in front of the rock, and said to them, "Listen, you rebels, shall we bring you water out of this rock?" Moses raised his hand and struck the rock twice with his staff. Water gushed forth in abundance, and they all drank, men and beasts.
>
> But the Lord said to Moses and Aaron, *"Because you did not believe in Me to sanctify Me in the eyes of the Children of Israel,* therefore you shall not lead this assembly into the land which I promised to give them." (Num. 20:6–12)

What had Moses done wrong? What was his sin? What offence could warrant so great a punishment as not to be privileged to see the conclusion of the mission he had been sent by God?

Few passages have generated so much controversy among the commentators. Each offers his own interpretation and challenges the others. So many were the hypotheses that the nineteenth-century Italian exegete Rabbi Shmuel David Luzzatto was moved to say, "Moses committed one sin, yet the commentators have accused him of thirteen or more – each inventing some new iniquity!"[1] One modern scholar[2] lists no less than twenty-five lines of approach, and there are many more. The following are the most significant:

1. Rashi, offering the simplest and best-known explanation, says that Moses' sin lay in striking the rock rather than speaking to it. Had Moses done as he was commanded, the people would have learned an unforgettable lesson: "If a rock, which neither speaks nor hears nor is in need of sustenance, obeys the word of God, how much more so should we" (Rashi to Num. 20:12).

2. Maimonides says that Moses' sin lay in his anger – his intemperate words to the people, "Listen, you rebels." To be sure, in anyone else, this would have been considered a minor offence. However, the greater the person, the more exacting are the standards God sets. Moses was not only a leader but the supreme role model of the Israelites. Seeing his behaviour, the people may have concluded that anger is permissible – or even that God was angry with them, which He was not.[3]

3. Nahmanides, following a suggestion of Rabbenu Hananel, says that the sin lay in saying, "Shall *we* bring you water out of this rock?" – implying that what was at issue was human ability rather than divine miracle and grace (commentary to Num. 20:8).

4. Rabbi Joseph Albo and others (including Ibn Ezra) suggest that the sin lay in the fact that Moses and Aaron fled from the congregation and fell on their faces, rather than standing their ground, confident that God would answer their prayers.[4]

---

1. Rabbi Shmuel David Luzzatto, commentary ad loc.
2. Rabbi Aaron Rother, *Shaarei Aharon* ad loc.
3. Maimonides, *Shemoneh Perakim*, ch. 4.
4. Albo, *Sefer HaIkkarim* IV:22.

5. Abrabanel makes the ingenious suggestion that Moses and Aaron were not punished for what they did at this point. Rather, their offences lay in the distant past. Aaron sinned by making the Golden Calf. Moses sinned in sending the spies. Those were the reasons they were not privileged to enter the land. To defend their honour, however, their sins are not made explicit in the biblical text. Their actions at the rock were the *proximate* rather than *underlying* cause (a hurricane may be the proximate cause of a bridge collapsing; the underlying cause, however, was a structural weakness in the bridge itself).

6. More recently, Rabbi Elazar Shach suggested that Moses may have been justified in rebuking the people, but he erred in the sequence of events. First he should have given them water, showing both the power and providence of God. Only then, once they had drunk, should he have admonished them.

Difficulties, however, remain. The first is that Moses himself attributed God's refusal to let him enter the land to His anger with the people, not just with himself:

> At that time, I pleaded with the Lord, "O Lord God, You have begun to show Your servant Your greatness and Your strong hand.... Let me cross over and see the good land that is on the other side of the Jordan, the fine hill country and the Lebanon." But God was angry with me *because of you*... (Deut. 3:26).

Similarly, Psalms 106:32 states, "By the waters of Meriva they angered the Lord and trouble came to Moses *because of them*."

Second: However we identify Moses' sin, disproportion remains between it and its punishment. Because of Moses' prayers, God forgave the Israelites. Could He not forgive Moses? To deprive him of seeing the culmination of a lifetime's efforts was surely unduly harsh. According to the Talmud, when the angels witnessed R. Akiva's death, they said, "Is this the Torah, and this its reward?" (Berakhot 61b). They might have asked the same question about Moses.

Third is the tantalising fact that, on a *previous* occasion in similar circumstances, God had told Moses to take his staff and strike the rock – precisely the act for which (for Rashi and many others) he was now punished:

> The people were thirsty for water there, and they grumbled against Moses, saying, "Why did you bring us out of Egypt to make us and our children and livestock die of thirst?" Then Moses cried out to the Lord, "What am I to do with these people? Before long they will stone me." The Lord answered Moses, "Walk on ahead of the people. Take with you some of the elders of Israel and take in your hand the staff with which you struck the Nile, and go. I will stand before you by the rock at Horeb. *Strike the rock*, and water will come out of it for the people to drink." (Ex. 17:3–6)

With this in mind, it seems difficult to hazard a new explanation of so debated a text, but there may be a way of seeing the entire episode that ties the others together and makes sense of what otherwise seems like an impenetrable mystery.

The Talmud contains the following statement of Resh Lakish:

> What is the meaning of the verse, "This is the book of the generations of Adam"? Did Adam have a book? Rather, it teaches that the Holy One, Blessed Be He, showed Adam [in advance] each generation and its interpreters, each generation and its sages, each generation and its leaders. (Avoda Zara 5a)

One of the most striking features of Judaism is that it is not centred on a single figure who dominates its entire history. To the contrary, each age gave rise to its own leaders, and they were different from one another, not only in personality but in the *type* of leadership they exercised. First came the age of the patriarchs and matriarchs. Then came Moses and his disciple Joshua. They were followed by a succession of figures known generically as "judges," though their role was more military than judicial.

With Saul, monarchy was born – though even then, kings were not the only leaders; there were prophets and priests as well. With Ezra a new figure emerges: the "scribe," *the teacher as hero.* Then came elders, sages, masters of halakha and aggada. During the Mishnaic period the leader of the Jewish people was known as *nasi* (and later, in Babylon, as *resh galuta* or exilarch). Ḥatam Sofer (Rabbi Moses Sofer; Bratislava, 1762–1839), in one of his responsa, notes that though the *nasi* was a scholar, his role was as much political as educational and spiritual.[5] He was, in fact, a surrogate king. The Middle Ages saw the emergence of yet more new types: commentators, codifiers, philosophers, and poets, alongside a richly varied range of leadership structures, some lay, some rabbinic, others a combination of both.

Leadership is a function of time. There is a famous dispute about Noah, whom the Torah describes as "perfect in his generations" (Gen. 6:9). According to one view, had Noah lived in a more righteous age, he would have been greater still. According to another, he would have been merely one of many.[6] The fact is that each generation yields the leadership appropriate to it. The Talmud says that Ezra was worthy of bringing the Torah to Israel, had Moses not preceded him (Sanhedrin 21b). In another passage, it says that Moses himself asked God to give the Torah through R. Akiva rather than himself (Menaḥot 29b).

One can speculate endlessly about the might-have-beens of history, but we are each cast into the world at a time not of our choosing, and we have no choice but to live within its particular challenges and constraints. For that reason, we do not compare leaders – for there are no timeless standards by which to judge them. "Jerubaal in his generation was like Moses in his generation; Bedan in his generation was like Aaron in his generation; Yiftaḥ in his generation was like Samuel in his generation" (Rosh HaShana 25b).

Each age produces its leaders, and each leader is a function of an age. There may be – indeed there are – certain timeless truths about leadership. A leader must have courage and integrity. He or she must be able, say the sages, to relate to each individual according to his or

---

5. *Responsa Ḥatam Sofer, Oraḥ Ḥayim,* 12.
6. *Midrash Tanḥuma, Parashat Noaḥ* 6:6.

her distinctive needs. Above all, a leader must constantly learn (a king must study the Torah "all the days of his life"; Deut. 17:19). But these are necessary, not sufficient, conditions. A leader must be sensitive to the call of the hour – *this* hour, *this* generation, *this* chapter in the long story of a people. And because he or she is of a specific generation, even the greatest leader cannot meet the challenges of a different generation. That is not a failing. It is the existential condition of humanity.

The remarkable fact about Moses and the rock is the way he observed precedent. Almost forty years earlier, in similar circumstances, God had told him to take his staff and strike the rock. Now too, God told him to take his staff. Evidently Moses inferred that he was being told to act this time as he had before, which is what he did. He struck the rock. What he failed to understand was that *time had changed* in one essential detail: he was facing a new generation. The people he confronted the first time were those who had spent much of their lives as slaves in Egypt. Those he now faced were born in freedom in the wilderness.

There is a critical difference between slaves and free human beings. Slaves respond to orders. Free people do not. They must be educated, informed, instructed, taught – for if not, they will not learn to take responsibility. Slaves understand that a stick is used for striking. That is how slave-masters compel obedience. Indeed that was Moses' first encounter with his people, when he saw an Egyptian beating an Israelite. But free human beings must not be struck. They respond not to power but persuasion. They need to be spoken to. What Moses failed to hear – indeed to understand – was that the difference between God's command then and now ("strike the rock" and "speak to the rock") was of the essence. The symbolism in each case was precisely calibrated to the mentalities of two different generations. You *strike* a slave, but *speak* to a free person.

Moses' inability to hear this distinction was not a failing, still less was it a sin. It was an inescapable consequence of the fact that he was mortal. *A figure capable of leading slaves to freedom is not the same as one able to lead free human beings from a nomadic existence in the wilderness to the conquest and settlement of a land.* These are different challenges, and they need different types of leadership. Indeed the whole biblical story of how a short journey took forty years teaches us just this truth. Great

change does not take place overnight. It takes more than one generation – and therefore more than one type of leader.

Moses could not become a Joshua, just as Joshua could not be
another Moses. The fact that at a moment of crisis, Moses reverted to
an act that had been appropriate forty years before showed that the time
had come for the leadership to be handed on to a new generation. It is
a sign of his greatness that Moses, too, recognised this fact and took the
initiative in asking God (Num. 27:15–17) to appoint a successor.

If this interpretation is correct, then Moses did not sin, nor was
he punished. To be sure, the Torah uses the language of sin: "You did not
have enough faith in Me to sanctify Me" (Num. 20:12); "You rebelled
against My word" (Num. 20:24); "You disobeyed My commandment"
(Num. 27:14); "You broke faith with Me....You did not sanctify Me"
(Deut. 32:51). This is not the language of innocence.

The simplest explanation is that given by Abrabanel in his tenth
interpretation, and by Luzzatto. God was referring not to Moses and
Aaron as individuals but to the people as a whole. As its leaders they
bore collective responsibility for what they had done. That would explain
why Moses said that "God was angry with me *because of you.*"

There is, though, another poignant possibility. At the start of
Moses' mission, when he encountered God at the burning bush, he
said, "But they (the Israelites) will not believe in me" (Ex. 4:1). Shortly
thereafter Moses' hand became leprous. The sages gave a radical interpretation to this incident. They said that Moses was being punished for
doubting the people. They said that God replied: "They are believers,
the children of believers, but in the end it will be you who does not
believe" (Shabbat 97a).

*It was not that Moses failed to believe in God. He failed to believe
in the people.* One can hardly call that a sin. The people did fall short
time and again. On several occasions God lost patience with them and
threatened to destroy them, and might have done so had Moses not
prayed on their behalf. But forty years had passed. They were no longer
the same people. They were a new generation. If you do not believe in
the people, you cannot be their leader. What God was saying to Moses
was: Your failure to believe in them is ultimately a failure to believe in
Me, since I have faith in them.

The fact that Moses was not destined to enter the Promised Land was not a punishment but the very condition of his (and our) mortality. For each of us, there is a Jordan we will not cross, however long we live, however far we travel. But this is not inherently tragic. What we begin, others will complete – if we have taught them how.

Moses was the greatest Jewish leader of all time. But he was also the supreme teacher. The difference is that his leadership lasted for forty years, while his teachings have endured for more than three thousand years (that, incidentally, is why we call him *Moshe Rabbenu*, "Moses our teacher," not "Moses our leader"). This is not to devalue leadership; to the contrary: had Moses only taught, not led, the Israelites would not have left Egypt. The message of the rock is not that leadership does not matter. It is that *leadership must be of its time*. A teacher may live in the world of ancient texts and distant hopes, but a leader must hear the call of the age and address the needs and possibilities of now.

The great leaders are those who, knowledgeable of a people's past and dedicated to its ideal future, are able to bring their contemporaries with them on the long journey from exile to redemption, neither longing for an age that was nor rushing precipitously into an age that cannot yet be. And, as Moses understood more deeply than any other human being, the great leaders are also teachers, empowering those who come after them to continue what they have begun.

Losing Miriam

I
t is a scene that still has the power to shock and disturb. The people complain. There is no water. It is an old complaint and a predictable one. That is what happens in a desert. Moses should have been able to handle it in his stride. He has been through far tougher challenges in his time. Yet suddenly he explodes into vituperative anger: "'Listen, you rebels, shall we bring you water out of this rock?' Moses raised his hand and struck the rock twice with his staff" (Num. 20:10–11). In the previous essay I argued that Moses did not sin. It was simply that he was the right leader for the generation that left Egypt but not the right leader for their children who would cross the Jordan and engage in conquering a land and building a society. The fact that he was not permitted to lead the next generation was not a failure but an inevitability. A group of slaves needed a strong leader capable of contending with them and with God. Builders of a new society need a leader who will *not* do the work for them but will inspire them to do it for themselves.

The face of Moses, we saw earlier, was like the sun; that of Joshua like the moon (Bava Batra 75a). The difference is that sunlight is so strong it leaves no work for a candle to do, whereas a candle can illuminate when the only other source of light is the moon. Joshua empowered his generation more than a figure as strong as Moses would have done.

But there is another question altogether about the episode at Mei Meriva, "the waters of contention." What made this trial different? Why did Moses momentarily lose control? Why then? Why there? He had faced just this challenge before. The Torah mentions two previous episodes. One took place at Mara, almost immediately after the division of the Red Sea. The people found water but it was bitter. Moses prayed to God, God told him how to sweeten the water, and the episode passed.

The second occurred at Rephidim (Ex. 17:1–7). This time there was no water at all. Moses rebuked the people: "Why are you quarrelling with me? Are you trying to test God?'" He then turned to God and said, "What am I to do with this people? Before long they will stone me!" God told him to go to a rock at Horeb, take his staff, and hit the rock. Moses did so, and water came out. There was drama, tension, but nothing like the emotional distress evident in *Parashat Ḥukkat*. Surely Moses, by now almost forty years older, with a generation of experience behind him, should have coped with this challenge without drama. He had been there before.

The text gives us a clue, but in so understated a way that we can easily miss it. The chapter begins thus: "In the first month, the whole Israelite community arrived at the desert of Zin, and they stayed at Kadesh. There Miriam died and was buried. Now there was no water for the community…" (Num. 20:1–2). Many commentators see the connection between this and what follows in terms of the sudden loss of water after the death of Miriam. Tradition tells of a miraculous well that accompanied the Israelites during Miriam's lifetime in her merit.[1] When she died, the water ceased.

There is, though, another way of reading the connection. *Moses lost control because his sister Miriam had just died.* He was in mourning for his eldest sibling. It is hard to lose a parent, but in some ways it is even harder to lose a brother or sister. They are your generation. You feel the Angel of Death come suddenly close. You face your own mortality.

---

1. Rashi, Commentary to Num. 20:2; Taanit 9a; Song of Songs Rabba 4:14, 27.

Miriam was more than a sister to Moses. She was the one, while still a child, to follow the course of the wicker basket holding her baby brother as it drifted down the Nile. She had the courage and ingenuity to approach Pharaoh's daughter and suggest that she employ a Hebrew nurse for the child, thus ensuring that Moses would grow up knowing his family, his people, and his identity.

In a truly remarkable passage, the sages said that Miriam persuaded her father Amram, the leading scholar of his generation, to annul his decree that Hebrew husbands should divorce their wives and have no more children because there was a 50 per cent chance that any child born would be killed. "Your decree," said Miriam, "is worse than Pharaoh's. He only decreed against the males, yours applies to females also. He intends to rob children of life in this world; you would deny them even life in the World to Come."[2] Amram admitted her superior logic. Husbands and wives were reunited. Yokheved became pregnant and Moses was born. Note that this midrash, told by the sages, unambiguously implies that a six-year-old girl had more faith and wisdom than the leading rabbi of the generation!

Moses surely knew what he owed his elder sister. According to the Midrash, without her he would not have been born. According to the plain sense of the text, he would not have grown up knowing who his true parents were and to which people he belonged. Though they had been separated during his years of exile in Midian, once he returned, Miriam had accompanied him throughout his mission. She had led the women in song at the Red Sea. The one episode that seems to cast her in a negative light – when she "began to talk against Moses because of his Cushite wife" (Num. 12:1), for which she was punished with leprosy – was interpreted more positively by the sages. They said she was critical of Moses for breaking off marital relations with his wife Tzippora. He had done so because he needed to be in a state of readiness for divine communication at any time. Miriam felt Tzippora's plight and sense of abandonment. Besides which, she and Aaron had also received divine communication but they had not been commanded to be celibate. She may have been wrong, suggested the sages, but not

---

2. *Midrash Lekaḥ Tov* to Ex. 2:1.

maliciously so. She spoke not out of jealousy of her brother but out of sympathy for her sister-in-law.

So it was not simply the Israelites' demand for water that led Moses to lose control of his emotions, but rather his own deep grief. The Israelites may have lost their water, but Moses had lost his sister, who had watched over him as a child, guided his development, supported him throughout the years, and helped him carry the burden of leadership in her role as leader of the women.

It is a moment that reminds us of words from the book of Judges said by Israel's chief of staff, Barak, to its judge-and-leader Deborah: "If you go with me, I will go; but if you do not go with me, I cannot go" (Judges 4:8). The relationship between Barak and Deborah was much less close than that between Moses and Miriam, yet Barak acknowledged his dependence on a wise and courageous woman. Can Moses have felt less?

Bereavement leaves us deeply vulnerable. In the midst of loss we can find it hard to control our emotions. We make mistakes. We act rashly. We suffer from a momentary lack of judgement. These are common symptoms even for ordinary humans like us. In Moses' case, however, there was an additional factor. He was a prophet, and grief can occlude or eclipse the prophetic spirit. Maimonides answers the well-known question as to why Jacob, a prophet, did not know that his son Joseph was still alive, with the simplest possible answer: grief banishes prophecy. For twenty-two years, mourning his missing son, Jacob could not receive the divine word.[3] Moses, the greatest of all the prophets, remained in touch with God. It was God, after all, who told him to "speak to the rock." But somehow the message did not penetrate his consciousness fully. That was the effect of grief.

So the details are, in truth, secondary to the human drama played out that day. Yes, Moses did things he might not have done, should not have done. He struck the rock, said "we" instead of "God," and lost his temper with the people. The real story, though, is about Moses the human being in an onslaught of grief, vulnerable, exposed, caught in a vortex of emotions, suddenly bereft of the sisterly presence that had

---

3. Maimonides, *Shemoneh Perakim*, ch. 7.

been the most important bass note of his life. Miriam had been the precociously wise and plucky child who had taken control of the situation when the life of her three-month-old brother lay in the balance, undaunted by either an Egyptian princess or a rabbi-father. She had led the Israelite women in song, and sympathised with her sister-in-law when she saw the price she paid for being the wife of a leader. The Midrash speaks of her as the woman in whose merit the people had water in a parched land. In Moses' anguish at the rock, we sense the loss of the elder sister without whom he felt bereft and alone.

The story of the moment Moses lost his confidence and calm is ultimately less about leadership and crisis, or about a staff and a rock, than about a great Jewish woman, Miriam, appreciated fully only when she was no longer there.

Love in the End

Amid the epic themes of *Parashat Ḥukkat*, it is easy to miss the significance of a short passage towards the end. It is brief, cryptic, almost unintelligible, and certainly does not seem to represent a major idea. Yet the sages gave it an interpretation that sheds brilliant light on the culture they sought to create in Jewish life after the destruction of the Temple and the loss of Jewish power.

The context is this. After reporting the episode of water from the rock, the Torah resumes the larger narrative of the journey towards the Promised Land. By now, the Israelites were close to their destination. They had left the desert and were moving towards the area that today forms the state of Jordan. They began to encounter the people of the region whose territory they would have either to pass through or to circumnavigate. Approaching Edom, they asked for permission to travel through the land. The request was refused and the Israelites accepted the decision (the Edomites were descendants of Esau, whose territorial rights the Israelites were told to respect). They then waged a battle against the Canaanite kingdom of Arad, and came to the vicinity of Moab. At this point the text says:

> Therefore the book of the Wars of the Lord speaks of "Waheb in Suphah, and the wadis: the Arnon with its tributary wadis, stretched along the settled country of Ar, hugging the territory of Moab." (Num. 21:14–15)

That is the Jewish Publication Society's translation, but the text is so fragmentary and obscure that its meaning is largely a matter of conjecture.

To give just one example: What is meant by "the book of the Wars of the Lord"? According to *Targum Yonatan*, it was not a separate book at all; it merely refers to this section of the Torah. For Rashi it was a list of the miracles performed by God for the sake of Israel. Ḥizkuni holds that it was an actual book that existed in ancient times and was subsequently lost. Ibn Ezra says it was a record of the Israelites' history begun in the time of Abraham. Abrabanel argues that it was a non-Israelite text. Some modern scholars suggest that it was a collection of epic poems telling of Israel's battles. How we answer this question will affect how we understand the rest of the passage.

The sages, however, gave one midrashic interpretation that laid no claim to being the plain sense of the verse, but is nevertheless fascinating in its own right:

> Even a teacher and disciple, even a father and son, when they sit to study Torah together become enemies to one another. But they do not move from there until they have become beloved to one another. Therefore it says "Waheb in Suphah," meaning: there is love at the end. (Kiddushin 30b)

The rabbis read "Waheb" as a derivative of the root *a-h-b*, meaning "to love," and "Suphah" as related to the word *sof*, "an end." What makes this text so intriguing is the way the sages interpret the phrase "the Wars of the Lord" as a reference to the debates within the house of study, the dialogue and disputation about Jewish law and the meaning of sacred texts.

This, in and of itself, is testimony to the massive transformation of Jewish life after the destruction of the Second Temple and the collapse of the Bar Kokhba Revolt. By the time this interpretation was offered, Jews no longer fought wars on the battlefield. The wars they were familiar with were altogether different. They were intellectual, spiritual; they took place in the mind; their weapons were reason and tradition; their arena was the study hall; and their aim – to establish the meaning of God's word. Seldom has a people been so transformed.

Yet there is more to the statement than this. There is an awareness of human conflict. We disagree. The sages do not speak of the house of study in eirenic terms, as an environment of peace and harmony. Even the word of God does not unite us, for though we know what the Torah *says*, we do not know, simply and uncontroversially, what it *means*. Hillel and Shammai, R. Ishmael and R. Yehuda, Rav and Shmuel, Abaye and Rava did not simply converse. They argued.

Indeed the Mishnaic, Talmudic, and midrashic literature are, for the most part, anthologies of argument: "Rabbi X says this, Rabbi Y says that." There is no attempt to gloss over the differences. To the contrary: the texts preserve not the conclusion of the debate but the debate itself. And here, the exception proves the rule. In the twelfth century Moses Maimonides wrote the greatest of all codes of Jewish law, the *Mishneh Torah*. In so doing, he made a conscious editorial decision. He eliminated the debates and recorded only the final law. The *Mishneh Torah* is, as it were, the Talmud with the arguments edited out. History ruled, in this respect, against Maimonides. The *Mishneh Torah* attracted more dispute and debate, commentaries and counter-commentaries, than almost any other work of Jewish law.

In Judaism, argument is not an accident but of the essence. As we saw in an earlier essay, the sages gave this a name – *argument for the sake of Heaven* – and thus attached to it a spiritual dignity of its own.[1] They went so far as to portray God as saying about the protagonists and their divergent views, "These and those are the words of the living God."[2] God *lives* in the cut and thrust of the house of study. He does not say: "X is right, and Y is wrong." He does not deliver the verdict; He empowers His sages to do that. The word of the Lord gives rise to the wars of the Lord – but wars without violence, bloodshed, or conquest.

1. See above, "Argument for the Sake of Heaven."
2. Eiruvin 13b; Gittin 6b.

In the passage we are discussing, the sages took a further step. They said: "There is love in the end." By this they were making a radical assertion. When two sides fight, not with weapons but with ideas, they recognise that their very disagreement presupposes an agreement – about the value of argument itself. Two sages who dispute the interpretation of a text disagree on a detail but agree on fundamentals: that the text is holy and binding, and we, who interpret it, revere both God and His word.

There are times when we read a rabbinic interpretation of a biblical text and wonder what exactly the sages were doing ascribing a meaning to a verse so far from its plain sense. Rarely, though, is this mere intellectual play, and the present instance is a fine example. The sages were well aware that the book of Numbers – especially the central section that comes to an end here – was about destructive arguments among the Israelites that cost an entire generation its chance to enter the land. They also knew that the fragmentation of the Jewish people in the late Second Temple period subsequently resulted in two of its worst catastrophes: the Roman destruction of the Temple and the persecutions following the failure of the Bar Kokhba Revolt. Yet there was never a serious attempt made to limit disagreement among Jews. They relished argument and debate and saw it as one of Judaism's greatest strengths. What they were saying here is profoundly moving. If we can take disagreement into the house of study and reconceptualise it as "argument for the sake of Heaven," then we can turn otherwise destructive conflict into the collaborative pursuit of truth, and make of it a spiritual experience that leads eventually to friendship and love.

There is a poignant Talmudic passage that tells of what can happen if we lose, even momentarily, the respect for difference implicit in the ethic of argument for the sake of Heaven. It concerns two third-century sages, R. Yoḥanan and Resh Lakish. The background to it is that, according to tradition, Resh Lakish was originally an outlaw, a highwayman, who was persuaded by R. Yoḥanan, the leading sage in the land of Israel at the time, to devote his life to Talmudic study.

One day, in the house of study, the question arose as to when instruments like swords, spears, daggers, and knives are considered complete, and thus capable of becoming ritually unclean. R. Yoḥanan said: They are complete when they have been tempered in a furnace. Resh Lakish said: They are not complete until they have been quenched in water. In the heat of the argument, R. Yoḥanan said, "Trust a robber to be expert in his trade." Resh Lakish, wounded by the jibe, turned on R. Yoḥanan, and said, "What benefit have you conferred on me [by persuading me to give up robbery and become a rabbi]? There [among robbers] I was called master, and here [in the house of study] I am called master." R. Yoḥanan responded, "I conferred on you the benefit of bringing you under the wings of the Divine Presence." Scarred by this encounter, Resh Lakish became ill and eventually died.

R. Yoḥanan grieved for him so much that the other sages feared for his health. They decided that he needed another study partner, and sent him R. Elazar b. Pedat, known for his expertise in Jewish law. This is how the passage continues:

> R. Elazar went and sat before R. Yoḥanan. To whatever R. Yoḥanan said, R. Elazar said, "There is a *baraita*, a rabbinic teaching, that supports you." R. Yoḥanan said, "Do you think you are like Resh Lakish? Whenever I would state something, Resh Lakish would raise twenty-four objections, to which I would respond with twenty-four rebuttals, with the result that we more fully understood the tradition. But all you say is, 'There is a *baraita* that supports you,' as if I did not know on my own that my view was correct." (Bava Metzia 84a)

Here in all its depth and pathos is the rabbinic ethic of the pursuit of knowledge as an extended argument between differing views within a fellowship of learning. The text is candid about the dangers. In the heat of the moment, R. Yoḥanan and Resh Lakish both say things they subsequently regret, with devastating consequences. But R. Yoḥanan remains insistent that the search for truth can be no less important than the truth itself, that scholarship thrives on challenge, and that, as the sages put it, "rivalry between scribes increases wisdom" (Bava Batra 21a, 22a). Merely to be told that you are correct adds nothing. Understanding – *religious* understanding – comes from the willingness to be challenged.

Reflecting on the many destructive arguments within the Jewish people, typified by the clashes in the book of Numbers, the sages nonetheless held unshakably to their belief in *the dignity of dissent*. That is what is happening in the great dialogues between Abraham, Moses, Jeremiah, and Job with God Himself. It is continued in the canonical texts of rabbinic Judaism, both halakhic and midrashic. Dismiss a contrary view, as R. Yoḥanan did to Resh Lakish, and you impoverish an entire culture.

The sages, in short, were articulating a principled form of what we would now call *conflict resolution*. Its rules were these:

1. Respect different perspectives.
2. Listen actively to your opponent and try to understand the logic of his or her position.
3. Never use force, physical or psychological. The only legitimate weapons are logic, argument, tradition, and persuasion.
4. Be open to the outcome. You may be right, but you must be prepared to be proved wrong.
5. See disagreement not just as conflict but as collaborative activity in pursuit of honesty and truth.
6. Accept it as a legitimate, even holy, part of life.
7. Keep talking.

For even though the participants may feel as if they are enemies to one another, "Waheb in Suphah" – there is love in the end.

Balak
בלק

Balak, king of Moab, fears the approach of the Israelites. Together with the elders of Midian, he attempts to hire the well-known Mesopotamian prophet Balaam to curse them. Balaam consults with God, who tells him not to go, but the Moabites and Midianites return with another offer. This time God instructs Balaam to accompany them but only to say the words He puts in his mouth. After a strange episode in which Balaam's donkey sees an angel blocking the way, Balaam and Balak ascend a mountain overlooking the Israelites' camp.

Three times at different places they prepare altars and sacrifices, but each time, Balaam utters blessings instead of curses. Balak leaves in anger and frustration. Having been spared Balaam's curses, however, the Israelites bring disaster on themselves through adultery and idolatry, seduced by the local women. Twenty-four thousand people die in a plague that strikes the camp until Pinhas, in an act of zealotry, rises up against one of the wrongdoers.

In the essays that follow, I examine first God's apparent changes of mind in relation to Balaam's mission. The second essay examines one of the most famous of Balaam's blessings, of Israel as "a people that dwells alone." The third explores the flaw in Balaam's character. The fourth asks about the place of the episode in the worldview of Tanakh as a whole. The fifth is about the aftermath, the sins of the Israelites with the Moabite and Midianite women.

The Hardest Word to Hear

The story of Balaam, the pagan prophet, begins with a bewildering set of non-sequiturs – a sequence of events that seems to have no logic.

The context is that the Israelites were approaching the end of their forty years in the wilderness. Already they had fought and won wars against Sihon king of the Amorites and Og king of Bashan. They had arrived at the plains of Moab – today, southern Jordan at the point where it touches the Dead Sea.

Balak king of Moab was concerned, and shared his distress with the elders of Midian. The language the Torah uses at this point is precisely reminiscent of the reaction of the Egyptians at the beginning of the book of Exodus.

EGYPT: [Pharaoh] said to his people: "Here, the Children of Israel is more *numerous* [*rav*] and powerful than we ...." And [the Egyptians] *felt a disgust* [*vayakutzu*] at the Children of Israel. (Ex. 1:9, 12)

MOAB: And Moab was very fearful because of the people because it was *numerous* [*rav*], and Moab *felt a disgust* [*vayakatz*] at the Children of Israel. (Num. 22:3)

The strategy Balak adopted was to seek the help of the well-known seer and diviner Balaam. In fact, the historical background to the Balaam narrative is well attested. Several Egyptian pottery fragments dating from the second millennium BCE have been found containing execration texts – curses – directed against Canaanite cities.[1] It was the custom among pre-Islamic Arabs to hire poets thought to be under divine influence to compose curses against their enemies.

As for Balaam himself, a significant discovery was made in 1967. A plaster inscription on the wall of a temple at Deir Alla in Jordan, dated to the eighth century BCE, was found to make reference to the night vision of a seer called Balaam ben Beor – the earliest reference in archaeological sources to a named individual in the Torah.[2] Thus, though the story itself contains elements of parable, it belongs to a definite context in time and place. (Another curious fact: the first-ever telegraph message – from Washington, May 24, 1844 – quoted the words of Balaam [Num. 23:23]: "What hath God wrought.")

The character of Balaam remains ambiguous, both in the Torah and subsequent Jewish tradition. Was he a diviner reading omens and signs, or a sorcerer practising occult arts? Was he a genuine prophet or a fraud? Did he assent to the divine blessings placed in his mouth, or did he secretly wish to curse Israel? According to some midrashic interpretations he was a great prophet, equal in stature to Moses. According to others, he was a pseudo-prophet with an "evil eye" who sought Israel's downfall.[3]

In this essay I want to examine neither Balaam nor his blessings, but rather the preamble to the story, for it is here that one of the deepest problems arises, namely: What did God want Balaam to do? It is a drama in three scenes.

---

1. See John Gray, *The Legacy of Canaan: The Ras Shamra Texts and Their Relevance to the Old Testament* (Leiden: E. J. Brill, 1965).
2. Bill Arnold and Bryan Beyer, *Readings from the Ancient Near East: Primary Sources for Old Testament Study* (Grand Rapids, MI: Baker Academic, 2002), 225.
3. See below, "The Man Without Loyalties."

In the first, emissaries arrive from Moab and Midian. They state their mission. They want Balaam to curse the Israelites. Balaam's answer is a model of propriety: Stay the night, he says, while I consult with God. God's answer is unequivocal: "But God said to Balaam, '*Do not go with them*. You must not put a curse on those people, because they are blessed'" (Num. 22:12).

Obediently, Balaam refuses. Balak redoubles his efforts. Perhaps more distinguished messengers and the promise of significant reward will persuade Balaam to change his mind. The second scene unfolds. This time a new and more impressive set of emissaries arrives, offering "very great honour" (Num. 22:17) should Balaam agree. Again his reply is exemplary: "Even if Balak were to give me his palace filled with silver and gold, I could not do anything great or small to go beyond the command of the Lord my God" (22:18). However, he adds a fateful rider: "Now stay here tonight as the others did, and I will find out what else the Lord will tell me" (22:19).

The implication is clear. Balaam is suggesting that God may change His mind. But this seems impossible. That is not what God does. Yet to our surprise, that is precisely what God appears to do: "That night God came to Balaam and said, 'Since these men have come to summon you, *go with them*, but do only what I tell you'" (Num. 22:20).

Initially God had said, "Do not go." Now He says, "Go." A second difficulty appears immediately in the next scene: "Balaam got up in the morning, saddled his donkey, and went with the princes of Moab. But *God was very angry when he went*, and the angel of the Lord stood in the road to oppose him" (Num. 22:21–22).

The previous night God had said, "Go." Balaam went. Then God became "very angry." Had God changed His mind not once but twice in the course of a single narrative? The mind reels. What is going on here? What was Balaam supposed to do? What did God want? The text offers no explanation. Instead the narrative shifts to the famous scene of Balaam's donkey – itself a mystery in need of interpretation:

Balaam was riding on his donkey, and his two servants were with him. When the donkey saw the angel of the Lord standing in the road with a drawn sword in his hand, it turned off the road into a field. Balaam beat it to get it back on the road.

Then the angel of the Lord stood in a narrow path between two vineyards, with walls on both sides. When the donkey saw the angel of the Lord, it pressed close to the wall, crushing Balaam's foot against it. So he beat it again.

Then the angel of the Lord moved on ahead and stood in a narrow place where there was no room to turn, either to the right or to the left. When the donkey saw the angel of the Lord, it lay down under Balaam, and he was angry and beat it with his staff. Then the Lord opened the donkey's mouth, and it said to Balaam, "What have I done to you to make you beat me these three times?"

Balaam answered the donkey, "You have made a fool of me! If I had a sword in my hand, I would kill you right now."

The donkey said to Balaam, "Am I not your own donkey, which you have always ridden, to this day? Have I been in the habit of doing this to you?" "No," he said.

Then the Lord opened Balaam's eyes, and he saw the angel of the Lord standing in the road with his sword drawn. So he bowed low and fell facedown. (Num. 22:22–31)

The commentators offer various ways of resolving the apparent contradictions between God's first and second reply. According to Nahmanides, God's first statement, "Do not go with them," meant, "Do not curse the Israelites." His second – "Go with them" – meant, "Go, but make it clear that you will only say the words I will put in your mouth, even if they are words of blessing." God was angry with Balaam not because he went, but because he did not tell them of the proviso.[4]

In the nineteenth century, Malbim and Rabbi Zvi Hirsch Mecklenburg suggested a different answer based on close textual analysis.[5] The Hebrew text uses two different words for "with them" in the first and

---

4. Nahmanides, Commentary to Num. 22:20.
5. Malbim, Commentary to Num. 22:21; Mecklenburg, *HaKetav VeHaKabbala* to Num. 22:12.

second divine replies. When God says, "Do not go with them" the Hebrew is *imahem*. When He later says, "Go with them," the corresponding word is *itam*. The two prepositions have subtly different meanings. *Imahem* means "with them mentally as well as physically," going along with their plans. *Itam* means "with them physically but *not* mentally" – in other words Balaam could accompany them but not share their purpose or intention. God was angry when Balaam went, because the text states (Num. 22:21) that he went *im* them – in other words, he identified with their mission.

This is an ingenious solution. The only difficulty is verse 35, in which the angel of God, having opened Balaam's eyes, finally tells Balaam, "Go with [*im*] the men." According to Malbim and Mecklenburg, this is precisely what God did *not* want Balaam to do.

There is, however, an alternative answer: *The hardest word to hear in any language is the word no*. Balaam had asked God once. God had said "No." That should have sufficed. Yet Balaam asked a second time. In that act he betrayed his essential character. He knew that God did not want him to go. Yet he invited the second set of messengers to wait overnight *in case God had changed His mind*.

God does not change His mind. Therefore Balaam's delay said something not about God but about himself. *He had not accepted the divine refusal*. He wanted to hear the answer yes – and that is indeed what he heard. *Not* because God wanted him to go, but because God speaks once, and if we refuse to accept what He says, God does not force His will upon us. As the sages of the Talmud put it: "Man is led down the path he chooses to tread" (Makkot 10b).

The true meaning of God's second reply, "Go with them," is, "If you insist, then I cannot stop you going – but I am angry that you should have asked a second time." God did not change His mind at any point in the proceedings. In scenes 1, 2, and 3, God did not want Balaam to go. His "yes" in scene 2 meant "no" – but it was a "no" Balaam was not prepared to hear. *When God speaks and we do not listen, He does not intervene to save us from our choices*: "Man is led down the path he chooses to tread."

But God was not prepared to let Balaam proceed as if he had divine consent. Instead He arranged the most elegant possible demonstration of the difference between true and false prophecy. The false prophet speaks. The true prophet listens. The false prophet tells people what they want to hear. The true prophet tells them what they need to hear. The false prophet believes in his own powers. The true prophet knows that he has no power. The false prophet speaks in his own voice. The true prophet speaks in a voice not his. "I am not a man of words," said Moses (Ex. 4:10). "I cannot speak for I am a child," said Jeremiah (Jer. 1:6).

The episode of Balaam and the talking donkey is pure humour. One thing provokes divine laughter in Tanakh, namely human pretension.[6] Balaam had won renown as the greatest prophet of his day. His fame had spread to Moab and Midian. He was known as the man who held the secrets of blessing and curse. God now proceeds to show Balaam that when He so chooses, even Balaam's donkey is a greater prophet than he. The donkey sees what Balaam cannot see: the angel standing in the path, barring the way. God humbles the self-important, just as He gives importance to the humble. When human beings think they can dictate what God will say, God laughs. And, on this occasion, so do we.

Some years ago, in the course of making a television programme for the BBC, I faced the following problem: I wanted to make a documentary about *teshuva*, repentance, but I had to do so in a way that would be intelligible to non-Jews as well as Jews, including those who had no religious belief at all. What secular counterpart could I choose that would illustrate the point?

I decided that the best way of doing so was to look at drug addicts. They had developed behaviour that they knew was self-destructive, but it was also addictive. To break the habit would involve immense reserves of will. They had to acknowledge that the life they led was harming them and they had to change. They had, in other words, to go through a secular equivalent of *teshuva*.

I spent a day in a rehabilitation centre, and it was heartbreaking. The young people there – they were aged between sixteen and eighteen – all came from broken families. Many had suffered abuse. Other than the workers at the centre, they had no networks of support. The staff was made up of exceptional people. Their task was mind-numbingly difficult. They

6. See *Covenant and Conversation: Exodus – The Book of Redemption* (Jerusalem: Maggid, 2009), 53–58.

would succeed in getting the addicts to break the habit for days, weeks at a time, and then they would relapse and the whole process would have to begin again. I began to realise that their patience was little less than a human reflection of God's patience with us. However many times we fail and have to begin again, God does not lose faith in us, and that gives us strength. Here were people doing God's work.

I asked the head of the centre, a social worker, what it was that she gave the young people that made a difference to their lives and gave them the strength to change. I will never forget her answer, because it was one of the most beautiful I ever heard. "We are probably the first people they have met who care for them unconditionally. And we are the first people in their lives who *cared enough to say no.*"

"No" is the hardest word to hear, but it is also often the most important – and the sign that someone cares. That is what Balaam, humbled, eventually learned, and what we too must discover if we are to be open to the voice of God.

A People That Dwells Alone

One of the most profound and influential comments ever made about Jewish destiny was made by the pagan prophet Balaam in *Parashat Balak*:

> As I see them from the mountain tops,
> Gaze on them from the heights,
> Behold it is a people that dwells alone,
> Not reckoned among the nations. (Num. 23:9)

To many – Jews and non-Jews, admirers and critics alike – that has seemed to epitomise the Jewish situation: a people that stands outside history and the normal laws governing the fate of nations. For Jews it was a source of pride. For non-Jews, it was all too often a source of resentment and hate. For centuries, Jews in Christian Europe were treated, in Max Weber's phrase, as a "pariah people."[1] All agreed, though, that Jews were different. The question is: How and why? The biblical answer is surprising and profound.

1. Max Weber, *Ancient Judaism*, trans. and ed. Hans H. Gerth and Don Martindale (New York: Free Press, 1967).

It is not that Jews alone knew God. That is manifestly not the case. Balaam – the very prophet who uttered these words – was not an Israelite. Nor were Avimelekh or Laban, to whom God appears in the book of Genesis. Abraham's contemporary, Melchizedek, king of Shalem (the city that later became Jerusalem), is described as a priest of God Most High. Yitro, Moses' father-in-law, was a Midianite high priest, yet the *parasha* that contains the supreme moment of Jewish history – the revelation at Mount Sinai – bears his name. Even the Pharaoh who ruled Egypt in the days of Joseph said of him, "Can we find anyone like this man, one in whom is the spirit of God?" (Gen. 41:38).

God does not appear only to Jews, members of the covenantal nation. Nor does He answer only Jewish prayers. At the dedication of the Temple, King Solomon made the following request:

> As for the foreigner who does not belong to Your people Israel but has come from a distant land because of Your name – for men will hear of Your great name and Your mighty hand and Your outstretched arm – when he comes and prays towards this Temple, then hear from heaven, Your dwelling place, and do whatever the foreigner asks of You, so that all the peoples of the earth may know Your name and fear You, as do Your own people Israel, and may know that this house I have built bears Your name. (I Kings 8:41–43)

The sages continued this great tradition when they said that "the righteous of the nations of the world have a share in the World to Come."[2] Yad Vashem, the Holocaust museum in Jerusalem, contains the names of more than twenty thousand righteous gentiles who saved lives during the Holocaust years.

Nor is it that God's covenant with the Children of Israel means that they are more righteous than others. Malachi, last of the prophets, has striking words to say on the subject:

---

2. *Mishnat Rabbi Eliezer* 6 (121); Maimonides, *Mishneh Torah, Hilkhot Teshuva* 3:5; *Hilkhot Melakhim* 8:11.

From where the sun rises to where it sets, My name is honoured among the nations, and everywhere incense and pure oblation are offered to My name, for My name is honoured among the nations, says the Lord of hosts. But you profane it. (Mal. 1:11–12)

Nor did any of the major strands in Jewish thought ever see Jewish chosenness as a privilege. It was, and is, a responsibility. The key verse here is the famous prophecy of Amos:

You alone have I singled out
Of all the families of the earth –
That is why I will call you to account
For all your iniquities. (Amos 3:2)

Where then did Jewish singularity lie? The clue lies in the precise wording of Balaam's blessing: "Behold it is *a people* that dwells alone." For it was *as a people* that God chose the descendants of Abraham; as a people that He made a covenant with them at Mount Sinai; as a people that He rescued them from Egypt, gave them laws, and entered into their history. "You will be to Me," He said at Sinai, "a kingdom of priests and a holy nation" (Ex. 19:6). Judaism is the only religion to place God at the centre of its self-definition as a nation. Jews are the only nation whose very identity is defined in religious terms.

There were many nations in the ancient world who had national gods. There were other religions – Judaism's two daughter faiths, Christianity and Islam – that believed in a universal God and a universal religion. Only Judaism believed, and still believes, in a universal God accessible to all, yet peculiarly manifest in the way of life, fate, and destiny of a single and singular people: "You are My witnesses, declares the Lord, and My servant whom I have chosen....You are My witnesses, declares the Lord, that I am God" (Is. 43:10–12).

Israel, in its history and laws, would be God's witness. It would testify to something larger than itself. So it proved to be. The historian Barbara Tuchman wrote:

> The history of the Jews is … intensely peculiar in the fact of having given the Western world its concept of origins and monotheism, its ethical traditions, and the founder of its prevailing religion, yet suffering dispersion, statelessness, and ceaseless persecution, and finally in our times nearly successful genocide, dramatically followed by fulfillment of the never-relinquished dream of return to their homeland. Viewing this strange and singular history one cannot escape the impression that it must contain some special significance for the history of mankind, that in some way, whether one believes in divine purpose or inscrutable circumstance, the Jews have been singled out to carry the tale of human fate.[3]

Why, if God is the God of the universe, accessible to every human being, should He choose *one nation* to bear witness to His presence in the human arena? This is a profound question, to which there is no short answer. But at least part of the answer, I believe, is this: *God is wholly Other; therefore He chose a people who would be humanity's "other."* That is what Jews were, and in many ways still are – outsiders, different, distinctive, a people who swam against the tide and challenged the idols of the age. *Judaism is the counter-voice in the conversation of humankind.*

During two thousand years of dispersion, Jews were the only people who, as a group, refused to assimilate to the dominant culture or convert to the dominant faith. They suffered as a result – but what they taught was not for themselves alone. They showed that a nation does not need to be powerful or large to win God's favour. They showed that a nation can lose everything else – land, power, rights, a home – and yet still not lose hope. They showed that God is not necessarily on the side of great empires or big battalions. They showed that a nation can be hated, persecuted, reviled – and yet still be loved by God. They showed that to every law of history there is an exception and what the majority believes at any given moment is not necessarily true. Judaism is God's question mark against the conventional wisdom of the age.

It is neither an easy nor a comfortable fate to be "a people that dwells alone," but it is a challenging and inspirational one.

---

3. Barbara Tuchman, *Bible and Sword* (New York: Ballantine, 1984), ix–x.

The Man Without Loyalties

What kind of man was Balaam, the pagan prophet hired to curse Israel? The text suggests that the Torah saw him as a genuine prophet, not merely a sorcerer. He addressed himself to God, not to one of the idolatrous gods of the nations (the text frequently uses the Tetragrammaton, that is, the holy four-letter name by which God was known to the prophets of Israel). God spoke to him and placed in his mouth some of the loveliest phrases ever spoken about Israel and its destiny.

Repeatedly, Balaam made clear to Balak and his representatives that he could not disobey God's command. When emissaries came a second time to persuade him to undertake the mission, he said, "Even if Balak were to give me his palace filled with silver and gold, I could not do anything great or small to go beyond the command of the Lord my God" (Num. 22:18). When he finally came to Balak, he insisted, "But can I say just anything? I must speak only what God puts in my mouth" (22:38). Again, when he delivered his first oracle, he said: "How can I curse those whom God has not cursed? How can I denounce those whom the Lord has not denounced?" (23:8). In all this he figures positively.

The rabbinic literature includes some astonishingly positive evaluations. On the phrase "no other prophet has risen in Israel like Moses, whom the Lord knew face-to-face" (Deut. 34:10), the sages said: "*In Israel there was no other prophet as great as Moses, but among the nations there was. Who was he? Balaam.*"[1] There is even a midrashic source that maintains that Balaam was a *greater* prophet than Moses.[2]

Yet the ultimate verdict on Balaam is negative. In chapter 25, we read of the massively ironic sequel to the Balaam episode. The Israelites, having been saved by God from the would-be curses of the Moabites and Midianites, suffer a self-inflicted tragedy, allowing themselves to be enticed by the women of the land. God's anger burns against them. Several chapters later (Num. 31:16), it emerges that it was Balaam who devised this strategy: "They were the ones *who followed Balaam's advice and were the means of turning the Israelites away from the Lord* in what happened at Peor, so that a plague struck the Lord's people." Having failed to curse the Israelites, Balaam eventually succeeded in doing them great harm.

So the picture that emerges from the Jewish sources is that Balaam is a figure of great gifts, a genuine prophet, a man whom the sages compared with Moses himself – yet at the same time a man of flawed character. This character would eventually lead to his downfall, to his reputation as an evildoer, and to his name being mentioned by the Mishna as having been denied a share in the World to Come (Mishna Sanhedrin 10:2).

Why? What was the flaw in his character? There are many speculations, but one suggestion given in the Talmud infers the answer from his name. What is the meaning of Balaam? The answer given by the Talmud is that it means "a man without a people" (*belo am*; Sanhedrin 105a).

Balaam was *the man without loyalties*. Balak sent for him with these words: "Now come and put a curse on these people, because they are too powerful for me.... *For I know that those you bless are blessed, and those you curse are cursed*" (Num. 22:6). Balaam was a prophet for hire. So, at any rate, must have been his reputation if Balak sent for him to perform this task. He had earned a name for his supernatural powers. He could bless someone and that person would succeed. He could curse

1. Sifre, *Devarim* 357.
2. *Eliyahu Rabba* 26; *Eliyahu Zuta* 10.

someone and that person would be blighted by misfortune. But there is no hint in any of the reports, biblical or otherwise, that Balaam was a prophet in the *moral* sense – that he was concerned with justice, desert, the rights and wrongs of those whose lives he affected. Like a contract killer of a later age, Balaam was a loner whose services could be bought. He had skills and used them to devastating effect. But he had no commitments, no loyalties, no rootedness in humanity. He was the man *belo am*, without a people.

The Hebrew word *emuna* is usually translated as "faith." In the Middle Ages it came to have that connotation (as in the summary of Maimonides' principles printed in most siddurim after the morning service: *Ani maamin be'emuna shelema*, "I believe with perfect faith"). But in Tanakh[3] it does not have that meaning. It is not a cognitive term but a moral one.

The concept of *brit*, "covenant," in the Torah – whether between two or more human beings, or, as at Sinai, between a nation and God – means a mutually binding pledge. Two parties undertake responsibilities to one another. They agree to join their destinies. The key virtue in an ethic defined by covenant is *loyalty* – being true to your word, trusting the other party to be true to his, and acting in such a way as to honour that commitment. *Emuna* means faithfulness, solidity, reliability. It means not walking away from the other party when times are tough. *Emuna*, in short, means loyalty. That is what Balaam lacked.

In the end – not only in the religious life but in life as a whole – moral qualities count for more than intellectual or even spiritual ones. There are all too many people blessed with great gifts who somehow achieve less than they hoped or others expected. Cleverer than other people, they tend to look down on others. They lack the basic qualities of human solidarity. What they do, they do brilliantly. But often they do the wrong things. They even commit crimes because they are convinced that they can get away with them.[4] Knowing how quick they

---

3. As in Deut. 32:4; Is. 59:4; Jer. 5:1; Hos. 2:22; Ps. 33:4; and other places.
4. On this, see the interesting study by Dacher Keltner, *The Power Paradox* (London: Allen Lane, 2016). The paradox in question is that good people become leaders, but leadership can corrupt good people.

are – and how slow others are – to understand, they come to believe that they can do wrong without anyone noticing, or at least identifying them as the culprit.

The classic case was Balaam himself. He knew he could not curse in the name of God those whom God sought to bless. But somehow he persuaded himself that he could give advice to the Midianites and Moabites – use non-Israelite women to lure the Israelite men – without God knowing. After all, what did Balaam do? He merely shared some thoughts with some important people. It was not he who actually carried out the plan. He could have claimed innocence. He forgot two things: that you cannot hide a crime from the God who sees all, and that you cannot in the long run hide a crime even from human beings. They may be slow to find you out, but eventually they will.

The Torah is about more than merely abstract principles and universal truths. It is also about marriage and the family, a people and its history, a nation and its destiny. More than almost any other religious tradition, Judaism is about the universality of justice but the particularity of love.[5] *Pace* Immanuel Kant, who argued that morality is of its essence universal, there are fundamental dimensions of the moral life that have to do with particularity: with the responsibilities that I have to my marriage partner, my child, my family, my community, my people, and my faith, and not just to humanity in its thin, abstract universality. It is in families and communities that loyalty is born – and without loyalty there can be no trust, no commitment, no *emuna*, no faithfulness.

What matters in the long run is not what gifts we have, but what use we put them to. We cannot choose the gifts we have. That is partly a matter of genetics or luck or fate or providence. But we can choose what we do with them. Balaam lost the high reputation he might have had because he lacked a basic commitment to moral principle.

A prophet without loyalty is not a prophet. A person without loyalty is not a mensch.

---

5. On this, see Jonathan Sacks, *Not in God's Name* (New York: Schocken, 2015), 189–206.

Let Someone Else Praise You

There is a fundamental question to be asked about the whole perplexing story of Balaam. Why is it here? Why was it included in the biblical narrative? Why does the Torah devote significant space to the words of a shaman who may or may not have been a genuine prophet? What does the episode signify? If God wished Israel to be blessed, why use a pagan prophet, and one who, as we see later in the story (Num. 31:16), did not wish them well?

The question is deepened by the fact that the episode is regarded by Tanakh as a whole as a highly significant one. It is referred to time and again – by Moses in Deuteronomy, by Joshua at the end of his mission, later by the prophet Micah, and later still, after the Babylonian exile and return, by Nehemiah:

> However, the Lord your God did not listen to Balaam but turned the curse into a blessing for you, because the Lord your God loves you. (Deut. 23:6)

> When Balak son of Zippor, the king of Moab, prepared to fight against Israel, he sent for Balaam son of Beor to put a curse on

you. But I would not listen to Balaam, so he blessed you again and again, and I delivered you out of his hand. (Josh. 24:9–10)

My people, remember what Balak king of Moab plotted and what Balaam son of Beor answered. (Mic. 6:5)

On that day the book of Moses was read aloud in the hearing of the people and there it was found written that no Ammonite or Moabite should be admitted into the assembly of God, because they had not met the Israelites with food and water but had hired Balaam to call a curse down on them. Our God, however, turned the curse into a blessing. (Neh. 13:2).

The answer is, surely, that some basic themes of Jewish faith are at stake. First, the Torah is telling us that no supernatural force directed against Israel can succeed, that "the guardian of Israel neither slumbers nor sleeps" (Ps. 121:4). God protects Israel from those who seek to do it harm. Balak and Balaam must repeatedly discover the absurdity of trying to curse Israel against the wishes of God.

Second, we are being reminded of a truth about prophecy. As God had already said to Moses at the burning bush when he said he was not a man of words: "'Who gave man a mouth?' asked God. 'Who makes a person dumb or deaf? Who gives a person sight or makes him blind? Is it not I – God? Now go! I will be with your mouth and teach you what to say'" (Ex. 4:12).

God speaks through those He chooses, as He chooses, and when He chooses. What is important is what is said, not who is saying it. The word of God is not the word of the prophet about God but the word of God through the prophet. God can choose a hero like Moses, a villain like Balaam, or even – this is the point of the story about the talking donkey – an animal. The prophet is not the author of his or her words, merely the vehicle.

The third point is suggested by a comment in *Midrash Rabba*:

It would have been appropriate for the reprimands [delivered to Israel] to have been said by Balaam and the blessings by Moses. However, if Balaam had spoken the reprimands, the Israelites would have said, "Our enemy is reprimanding us." And had Moses delivered the blessings, the nations of the world would have said, "One who loves them is blessing them." Therefore, said the Holy One, Blessed Be He, "Let Moses who loves them reprimand them; and let Balaam who hates them, bless them, so that both the reprimands and the blessings make a clear impression on Israel."[1]

When people say what they are expected to say, their words tend to be discounted. "Well, he would say that, wouldn't he?" Friends praise and bless. Enemies criticise and curse. Hence, to make an impression, to be effective, ultimately to be credible, the order had to be reversed.

It was important that the hard and harsh words – of critique, challenge, warning, and reproof – were said by those whose orientation to the Jewish people was that of love. That is why the prophets of Israel had to love Israel, for it was their task to reprimand the people, and criticism is effective only when delivered out of love.[2] That is why the command to deliver reproof is almost immediately followed by the command to love: "You must reprove your neighbour and not bear sin because of him…. You shall love your neighbour as yourself; I am God" (Lev. 19:17–18).

The corollary also follows. It takes an outsider to deliver praise. As the book of Proverbs puts it: "Let someone else praise you, and not your own mouth; a stranger, and not your own lips" (Prov. 27:2).

The fourth point has to do with the promise made by God to Abraham at the very outset of the Jewish story:

> I will make you into a great nation, and I will bless you; I will make your name great, and you will be a blessing. I will bless those who bless you, and whoever curses you, I will curse; and all peoples on earth will be blessed through you.[3]

1. Deuteronomy Rabba 1:4.
2. See on this, two works on prophecy and social criticism by the political philosopher Michael Walzer: *Interpretation and Social Criticism* (Cambridge, MA: Harvard University Press, 1987), and *Company of Critics* (New York: Basic Books, 1988).
3. Gen. 12:2–3. See also Gen. 18:18; 22:18; 26:4; 28:14.

To be sure, Abraham was indeed blessed, by Melchizedek king of Shalem (Gen. 14:18). But when, thereafter, do we hear of the Israelites being blessed by others? That is what makes Balaam's blessings so important. They are the fulfilment of that earlier divine promise. As if to emphasise this, Balaam makes the point no less than three times, once in each of his three speeches of blessing:

> Balak brought me from Aram, the king of Moab from the eastern mountains. "Come," he said, "curse Jacob for me; come, denounce Israel." How can I curse those whom God has not cursed? How can I denounce those whom the Lord has not denounced? (Num. 23:7–8)

> God is not human, that He should lie, not a human being, that He should change his mind. Does He speak and then not act? Does He promise and not fulfil? I have received a command to bless; He has blessed, and I cannot change it. (Num. 23:19–20)

> May those who bless you be blessed, and those who curse you be cursed! (Num. 24:9)

There is a further point, by far the most tantalising. As we read the book of Numbers we read, in seemingly endless variations, a story of the fickleness, ingratitude, and immaturity of the Israelites in the desert. Led by God, protected, nourished, and sustained by Him, all they seem able to do is to complain. Where is their thanksgiving, their faithfulness, their acknowledgement? *Why did God choose this people?*

Even when Moses prays on their behalf, he does not invoke their merits. He speaks of God's promise to the patriarchs. He reminds God of the potential desecration of His name in the eyes of the nations if His people perish. He also appeals simply to God's compassion and forgiveness. From the beginning of Exodus to the end of Numbers, not a word is spoken in praise of the Israelites – *except by Balaam*. Nor are these faint praises:

> No wrongdoing is seen in Jacob, no vice observed in Israel. The Lord their God is with them; the shout of the King is among them. (Num. 23:21)

How beautiful are your tents, Jacob, your dwelling places, Israel. Like valleys they spread out, like gardens beside a river, like aloes planted by the Lord, like cedars beside the waters. (24:5–6)

I see him, but not now; I behold him, but not near. A star will come out of Jacob; a sceptre will rise out of Israel. (24:17)

Who said these words? Ostensibly Balaam. But we know he is only speaking the words God put in his mouth. Might this whole passage not be God's oblique way of expressing His love for the people He has taken as His own? Might God not have placed in the mouth of Balaam precisely what He would like to say to them Himself but cannot do so, for they are not yet ready for such words, as immediately becomes apparent when the people, having been saved from Balaam's curses, then start committing adultery and idolatry with the women of Moab and Midian?

Might the whole Balaam/Moses dialectic – Moses reprimanding the people, Balaam singing their praises – represent the duality within the mind of God, between Hashem and Elokim, love and justice, the love God feels for this people yet the justice He demands that they live up to if they are to be His witnesses to the world?

Is this not precisely the divine pathos, that more than Israel loves God, God loves Israel? Surely this is the underlying theme of most of the prophetic literature – what A. J. Heschel called the "divine pathos."[4] Might not the entire Balaam episode be God's way of comforting a people who have been condemned to a forty-year wait in the wilderness? Who have just lost two of their three greatest leaders, Miriam and Aaron? Who are about to enter the home He has been keeping for them since He promised it centuries earlier to Abraham? Might Balaam, who is speaking God's words, not be God's mouthpiece obliquely delivering the praise the Israelites have not yet earned but which God wants recorded for posterity?

Might this not be the explanation for the otherwise altogether remarkable fact that more than any other national literature, the Hebrew Bible records Israel's failings, its shortcomings, its sins, its faults? It is a literature of unparalleled self-criticism. Somehow, somewhere, the

4. See A. J. Heschel, *The Prophets* (New York: Harper and Row), 1962.

people must be assured that they are loved not just for their ancestors but for themselves. Without it we would be left altogether without an explanation for the love of God for this people with whom He is so often angry but for whom He never ceases to care.

Balaam is God's messenger delivering a love letter to His people in such a way as to leave no doubt that the message came directly from God – since there is nothing in Balaam's character and conduct that would explain it in any other way. Balaam is, if one can say such a thing, God's way of fulfilling Proverbs' principle: "Let someone else praise Your people, and not Your own mouth; a stranger, and not Your own lips."

Balaam is the most unlikely messenger but the one who delivers the most beautiful of messages.

Tragic Irony

The story of Balak and Balaam has an ending that is devastating and unexpected. Recall what happened: The Moabites and Midianites were terrified by the approaching Israelites. Balak the Moabite king approached the Midianites and suggested that they hire Balaam to curse the Israelites. If, as they feared, the Israelites derived their strength from a supernatural force, then it made sense to counter it with another supernatural force. The plan failed spectacularly. Instead of cursing the Israelites, Balaam blessed them. Chapter 24 then ends with the words, "Balaam got up and returned home, and Balak went his own way" (Num. 24:25).

This should have been the end of the story. But it was not. Instead, in the very next verses we read:

> While Israel was staying in Shittim, the men began to indulge in sexual immorality with Moabite women, who invited them to the sacrifices to their gods. The people ate the sacrificial meal and bowed down before these gods. So Israel yoked themselves to the Baal of Peor. And the Lord's anger burned against them. (Num. 25:1–3)

This could not be more serious. It is the first time the Israelites commit the cardinal sin of idolatry. Most of the commentators do not regard the Golden Calf as an idol. It was intended as a substitute Moses – a vehicle for receiving divine messages – rather than an object of worship in its own right. But the idolatry at Shittim was real. For the first time we see the Israelites bowing down to Baal, the Canaanite god. It was a betrayal of everything they should have stood for.

What is more, this was the first time the Israelites sinned gratuitously, as it were. Previously they had been driven by fear or hunger or thirst or disappointment. None of these was operative in the case of the Moabite women. This was sheer sexual self-indulgence, yielding to temptation unthinkingly. Even the idolatrous act was undertaken not in any spirit of rebelliousness, but almost as an afterthought: first sex, then food, then pagan worship. If the first, why not the second and the third? The casualness of it almost beggars belief.

Worse: This was the first occasion they had had real contact with the people who would become their neighbours. They were no longer in the desert, far from cities and civilisation. They were approaching the holy land. That they could fall so quickly was a frightening sign of how little they had learned about the nature of their mission as an exemplary people.

Worse still: The sinners were not the usual suspects, the people who came out of Egypt. A generation had passed. Aaron and Miriam had died. So had most of their contemporaries. The Israelites were coming close to their destination. This was the new generation in which all the hopes of the future were invested. Yet they too stumbled at the first fence, fell in the first trial.

Worst of all, it began with sex. To understand the significance of this, recall the book of Genesis. We would have expected it to be either an affirmation of monotheism or a critique of idolatry. But it is neither. It is a critique of the sexual mores of the surrounding culture. Abraham and Isaac feared that they would be murdered for their wives. The people of Sodom surrounded Lot's house, bent on committing an act of homosexual rape. Shechem raped and abducted Jacob's daughter Dina. Potiphar's wife tried to seduce Joseph, and when she failed, had him imprisoned on a false charge of rape.

The implicit argument is profound. What is wrong with idolatry is that it is worship of power – and in human terms the worship of power translates into the untrammelled pursuit of sexual desire. To paraphrase Thucydides, the strong do what they wish and the weak suffer as they must. For Israel to slip into the same sin at the first opportunity is ominous and bodes ill for the future. It also makes a nonsense of Balaam's blessing, "How goodly are your tents, Jacob, your dwelling places, Israel" (Num. 24:5), if, as the rabbis thought, this refers to the modesty of Israel's family life (Rashi to Num. 24:5).

So we brace ourselves for divine anger, and it duly comes.

> The Lord said to Moses, "Take all the leaders of these people, and hang them before the Lord, facing the sun, so that the Lord's fierce anger may turn away from Israel." So Moses said to Israel's judges, "Each of you is to put to death those of your people who have yoked themselves to the Baal of Peor." (Num. 25:4–5)

It was a sharp and painful punishment designed to restore order to the camp. But it failed to do so. One of the tribal leaders, Zimri from the tribe of Simeon, proceeded to bring a Midianite woman into the centre of the camp and cohabit with her in full view of the people, as brazen an offence as we have seen since Datan and Aviram joined the Korah rebellion. Only the zealousness of Pinhas – killing them both as they were cavorting – saved the day.

Where was Moses? The rabbis were surely right to suggest that it was Moses' own background that rendered him powerless in the given situation, for he had himself married a Midianite woman, the daughter of one of their priests (Sanhedrin 82a). Any attempt on Moses' part to do what Pinhas did would have exposed him to the charge of hypocrisy, and made the situation worse, not better.

That said, however, it is hard to avoid the sense that Moses had reached almost the end of the line as a leader. He was old. He was a member of an earlier generation that had proved incapable of meeting the challenge of entering the land. The previous challenges – the episode of the quails, the spies, the Korah revolt, and finally the moment when he struck the rock – sapped his strength. This was true if not spiritually then emotionally, if not in his relationship with God then at least in his relationship with the people.

But the real issue in the story of Balaam is one in which we the readers stand in a privileged position vis-à-vis the participants. For we know, as the people at the time did not, what had previously transpired between God, Balaam, and Balak. No Israelite was present at any point in the events described in the previous chapters. They could not have known the danger they were in, of being cursed by one of the spiritual virtuosi of the time. They could not have known how God Himself had intervened to turn the curses into blessings.

The Oxford English Dictionary defines tragic irony as "a literary technique, originally used in Greek tragedy, by which the full significance of a character's words or actions is clear to the audience or reader although unknown to the character." Tragic irony is rare in the Hebrew Bible. One might almost say it is foreign to the spirit of Judaism, whose defining principle is hope. Yet Numbers 25 is precisely this: a study in tragic irony. Not knowing that they had just been saved from serious danger, the Israelites proceeded to fall into a simple and obvious trap. Having been steered away from the abyss, they slipped on a banana skin. We, the readers, understand this even more deeply than the Israelites at the time.

The Torah is a subtle book, and in the story of Balaam it uses one of its most delicate techniques. Only several chapters later (Num. 31:16), in the course of the war the Israelites eventually waged against the Midianites, do we discover that the entire episode of sexual and spiritual betrayal at Shittim was planned and conceived by Balaam himself.

When the Torah withholds a fact essential to understanding a passage and reveals it only later, it is forcing us to realise that events are not always what they first seem. In this case, certain puzzling aspects of the Balaam story now become clear. We now understand why God was angry with Balaam for going along with the Moabites and Midianites despite the fact that He had given him permission to do so. Evidently God detected in Balaam's mind a persisting malevolence towards Israel, which eventually found expression in the plan to have the women seduce the Israelite men.

We also understand the ambiguity of some of the blessings themselves, including the famous line, "It is a people that dwells alone [*levadad*], not reckoned among the nations" (Num. 23:9). Recall how many centuries later the book of Lamentations used the same word to describe not the uniqueness of Israel but its isolation: "How lonely [*vadad*] lies the city once so full of people!" (Lam. 1:1). The sages went so far as to say that, with one exception, all the blessings pronounced by Balaam eventually turned into curses (Sanhedrin 105b).

The real effect of concealing the information about Balaam is, though, to focus attention on the Israelites. It was they who sinned. Had Balaam's name been mentioned at the outset, we would have focused on him. It would have been his malice, his cunning, his defiance of God's purposes that would have been the story. The Torah is signalling to us that it was not the story. That is not where the Torah wants our attention to be directed. It wants us to focus relentlessly on the Israelites.

The message of the story of Balaam as a whole is this: God saves Israel from its enemies but even God cannot save Israel from itself.

To be defended by the Holy One, Israel must be holy, and that includes – as Leviticus insists in chapters 18 and 20 – a strict sexual ethic. Lose that and the nation will lose everything. If the Israelites act like the Canaanites, they will suffer the fate of the Canaanites. If, on the other hand, it values marriage, honours and sanctifies fidelity between husband and wife and tender care between parents and children, then Israel will eventually be blessed even by its enemies. But if it is unworthy, it can expect no special indulgence from God. To the contrary, as Amos said: "You alone have I singled out of all the families of the earth – that is why I will call you to account for all your iniquities" (Amos 3:2). Loyalty begins in our most intimate relationships, and extends outwards to the nation and upwards to God. Disloyalty, as the Israelites showed in Shittim, can only end in disaster.

The whole book of Numbers has been a counterpoint between order and chaos, law and narrative, God's faith and the people's faithlessness, the blessings God brings forth from the mouth of an enemy and the curses the people bring upon themselves. This is history, but not in a conventional sense. Numbers is less a chronicle of what happened in the course of forty years than a tutorial in what it is to find or lose direction in the wilderness of time.

The enduring lesson remains. God may save us from our enemies, but only we can save us from ourselves.

Pinḥas
פנחס

Parashat Pinḥas begins by completing the episode which began in *Parashat Balak*: Pinhas had ended the plague that was devastating the Israelites while they were seduced into idolatry by the Moabite and Midianite women. Pinhas' reward for his zealotry was a "covenant of peace" (Num. 25:12) and "lasting priesthood" (25:13).

The *parasha* then moves on to the second census in the book, this time of the new generation that would enter the land. There then follow two narratives, one about the daughters of Tzlofhad and God's positive reply to their request for a share in the land, the second about Moses' request that God appoint a successor. The *parasha* ends with two chapters about the sacrifices to be brought at different times, daily, weekly, monthly, and on festivals.

The first of the essays looks at Judaism's understanding of the zealot, typified by Pinhas and in a later age by the prophet Elijah. The second analyses why the act of a zealot cannot serve as the basis for a general rule of conduct. The third is about an unusual feature of the Torah text at the beginning of chapter 26, immediately prior to the census. It contains a *piska be'emtza pasuk*, a chapter break in the middle of a sentence. I argue that this is a kind of audible silence in the narrative, marking a point at which words fail. The fourth asks whether a positive message may be inferred from the fact that Moses was unable to hand on his leadership role to either of his sons. The fifth suggests some of the leadership lessons to be learned from the narrative in which Joshua is chosen as Moses' successor. The sixth analyses an apparently redundant text from which, I argue, an important leadership principle can be inferred.

The Zealot

With Pinhas, a new type of character entered the world of Israel: the zealot. "Pinhas son of Eleazar, son of Aaron, the priest, has turned My anger away from the Israelites by being zealous with My zeal in their midst so that I did not put an end to them in My zeal" (Num. 25:11). He was followed, many centuries later, by the one other figure in Tanakh described as a zealot, the prophet Elijah. Asked by God on Mount Horeb, "What are you doing here, Elijah?" Elijah replied, "I have been very zealous for the Lord God Almighty" (I Kings 19:14). In fact, tradition associates these two men: "Pinhas *is* Elijah," say the sages.[1] Pinhas, says a *Targum*, "became an angel who lives forever and will be the harbinger of redemption at the End of Days."[2]

What is fascinating is how Judaism – both biblical and post-biblical – dealt with the idea of the zealot. Recall the two contexts. First was that of Pinhas. Having failed to curse the Israelites, Balaam eventually devised a strategy that succeeded. He persuaded the Moabite women

---

1. *Yalkut Shimoni* I:771.
2. *Targum Yonatan* to Num. 25:12.

to seduce Israelite men and then lure them into idolatry.[3] This evoked intense divine anger, and a plague broke out among the Israelites.

To make matters worse, Zimri, a leader of the tribe of Simeon, brought a Midianite woman into the camp where they flagrantly and publicly engaged in intimacy. This was an extraordinary breakdown of order within the camp. God had already told Moses to punish the leaders of the people in full view of the nation as a whole to restore order. In light of this, Zimri's defiance was one of the most blatant in the Torah, comparable to that of Datan and Aviram at the time of the Korah rebellion. Only radical action could save the people at that moment.

That is what Pinḥas did. Sensing that Moses felt powerless – he had himself married a Midianite woman[4] – Pinḥas seized the initiative and stabbed and killed both Zimri and the woman, Cozbi. This stopped the plague, brought by divine anger, in which 24,000 Israelites had already died. The text makes clear what might have happened otherwise. God told Moses, "Pinḥas son of Eleazar, son of Aaron, the priest, has turned My anger away from the Israelites by being zealous with My zeal in their midst so that *I did not put an end to them in My zeal*" (Num. 25:11). Pinḥas, in other words, saved the people from destruction.

The story of Elijah is set many centuries later. It begins with the accession of Ahab to the throne of the northern kingdom, Israel. The king had married Jezebel, daughter of the king of Sidon, and under her influence introduced Baal worship into the kingdom, building a pagan temple and erecting a pole in Samaria honouring the Ugaritic mother goddess Asherah. Jezebel, meanwhile, was organising a programme of killing the prophets of the Lord (I Kings 18). The Bible says of Ahab that "he did more evil in the eyes of the Lord than any of those before him" (16:30).

Elijah announced that there would be a drought to punish the king and the Baal-worshipping nation. Confronted by Ahab, Elijah challenged him to gather the 450 prophets of Baal to a test at Mount Carmel. When all were present, Elijah set out the terms of the test. They and he would prepare sacrifices and call on God. The one who sent fire from

---

3. See Num. 31:16.
4. According to the sages (Sanhedrin 82a), it was this fact, that Moses had married a Midianite woman, that caused him to forget the law that Pinḥas remembered.

heaven would be demonstrated to have been the true God. The Baal prophets did so and called on their god, but nothing happened. In a rare show of scornful jesting – zealots are not often known for their sense of humour – Elijah told them to cry louder. Maybe, he said, Baal is busy or travelling or having a sleep. The false prophets worked themselves into a frenzy, gashing themselves until their blood flowed, but still nothing happened. Elijah then prepared his sacrifice and had the people douse it three times with water to make it harder to burn. He then called on God. Fire immediately descended from heaven, consuming the sacrifice. The people, awestruck, cried out, "The Lord – He is God! The Lord – He is God!" (I Kings 18:39), words we say nowadays at the climax of *Ne'ila* at the end of Yom Kippur. The people then killed the prophets of Baal. God had been vindicated, and idolatry shown to be a sham.

Pinhas and Elijah were religious heroes. They stepped into the breach at a time when the nation was facing religious and moral crisis and palpable divine anger. They acted while everyone else, at best, watched. They risked their lives by so doing. There can be little doubt that the mob might have turned against them and attacked them. Indeed, after the trial at Mount Carmel, Jezebel let it be known that she intended to have Elijah killed. Both men acted for the sake of God and the religious welfare of the nation. And God Himself is called "zealous" many times in the Torah. Zealousness must therefore be a virtue, or so it seems.

Yet the treatment of the two men in both the Written and Oral Torah is deeply ambivalent. God rewarded Pinhas by giving him "My covenant of peace" (Num. 25:12), intimating that God would ensure that he never again acted the part of a zealot. Indeed, some years later in the days of Joshua, he played a vital role as a diplomatic man of peace by averting a civil war between the rest of the Israelites and the two-and-a-half tribes – Reuben, Gad, and half of Menashe – who had settled to the east of the Jordan (Josh. 22).

As for Elijah, he was implicitly rebuked by God in one of the great scenes of the Bible. He had won the confrontation at Mount Carmel. But the story does not end there. Jezebel issued a warrant for his death. Elijah escaped to Mount Horeb. There he received a unique vision. He witnessed a whirlwind, then an earthquake, then a fire. But he was led to understand that God was not in these things. Then God spoke to him in a "still, small voice," and told him to appoint Elisha as his successor (I Kings 19:9–16).

The episode is enigmatic, and made all the more so by a strange feature of the text. Immediately *before* the vision, God asked, "What are you doing here, Elijah?" and Elijah replied, "I am moved by zeal for the Lord, the God of Hosts" (I Kings 19:9–10). Immediately *after* the vision, God asked the same question, and Elijah gave the same answer (I Kings 19:13–14). A midrash turns the text into a dialogue:

> Elijah: *The Israelites have broken God's covenant.*
> God: Is it then *your* covenant?
> Elijah: *They have torn down Your altars.*
> God: But were they *your* altars?
> Elijah: *They have put Your prophets to the sword.*
> God: But you are alive.
> Elijah: *I alone am left.*
> God: Instead of hurling accusations against Israel, should you not have pleaded their cause?[5]

The meaning of the midrash is that God expects His prophets to be defenders, not accusers. The prophetic task of getting people to change is best done not through violent confrontation, but by gentleness and the word softly spoken. Elijah, by giving the same answer after the vision as he had done before it, showed that he had not understood that God was telling him to adopt the way of the "still, small voice" in the future. As a result, God then told him that someone else must take his place. Elijah must hand his mantle on to Elisha. We can now define both what is great about the zealot and what is intensely dangerous. *The zealot acts the part of God.* Rashi, commenting on the phrase, "Pinḥas…has turned My anger away from the Israelites by being *zealous with My zeal*," interprets this to mean that God was saying that Pinḥas had "executed My vengeance and showed the anger I should have shown" (Rashi to Num. 25:11). He had done what normally only God would do. The zealot, on his own initiative, acts on behalf of God. But human beings are not

5. Song of Songs Rabba 1:6.

God. They do not know what God knows. That is why, in the biblical age in general, people either awaited God's instruction or availed themselves of the normal process of the law.

Pinhas and Elijah did not wait. In their view, the nation was facing an immediate crisis and they had to act firmly, decisively, and without mercy. They were heroes of the spiritual life. Yet both were implicitly reprimanded by God. God did not say that they were wrong to do what they did. To the contrary, God praised Pinhas and answered Elijah's prayer. But He also made it clear that once was enough. Pinhas was now to take on the role of priesthood and the way of peace. Elijah was told that the time had come to appoint his successor.

In general we are commanded to "walk in God's ways" and imitate His attributes. "Just as He is merciful and compassionate, so you be merciful and compassionate."[6] But note that the command specifies mercy and compassion. It does not include vengeance and punishment. God, who knows all, may execute sentence without a trial, but we, being human, may not. Punishment "by the hand of Heaven" does not operate on the same logic as punishment "by human hand." There are forms of justice that are God's domain, not ours.

There is, of course, an exception – namely, the law of *rodef*, the "pursuer." If you see someone about to kill someone else, you may and should stop him, even, if there is no other alternative, at the cost of his life (Sanhedrin 73a). The *rodef*, by actively endangering the life of another, has to that extent forfeited his own right to life. The question is: Can there be a *rodef* vis-à-vis society as a whole? That, it seems, is how Pinhas regarded Zimri, and Elijah the prophets of Baal. They were actively endangering the nation. The danger posed by a *rodef* is immediate. It cannot be dealt with by normal processes of the law. That is why Pinhas and Elijah acted as they did.

Both were vindicated by God. But God also made it clear that they should never act that way again. The zealot who takes the law into his own hands is embarking on a course of action fraught with moral danger. Only the most holy may do so, only once in a lifetime, and only in the most dire circumstances: when the nation is at risk, when there

---

6. *Mekhilta, Parashat Beshallaḥ* 3.

is nothing else to be done and no one else to do it. As we will see in the next essay, the rabbis ruled that Pinḥas' act was a case of *halakha ve'ein morin ken*, meaning that it may have been within the law, but if someone were to ask whether he or she may act likewise, the answer would be no.

There were times when zealots saved the Jewish people. The most obvious example is the uprising of the Maccabees against the Seleucid Greeks in the war we commemorate on Ḥanukka. But there were other times when zealots did great harm. One such case was the assassination of Gedalia ben Ahikam, appointed by the Babylonians as governor of Judea after the destruction of the First Temple. Gedalia had begun the reconstruction of Jewish life after the catastrophe of conquest, but was regarded by some extremists as a traitor and a servant of Israel's enemies. As a result of the assassination, many of the Jews still in Judea were forced to flee to Egypt, devastating Jewish life in what remained of the holy land.

A second disaster was the campaign of the Jewish zealots against the Romans in late Second Temple times. Just as the people had ignored the advice of the prophet Jeremiah in the sixth century BCE, so they ignored the advice of moderates like Rabban Yoḥanan b. Zakkai in the first century CE, and the result was the destruction of the Second Temple. Josephus, an eyewitness to the Roman siege of Jerusalem, tells us that the zealots spent much of their time attacking their fellow Jews, thus weakening the nation when strength was essential.

A third example, in our own times, was the assassination of the prime minister of Israel, Yitzhak Rabin, by a zealot, Yigal Amir, who apparently believed that Rabin was a *rodef* who was endangering the nation by pursuing a peace process that might put Israel's future safety at risk.

Not everyone is a Pinḥas or an Elijah, and even Pinḥas and Elijah were not allowed to repeat their zealous deeds. It is exceptionally dangerous to believe you have privileged access to the mind of God and that you have the right to act on His behalf. God is God and humans are all too human. That is why legal and political processes exist, and why the zealot, who circumvents both, is often more of a danger than the danger he claims to avert.

Not by accident did tradition fix the *parasha* break between *Parashat Balak* and *Parashat Pinḥas* at the most counterintuitive point, *between* Pinhas' act (Num. 25:6–9) and the divine verdict on the act (Num. 25:10–15). The result is that we are forced to wait a week before hearing whether he did right or wrong. It is as if the sages wanted us to live with that ambiguity so that we would not too readily conclude that Pinhas was a hero. He was, but his act was fraught with moral hazard. How so is the subject of the next essay.

Acts and Consequences

One of the most interesting features of Pinhas' act of zealotry is how it was understood from the perspective of halakha, Jewish law. To what extent did it constitute a precedent? Pinhas saved the nation from what we can only assume would have been dire consequences. Twice before, in the context of the Golden Calf and then again in the case of the spies, God had threatened to destroy the whole people. Only the impassioned prayers of Moses had swayed the verdict from retribution to compassion. It is hard to underestimate the consequences of a third offence that was at least as serious as those that had gone before.[1] Indeed, the biblical text is explicit about this. God told Moses: "Pinhas son of Eleazar, son of Aaron, the priest, has turned My anger away from the Israelites by being zealous with My zeal in their midst so that *I did not put an end to them in My zeal*" (Num. 25:11). He saved the people by his act, as Moses had previously done by his prayers. A psalm praises his behaviour in the highest of terms:

---

1. By consorting with the Midianite women and then joining in the worship of their gods, the people had been guilty of both sexual immorality and idolatry, a potentially more serious breach of the covenant than either the Golden Calf or the episode of the spies.

They yoked themselves to the Baal of Peor and ate sacrifices offered to lifeless gods; they aroused the Lord's anger by their wicked deeds, and a plague broke out among them. But Pinhas stood up and intervened, and the plague was checked. *This was credited to him as righteousness for endless generations to come.* (Ps. 106:28–31)

The reasonable assumption, therefore, is that he would be held as a role model of heroic action in defence of the nation.

Yet Jewish law placed three sharp limitations on what could be inferred from the episode. The first is that, had Zimri turned around and killed Pinhas instead, Zimri would be deemed innocent since he would have been acting in self-defence (Sanhedrin 82a).

Second, Pinhas was only warranted in what he did because he acted while Zimri and Cozbi were still engaged in their sexually immoral act. Had he delayed for even a moment after they had separated from one another, he would not be permitted to do what he did, and had he done so he would have been guilty of murder (Sanhedrin 82a).

Third, as we saw in the previous essay, had Pinhas asked a halakhic authority – Moses, or any of the judges – whether he was permitted to do what he was about to do, the answer would have been no. This is a rare instance of the rule called *halakha ve'ein morin ken*, "It is a law that is not taught" (Sanhedrin 82a).

The Jerusalem Talmud goes further still. It says that the sages of the time *sought to excommunicate Pinhas*, and would have done so had not the Holy Spirit hastened to say, "He and his descendants will have a covenant of a lasting priesthood, because he was zealous for the honour of his God and made atonement for the Israelites" (Num. 25:12).[2]

This is all deeply puzzling. If Pinhas was wrong in what he did, why do the Torah and the book of Psalms praise him in so fulsome a way? But if he was right and acted in accordance with the law, then his conduct should serve as a positive role model for future generations, and the law ought to be taught. That, after all, is the purpose of law: to guide us, especially in situations of dilemma like the one Pinhas faced.

2.   Y. Sanhedrin 9:7.

Ideally, no doubt, he or others should have brought Zimri to court. But this was no time to go through standard legal procedures. A plague was raging. People were dying in their thousands. It was clear that something had to be done immediately. Why does Jewish law rule that in such a case, though the act is permitted, the court or a halakhic authority is allowed to say that it is not permitted?

The rabbis were evidently also troubled by the fact that, while Zimri and Cozbi's act was committed in the sight of the whole nation, Pinhas seems to have acted on his own initiative. Why did Moses not act? Did Pinhas ask permission from him before he acted, or not? If he did not, then surely he was guilty of precisely the sin for which two of his uncles, Nadav and Avihu, died on the day the Sanctuary was consecrated, namely acting spontaneously without first asking permission. But if he did ask Moses, and Moses gave him permission to act, then how could the rabbis conclude that this was a case of *halakha ve'ein morin ken*, where we are not allowed to disclose the law? The Babylonian Talmud, sensitive to these difficulties, tells the following story:

> Zimri seized Cozbi by her coiffure and brought her before Moses. "Son of Amram," he said, "Is this woman forbidden or permitted? And should you say, 'She is forbidden,' then who permitted you to marry the daughter of Yitro?" At that moment Moses forgot the halakha [concerning intimacy with a heathen woman], and all the people burst into tears. That is why it is written that the people were weeping before the door of the Tabernacle of the congregation. It is also written, "And Pinhas son of Eleazar, son of Aaron, the priest, saw it." What was it that he saw? Rav said: He saw what was happening and remembered the halakha, and said to him, "Great-Uncle, did you not teach us this when you came down from Mount Sinai: he who cohabits with a heathen woman is punished by zealots?" Moses replied, "He who reads the letter, let him be the agent to carry it out." Shmuel said: He saw that there is neither wisdom nor understanding nor counsel against the Lord; whenever the divine name is being profaned, honour must not be paid to one's teacher. R. Yitzhak said in R. Elazar's name: He saw the angel wreaking destruction amongst the people. (Sanhedrin 82a)

As we noted, the reason Moses did not act, according to the sages, was that he himself had married a Midianite woman. He would have been accused of hypocrisy by the people and would have failed to halt the breakdown of order. The Talmud then gives three alternative accounts of what happened and why. Rav said that Pinhas did consult with Moses, who answered him obliquely, not saying but clearly implying that he should act. This is consistent with the principle that the law in question is a case of *halakha ve'ein morin ken*, a law that is not taught but may be hinted at.

Shmuel invokes a different principle altogether, that Pinhas acted on the basis of the rule that where there is *ḥillul Hashem*, a desecration of God's name, it is not necessary to ask permission of one's teacher or any other halakhic authority. To do so would be putting the honour of another human being before the honour of God. R. Elazar suggests, simply, that it was none of these considerations that were at stake but something else altogether, namely *pikuaḥ nefesh*, saving lives. A plague was raging and Pinhas acted to bring it to a halt.

The halakhic discussion is complex, and my concern here is not to analyse the various views but to suggest one way of thinking about the ethical issues involved.

Pinhas was not acting within the normal parameters of the law. Zimri, by cohabiting with Cozbi, may or may not have committed a sin that carried the death sentence, but if he did, then Pinhas was executing punishment without a trial. There are extenuating circumstances in Jewish law in which either the king or the court may execute non-judicial punishment to secure social order.[3] But Pinhas was neither a king nor acting as a representative of the court.

Whether or not he received tacit permission from Moses, he was a private individual acting on his own initiative, not as an agent of the court or an official representative of the people. That is why, had Zimri turned round and killed Pinhas before Pinhas had a chance of killing him, he would have been deemed innocent of murder since he was acting in self-defence. Zimri had not been found guilty by a court of law. Therefore he had not forfeited any of his rights, including the right to self-defence.

3. See Maimonides, *Mishneh Torah, Hilkhot Sanhedrin* 24:4; *Hilkhot Melakhim* 3:10.

Likewise, it was essential that Pinhas acted while Zimri and Cozbi were engaged in their act. Normally a judicial procedure is necessary to establish, on the basis of witnesses, that the accused has committed the act for which he stands indicted. However, in this case Zimri and Cozbi were actually engaged in the act at the time, and were doing so in full public view. The entire community was witness to it. This is what Rashi meant when he said that "everyone could see that he did not kill them without just cause" (commentary to Num. 25:8).

It may be, however, that Pinhas killed Zimri not because he was guilty of a specific offence, but because his behaviour was endangering the entire community, who had already incurred divine anger, and would do so even more were he and Cozbi allowed to continue in their defiance without anyone acting to prevent them. He was, in other words, a *rodef*, a "pursuer," vis-à-vis the community as a whole.[4] A "pursuer" may be killed extrajudicially to save the life of the pursued if this is the only way of stopping him from killing. But this only applies while he is actually pursuing, not subsequently when the damage has already been done.

There is, however, a simpler way of understanding the moral issue involved. To do so, we need to take a brief detour into ethical theory. It was Jeremy Bentham who famously argued that an action is right if it leads to the greatest happiness for the greatest number. Without going into details, what is distinctive about this way of seeing the moral life is that it focuses, not on law, or duty, or conscience, or virtue, but rather on the *consequences* of our actions.

There are two ways of thinking about consequences when it comes to making moral choices. The simple, direct way is to ask, "Will *this act* bring about the best possible consequences?" This is known as act utilitarianism. However, as many philosophers have pointed out, there are serious problems with act utilitarianism.

---

4. This, according to Rabbi Zvi Hirsch Chajes, is why a king or the Sanhedrin are able to impose the death penalty for certain acts that threaten the social order, even if they are not capital offences in biblical law. See his *Torat HaNevi'im, Kol Sifrei Maharatz Chajes*, vol. 1 (Jerusalem: 1958), 48.

Imagine a situation in which a judge can prevent riots that will cause many deaths if he convicts an innocent individual and sentences him to a harsh punishment. According to act utilitarianism, he should do so. One person's loss of liberty and justice is outweighed by the saving of many lives. Or imagine a doctor who can save five lives by killing a healthy individual whose organs he then uses to perform life-saving transplants. The saving of five lives outweighs the loss of one.

Every ethical instinct within us recoils from such conclusions. Morality is not a form of expediency. You cannot reduce the moral life to such calculations of loss and gain. That is why many thinkers attracted by Bentham's idea have formulated a different version known as rule utilitarianism. This says that we should act only in accordance with rules, but the rules themselves are justified because they produce the best possible consequences.

Judaism has a place for rule utilitarianism in its overall moral vision. Whether or not it applies to biblical law, it certainly applies to enactments made by the king or the Sanhedrin for the sake of *tikkun olam* (social order), *darkhei shalom* (good community relations), and other such principles. They were enacted because they made life better for the members of society. They promoted the greatest good for the greatest number. However, there are rare circumstances in which act utilitarianism does enter the picture, in any moral system, not just that of the Torah. One famous theoretical example was introduced into the philosophical literature by one of my own tutors, the late Philippa Foot. It is a thought experiment known as the "trolley problem."[5]

Imagine there is a runaway trolley careering down a railway track. There are five people tied to the track, unable to move. You are watching this happen from the signal box. If you do nothing, the five will die. Beside you is a lever that, if you pull it, will switch the trolley to another track. To that other track one person is tied. Do you pull the lever, so that one person dies but five live? Or do you do nothing, because you do not wish to be responsible for the death of anyone? Act utilitarianism

---

5. Philippa Foot, "The Problem of Abortion and the Doctrine of the Double Effect," *Oxford Review* 5 (1967): 5–15, reprinted in Philippa Foot, *Virtues and Vices* (Oxford: Blackwell, 1978).

tells you to pull the lever. True, you would be responsible for one death, but at the same time you would have saved five lives.

Judith Jarvis Thompson broadened the discussion by imagining a similar but different case.[6] This time you are not in the signal box but on a bridge above the track. You see the trolley coming, and you see the five people tied to the track. Only by putting something heavy on the track can you stop the trolley and save their lives. Next to you on the bridge is a fat man. Should you push him over the bridge? He will die, but the trolley will be stopped and five lives saved. Again, act utilitarianism suggests you should push him.[7] The difference between this case and the previous one seems to be that here you are deliberately causing someone's death to save other people's lives, whereas there you are saving other people's lives, and the fact that someone else will die was not part of your intention. It is an unwanted and unintended consequence of pulling the lever to switch the tracks.

Many people are inclined to pull the lever, but disinclined to throw the fat man off the bridge. What, though, if the fat man was not an innocent bystander, but rather the person who tied the five people to the track, or at least one of a gang who had done so? Here, we might well feel that we ought to throw him off the bridge to save the five lives. By his guilt, he has forfeited his rights.

What is happening in these cases is that we are using act utilitarianism not as the basis of the moral life in general, but as a way of deciding how best to act in a situation in which there are no clean choices. Whichever way you act, you will be breaking a rule that in ordinary circumstances you should abide by. You should not stand idly by and do nothing when you could save five lives. But you should not cause someone to die by pulling a lever or throwing him off a bridge. You face, in the literal sense, a *dilemma*, that is, a choice between two courses of action, both of which are undesirable or, ordinarily, just plain wrong.

6. Judith Jarvis Thomson, "Killing, Letting Die, and the Trolley Problem," *The Monist* 59 (1976): 204–217.
7. We are assuming that you are too light to throw yourself over the bridge and stop the trolley. Otherwise, the moral dilemma would be different. It would be about the moral limits of self-sacrifice for the general good.

That is what was happening in the case of Pinḥas. He had a simple choice: either do nothing and let more people die, or act extrajudicially and kill the two key culprits, Zimri and Cozbi. Pinḥas' act cannot be made the basis of a law, because of the unique circumstances in which he did what he did. He did not act on the basis of rule utilitarianism, because he was faced with two rules which clashed: (1) do not stand idly by while innocent people die, and (2) do not put an offender to death without a properly constituted trial. His behaviour was a classic instance of act utilitarianism, *and the essence of act utilitarianism is that it is about specific situations, not general rules.*

That is what the sages meant when they called it a case of *halakha ve'ein morin ken*, a law which should not be taught. It is why they hedged it around with qualifications. It only applied when the offence was committed in public, when the sentence was carried out while the sin or crime was being committed, and only if the person carrying it out was a "zealot."

The truth is that an act like that of Pinḥas can only be justified in retrospect, when it does actually produce the consequences it was intended to achieve. What is more, it is essential that it never becomes the basis of a general rule, because act utilitarianism has the effect of undermining all rules. Were a doctor to kill a patient to save five lives, no one would ever trust a doctor again. Were a judge to punish an innocent man to prevent a riot, no one would ever trust the judicial system again.

That is why, in praising Pinḥas for his courage and zeal, God ensured that he would never act that way again, by making with him "My covenant of peace." Rare indeed are the circumstances in which Pinḥas-like zealotry is justified, and if anyone asks whether he may do so, the answer must always be, "No."

When Words Fail

The Greeks had a word for it. They called it *aposiopesis*, which means "becoming silent." This was later adopted as a literary term for a sentence that, for rhetorical effect, is broken off in the middle, often to indicate that the speaker, overcome by emotion, cannot complete it.

Shakespeare gave us a classic example in the case of King Lear, overcome with rage at the way he had been treated by his daughters:

> I will have such revenges on you both
> That all the world shall – I will do such things –
> What they are yet, I know not; but they shall be
> The terrors of the earth![1]

He is twice rendered speechless by his anger. A more profound and poignant instance occurs in Psalms 27:13: "Were it not for my faith that I shall see the Lord's goodness in the land of the living...." The sentence is left unfinished. The psalmist had said in the previous verse, "Do not

---

1. *King Lear*, act IV, scene 2.

abandon me to the will of my foes, for false witnesses have risen against me, breathing violence" (27:12). Now he says that it is only his faith in God that allows him to continue. Were it not for that.... He leaves the next words left unsaid, as if overcome by a sense of the unspeakable despair that would follow. Then he continues, rallying himself: "Hope in the Lord. Be strong and of good courage, and hope in the Lord!" (27:14). The effect is powerful, as the psalmist wrestles with his fears and eventually defeats them.

There are certain rare occasions when the Torah itself signals a break in the sequence of words. It uses what is known as a *piska be'emtza pasuk*, a "paragraph break in the middle of a sentence."[2] There are only a handful of such cases, and there are varying traditions about some of them.

One such case, not marked as such in our texts but signalled in some ancient manuscripts, is Genesis 4:8: "And Cain said to Abel his brother... and it came to pass that, when they were in the field, Cain rose against his brother and killed him."

With or without an actual *piska be'emtza pasuk* the ellipsis – the gap in the middle of the sentence – is obvious. The text says that Cain said, but it does not tell us what he said. The commentators offer various explanations. Some fill in the gap. They say that Cain had an argument with his brother, and there are several suggestions as to what it was about.[3] The Samaritan text and early translations simply add the phrase, "Let us go out into the field." However, the simplest explanation is that the text is deliberately fractured to suggest, in the most dramatic way,

---

2.   See David B. Weisberg, "Break in the Middle of a Verse: Some Observations on a Massoretic Feature," in *Pursuing the Text: Studies in Honor of Ben Zion Wacholder*, ed. John C. Reeves and John Kampen (Sheffield: Sheffield Academic Press, 1994), 34–45, and the literature cited there.

3.   Another suggestion made by some commentators is that Cain was replying to God who had just warned him: "Why are you angry? Why is your face downcast? If you do what is right, will you not be accepted? But if you do not do what is right, sin is crouching at your door; it desires to have you, but you must rule over it" (Gen. 4:7). On this reading, the first part of the verse should be read, "And Cain spoke [to God, in reply to God's warning] against Abel his brother," meaning that he blamed Abel for his anger.

that words failed. Speech broke down. Cain was no longer able to speak to his brother. And *where words end, violence begins.*[4]

However, the two most striking instances of a paragraph break in the middle of a sentence are in Genesis 35 and in our *parasha.* Numbers 25 describes the terrible events at Shittim. Enticed by the women of Moab and Midian, the Israelite men began worshipping the local idols. There was chaos in the camp, and divine anger. Leaders were sentenced to death. Pinhas killed Zimri and Cozbi, who were cohabiting within full view of the people. Twenty-four thousand people died in a plague. God told Moses to take revenge against the Midianites. Then we read: "And it came to pass after the plague...." (Num. 26:1).

At that point there is a *piska be'emtza pasuk,* a paragraph break. In a Torah scroll, the writing breaks off and the rest of the line is left empty. The text then continues:

> ...God spoke to Moses and Eleazar, son of Aaron the priest, saying, "Take a census of the entire Israelite community by paternal lines, [counting] every male over twenty years old who is fit for duty." (Num. 26:1–2)

The example in Genesis occurs after the death of Rachel. The text says:

> While Israel was living in that land, Reuben went and slept with Bilha, his father's concubine, and Israel heard about it...

> Jacob had twelve sons. (Gen. 35:22)

In both cases, there is no obvious ellipsis. It would have made perfectly good sense to have Numbers 26:1 run without a break. It would simply

---

4. There is a further instance, signalled in our text as a closed paragraph break – that is, an empty space in the middle of a line in the Torah scroll – in Deut. 2:8: "So we went on past our kinsmen the descendants of Esau living in Se'ir, left the road through the Arava from Eilat and Etzion-Gever [pause], and turned to pass along the road through the desert of Moab." Here the pause seems simply to indicate a change in the direction of the Israelites' journey. Until then, they had been travelling in a southerly direction, *away* from the land. Now they turned north, *towards* the land.

say that after the plague in which 24,000 people died, God ordered a census so that the people would know the number of the survivors. That is one way in which Rashi explains the verse.[5]

In the case of Genesis 35, it would have made sense to end the verse after, "And Israel heard about it." There is a break in the subject matter at that point. Why then the paragraph break in the middle of the sentence?

Some suggest, on the basis of Mesopotamian parallels,[6] that the break indicated a belief, on the part of the scribes, that there might be words missing from the text at these points. They would not have added them. Any tampering with the received text was absolutely forbidden. Nonetheless, by leaving the rest of the line empty, they hinted that there might once have been an additional phrase in the text.

This, though, is unlikely in the case of the Torah. More probably, the break was there to signal an *oral* tradition that did not belong to the written text but was nonetheless essential to understanding it. The sages, for instance, explained the behaviour of Reuben by saying that he did not sleep with Bilha. He merely removed his father's bed from her tent and shifted it to that of his mother Leah. He believed that if, after Rachel's death, Jacob slept with Bilha, her handmaid, this would be an unforgivable slight to Leah.[7]

Likewise, in the case of the plague in our *parasha*, the break might be there to hint at the tradition, included in *Targum Yonatan*, that God was then moved to compassion and resolved to make this the last punishment the Israelites suffered in the wilderness. Along similar lines,

---

5. It is, in fact, his first interpretation. His second is that the text alludes not to what preceded it but what would shortly follow, namely Moses' request that God appoint a successor. Just as the people were numbered at the start of Moses' career as a leader, so they were numbered at the end.

6. See Weisberg, above, note 2.

7. See Shabbat 55b. The Reuben-Bilha episode was a much-interpreted text in ancient times. See James Kugel, *The Ladder of Jacob: Ancient Interpretations of the Biblical Story of Jacob and His Children* (Princeton, NJ: Princeton University Press, 2006), 81–114. Kugel's footnotes contain references to further scholarly studies of the *piska be'emtza pasuk*.

Ḥizkuni writes that this is why a census followed. Everyone counted at that time lived to enter the Promised Land.[8]

It may be that the paragraph break in the middle of a sentence is there *not to break but to join*. By continuing the sentence despite the beginning of a new paragraph, the text is telling us not to see them as two separate subjects, but rather as integrally related. Thus Jacob had twelve sons *because* Reuben had slept with Bilha, or rearranged the beds. This event so disturbed Jacob that he never slept with the handmaids (or Leah) again. That is why he had no more children.[9] So too in the case of our *parasha*, the Torah wants us to understand that it was not merely *after* the plague but also *because* of it that God ordered a new census.

Thus far, tradition and contemporary scholarship. Yet it seems to me that what we have here is not simply a scribal device but rather an integral element of the text itself. The *piska be'emtza pasuk* is an instance of *aposiopesis*, an audible silence within the text, a point at which language fails. In fact, the two stories, Reuben's apparent intimacy with Bilha and the Israelites' adultery and idolatry with the Moabite and Midianite women, are deeply connected and give rise to the same, almost unbearably powerful emotions.

Think first of Jacob in Genesis 34–35. He has just come through the trauma of his encounter with his brother Esau. The meeting itself was something of an anticlimax, but the anxiety Jacob felt beforehand was palpable, reaching a height in the nighttime struggle with an angel. We feel, at the end of Genesis 33, a sense of relief. Jacob has safely returned home.

Then comes the terrible episode of the rape and abduction of Dina. Simeon and Levi, Jacob's second and third sons, rescue her, but at the brutal cost of the killing of all the males of Shechem, and the looting of all their property. Jacob, appalled, rebukes them, but they are unapologetic: "Should he have treated our sister like a prostitute?" (Gen. 34:31).

---

8. Alternatively, it may be a signal to indicate that the narrative, considered in historical sequence, continues elsewhere. The Torah has just told us that God told Moses to take vengeance against the Midianites (Num. 25:17–18). However, that does not happen until Numbers 31. The paragraph break may thus be a way of signalling that what follows for the next five chapters is in parentheses.
9. Kugel, on the basis of Jubilees 33, in *The Ladder of Jacob*, 96-97.

Then Jacob's wife Rachel dies while giving birth to her second son, Benjamin. We can hardly begin to imagine Jacob's grief. Rachel was the love of his life, and now she is gone. Immediately after this we read that "Reuben went and slept with Bilha, his father's concubine, and Israel heard about it." Whatever actually happened – we noted above the rabbinic interpretation that Reuben was doing no more than moving the beds – Jacob evidently suspected the worst and said so on his deathbed, cursing Reuben:

> Unstable as water, you will not excel,
> for you went up onto your father's bed,
> onto my couch and defiled it. (Gen. 49:4)

However, the real offence was far worse. We learn from the book of Samuel (II Sam. 16:21–22) that sleeping with your father's concubine is tantamount to throwing off his authority and declaring yourself head of the household (or the nation) in his place. Short of murder, it is the ultimate Oedipal act.

Hence the silence. It is as if there are no words to describe Jacob's feelings of grief and betrayal. He had survived Esau, only to lose Rachel and discover that his second and third sons were brutal killers, while his firstborn Reuben had seemingly usurped him within his own household.

That is surely the mood in Numbers 23–25. God had saved the Israelites from their enemies who had sought out Balaam to curse them, only to discover that they then allowed themselves to be seduced by the Moabite women, first sexually, then religiously, worshipping the local god Baal Peor. It was the ultimate betrayal. Seemingly unable to resist the slightest temptation, the Israelites had abandoned their King and Redeemer for a minor local deity before they had even entered the holy land. It is as if the Torah were telling us that there are times when even God is lost for words, when even Heaven is silent, because there is nothing to be said in the people's defence with the sole exception of Pinhas' single act of zeal.

The *piska be'emtza pasuk* is a deliberate pause in the flow of words until we can feel the pressure of sheer silence and begin to take in the enormity of the offence that has just been committed.

What the text does next is similar in both cases. After the silence comes a genealogy – in Genesis, a listing of Jacob's twelve sons, in Numbers a census itemising the number in each of the twelve tribes. It is as if the Torah were consciously beginning again. A silence has been observed. We now know how close the story came to complete derailment. Seeing what his first three sons had done, Jacob might have given up. Seeing what His people had done, God might have destroyed almost the entire people as He had threatened to do twice before. But now, after the silence, comes a new beginning. There are acts that are unforgivable, but the story must continue somehow. That is what the Torah is telling us through these two paragraph breaks in the middle of a verse. They are audible silences. In them, the absence of words speaks more powerfully than any words could do.

That, for me, is Jewish history after the Holocaust. "And it came to pass after the plague...." There is nothing you can say. There is a reverberating silence, a black hole that swallows speech. And then you count the survivors and begin Jewish history again. The pain is undiminished, the grief unhealed, history unredeemed. But there is no choice but to begin again. That is what faith is.

The Crown All Can Wear

Midrash is, among other things, the ability to listen to the Torah's silences. Sometimes they contain great dramas.

What is the meaning of Abraham's silence as he rides for three days with Isaac towards the mountain and the great trial? Or Isaac's as he lies bound on the altar? Or Jacob's when he sees that his son Reuben has defiled his bed? These are eloquent silences – not a mere absence of words but a reticence, a concealment, a beckoning to those who hear them to explore, conjecture, enter into the mind of the characters involved. The Torah does not bear all its meanings on the surface, just as a person does not – and at its deepest level, the Torah is a profound meditation on what it is to be a person in the image of God-who-is-a-person.

So it is with the astonishingly understated narrative of Moses' request to God to appoint a successor:

> Moses said to the Lord, "May the Lord, God of the spirits of all flesh, appoint a man over this community to go out and come in before them, one who will lead them out and bring them in, so the Lord's people will not be like sheep without a shepherd." (Num. 27:15–17)

On the surface, there was no drama, no passion, no inner conflict. Yet the rabbis were right to detect here a silence to be decoded. The immediate context is Moses' knowledge of his own mortality, of the fact that he would not live to cross the Jordan and enter the land:

> Then the Lord said to Moses, "Go up this mountain in the Abarim range and see the land I have given the Israelites. After you have seen it, you too will be gathered to your people, as your brother Aaron was." (Num. 27:12–13)

Miriam had died. So had Aaron. Now Moses himself was within sight of the Angel of Death. Who would be his successor? Did he have no thoughts on the matter? With profound attentiveness, the sages listened to the immediately previous passage, and there they found the clue. It is the story of the daughters of Tzlofhad, who claim their rights of inheritance in the land, despite the fact that inheritance passed through the male line and their father had left no sons. Moses brought their request to God, who answered that it was to be granted.

Against this background, the Midrash interprets Moses' thoughts as he brings his own request to God, that a successor be appointed:

> What was Moses' reason for making this request after declaring the order of inheritance? Just this, that when the daughters of Tzlofhad inherited from their father, Moses reasoned: The time is right for me to make my own request. If daughters inherit, it is surely right that my sons should inherit my glory. The Holy One, Blessed Be He, said to him, "He who keeps the fig tree shall eat its fruit" (Prov. 27:18). Your sons sat idly by and did not study the Torah. Joshua served you faithfully and showed you great honour. It was he who rose early in the morning and remained late at night at your House of Assembly. He used to arrange the benches and spread the mats. Seeing that he has served you with all his might, he is worthy to serve Israel, for he shall not lose his reward.[1]

---

1. Numbers Rabba 21:14.

This is the unspoken drama. Not only was Moses fated not to enter the land, but he was also destined to see his sons overlooked in the search for a successor. That was his second personal tragedy.

But it is precisely here that we find, for the first time, one of Judaism's most powerful propositions. Biblical Israel had its dynasties. Both priesthood and, in a later age, kingship were handed down from father to son. Yet there is a profoundly egalitarian strand in Judaism from the outset. Ironically, it is given one of its most powerful expressions in the mouth of the rebel, Korah: "All the congregation are holy and the Lord is in their midst. Why then do you set yourselves above the congregation?" (Num. 16:3).

But it was not only Korah who gave voice to such a sentiment. We hear it in the words of Moses himself: "Would that all the Lord's people were prophets and that the Lord would put His spirit on them" (Num. 11:29).

We hear it again in the words of Hannah when she gives thanksgiving for the birth of her son:

> The Lord sends poverty and wealth;
> He humbles and He exalts.
> He raises the poor from the dust
> and lifts the needy from the ash heap;
> He seats them with princes
> and has them inherit a throne of honour. (I Sam. 2:7–8)

It is implicit in the great holiness command: "The Lord said to Moses, 'Speak to the entire assembly of Israel and say to them: Be holy, because I, the Lord your God, am holy'" (Lev. 19:2).

This is not a call to priests or prophets – a sacred elite – but to an entire people. There is, within Judaism – as we discussed in an earlier chapter[2] – a profound egalitarian instinct: the concept of a nation of individuals standing with equal dignity in the presence of God.

Korah was wrong less in what he said than in why he said it. He was a demagogue attempting to seize power. But he tapped into a deep

---

2. See "The Egalitarian Impulse in Judaism."

reservoir of popular feeling and religious principle. Jews have never been easy to lead because each is called on to be a leader. What Korah forgot is that to be a leader it is also necessary to be a follower. Leadership presupposes discipleship. That is what Joshua knew, and what led to him being chosen as Moses' successor. "He who keeps the fig tree shall eat its fruit.... Joshua served you faithfully and showed you great honour.... Seeing that he has served you with all his might, he is worthy to serve Israel."

The tradition is summed up in the famous Maimonidean ruling we saw earlier:

> With three crowns was Israel crowned – with the crown of Torah, the crown of priesthood, and the crown of kingship. The crown of priesthood was bestowed on Aaron and his descendants. The crown of kingship was conferred on David and his successors. But the crown of Torah is for all Israel. Whoever wishes, let him come and take it. Do not suppose that the other two crowns are greater than that of Torah.... The crown of Torah is greater than the other two crowns.[3]

This had immense social and political consequences. Throughout most of the biblical era, all three crowns were in operation. In addition to prophets, Israel had kings and an active priesthood serving in the Temple. The dynastic principle – leadership passing from father to son – still dominated two of the three roles. But with the destruction of the Second Temple, kingship and a functioning priesthood ceased. Leadership passed to the sages who saw themselves as heirs to the prophets. We see this in the famous one-sentence summary of Jewish history with which Tractate Avot (Ethics of the Fathers) begins: "Moses received the Torah from Sinai and handed it on to Joshua, who handed it on to the elders, the elders to the prophets, and the prophets to the men of the Great Assembly" (Mishna Avot 1:1).

Conspicuously missing from this list are the priests. In biblical Israel, they were the primary guardians and teachers of Torah. Why did

---

3. Maimonides, *Mishneh Torah, Hilkhot Talmud Torah* 3:1.

the rabbis not see themselves as heirs to Aaron and the priesthood? That would, on the face of it, have been far more natural than defining themselves as successors to the prophets. There are many reasons, but one is surely this: the priesthood was a dynasty. It was not open to everyone. It was restricted by birth. Prophetic leadership, by contrast, could never be predicted in advance. The proof was Moses. The very fact that his children did not succeed him as leaders of the people may have been an acute distress to him but it was a deep consolation to everyone else. It meant that anyone, by discipleship and dedication, could aspire to rabbinic leadership and the crown of Torah.

Hence we find in the sources a paradox. On the one hand, the Torah describes itself as an inheritance: "Moses commanded us the Torah as an inheritance [*morasha*] of the congregation of Jacob" (Deut. 33:4). On the other, the sages were insistent that Torah is *not* an inheritance: "R. Yose said: Prepare yourself to learn Torah, for it is not given to you as an inheritance [*yerusha*]" (Mishna Avot 2:12).

The simplest resolution of the contradiction is that there are two kinds of inheritance. Biblical Hebrew contains two different words for what we receive as a legacy: *yerusha/morasha* and *nahala*. *Nahala*, as we noted earlier, is related to the word *nahal*, "a river." It signifies something passed down automatically across the generations, as river water flows downstream. *Yerusha* comes from the root *yarash*, meaning "to take possession." It refers to something to which you have legitimate title, but which you need positive action to acquire.

A hereditary title, such as being a duke or an earl, is passed from father to son. So too is a family business. The difference is that the first needs no effort on the part of the heir, but the second requires hard work if the business is to continue to be worth something. Torah is like a business, not a title. It must be earned if it is to be sustained.

The sages themselves put it more beautifully: "'Moses commanded us the Torah as an inheritance [*morasha*] of the congregation of Jacob' – read not 'inheritance [*morasha*]' but 'betrothed [*meorasa*]'" (Berakhot 57a). By a simple change in pronunciation – turning a *shin* [="sh"] into a *sin* [="s"], "inheritance" into "betrothal" – the rabbis signalled that, yes, there is an inheritance relationship between Torah and the Jew, but the former has to be loved if it is to be earned.

The sages were fully aware of the social implications of R. Yose's dictum that the Torah "is not given to you as an inheritance." It meant that literacy and learning must never become the preserve of an elite:

> They sent word from there [Israel].... Be careful [not to neglect] the children of the poor, because from them Torah goes forth....
>
> And why is it not usual for scholars to give birth to sons who are scholars?
>
> R. Yosef said: So that it should not be said that the Torah is their inheritance.
>
> R. Shisha b. R. Idi said: So that they should not be arrogant towards the community.
>
> Mar Zutra said: Because they act highhandedly against the community.
>
> R. Ashi said: Because they call people asses.
>
> Ravina said: Because they do not first utter a blessing over the Torah. (Nedarim 81a)

In these dicta we see the full range of rabbinic meditation on why the crown of Torah was not hereditary – because it might become the prerogative of the rich; because children of great scholars might take their inheritance for granted; because it could lead to arrogance and contempt for others; and because learning itself might become a mere intellectual pursuit rather than a spiritual exercise ("because they do not first utter a blessing over the Torah").

The very fact that the sages said these things is evidence that they had to be constantly on their guard against exclusivist attitudes to Torah. Equality is never preserved without vigilance – and indeed there were contrary tendencies. We see this in one of the debates between the schools of Hillel and Shammai:

> "Raise up many disciples" – The school of Shammai says: A person is to teach only one who is wise, humble, of good stock, and rich.
>
> But the school of Hillel says: Everyone is to be taught. For there were many transgressors in Israel who were attracted to the study of Torah, and from them sprang righteous, pious,

and worthy men. To what may it be compared? "To a woman who sets a hen to brood on eggs – out of many eggs, she may hatch only a few, but out of a few [eggs], she hatches none at all."[4]

One cannot predict who will achieve greatness. Therefore Torah must be taught to all. A later episode illustrates the virtue of teaching everyone:

> Once Rav came to a certain place where, though he had decreed a fast [for rain], no rain fell. Eventually someone else stepped forwards in front of Rav before the ark and prayed, "Who causes the wind to blow" – and the wind blew. Then he prayed, "Who causes the rain to fall" – and the rain fell.
>
> Rav asked him: What is your occupation [i.e., what is your special virtue that causes God to answer your prayers]? He replied: I am a teacher of young children. I teach Torah to the children of the poor as well as to the children of the rich. From those who cannot afford it, I take no payment. Besides, I have a fish pond, and I offer fish to any boy who refuses to study, so that he comes to study. (Taanit 24a)

It would be wrong to suppose that these attitudes prevailed in all places at all times. No nation achieves perfection. An aptitude for learning is not equally distributed within any group. There is always a tendency for the most intelligent and scholarly to see themselves as more gifted than others and for the rich to attempt to purchase a better education for their children than the poor. Yet to an impressive – even remarkable – degree, Jews were vigilant in ensuring that no one was excluded from education and that schools and teachers were paid for by public funds. By many centuries, indeed millennia, Jews were the first to democratise education. The crown of Torah was indeed open to all.

Moses' tragedy was Israel's consolation. "Why is it not usual for scholars to give birth to sons who are scholars? ... So that it should not be said that the Torah is their inheritance." The fact that his successor was not his son, but Joshua, his disciple, meant that one form

4. *Avot DeRabbi Natan*, version 2, ch. 4.

of leadership – historically and spiritually the most important of the three crowns – could be aspired to by everyone. Dignity is not a privilege of birth. Honour is not confined to those with the right parents. In the world defined and created by Torah, everyone is a potential leader. We can all earn the right to wear the crown.

Lessons of a Leader

In a brief but instructive passage, *Parashat Pinḥas* describes one of the key transitional moments in biblical history. Moses, aware that his life is drawing to a close and that he will not have the privilege of leading the people into the Promised Land, asks God to appoint a successor.

This is, in itself, a significant lesson. *Great leaders care about succession.* What matters to them as they face their mortality is that the work should continue. In *Parashat Ḥayei Sara*, after the death of Sarah, Abraham instructed his servant to find a wife for Isaac so that there would be continuity for the family of the covenant. David chose Solomon. Elijah, at God's bidding, appointed Elisha. Unlike most other religions, Judaism is not about a single transformative moment in history, to which all the rest of time is either before or after. We believe that the work of the covenant is an ongoing process, a continuing journey, an effort that must be renewed in every generation. Succession is vital, and Moses knew it.

We saw in the previous essay that there was a measure of poignancy, even disappointment, at Moses' realisation that he would not be succeeded by either of his sons, Gershom or Eliezer. There was, we noted, a positive reason for this: to teach us that the "crown of Torah" is not an inheritance. It has to be earned; it cannot be conferred by descent.

That said, there are important lessons to be learned from Moses' request and God's reply. Here we focus on three of them. The first is hinted at in the strange, circumlocutory way in which Moses frames his request:

> May the Lord, *God of the spirits of all flesh*, appoint a man over this community to go out and come in before them, one who will lead them out and bring them in, so the Lord's people will not be like sheep without a shepherd. (Num. 27:16)

Why, asked the sages, did Moses add the phrase, "God of the spirits of all flesh"? The answer, given by Rashi quoting a midrash, is that he was signalling what he saw as an essential quality of anyone leading the Jewish people: "Master of the universe, the character of each person is revealed to You, and no two are alike. Appoint over them a leader *who will bear with each person according to his individual character*."[1] A leader, even as he or she seeks to communicate a shared vision and common purpose, is nonetheless sensitive to the differences between people.

Maimonides says that this is a basic feature of the human condition. Homo sapiens is the most diverse of all life forms. Therefore cooperation is essential – because where some are weak, others are strong – but it is also difficult, because we respond to challenges in different ways. That is what makes leadership necessary, but also demanding:

> This great variety and the necessity of social life are essential elements in man's nature. But the well-being of society demands that there should be a leader able to regulate the actions of man; he must complete every shortcoming, remove every excess, and prescribe for the conduct of all, so that the natural variety should be counterbalanced by the uniformity of legislation, and the order of society be well established.[2]

---

1. Rashi to Num. 27:16, based on *Midrash Tanḥuma, Parashat Pinḥas* 11.
2. Maimonides, *Guide for the Perplexed*, II:40.

This is a universal principle. Yet there remains something distinctively Jewish about it. One of the most striking facts about Judaism is its insistence on *the dignity of difference*. No two human beings are exactly alike. Even identical twins, who share the same genetic endowment and who are sometimes hardly identifiable from one another, nonetheless share only 50 per cent of their behavioural characteristics. This, we believe, is not something to be lamented, but to be honoured. It is the basis of one of the most striking sentences in the Mishna, that "a single soul is like a universe" (Mishna Sanhedrin 4:5), meaning that none of us is substitutable for any other.

We are each unique, therefore irreplaceable, therefore sacrosanct, and a leader must honour this fact. He or she must respect differences and then, like the conductor of an orchestra, integrate them, ensuring that the many different instruments play their part in harmony with the rest. True leaders do not seek to impose uniformity. They honour diversity.

Hence rule 1: *Leaders respect difference. They recognise our distinctive gifts and help us realise them. They understand our role in the team. They help us make the contribution only we can make to the project we all share.*

The second principle is hinted at by the word that appears both in Moses' request and God's reply: the word *ish*, "a man." Moses asked God to appoint "a man [*ish*] over the congregation." God replied, "Take for yourself Joshua, son of Nun, a man [*ish*] of spirit" (Num. 27:18).

We might reasonably conclude that Moses was talking about gender, meaning, a man, not a woman. However, Jewish tradition did not read it this way. There were prophetesses as well as prophets. There was a woman leader, namely Deborah, in the era of the judges. *Ish* in this context does not mean a man as opposed to a woman. What it does mean can be inferred from the two places in the Torah where we find the phrase *ha'ish Moshe*, "the man Moses." One occurs in the story of the Exodus: "The man Moses was highly respected [*gadol meod*, literally, 'very great'] in the land of Egypt, in the eyes of Pharaoh's servants and the people" (Ex. 11:3). The other appears in the episode in which his own sister and brother, Miriam and Aaron, criticise him: "Now the man Moses was very humble [*anav meod*], more so than anyone else on the face of the earth" (Num. 12:3).

These are two characteristics – greatness and humility – that we often think of as opposed. People whom the world considers great are rarely humble, and those who are humble rarely achieve greatness, at least in the public eye. But Moses was both. The Torah goes out of its way to apply the same adverb, *meod*, "very," to both attributes. He was very great and at the same time very humble.

It is just this combination of attributes that R. Yoḥanan attributed to God Himself: "Wherever you find God's greatness, there you find His humility."[3] Here is one of his prooftexts:

> For the Lord your God is God of gods and Lord of lords, the great God, mighty and awesome, who shows no partiality and accepts no bribes. He defends the cause of the fatherless and the widow, and loves the stranger residing among you, giving them food and clothing. (Deut. 10:17–18)

The word *ish* in the context of leadership does not mean "a man" but rather, "a mensch," one whose greatness is lightly worn, who cares about the people others often ignore, "the fatherless, the widow, and the stranger," who spends as much time with the people at the margins of society as with the elites, who is courteous to everyone equally and who receives respect because he or she gives respect.

That humility was palpable in the case of Joshua. After the making of the Golden Calf, he was waiting for Moses at the foot of the mountain so he could inform him about what had happened in his absence (Ex. 32:17). When Eldad and Medad began prophesying, which Joshua saw as a potential threat to Moses' leadership, his concern for Moses was immediate and deeply felt (Num. 11:28). Together with Caleb, he refused to side with the ten spies who brought a demoralising report about the land and its inhabitants (Num. 14:6). Yet when Moses told him to assemble a military force and fight the Amalekites, he did so without demur, and won an important victory (Ex. 17:9–13).

Humility remains one of the most important qualities of a leader. In his classic business text, *Good to Great*, Jim Collins argues for what he

---

3. From the liturgy on Saturday night. The source is *Pesikta Zutreta, Parashat Ekev.*

calls "level 5 leadership," which he defines as "an individual who blends extreme personal humility with intense professional will." His research revealed that individuals of this specific type were to be found at the helm of every outstandingly successful company. What they shared was an ability to channel their ego needs away from themselves and focus instead on the people and the institution they were leading.[4]

Hence rule 2: *Leaders care about others, not themselves. Their focus is on the team, the mission, and the ideals. They may be driven people, and they certainly drive others, but what matters is not their own honour or success but that of those they lead.*

Third is the startling comment of Rashi on the phrase in which God told Moses to take Joshua and "make him stand before Eleazar the priest and the entire assembly and *you shall command him* in their presence" (Num. 27:18–19). On this, Rashi says, "You shall command him about the Israelites, saying, '*Be aware that they are troublesome and obstinate.* [You may be their leader only] on condition that you accept this.'"[5]

This comment, based on a midrash, is a rabbinic anticipation of Ronald Heifetz's theory of adaptive leadership, which has been a constant underlying theme of our study of Numbers as a whole.[6] Adaptive leadership is needed when, to meet a new challenge, the people have to change. This cannot be done by the leader alone. He has to educate the people, and to a certain degree, hand the challenge back to them.

People resist change, especially when that means giving up long-standing habits that have become deeply embedded in their character. They can go through all the emotions associated with loss: denial, anger, bargaining, and depression.[7] That is one of the bass notes of Numbers: the people's anger at Moses for forcing them to face the responsibilities of freedom. Hence their frequent false nostalgia about how things were in Egypt, and their regret that they ever left.

---

4. Jim Collins, *Good to Great* (New York: HarperCollins, 2001), 21.
5. Rashi to Num. 27:19; see Sifre, *Parashat Behaalotekha* 91; Exodus Rabba 7:3.
6. See "The Adaptive Challenge."
7. These are four of the five stages in Elisabeth Kübler-Ross' analysis of grief in *On Death and Dying* (New York: Macmillan, 1969).

Moses lived through this time and again. Perhaps this was why he was initially so reluctant to accept the role of leader at all. But this – being exposed to people's anger – is the price leaders have to pay if they are to move a people from where they are to where they need to be. The highest form of leadership is the kind that changes people by a combination of vision, education, and giving people a sense of possibility and responsibility – helping them to achieve greatness. When the leader is good, people say, "The leader did it." When the leader is great, they say, "We did it ourselves."[8] That is because, in a real sense, a great leader is one who persuades or provokes people to do it themselves.

But this always carries a price, because people usually want the leader to do it for them. When they realise it will not happen this way, that the leader cannot relieve people of responsibility, there is anger. That is what the sages meant when they said that God told Moses to inform Joshua that the people "are troublesome and obstinate" and that being their leader came with the condition that "you accept this."

Ronald Heifetz and Marty Linsky remind us how intense an emotional burden this is. Learning to "take the heat" and live with people's anger is one of the hardest tasks of leadership, but it is absolutely essential. The leader has, they say, to hold steady, be respectful of people's pain, and defend the vision without becoming personally defensive. "Receiving anger" is, in their words, "a sacred task."[9]

Rule 3: If you undertake the task of adaptive leadership – of getting people to own their own problem and rise to the challenge of change and growth – you must expect anger along the way. That is one of the conditions of the role.

Yet rabbinic commentary did not let the episode go without a positive note. On the phrase, "Take Joshua son of Nun," Rashi says, "Persuade him, saying, 'Happy are you to merit leading the children of God.'"[10] In the end, leadership is a privilege. It is one of the richest sources of meaning in life.

8. A similar sentiment is attributed to the great Chinese thinker Lao-Tzu.
9. Heifetz and Linsky, *Leadership on the Line* (Boston: Harvard Business Press, 2002), 146.
10. Rashi to Num. 27:18, quoting Sifre, *Parashat Pinḥas* 23.

Walter Lippmann once wrote, "The final test of a leader is that he leaves behind him in other men the conviction and the will to carry on."[11] The measure of Moses' greatness is that he not only inspired Joshua to continue the task he had begun, but did so to an unending flow of prophets, sages, and people of spirit who, lifted by his vision, carried it forwards in generation after generation. In his lifetime he knew the bitterness of failure, but few if any have inspired so many for so long.

11. Walter Lippmann, "Roosevelt Has Gone," *New York Herald Tribune*, April 14, 1945.

Leadership and the Art of Pacing

There are three kinds of Torah: the Torah we learn from books, the Torah we learn from teachers, and the Torah we learn from life. The first two are straightforward. That is how most of us learn. But the third can sometimes be the deepest and most personal. We learn because something happens to us or through us that gives us a new insight into what the Torah is trying to teach us to see.

In my own years as a leader, there was one phrase in *Parashat Pinḥas* I only understood through the experience of leadership itself. It appears in the course of Moses' request of God that He designate his successor. He said:

> May the Lord, God of the spirits of all flesh, appoint someone over this community *who will go out before them and come in before them, who will lead them out and bring them in.* Let the Lord's people not be like sheep without a shepherd. (Num. 27:16–17)

The italicised words seem to be saying the same thing twice. Why the repetition? The meaning of the first phrase, "who will go out before them and come in before them," is clear. It means one who will lead from the front, who will not send his people into battle while staying behind in safety himself. Rashi quotes a verse (I Sam. 18:16) in which the Torah says: "All Israel and Judah loved David *because he went out and came back in front of them.*" The watchword of Israel's leaders has always been *Aḥarai,* "After me."

It is the second phrase that is difficult: "who will lead them out and bring them in." Surely that follows from the first without saying anything new. Rashi is forced to offer two different explanations. One is that it means, "who will lead them [to victory] *through his merits.*" This is a possible reading but it is not the plain sense of the verse.[1] The other is sardonic. Moses, says Rashi, was protesting to God: "Do not do to my successor what You did to me, denying me the chance to lead the people into the land."[2] Let Joshua, unlike me, reach his destination. This is very striking, but even less the plain sense of the verse.

Thus far Rashi. But there is another interpretation – one I only discovered through the life of leadership itself. A leader must indeed lead from the front. But he or she must also understand the pace at which people can go. Leadership is not effective *if leaders are so far ahead of those they lead that when they turn their heads round, they discover that there is no one following.* Leaders must go out in front and come back in front. But they must also "lead the people out and bring them back," meaning, they must take people with them. They must make sure that the people are keeping up with them. They must pace the challenge.

Moses discovered this through the episode of the spies. He was ready to enter the Promised Land. So were two of the spies, Joshua and Caleb. But the rest of the people were not, including ten of the spies. For them it was too much, too soon. The spies raised doubts. The people despaired. Some regretted the fact that they had ever left Egypt. We recall Maimonides' explanation in *Guide for the Perplexed* that human nature changes at best gradually, never suddenly.[3] It proved too much to expect that a generation born in slavery would be able to fight the battle of freedom. It would take forty years – an entire generation. Their children,

---

1. Rashi is quoting Sifre ad loc.
2. The source is *Midrash Yelamdenu* (i.e., *Midrash Tanḥuma,* Buber) ad loc.
3. Maimonides, *Guide for the Perplexed,* III:32.

born in freedom and toughened by the experience of the desert, would have the strength their parents lacked.

Recall, though, what happened next. No sooner had Moses told the people of the forty-year delay than they regretted their reaction and wanted to begin the conquest of the land immediately. Moses warned them it would end in disaster, but they refused to listen:

> Early the next morning, [the people] began climbing towards the top of the hill, declaring, "We are now ready! We shall go forwards to the place that God described. We [admit that] we were mistaken." "Why are you going against God's word?" said Moses. "It will not work! Do not proceed; God is not with you. Do not be killed by your enemies!"... [But the people] defiantly climbed towards the top of the hill, though neither the Ark of God's covenant nor Moses moved from the camp. The Amalekites and Canaanites who lived in that hill country came down and defeated [the Israelites], pursuing them with crushing force all the way to Hormah. (Num. 14:40–45)

First the people thought the conquest could not be done at all, then they thought it could be done immediately. What they lacked was a sense of pace and timing. They failed to understand how much preparation, mental and physical, would be needed. It was this experience, I suspect, that lay behind Moses' twofold request. He asked God to appoint a successor who would lead from the front, but who would also understand that he had to go at a speed at which the people could keep up with him.

Not all forms of leadership require this. The great prophets were often centuries ahead of their time. That is what made them prophets. It is also the reason that they were often unheeded during their lifetime. Today we still find the words of Amos and Hosea, Isaiah and Jeremiah, challenging. They saw the far horizon, but to their contemporaries it was too distant, a destination too remote, a mountain too high to climb.

There are secular examples. The great artists were often ahead of their time. Beethoven's late quartets were almost unintelligible for a century. The first Impressionist exhibition was panned by the critics. Van Gogh sold only one painting in his lifetime. The audience at the first performance of Stravinsky's *Rite of Spring* expressed their disapproval with catcalls and whistles.

An artist *may* be ahead of his time; a prophet *must* be ahead of his time. But they are not leaders of people. They are leaders of ideas. Often they are reclusive. Only a few of their contemporaries understand what they are trying to do, but that is enough for them. Eventually, long after their lifetime, their ideas penetrate a wider circle. But a leader to follow Moses and lead the people across the Jordan and into the land had to be able to connect with people. That is why Moses prayed to God for a successor who would go out in front – but not too far, too fast.

God chose Joshua, a man who had served Moses faithfully throughout, and who had led the people into battle against the Amalekites after the crossing of the Red Sea. Joshua was not another Moses. As we noted earlier, the sages said that "the face of Moses was like the sun, while that of Joshua was like the moon" (Bava Batra 75a). In fact, as the Torah says explicitly, there never was another Moses (Deut. 34:10–12). However, that is precisely why Joshua was the right leader for the next generation.

Moses was the archetype of the strong leader, the man who – with God's help – did it all. It was he who confronted Pharaoh, led the people out of Egypt, took them through the sea, and led them to Mount Sinai. He was the voice of God to the people, and the voice of the people when he prayed to God. Strong leaders make history. Books are written about them. Thomas Carlyle's *On Heroes, Hero-Worship, and the Heroic in History* (1840)[4] is the classic text on the "great man" theory of leadership: history is made by rare, inspired individuals capable of moving people from their accustomed orbit into a new trajectory. That, translated into Judaic terms, is what Moses was.

But great individuals do not necessarily turn those they lead into great individuals. Like the sun, they burn too brightly for others to be able to see them face to face. This was literally so in the case of Moses. When he came down from the mountain with the second set of tablets, the Torah says, "he was not aware that his face was radiant" because he had spoken with God (Ex. 34:29–35). Thereafter he had to wear a veil because people were fearful of looking at him directly.

4. London: Cassell, 1908.

When people are led by "great men," they can easily become passive, dependent, lacking in a sense of personal and collective responsibility. When there is a crisis, they expect the leader to deal with it. They do not expect him or her to challenge them to do it themselves. Moses' greatness, never subsequently repeated, was both good news and bad. Without his strength the people would never have left Egypt, but dependent on his strength they would never develop the independence they needed to conquer the land.

It was precisely *because* Joshua was like the moon to Moses' sun that he was the right leader for the next generation. He left space for people to fill, room for them to grow. Because they had to shoulder responsibilities, they acquired a sense of timing and pace. Throughout Joshua's leadership the people never complained that he was going too fast or too slow.

A leader must have vision, but also realism. He or she must think the impossible but know the possible. Because leaders are often figures of great ability, they can sometimes forget that not everyone can travel as fast as they can. A leader can be too far ahead of his or her time. People are slow to change, and a leader who understands the need for change may try to force the pace faster than the people can go.

That is why some of the greatest leaders – Lincoln, Gandhi, John F. and Robert Kennedy, Martin Luther King Jr., Anwar Sadat, Yitzhak Rabin – were assassinated. In retrospect they are seen as heroes. But at the time, they were often regarded as traitors, betrayers. They forced people out of their comfort zone, usually by trying to turn enemies into friends. They were driving people faster than they could go. There were times when Moses himself feared for his life.[5]

That is what Moses was saying. Let the Israelites be led by one who will "go out before them and come in before them," leading from the front – but *also* one who will "lead them out and bring them in," meaning one who will carry the people with him, not going so fast that they cannot keep up.

A leader of the people must go at the people's pace. He or she must educate them, prepare them for the challenges ahead, listen to

5. See, e.g., Ex. 17:4.

359

their grievances, give them courage, lift their sights, and be prepared to slow down if they are unable to accelerate. He or she must be impatient and patient all at once – a difficult balancing act. But there is no choice. Leaders must not go on ahead so far and fast that, nearing their destination, they find themselves alone.

Matot
מטות

Parashat Matot begins with an account of how Moses instructed the leaders of the tribes about vows and oaths – how they should be kept and how they may be annulled. The Israelites are commanded to wage war against the Midianites because of their hostility. There is an account of what is to be done with the spoils of war.

Two tribes, Reuben and Gad, together with half the tribe of Menashe, ask permission to stay east of the Jordan where the land is ideal pasture for their cattle. Moses is initially angered, but eventually agrees on condition that they first join and lead in the battles for the land west of the Jordan.

The first essay in this section looks at the laws of vows and oaths, asking why this section appears here rather than elsewhere. The second focuses on a detail of the negotiation between Moses and the leaders of Reuben and Gad that throws light on a fundamental principle of Judaism. The third is about the negotiation itself as an example of what later became known in Game Theory as *non-zero*, that is, an agreement from which both sides gain. The fourth is about a phrase in the course of those negotiations that became the basis for a principle of Jewish law – that one should be "above suspicion."

The World We Make with Words

T urning to the beginning of *Parashat Matot*, as so often when reading the book of Numbers, we find ourselves asking: *What is going on?* It begins with a set of legal instructions, delivered by Moses to the heads of the tribes, about vows and oaths – how they should be honoured and under which circumstances they can be annulled. The key principle is: "When a man makes a vow to the Lord or takes an oath to obligate himself by a pledge, he must not break his word but must do everything he said" (Num. 30:3). Doing what you say you will do is undeniably important, but why state it now? What does it have to do with this particular juncture of the Israelites' history?

Recall the context: The people's forty-year journey across the desert is nearing its end. The Israelites are approaching their destination. They have fought some early battles, against Arad, Sihon, and Og. A second census has been taken of the people, because – with the exceptions of Caleb and Joshua – they are no longer the same people who were counted in the first census at the beginning of the book. Instructions have been given as to how the land should be divided between the tribes. There has been a change of the generations. A new leader, Joshua, has been designated as Moses' successor. The people will shortly fight another battle, this time against the Midianites. But before they do so, Moses instructs "the heads of the tribes" about vows and oaths. Why then, why there? What is this particular legal passage doing at this point in the Jewish story?

The answer will depend on how we understand Numbers as a whole. It may be that the entire book is simply a sequence of narratives interrupted by laws. There may be no specific connection between the two. Or the connection may not be substantive but simply *mnemonic*, that is, B follows A because A helps you remember B. Memory is important even in the case of a written text like the Torah, since for much of Jewish history people learned these texts by heart. So, for example, it is relatively straightforward to remember a psalm or poem – like *Ashrei* or *Eshet Ḥayil* or *Anim Zemirot* – that is written as an alphabetical acrostic. If you remember the first line that begins with an *aleph*, you know that the next line will begin with a *beit*, and so on.

That is a possibility here. In the case of the laws of vows there is a verbal connection between them and the previous laws about sacrifices. The penultimate verse of the previous *parasha* states: "These shall you offer to the Lord at the appointed times, in addition to *your vows* and your freewill offerings..." (Num. 29:39). Having mentioned vows, the Torah now states the laws that apply to them. It is an easily remembered sequence. That is one explanation.

However, there is a second and more substantive possibility,[1] namely that these laws have everything to do with the fact that the Israelites are now close to the land that they will eventually conquer and settle. They will then confront one of the fundamental issues of the Torah as a whole, namely *the tension between order and freedom.*

Can they build a society that is both free and ordered? Early in its story of humanity, the Torah has shown us the alternatives. There can be freedom without order. That was the world "full of violence" before the Flood. It is the condition of many failed or failing states

---

1. There is a third possibility that I do not discuss in the essay, namely that as the Israelites approach the land they are about to fight many battles, and people tend to make vows of various kinds before going into battle. See for instance Jacob's vow in Gen. 28:20–22.

today. Hobbes called this "the war of every man against every man" in which life is "solitary, poor, nasty, brutish, and short." That is *anarchy*.

Equally there can be order without freedom. That was Egypt of the Pharaohs, where the word of the ruler was law, and where the mass of humankind were, literally or substantively, slaves. That is *tyranny*.

The Torah rejects both. The third alternative, to which most of the Torah is dedicated, is *nomocracy*, "the rule of laws, not men." In it, people do what they do not simply because they want to and have the power to do so even against the will of others, but because it is the right, lawful, commanded thing to do. That is the Torah project: a society built on laws given by God Himself, accepted voluntarily at Mount Sinai, taught by parents to children, spoken of "when you sit in your house, when you walk on the way, when you lie down, and when you rise up," laws not just engraved in stone or inscribed on parchment but "written on their hearts" (Jer. 31:32).

But is law enough? The short answer is no. Think about our daily interactions. Few of them are about the kind of transaction about which we need to take legal or halakhic advice. Many of them, however, have to do with the issue of trust. Can I trust a workman to do the job for which I have paid him? Can I trust the au pair I leave alone in the house? Can I trust a colleague at work with whom I have shared ideas not to take all the credit for himself? Sociologists and economists nowadays call this *social capital*, and on it the smooth running of a free society depends.[2]

Anarchy is a low-trust condition. I never know where the next threat will come from, so I live in perpetual fear. Tyranny is also a low-trust condition. I am never entirely sure whether the person I take as a friend may not be a member of the secret police relaying my unguarded remarks to the state authorities. But democracies can also become low-trust societies if businesspeople and financiers are motivated solely by personal gain, if politicians seek only personal advantage, and if those who can get away without contributing to the common good do so. *If the only way of ensuring that your interests will be protected is to use law and lawyers at every stage, you have a low-trust, low-social-capital society.*

2. For a good account, see Francis Fukuyama, *Trust: The Social Virtues and the Creation of Prosperity* (London: Penguin, 1996).

It may have all the formal features of a free society, but it is one in which liberty is unlikely to last for long.

There is a classic example in Tanakh. It appears in the book of Jeremiah, where the prophet is describing the society of his time, when people could no longer be trusted to keep their word:

> They bend their tongues like bows;
> They are valorous in the land for treachery, not for honesty;
> They advance from evil to evil.
> They do not heed Me – declares the Lord.
> Beware of your friends;
> Trust not even a brother,
> For every one of them is a deceiver, and every friend a slanderer.
> Friend deceives friend, and no one speaks the truth.
> They have taught their tongues to lie; they weary themselves with sinning.
> You live in the midst of deceit; in their deceit they refuse to heed Me – declares the Lord. (Jer. 9:2–5)

Jeremiah had no doubt that such a society could not long endure. It was about to lose its freedom to the Babylonians. It did – and thereafter, it never fully recovered.

That, I believe, is why the laws of vows and oaths appear as the Israelites are on the brink of entering the land. They represent one of the most distinctive features of Judaism as a way of life, namely, its intense focus on *the way we create or destroy worlds by words*. With words, God created the world: "And God said, 'Let there be …' and there was." One of the gifts God gave the first human was language: the ability to name the animals (Gen. 2:19). When the Torah says that "God formed man from the dust of the earth and breathed into him the breath of life and man became a living being" (2:7), the *Targum* translates the last phrase as "and man became a *speaking* being." For Judaism, speaking is life itself.

There is one highly specialised use of language in which we use words not just to describe something that exists but to create something that does not yet exist. The Oxford philosopher J. L. Austin called this *performative utterance.*[3] It happens when we use language not to state something but to *do* something. So for instance, when a groom says to his bride under the *ḥuppa*, "Behold you are betrothed to me ...," he is not *describing* a marriage, he is *getting married*. When in ancient times the *Beit Din* declared the new moon, they were not making a statement of fact. They were *creating* a fact, they were *turning the day into* the new moon.

The key instance of a performative utterance is a promise. When I promise you that I will do something, I am creating something that did not exist before, namely an obligation. This fact, small though it might seem, turns out to lie at the very foundation of Judaism.

A mutual promise – X pledges himself to do certain things for Y, and Y commits himself to do other things for X – is called a *covenant*. Judaism is based on covenant, specifically the covenant made between God and the Israelites at Mount Sinai, which bound them and still to this day binds us. It is the supreme instance in human history of a performative utterance.

The philosopher who best understood the significance of the act of promising to the moral life was Nietzsche, who said this:

> To breed an animal with the prerogative to promise – is that not precisely the paradoxical task which nature has set herself with regard to humankind? Is it not the real problem *of* humankind? ... Man himself will really have to become *reliable, regular, necessary,* even in his own self-image, so that he, as someone making a promise is, is answerable to his own *future.* That is precisely what constitutes the long history of the origins of *responsibility.*[4]

What Nietzsche meant was that human affairs are fraught with unpredictability. That is because we are free. We do not know how other people will behave or how they will respond to an act of ours. So we can never be sure of the consequences of our own decisions. Freedom seems to rob

3. J. L. Austin, *How to Do Things with Words* (Oxford: Clarendon Press, 1975).
4. Friedrich Nietzsche et al., *On the Genealogy of Morality* (Cambridge: Cambridge University Press, 2007), Second Essay, 35–36.

the human world of order. We can tell how inanimate objects will behave under different conditions. We can be reasonably sure of how animals will behave. But we cannot tell in advance how humans will react. How then can we create an orderly society without taking away people's freedom?

The answer is *the act of promising*. When I promise to do something, I am freely placing myself under an obligation to do something in the future. If I am the kind of person who is known to keep his word, I have removed one element of unpredictability from the human world. You can rely on me, since I have given my word. When I promise, I voluntarily bind myself. It is this ability of humans voluntarily to commit themselves to do or refrain from doing certain acts that generates order in the relations between human beings without the use of coercive force.[5]

So it is no accident that the rule that one who makes a vow or takes an oath "must not break his word but must do everything he said" is stated shortly before the Israelites approach the Promised Land. The institution of promising, of which vows and oaths to God are a supreme example, is essential to the existence of a free society. *Freedom depends on people keeping their word.*

If trust breaks down, social relationships break down. Society will then depend on law enforcement agencies or some other use of force. When force is widely used, society is no longer free. The only way free human beings can form collaborative and cooperative relationships without recourse to force is by the use of verbal undertakings honoured by those who make them.

The temptation to break your word when it is to your advantage to do so can sometimes be overwhelming. That is why belief in a God who oversees all we think, say, and do and who holds us accountable to our commitments is so fundamental. Although it sounds strange to us now, the father of toleration and liberalism, John Locke, held that citizenship should not be extended to atheists because, not believing in God, they could not be trusted to honour their word.[6]

---

5. On this, see Hannah Arendt, *The Human Condition* (Chicago: University of Chicago Press, 1958), 243–244.
6. "Lastly, those are not at all to be tolerated who deny the being of a God. Promises, covenants, and oaths, which are the bonds of human society, can have no hold upon

There is a specific example in the *parasha* of how this works out in real life. Two of the tribes, Reuben and Gad, decided that they would rather live to the east of the Jordan where the land was more suitable for their livestock. After a fraught conversation with Moses, who accused them of shirking their responsibilities to the rest of the people, they agreed to be in the front line of the army until the conquest of the land was complete (Num. 32). Everything depended on them keeping their word.

The appearance of the laws of vows and oaths prior to the episode of the tribes of Reuben and Gad is like the appearance of the laws of the red heifer (purification after contact with the dead) before the story of the deaths of Miriam and Aaron and the announcement of the death of Moses. Both are instances of the rule that "God provides the cure before the disease."[7] The law is stated before the narrative to which it applies.

More generally, the insistence on honouring your word is axiomatic to the creation of the kind of society the Torah envisages in Israel, and the moral is still relevant today. A free society depends on trust, and trust depends on keeping your word. Only under very special and precisely formulated circumstances can you be released from your undertakings.

If you seek liberty, treat words as holy, vows and oaths as sacrosanct. When that happens, then, just as God used words to create the natural universe, so we use words to create a social universe. Words create moral obligations, and moral obligations, undertaken responsibly and honoured faithfully, create the possibility of a free society.

---

an atheist. The taking away of God, though but even in thought, dissolves all" (John Locke, *Letter Concerning Toleration* [Indianapolis: Hackett, 1983], 51).

7. Megilla 13b; *Midrash Lekaḥ Tov, Parashat Shemot*, 3:1.

Priorities

The Israelites were almost within sight of the Promised Land. They had successfully waged their first battles. They had just won a victory over the Midianites. There is a new tone to the narrative. We no longer hear the querulous complaints that had been the bass note of so much of the wilderness years.

We know why. That was the sound of the generation, born in slavery, that had left Egypt. By now, almost forty years have passed. The second generation, born in freedom and toughened by conditions in the desert, have a more purposeful feel about them. Battle-tried, they no longer doubt their ability, with God's help, to fight and win.

Yet it is at just this point that a problem arises, different in kind from those that had gone before. The people as a whole now have their attention focused on the destination: the land west of the river Jordan, the place that even the spies had confirmed to be "flowing with milk and honey" (Num. 13:27).

The members of the tribes of Reuben and Gad, though, began to have different thoughts. Seeing that the land through which they were travelling was ideal for raising cattle, they decided that they would prefer to stay there, to the east of the Jordan, and proposed this to Moses.

Unsurprisingly, he was angry at the suggestion: "Moses said to the Gadites and Reubenites, 'Are your brothers to go to war while you stay here? Why would you discourage the Israelites from going over into the land the Lord has given them?'" (Num. 32:6–7). He reminded them of the disastrous consequences of the earlier discouragement on the part of the spies. The whole nation would suffer. They would have shown not only that they were ambivalent about God's gift of the land but also that they had learned nothing from history.

The tribes did not argue with his claim. They accepted its validity, but they pointed out that his concern was not incompatible with their objectives. They suggested a compromise:

> Then they came up to him and said, "We would like to build sheepfolds for our flocks and towns for our children. But we will then arm ourselves and go as an advance guard before the Israelites until we have established them in their home. Meanwhile our children will live in fortified cities, for protection from the inhabitants of the land. We will not return to our homes until every Israelite has received his inheritance. We will not receive any inheritance with them on the other side of the Jordan, because our inheritance has come to us on the east side of the Jordan." (Num. 32:16–19)

We are willing, in other words, to join the rest of the Israelites in the battles that lie ahead. Not only this, but we are prepared to be the nation's advance guard, in the forefront of the battle. We are not afraid of combat, nor are we trying to evade our responsibilities to our people as a whole. It is simply that we wish to raise cattle, and for this, the land to the east of the Jordan is ideal. Warning them of the seriousness of their undertaking, Moses agreed. If they kept their word, they would be allowed to settle east of the Jordan. And so, indeed, it happened (Josh. 22:1–5).

That is the story on the surface. But as so often in the Torah, there are subtexts as well as texts. One in particular was noticed by the sages, with their sensitivity to nuance and detail. Listen carefully to what the Reubenites and Gadites said: "Then they came up to him and said, 'We would like to build *sheepfolds for our flocks and towns for our children.'"* Moses replied: "Build towns for your children, and sheepfolds for your flocks, but do what you have promised" (Num. 32:24).

The ordering of the nouns is crucial. The men of Reuben and Gad put property before people: they spoke of their flocks first, their children second.[1] Moses reversed the order, putting special emphasis on the children. As Rashi notes:

> They paid more regard to their property than to their sons and daughters, because they mentioned their cattle before the children. Moses said to them: "Not so. Make the main thing primary and the subordinate thing secondary. First build cities for your children, and only then, folds for your flocks." (Commentary to Num. 32:16)

A midrash[2] makes the same point by way of an ingenious interpretation of a verse in Ecclesiastes: "The heart of the wise inclines to the right, but the heart of the fool to the left" (Eccl. 10:2). The midrash identifies "right" with Torah and life: "He brought the fire of a religion to them from his right hand" (Deut. 33:2). "Left," by contrast, refers to worldly goods:

> Long life is in her right hand;
> in her left hand are riches and honour. (Prov. 3:16)

Hence, infers the midrash, the men of Reuben and Gad put "riches and honour" before faith and posterity. Moses hints to them that their priorities are wrong. The midrash continues: "The Holy One, Blessed Be He, said to them: 'Seeing that you have shown greater love for your cattle than for human souls, by your life, there will be no blessing in it.'"

1. Note also the parallel between the decision of the leaders of Reuben and Gad and that of Lot, in Genesis 13:10–13. Lot too made his choice of dwelling place based on economic considerations – the prosperity of Sodom and the cities of the plain – without considering the impact the environment would have on his children.
2. Numbers Rabba 22:9.

This turned out to be not a minor incident in the wilderness long ago, but rather, a consistent pattern throughout much of Jewish history. The fate of Jewish communities, for the most part, was determined by a single factor: *their decision, or lack of decision, to put children and their education first.* Already in the first century, Josephus was able to write: "The result of our thorough education in our laws, from the very dawn of intelligence, is that they are, as it were, engraved on our souls."[3] The rabbis ruled that "any town that lacks children at school is to be excommunicated" (Shabbat 119b). Already in the first century, the Jewish community in Israel had established a network of schools at which attendance was compulsory (Bava Batra 21a) – the first such system in history.

The pattern persisted throughout the Middle Ages. In twelfth-century France a Christian scholar noted: "A Jew, however poor, if he has ten sons, will put them all to letters, not for gain as the Christians do, but for the understanding of God's law – and not only his sons but his daughters too."[4]

In 1432, at the height of Christian persecution of Jews in Spain, a synod was convened at Valladolid to institute a system of taxation to fund Jewish education for all.[5] In 1648, at the end of the Thirty Years' War, the first thing Jewish communities in Europe did to re-establish Jewish life was to re-organise the educational system. In their classic study of the shtetl, the small townships of Eastern Europe, Zborowski and Herzog write this about the typical Jewish family:

> The most important item in the family budget is the tuition fee that must be paid each term to the teacher of the younger boys' school. Parents will bend in the sky to educate their son. The mother, who has charge of household accounts, will cut the family food costs to the limit if necessary, in order to pay for her son's schooling. If the worst comes to the worst, she will pawn

---

3. Josephus, *Contra Apionem*, ii, 177–178.
4. Beryl Smalley, *The Study of the Bible in the Middle Ages* (Notre Dame, IN: University of Notre Dame Press, 1952), 78.
5. Salo Baron, *The Jewish Community* (Philadelphia: Jewish Publication Society of America, 1945), 2:171–173.

her cherished pearls in order to pay for the school term. The boy must study, the boy must become a good Jew – for her the two are synonymous.[6]

In 1849, when Samson Raphael Hirsch became rabbi in Frankfurt, he insisted that the community create a school before building a synagogue. After the Holocaust, the few surviving yeshiva heads and hasidic leaders concentrated on encouraging their followers to have children and build schools.[7]

It is hard to think of any other religion or civilisation that has so predicated its very existence on putting children and their education first. There have been Jewish communities in the past that were affluent and built magnificent synagogues – Alexandria in the first centuries of the Common Era is an example. Yet because they did not put children first, they contributed little to the Jewish story. They flourished briefly, then disappeared.

Moses' implied rebuke to the tribes of Reuben and Gad is not a minor historical detail but a fundamental statement of Jewish priorities. Property is secondary, children primary. Civilisations that value the young stay young. Those that invest in the future have a future. It is not what we own that gives us a share in eternity, but those to whom we give birth and the effort we make to ensure that they carry our faith and way of life into the next generation.

6. Mark Zborowski and Elizabeth Herzog, *Life Is with People: The Culture of the Shtetl* (New York: Schocken, 1974), 87.
7. My book on this subject is Jonathan Sacks, *Will We Have Jewish Grandchildren?* (London: Vallentine Mitchell, 1994).

The Power of Non-Zero

Game theory was the invention of one of the most brilliant minds of the twentieth century, John von Neumann (1903–1957). A child prodigy, he went on to make original contributions to mathematics, economics, statistics, computing, and physics. One of his fascinations was decision-making under conditions of uncertainty, in fields as far removed from one another (or perhaps not) as poker, economics, and the logic of deterrence in war.

Before von Neumann, the dominant models in microeconomics tended to be displayed in graphs charting such factors as supply and demand, marginal cost, and marginal utility. Where the lines crossed, there was equilibrium. That was where production and consumption, or selling and buying, evened out. It was as precise and beautiful as a Bach sonata.

But life tends not to be like that. Rarely do we find total information, perfect competition, and unblemished rationality. Moreover, economic variables are often not specifiable in advance. The effect of one person's decision may well depend on how other people react to it. That is how bluffing works in poker. It is also how major financial decisions operate. The effectiveness of a rise or reduction in interest rates on the part of a central bank will depend on how the market reads it. If it generates confidence, it may well achieve its objectives, but if it is seen as an act of panic, it may prove counterproductive. Von Neumann's father was a senior banker, and the son had absorbed some of the complexities of such decisions by listening to his family's dinnertime conversations. He knew that existing models of decision-making failed to account for this level of complexity, in which the outcome is determined not only by what I do but also by how you react to what I do.[1] That was the basic insight on which game theory was based.

One of the simplest and most important distinctions in game theory is between *zero-sum* and *non-zero-sum* games. Zero-sum games are ones in which one person's gain is matched by the other person's loss. Either I win and you lose, or you win and I lose. Non-zero games are those in which the sum of the gains and losses is more, or less, than zero. It may be that both sides win or that both lose. What is fascinating is that the sages of the Talmud were well aware of this, and spelled it out in halakhic principles such as *zeh neheneh vezeh neheneh*, "both sides gain" (Kiddushin 22b), or *zeh neheneh vezeh lo ḥaser*, "one side gains but the other does not lose" (Bava Kamma 20b).

The idea is hugely important because it opens the way to creative forms of conflict resolution. A classic example is set out in our *parasha*. The Israelites were on the last stage of their journey to the Promised Land. They had arrived at the east bank of the Jordan, within sight of their destination. Two of the tribes, Reuben and Gad, who had large herds and flocks of cattle, felt that the land they were currently on was ideal for their purposes. It was good grazing country. So they approached Moses and asked for permission to stay there rather than take up their share in the land of Israel. They said: "If we have found favour in your eyes, let this land be given to your servants as our possession. Do not make us cross the Jordan" (Num. 32:5).

Moses immediately saw the dangers in this proposition. The two tribes were putting their own interests above those of the nation as a

---

1. A not-dissimilar idea was developed by George Soros, who called it "reflexivity." Soros' principle is that how people react to a situation depends on how they interpret the situation. The biblical narrative that best exemplifies this is the story of the spies (Num. 13–14).

whole. They would be seen as abandoning their fellow Israelites at the very time they were needed most. There were wars to be fought if the people were to inherit the land. As Moses put it to the tribes: "Are your brothers to go to war while you stay here? Why would you discourage the Israelites from going over into the land the Lord has given them?" (Num. 32:6–7).

The proposal was potentially disastrous. Moses reminded the men of Reuben and Gad what had happened when the spies demoralised the people. The result of that one episode was to condemn an entire generation to die in the wilderness and to delay the eventual conquest by forty years. "And here you are, a brood of sinners, standing in the place of your fathers and making the Lord even more angry with Israel. If you turn away from following Him, He will again leave all this people in the wilderness, and you will be the cause of their destruction" (Num. 32:14–15). Moses was blunt, honest, and confrontational.

What then followed is a model of non-zero negotiation. The Reubenites and Gadites accepted the justice of Moses' concerns, and proposed a compromise. Let us make provisions for our cattle and our families, they said, and we will then accompany the other tribes across the Jordan. Not only will we fight alongside them, we will go ahead of them. We will not return to our cattle and families until all the battles have been fought, the land has been conquered, and the other tribes have received their inheritance. We will gain by having good land for our cattle, and the nation as a whole will not lose because we will be in the army, in the front line, and we will stay until the war has been won.

Moses recognised that they had met his objections. He restated their position to make sure he and they both understood the proposal and were ready to stand by it. He extracted from them agreement to a *tenai kaful*, a double condition, both positive and negative: If we do this, these will be the consequences, but if we fail to do this, those will be the consequences.[2] He left them no escape from their commitment. The two tribes agreed. Conflict had been averted. The Reubenites and Gadites achieved what they sought, while the interests of the other tribes had been secured. It was a classic non-zero, win-win negotiation.

2. See Gittin 75a.

How justified Moses' concerns were became apparent many years later. The Reubenites and Gadites did indeed fulfil their promise in the days of Joshua. The rest of the tribes conquered and settled Israel while they (together with half the tribe of Menashe) established their presence in Transjordan. Despite this, within a brief space of time there was almost civil war.

Joshua 22 describes how, returning to their families and settling their land, the Reubenites and Gadites built "an altar to the Lord" on the east side of the Jordan. Seeing this as an act of secession, the rest of the Israelites prepared to do battle against them. Joshua, in a bold act of diplomacy, sent Pinhas, the former zealot, now man of peace, to negotiate. He warned them of the terrible consequences of what they had done by, in effect, creating a religious centre outside the land of Israel. It would split the nation in two.

The Reubenites and Gadites made it clear that this was not their intention at all. To the contrary, they themselves were worried that in the future, the rest of the Israelites would see them living across the Jordan and conclude that they no longer wanted to be part of the nation. That is why they had built the altar, not to offer sacrifices, not as a rival to the nation's Sanctuary, but merely as a symbol and a sign to future generations that they too were Israelites. Pinhas and the rest of the delegation were satisfied with this answer, and once again civil war was averted.

The negotiation between Moses and the two tribes brilliantly exemplifies the four principles arrived at by the Harvard Negotiation Project, set out by Roger Fisher and William Ury in their classic work, *Getting to Yes*.[3] First, Moses *separated the people from the problem*. He made it clear to the Reubenites and Gadites that the issue had nothing to do with them specifically and everything to do with the Israelites' experience in the past in the episode of the spies, in which everyone suffered and no one gained. The problem was not about this tribe or that but about the nation as a whole.

Second, Moses and the Reubenites and Gadites *focused on interests, not positions*. The Reubenites and Gadites were prepared to change

3. Roger Fisher and William Ury, *Getting to Yes: Negotiating Agreement Without Giving In* (London: Random House Business, 2012).

their plans for the sake of the nation as a whole, while Moses, in light of this, was willing to retract his opposition. It is striking how different this conflict was from that of Korah and his followers. There, the whole argument was about positions, not interests – about who was entitled to be a leader. The result was collective tragedy.

Third, the Reubenites and Gadites *invented an option for mutual gain.* By creative thinking, they formulated a proposal that would satisfy both their needs and those of the other tribes.

Fourth, Moses *insisted on objective criteria.* The Reubenites and Gadites would not return to the east bank of the Jordan until all the other tribes were safely settled in their territories. And so it happened, as narrated in the book of Joshua:

> Then Joshua summoned the Reubenites, the Gadites, and the half-tribe of Menashe and said to them, "You have done all that Moses the servant of the Lord commanded, and you have obeyed me in everything I commanded. For a long time now – to this very day – you have not deserted your fellow Israelites but have carried out the mission the Lord your God gave you. Now that the Lord your God has given them rest as He promised, return to your homes in the land that Moses the servant of the Lord gave you on the other side of the Jordan." (Josh. 22:1–4)

This was, in short, a model negotiation, a sign of hope after the many destructive conflicts elsewhere in the book of Numbers, as well as a compelling alternative to the many later conflicts in Jewish history that had such destructive outcomes. It succeeded not because either side was weak, or used ambiguous words and diplomatic evasions, but because *both were honest, principled, and focused on not only what was good for them but also on what was good for the other side.* That is the power of non-zero thinking.

Non-zero-sum-ness is more than a mathematical concept. It is fundamental to the theological principle of the dignity of difference and the miracle that unity in heaven creates diversity on earth.[4] Because

---

4. See, for example, Jonathan Sacks, *The Dignity of Difference* (London: Continuum, 2002), 45–66.

we are each finite, limited, and different, what I lack, someone else has. What someone else lacks, I have. Therefore when we come together in collaborative ways, we both benefit. When, to the contrary, we focus on positions, not interests – defining a conflict in win/lose, zero-sum terms – the result is usually violence from which both sides lose.[5] The human tendency to do just this is perennial, disastrous, and to be fought against in every generation.[6] It is by re-conceptualising difference from a source of conflict to one of mutual gain that we become agents for the greatest and hardest-to-achieve divine blessing of all: peace.

Peace is not a world where we are all the same. It is a world in which we use our differences to enlarge our understanding of God and our appreciation of those not like us. It is no accident that Numbers, an anthology of conflicts, moves towards a close with this story of conflict avoided, peace restored.

5. See on this A. O. Hirschman's important work, *The Passions and the Interests: Political Arguments for Capitalism Before Its Triumph* (Princeton, NJ: Princeton University Press, 1977).
6. It has to do with a specific set of reactions in the (predominantly male) brain that are sensitive to hierarchy and the role of the alpha male. It tends to dominate in honour-based cultures.

Above Suspicion

From the negotiation between Moses and the leaders of the tribes of Reuben and Gad – the subject of the previous two essays – the sages took a phrase and from it derived one of the great principles of Jewish law and life. Having reached an agreement with the tribes, Moses granted their request on condition that they fulfil their word: "Then when the land is then conquered before the Lord, you may return *and you shall be innocent before the Lord and before Israel* and this land will be yours as your permanent property before the Lord" (Num. 32:22).

The italicised phrase – "you shall be innocent/guiltless/free of further obligation before the Lord and before Israel" – became in the course of time an ethical axiom of Judaism. It is not enough to do what is right in the eyes of God. One must also act in such a way as to be seen to have done right in the eyes of one's fellow man. One must be above suspicion. That is the rule of *viheyitem nekiyim*, "You shall be innocent before the Lord and before Israel."

How did this translate itself into Jewish law and life? The Mishna in Shekalim speaks of the three periods in the year when appropriations were made from the collective donations stored in the Temple treasury. The Mishna states that the person who made the appropriation did not enter the chamber wearing a bordered cloak or shoes or *tefillin* or an amulet, so that if he subsequently became poor, people would not say that he became poor because he committed an offence in the chamber, and so that if he became rich people would not say that he did so by misappropriating contributions in the chamber – for we must be free of blame in the eyes of people just as we must be free of blame before God, as it is said, "You shall be innocent before the Lord and before Israel." (Mishna Shekalim 3:2)

Similarly, the Tosefta states: "When one went in to take up the offering of the chamber, they would search him when he went in and when he came out, and they continue chatting with him from the time he goes in until the time he comes out."[1] Not only must there be no wrongdoing when coins are taken from the Temple treasury; there must be no suspicion of wrongdoing. Hence the person who gathered the money should not wear any item of clothing in which coins could be hidden. He was to be searched before and afterwards, and even engaged in conversation so that he would not be tempted to secrete some of the money in his mouth.

Two rabbinic teachings from the Second Temple period speak of families famous for their role in Temple life and the lengths they went to so as to place themselves beyond suspicion. The Garmu family was expert in preparing the show bread. It was said of them that "their memory was held in high esteem because fine bread was never found in their children's homes, in case people might say, they feed from the preparation of the show bread."[2] Likewise the Avtinas family was skilled in making the incense used in the Temple. They too were held in high repute because "never did a bride of their family go forth perfumed, and when they married a woman from elsewhere, they stipulated that she was not to go out perfumed, in case people should say, 'They perfume themselves from the preparation of the Temple incense.'"[3]

1. Tosefta, Shekalim 2:2.
2. Tosefta, Yoma 2:5.
3. Tosefta, Yoma 2:6.

The general principle is stated in the Jerusalem Talmud:

> R. Shmuel b. Naḥman said in the name of R. Yonatan: In the Mosaic
> books, the Prophets, and the Writings, we find that a person must
> discharge his obligations before men just as he must discharge them
> before God. Where in the Mosaic books? In the verse, "You shall be
> innocent before the Lord and before Israel." Where in the Proph-
> ets? In "God, the Lord God, He knows and Israel too shall know."
> Where in the Writings? In the verse, "You shall find grace and good
> favour in the eyes of God and men." Gamliel Zoga asked R. Yose
> b. Avun, "Which verse says it most clearly?" He replied, "You shall
> be innocent before the Lord and before Israel." (Y. Shekalim 3:2)

This concern became the basis of two halakhic principles. The first is
known as *ḥashad*, "suspicion," namely that certain acts, permitted in
themselves, are forbidden on the grounds that performing them may lead
others to suspect one of doing something forbidden. Thus, for example,
R. Shimon b. Yoḥai held that one of the reasons why the Torah prescribes
that *pe'ah* (the corner of the field left unharvested for the poor) should
be left at the *end* of harvesting was because of suspicion. If the owner of
the field had set aside an unharvested corner at the beginning or middle,
the poor would come and take what was theirs before the end of harvesting, and a passer-by might think that no corner had been set aside
at all. Likewise the rabbis ordained that if a house has two doors on different sides, Ḥanukka candles should be lit at both so that a passer-by,
seeing one door but not the other, should not think that the owner of
the house had failed to fulfil the command.

A closely related halakhic principle is the idea known as *marit
haayin*, "appearances." Thus, for example, before milk substitutes became
common, it was forbidden to drink milk-like liquids (made, for example,
from almonds) together with meat on the grounds that people might
think it was milk itself. Similarly, it is forbidden on Shabbat to hang out
garments that became wet (for example, by falling into water) to dry, in
case people think that one has washed them on Shabbat. In general one
is not allowed to perform actions which, permitted in themselves, lend
themselves to misinterpretation.

The connection or contrast between these two principles is a matter of some debate in the rabbinic literature. There are those who see *ḥashad* and *marit haayin* as very similar, perhaps even two names for the same thing. Others however see them as different, even opposites. *Ḥashad* represents the possibility that people might think you have done something forbidden and thus think badly of you. *Marit haayin* concerns cases where people, knowing that you are not the sort of person to do something forbidden, draw the mistaken conclusion that because you are doing X, Y is permitted, because X is easily mistaken for Y. Thus, to take one of the cases mentioned above, people seeing you hanging out clothes to dry on Shabbat might conclude that it is permitted to wash the clothes, which it is not.

This concern for appearances is, on the face of it, strange. Surely what matters is what God thinks of us, not what people think of us. The Talmud tells us of a moving encounter between the dying Rabban Yoḥanan b. Zakkai and his disciples:

> They said to him: Master, bless us. He said to them: May it be God's will that the fear of Heaven should be as important to you as the fear of [the opinions of] human beings. They said: Is that all? He said: Would that you were able to attain this [level of spirituality]. You can see [how difficult it is] because when someone wants to commit a sin, he says, "I hope no one will see me" [thus placing his fear of human beings above the fear of God who sees all]. (Berakhot 28b)

How we appear to others, the rabbi was saying, is less important than how we appear to God, yet people tend to take the former more seriously. In any case, it is forbidden to suspect people of wrongdoing. The rabbis said, "One who suspects the innocent is [punished by being] bodily afflicted" (Shabbat 97a) and "One should always judge a person in the scale of merits" (Mishna Avot 1:6). Why, then, if the onus is on the observer not to judge harshly, should we – the observed – be charged with the duty of acting above suspicion?

The answer is that we are not allowed to rely on the fact that others will judge us charitably, even though they should. Rashi makes a sobering comment on the life of Moses: "If he left his tent early, people would say that he had had a row with his wife. If he left late, they would say, 'He is devising evil plots against us'" (commentary to Deut. 1:12).

Even Moses, who devoted his life with total selflessness to the People of Israel, was not able to avoid their suspicion. Rabbi Moses Sofer goes so far as to say that he was troubled throughout his lifetime by the challenge of the command, "You shall be innocent before the Lord and before Israel," adding that it was far easier to fulfil the first half of the command ("before the Lord") than the second ("before Israel").[4] Indeed he wondered if it was possible for anyone to fulfil it in its entirety. Perhaps, he said, that is what Ecclesiastes meant when he said, "There is not a righteous man on earth who only does what is right and never sins" (Eccl. 7:20). There is no one who is fully innocent in the eyes of others.

Yet there is a profound idea embedded in the concept of *viheyitem nekiyim*, "You shall be innocent." The Talmudic sage Rava was scathing of those who stood in the presence of a Torah scroll but not in the presence of a Torah sage (Makkot 22b). *To be a Jew is to be summoned to become a living sefer Torah.* People learn how to behave not only from the books they study but also – perhaps more so – from the people they meet. Jewish educators speak of "text-people" as well as "text-books," meaning that we need living role models as well as formal instruction. For that reason, R. Akiva used to follow R. Yehoshua to see how he conducted himself in private, saying "This too is Torah, and I need to learn" (Berakhot 62a). The twin principles of *ḥashad* and *marit haayin* mean that *we should act in such a way as to be held as a role model* (by being above suspicion – the rule of *ḥashad*) and that, just as a book of instructions should be unambiguous, so should our conduct (by not laying itself open to misinterpretation – the idea of *marit haayin*). People should be able to observe the way we behave and learn from us how a Jew should live.

The fact that these rules apply to every Jew, not just to religious leaders, is testimony to the spiritual egalitarianism of the halakha. *Each of us is bidden to become a role model.* That these rules exist despite the fact that we are commanded not to suspect others of wrongdoing tells us something else about Judaism, namely that it is a system of duties,

4. *Responsa Ḥatam Sofer*, vol. 6, *Likkutim* 59.

not just of rights. We are not allowed to say, when we have acted in a way conducive to suspicion, "I have done nothing wrong; to the contrary, the other person, by harbouring doubts about me, is in the wrong." To be sure, he is. But that does not relieve us of the responsibility to conduct our lives in a way that is above suspicion. Each of us must play our part in constructing a society of mutual respect.

This brings us back to where we began, with the request of the tribes of Reuben and Gad to settle the land east of the Jordan. Moses granted their request on condition that they first joined the other tribes in their battles. They did so. Years later, Joshua summoned them and told them that they had fulfilled their promise and were now entitled to return to the place where they had built their homes (Josh. 22).

However, in a deep historical irony, suspicion was aroused again, this time for a quite different reason, namely that they had built an altar in their territory. The other tribes suspected that they were breaking faith with the God of Israel by constructing their own place of worship. Israel was on the brink of civil war. The suspicion was unfounded. The Reubenites and Gadites explained that the altar they had built was not intended to be a place of worship, but rather a sign that they too were part of the Israelite nation – a safeguard against the possibility that one day, generations later, the tribes living in Israel proper (west of the Jordan) would declare the Reubenites and Gadites to be foreigners since they lived on the other side of the river:

> That is why we said, "Let us get ready and build an altar – but not for burnt offerings or sacrifices." On the contrary, it is to be a witness between us and you and the generations that follow, that we will worship the Lord before Him with our burnt offerings, sacrifices, and fellowship offerings. Then in the future your descendants will not be able to say to ours, "You have no share in the Lord." And we said, "If they ever say this to us or to our descendants, we will answer: 'Look at the replica of the Lord's altar which our fathers built, not for burnt offerings and sacrifices, but as a witness between us and you.'" (Josh. 22:26–28)

Civil war was averted, but only just.

Suspicion is a pervasive feature of social life and it is intensely destructive.[5] Judaism – a central project of which is the construction of a gracious society built on responsibility and trust – confronts the problem from both directions. On the one hand it commands us not to harbour suspicions but to judge people generously, giving them the benefit of the doubt. On the other, it bids each of us to act in a way that is above suspicion, keeping [as the rabbis put it] "far from unseemly conduct, from whatever resembles it, and from what may merely appear to resemble it."[6]

Being innocent before God is one thing; being innocent before one's fellow human beings is another, and far more difficult. Yet that is the challenge – not because we seek approval (that is pandering) but because we are summoned to be role models, exemplars, living embodiments of Torah. We are called on to be a unifying, not a divisive, presence in Jewish life. As Ḥatam Sofer said, we will not always succeed. Despite our best endeavours, others may still accuse us (as they accused Moses) of things of which we are genuinely innocent. Yet we must do our best by being charitable in our judgement of others and scrupulous in the way we conduct ourselves.

5. See Cass Sunstein, *On Rumours* (London: Allen Lane, 2009).
6. Numbers Rabba 10:8.

Masei

מסעי

Parashat Masei begins with an itinerary of the forty-two stopping points of the Israelites on their forty-year journey through the wilderness, culminating in their encampment on the plains of Moab, where they will stay until the death of Moses.

Their destination already close, the *parasha* sets out the boundaries of the Promised Land, as well as specifying certain places that will become cities of refuge where people guilty of manslaughter are to be protected against possible vengeance on the part of a relative of the person who died.

The *parasha* ends with a claim on the part of the leaders of the tribe of Menashe that the ruling in favour of the daughters of Tzlofhad that they were entitled to inherit their late father's share in the land could mean that the land was lost to the tribe if any of them married members of another tribe. A divine ruling resolves the conflict: the daughters have a right to inherit the land but must marry only within the tribe. With this, the book of Numbers ends.

The first of the essays explains why the Torah finds it necessary to detail at length the various stages of the Israelites' journey. The second asks why those exiled to a city of refuge were allowed home on the death of the high priest. The third looks at one detail of the laws of the cities of refuge that sets the life of an individual above the good of the community as a whole. The fourth, by contrast, shows how the second half of the story of the daughters of Tzlofhad emphasises group rights alongside the rights of individuals. The fifth is about the religious significance of the land and State of Israel. The sixth is about the prophetic voice in Judaism, as exemplified by the *haftarot* read during the three weeks between *Shiva Asar BeTammuz* and Tisha B'Av, which always coincide with the end of Numbers and the beginning of Deuteronomy.

The Long Walk to Freedom

Than he Israelites set out from Rameses on the fifteenth day of the first month, the day after the Passover. They marched out defiantly in full view of all the Egyptians.... The Israelites left Rameses and camped at Sukkot" (Num. 33:3–5). So begins the almost mind-numbing recitation of the forty-two journeys the Israelites made during their years in the wilderness. They journeyed from X and camped at Y. They journeyed from Y and camped at Z. It is for the most part a tedious recitation, deliberately so. Why then is it here?

The word Torah, the name given to the Five Books of Moses, means "instruction," "teaching," "guidance." It does not record events merely because they happened. Nowhere is this more manifest than in the book of Numbers, where almost thirty-eight of the forty wilderness years are passed over in silence, evidently because, although things happened in those years, they were mere events with no teaching to be drawn for the generations. Where then is the teaching in this list of place names?

The sages made a brave suggestion.

> It is like the case of a king whose son was ill. He took him to a certain place to be cured. On their return journey, his father

393

began to recount all the stages, saying: "Here we slept. Here we cooled ourselves. Here you had a headache." So the Holy One, Blessed Be He, said to Moses: Recount to them all the places where they provoked Me.[1]

Yet this remains challenging for a number of reasons. First, many of the places listed here are not mentioned elsewhere in the biblical text. If significant events occurred there – and all the more so if they were places where the people provoked God – then these stories are missing.[2] What is more, there is no mood of rebuke at this point in the narrative, no deliberate attempt to remember places where the people provoked God. That is the task of the early chapters of the book of Deuteronomy, where Moses does indeed take the people to task, getting them to know the shortcomings of their parents' generation so that they will not repeat their mistakes.

More likely, what we have here is a reminder for all time of what Nelson Mandela called *the long walk to freedom*.[3] Look at a map and you will see that the distance between Egypt and the land of Israel is not far. They are today bordering countries. Even in biblical times, the journey was not a major one. In Genesis 12 we read of how Abraham travelled there after arriving in the land of Canaan because there was a famine and he needed to buy food. The same thing happened in the days of Jacob and Joseph. The physical journey is a matter of weeks, not years.

The real journey to freedom, however, is not a physical one. It is a mental, moral, and spiritual one. It is long, arduous, and demanding, and there are challenges and failures along the way. That is what the book of Numbers has been all about. God was with the people. Yet they lacked the faith in themselves or in God to take the challenges in their stride.

1. Numbers Rabba 33:3.
2. Equally interesting is the fact that one of the places where the people provoked God is *not* included in this list, namely Taberah (Num. 11:3). Ibn Ezra (to Deut. 9:22) and Nahmanides (to Num. 11:3) both explain that it was not one of the places where the people encamped. They merely stayed there briefly on their way to their next stopping point, *Kivrot HaTaava*.
3. Nelson Mandela, *The Long Walk to Freedom* (Boston: Little, Brown, 1994).

There is an air of petulance about the people still, when they complain about the manna, or the water, or this or that aspect of Moses' leadership.

This was signalled at the outset. We read, in Exodus, that "when Pharaoh let the people go, God did not lead them on the road through the Philistine country, though that was shorter. For God said, 'If they face war, they might change their minds and return to Egypt'" (Ex. 13:17). We now know what this meant. The direct route meant travelling along the coast from the Nile Delta eastwards and northwards. Rameses II maintained a series of garrisons there, ready to repel an attack from the Hittites in the north. Had the Israelites taken this route they would have faced well-trained forces of the Egyptian army, ready to overwhelm them and take them back to Egypt.[4]

Yet the indirect route turned out not to save the people from war. Within days, the Egyptian army was pursuing them in chariots, the most powerful military technology of the time, which gave Egypt its unique strength. The people did indeed regret having left Egypt:

> Was it because there were no graves in Egypt that you brought us to the desert to die? What have you done to us by bringing us out of Egypt? Did we not say to you in Egypt, "Leave us alone; let us serve the Egyptians"? It would have been better for us to serve the Egyptians than to die in the desert! (Ex. 14:11–12)

This encounter was not accidental. The Torah states that God deliberately provoked Pharaoh to pursue after them (Ex. 14:4).

Nor was this all. Within days of crossing the sea, the people were attacked by the Amalekites. This time the battle was not fought for them by God; they had to fight it themselves. Even so, there is something unexpected in the negative report of the spies and the immediate demoralisation of the people. Everything we read in the Torah and the book of Joshua suggests that the people of the land were terrified of the Israelites, not

---

4. See James K. Hoffmeier, *Israel in Egypt: The Evidence for the Authenticity of the Exodus Tradition* (New York: Oxford University Press, 1996), 164–198. See also K. A. Kitchen, *On the Reliability of the Old Testament* (Grand Rapids, MI: Eerdmans, 2003), 266–267.

the other way around. The people knew that with God on their side, they could not lose. Yet fear overwhelmed their capacity for rational thought.[5]

This led Maimonides to suggest, in *Guide for the Perplexed*, that God deliberately led the people through the wilderness in order to put them in a situation where, by sheer necessity, they would acquire strength and endurance:

> It is a well-known fact that travelling in the wilderness without physical comforts such as bathing produces courage, while the opposite produces faintheartedness. Besides this, another generation rose during the wanderings that had not been accustomed to degradation and slavery.[6]

Maimonides makes this point in the course of his larger argument that it is impossible in human nature to go from one extreme to another, from the established way of doing things to a completely new one. That is why the Torah does not propose a series of radical breaks with what the Israelites had become accustomed to in Egypt. The Torah works through "the cunning of history." It produces its effect slowly and gradually.

If so, then the forty-two stopping points on the way are a literary device to communicate just how many stages we must go through to get from here to there when the destination is liberty itself. *The road from slavery to freedom is as long or short as it takes for people to develop the habits of responsibility for their and their children's future.* Freedom means making sacrifices in the present for the sake of peace and prosperity in the future. It means obeying laws for the sake of the common good. It involves virtue on the part of its citizens, and courage, and discipline. That is what the list in *Parashat Masei* is all about: the many small journeys it took before the people were ready to enter the land and begin to construct a society of freedom under the sovereignty of God.

Rousseau was blunt about the need to train people for liberty at the beginning of the journey to freedom. In one of the most powerful

---

5. This is what Daniel Goleman calls an "amygdala hijack." See D. Goleman, *Emotional Intelligence* (London: Bloomsbury, 1996), ch. 2.
6. Maimonides, *Guide for the Perplexed*, III:32.

passages in *The Social Contract,* he insists that a nation has to get this right at the outset, otherwise it will fail:

> Once customs are established and prejudices rooted, reform is a dangerous and fruitless enterprise; a people cannot bear to see its evils touched, even if only to be eradicated; it is like a stupid, pusillanimous invalid who trembles at the sight of a physician.... Free peoples, remember this maxim: liberty can be gained, but never *regained*.[7]

One of the most salient distinctions, made by all the early theorists of freedom in the seventeenth and eighteenth centuries, was the distinction between *liberty,* the freedom to do what we ought, and *licence,* the freedom to do what we like. This is roughly the same as the difference between the Hebrew terms *ḥerut* (law-governed liberty) and *ḥofesh* (the absence of someone else controlling what you do). The book of Judges contains a poignant sentence about Israel several centuries after Joshua's conquest: "In those days there was no king in Israel; everyone did what was right in his own eyes" (Judges 17:6; 21:25). That is the condition of licence. In it, liberty is at risk.

More relevant still to the book of Numbers than Rousseau's remark is an observation by a man who was critical of the French revolution that Rousseau's writings inspired, namely Edmund Burke. In his *Letter to a Member of the National Assembly,* he wrote:

> Men are qualified for civil liberty, in exact proportion to their disposition to put moral chains upon their own appetites.... Society cannot exist, unless a controlling power upon will and appetite be placed somewhere, and the less of it there is within, the more there must be without. *It is ordained in the eternal constitution of things, that men of intemperate minds cannot be free.* Their passions forge their fetters.[8]

7. Jean-Jacques Rousseau, *The Social Contract,* trans. Maurice Cranston (Harmondsworth: Penguin Classics, 1968), 88–89.
8. E. Burke, *Reflections on the Revolution in France* (Oxford: Oxford University Press, 1993), 289.

That is precisely the recurring theme of Numbers. It is why the Torah draws attention to the people's complaints about the manna and the water. It is why it tells the story of their seduction by the Moabite women, which led in turn to the embrace of idolatry (Num. 25:1–4). It is the key to understanding both parts of the story of the spies – both the lack of self-confidence of the people when they yielded to their demoralising report and the excess of self-confidence shown by the *maapilim*, the people who after God's decree impetuously set out on a military campaign only to be defeated by the Amalekites (Num. 14:40–45). The people had intemperate minds. They were wayward. They succumbed to the mood of the moment. They allowed themselves to be swayed by passing waves of emotion. Their passions forged their fetters. They were not yet fit to be free. In the end they had to leave that task to their children.

"They journeyed from X and camped at Y. They journeyed from Y and camped at Z" and so on – for forty-two stages. This is no mere reminiscence. Nor is it included for the sake of history alone. It is a way of reminding us in every generation *how long it takes to reach the Promised Land*. It has nothing to do with distance on the map and everything to do with self-control in the mind.

What Numbers is teaching us – and it will be the theme of one of the most remarkable political documents in history, the book of Deuteronomy – is that freedom is not what most civilisations have thought it is. It is not primarily a matter of structures of governance – democracy versus aristocracy, oligarchy, monarchy, and the rest. Democracy can lead to tyranny; indeed Plato thought it always would.

The most important guarantor of freedom is the "habits of the heart" of the people. That is one of the fundamental purposes of Torah: to train us, through the 613 commands touching on all aspects of life, in habits of self-control, moral responsibility, and a sense of justice and compassion. There were times when Jews lost their freedom. But they never lost their passion for it, or their ability to seize it when the chance came. Look at every movement for liberty in the modern world and you will find, somewhere in its inception, either Jews or Jewish ideas. To quote Heinrich Heine: "Since the Exodus, freedom has always spoken with a Hebrew accent."

In one of the great speeches of the twentieth century, American jurist Judge Learned Hand said this about "the spirit of liberty":

> I often wonder whether we do not rest our hopes too much upon constitutions, upon laws, and upon courts. These are false hopes; believe me, these are false hopes. Liberty lies in the hearts of men and women; when it dies there, no constitution, no law, no court can save it; no constitution, no law, no court can even do much to help it.[9]

There is an obvious question. If God wanted us to be free, why did He not make us law-abiding? Why did He not hardwire a disposition for justice into our genes? The answer is equally obvious. You cannot make someone free. That is something we each have to learn through education and experience. It is a contradiction in terms to think we can be forced to be free.[10] Maimonides makes the point forcibly in *Guide for the Perplexed*: God can force people to obey the law, but He has never done so nor will He ever do so. "If it were part of His will to change the nature of a person, the mission of the prophets and the giving of the Torah would have been altogether superfluous."[11]

The list of journeys at the beginning of *Parashat Masei* is there to teach us a principle that has been ignored for most of history, always with tragic results.[12] *There are no shortcuts to freedom.* You do not achieve it by deposing a tyrant or instituting democratic elections. You have to educate people to be free, and they have to learn and internalise its disciplines and responsibilities. *Parashat Masei* teaches us that the walk to

9. "The Spirit of Liberty," speech at "'I Am an American' Day" ceremony (Central Park, New York City, May 21, 1944).
10. That did not stop Rousseau from making this error: *Social Contract*, 64.
11. Maimonides, *Guide for the Perplexed*, III:32.
12. During the years this book was being written, uprisings took place in 2011 in many Middle East and North African countries. It became known as the "Arab Spring." The result as of 2016 is a series of failed states and the spread of terror, civil war, brutality, and religiously motivated barbarism that have destroyed what little freedom there was to begin with. Yet almost no one in those early months made the obvious point, that without the "apprenticeship of liberty," no change of ruler brings freedom – only a new tyranny.

freedom is long, and there are many stopping points along the way. It needs not just miracles from God but also self-transformation by human beings. There is only one way out of the wilderness, and that is learning to be free, however long it takes.

The Death of the High Priest

The book of Numbers draws to a close with an account of the cities of refuge, the six cities – three on each side of the Jordan – set apart as places to which people found innocent of murder, but guilty of manslaughter, were sent (Num. 35:9–34).

In early societies, especially non-urban ones that lacked an extensive police force, there was always a danger that people would take the law into their own hands, in particular when a member of their family or tribe had been killed. Thus would begin a cycle of vengeance and retaliation that had no natural end, one revenge killing leading to another and another, until the community had been decimated, a phenomenon familiar to us from literature, from the Montagues and Capulets of *Romeo and Juliet*, to the Sharks and Jets of *West Side Story*, to the Corleones and Tattaglias of *The Godfather*.[1]

The only viable solution is the effective and impartial rule of law. There is, though, one persisting danger. If Reuben killed Simeon and is deemed innocent of murder by the court – it was unintended, there was

1. On this, see René Girard, *Violence and the Sacred* (Baltimore: Johns Hopkins University Press, 1977).

no malice aforethought, the victim and perpetrator were not enemies – then there is still the danger that the family of the victim may feel that justice has not been done. Their close relative lies dead and no one has been punished.

It was to prevent such situations of "blood vengeance" that the cities of refuge were established. Those who had committed manslaughter were sent there, and so long as they were within the city limits, they were protected by law. There they had to stay until – according to this *parasha* – "the death of the high priest" (Num. 35:25).

The obvious question is: *What does the death of the high priest have to do with it?* There seems no connection whatsoever between manslaughter, blood vengeance, and the high priest, let alone his death.

Let us look at three quite different interpretations. They are each interesting in their own right, but more generally, they show us the range of thought that exists within Judaism.

The first is that the death of the high priest *atoned* for the lost life of the victim (Makkot 11b). To be sure, there was no malice aforethought. The killing was unintended. But it is precisely for unintended acts – sins committed *beshogeg*, unknowingly or unwittingly – that a sin offering had to be brought (Lev. 4). In the case of manslaughter, no sin offering is adequate. What has been lost is a life, and one life is like a universe. "When blood is shed in the land, it cannot be atoned for except through the blood of the person who shed it" (Num. 35:33). That is in the case of murder. In the case of manslaughter, it seems as if it is the death of the high priest that atones.

A second approach – or it may be a variant on the first – is that in some way the high priest shared in the responsibility for the death: "A venerable old scholar said: I heard an explanation at one of the sessional lectures of Rava that *the high priest should have implored divine grace for the generation, which he failed to do*" (Makkot 11a).

According to this, the high priest had a share, however small, in the guilt for the fact that someone died, albeit unintentionally. Murder is not something that could have been averted by the high priest's prayer. The murderer was guilty. He chose to do what he did, and no one else can be blamed. But manslaughter, precisely because it happens without anyone intending that it should, is the kind of event that might have been averted by the prayers of the high priest. Therefore it is not fully atoned for until the high priest dies. Only then can the manslaughterer go free.

Maimonides offers a completely different kind of explanation in *Guide for the Perplexed*:

> A person who killed another person unknowingly must go into exile because the anger of "the avenger of the blood" cools down while the cause of the mischief is out of sight. The chance of returning from the exile depends on the death of the high priest, the most honoured of men, and the friend of all Israel. By his death the relative of the slain person becomes reconciled (Num. 35:25); for it is a natural phenomenon that we find consolation in our misfortune when the same misfortune or a greater one has befallen another person. Amongst us no death causes more grief than that of the high priest.[2]

According to Maimonides, the death of the high priest has nothing to do with guilt or atonement, but simply with the fact that it causes great collective grief, in which people forget their own misfortunes in the face of larger national loss. That is when people let go of their individual sense of injustice and desire for revenge. It then becomes safe for the person found guilty of manslaughter to return home.

What is at stake between these profoundly different interpretations of the law? One element has to do with whether exile to a city of refuge is a kind of punishment or not. According to the Babylonian Talmud, it seems as if it was. There may have been no intent. No one was legally to blame. But a tragedy had happened at the hands of X, the person guilty of manslaughter, and even the high priest shared, if only negatively and passively, in the guilt. The key concept at work here is *atonement*, which presupposes that there was something to atone for. Only when the manslaughterer and the high priest had undergone some suffering, one by way of exile, the other by way of (natural, not judicial) death, would the moral balance be restored. The family of the victim felt that some sort of justice had been done.

2. Maimonides, *Guide for the Perplexed*, III:40.

Maimonides, however, does not understand the law of the cities of refuge in terms of guilt or punishment whatsoever. The only relevant consideration is safety. The person guilty of manslaughter goes into exile, not because it is a form of atonement or expiation, but simply because it is safer for him to be a long way from those who might be seeking vengeance. He stays there until the death of the high priest because only after national tragedy can you assume that people have given up thoughts of taking revenge for their own lost family member. This is a fundamental difference in the way we conceptualise the cities of refuge.

There is another and more fundamental difference. The Babylonian Talmud assumes a certain level of supernatural reality: had the high priest prayed hard and devotedly enough, there would have been no accidental deaths.

Maimonides' explanation is non-supernatural. It belongs broadly to what we would call social psychology. People are more able to come to terms with the past when they are not reminded daily of it by seeing the person who, perhaps, was driving the car that killed their son as he was crossing the road on a dark night, in heavy rainfall, on a sharp bend in the road.

There are deaths – like those of Princess Diana and of the Queen Mother in Britain – that evoke widespread and deep national grief. There are times – after 9/11, for example, or the Indian Ocean tsunami of December 26, 2004 – when our personal grievances seem simply too small to worry about. This, as Maimonides says, is "a natural phenomenon."

This fundamental difference between a *natural* and *supernatural* understanding of Judaism runs through many eras of Jewish history: sages as against priests, philosophers as against mystics, R. Ishmael as against R. Akiva, Maimonides in contradistinction to Judah Halevi, and so on to today.

It is important to realise that not every approach to religious faith in Judaism presupposes supernatural events – events, that is to say, that cannot be explained within the parameters of science, broadly conceived. God is beyond the universe, but His actions within the universe may nonetheless be in accordance with natural law and causation.

In this view, prayer changes the world because it changes us. Torah has the power to transform society, not by way of miracles, but by effects that are fully explicable in terms of political theory and social science. And the death of the high priest, with the communal grief it triggers, makes it possible for the manslaughterer to return home. This is not the only approach to Judaism, but it is Maimonides', and it remains one of the two great ways of understanding our faith.

Individual and Community

I t is no coincidence that the book of Numbers draws to a close with a statement of one of the fundamentals of Judaism: the sanctity of human life. As the people approach the land that will become holy, they are reminded: "Do not pollute the land in which you live; it is blood that pollutes the land" (Num. 35:33). With these words we are brought back almost to the beginning of the human story, to the scene in which the first child, Cain, murders the second, Abel, and is told by God, "The sound of your brother's blood is crying to Me from the ground" (Gen. 4:10). Likewise we recall the central law of the covenant with Noah: "He who sheds the blood of man, by man shall his blood be shed, for in the image of God did God make man" (Gen. 9:6). Since the human person is the image of God, murder is not merely a crime; it is sacrilege. It defiles the land. It desecrates something holy, namely human life itself.

Hence the law of the cities of refuge – the six towns, three on either side of the Jordan, set aside for the protection of those found guilty of manslaughter, those who caused a human death without murderous intent. They were there to protect manslaughterers from "blood vengeance" by a member of the family of the victim. The blood feud was one

407

of the primary drivers of violence in the ancient world.[1] On the one hand, the Torah recognises its existence by ruling that if, after a properly constituted trial, the accused is found guilty of murder, the death sentence is to be carried out by the *goel hadam*, the "blood avenger" (literally, "blood redeemer").[2] On the other, it equally recognises that the desire for revenge must not be allowed to interfere with the due process of the law. Therefore it becomes essential to protect the accused until he has first stood trial,[3] and if he is deemed innocent of murderous intent, to protect him thereafter.

The Torah tells us, however, that the protection afforded by the cities of refuge exists only so long as the manslaughterer actually stays inside. If he leaves, he forfeits his protection,[4] and therefore places his life at risk. This gives rise to a fascinating provision of Jewish law. This is how Maimonides, following the Talmud, states it:

> One who has been exiled does not leave the city of refuge at all, even to perform a mitzva, or to give evidence in a monetary or capital case, or to save someone by his testimony, or to rescue someone from a non-Jew or a river or a fire or a collapsed building. *Even if all Israel needs his help*, like Joab son of Zeruiah [King David's chief of staff], he never leaves the city of refuge until the death of the high priest, and if he leaves, he makes himself vulnerable to death.[5]

There is a principle here that sheds much light on Judaism's system of values. Outside the city of refuge, the person found guilty of manslaughter could be killed by the blood avenger: "But if the accused ever goes outside the limits of the city of refuge to which he has fled, and

1. See the previous essay and the book by René Girard cited there.
2. Num. 35:19; Maimonides, *Mishneh Torah, Hilkhot Rotze'aḥ* 1:2.
3. See Num. 35:12: "These cities shall serve you as a refuge from the avenger, so that a murderer not die until he can stand trial before the courts." In other words, the cities of refuge not only protected the manslaughterer – they also protected all those accused of murder until they could stand trial.
4. See Num. 35:26–28.
5. Maimonides, *Mishneh Torah, Hilkhot Rotze'aḥ* 7:8.

the avenger of blood finds him outside the city, the avenger of blood may kill the accused without being guilty of murder" (Num. 35:26–27).

Thus, to leave the city of refuge was to put one's life at risk. No one in Judaism is commanded to put his life at risk to save the life of another – even to save the entire Jewish people ("even if all Israel needs his help"). Despite the fact that Judaism is an intensely communal faith, nonetheless in Jewish law, the right to life is absolute and inalienable, and whenever it is at stake, *the individual takes priority over the community*.

Here is another example, codified by Maimonides:

> If idol worshippers say to a group of women, "Give us one of your women for immoral purposes, or we will violate you all," they must all allow themselves to be violated rather than hand over one Jewish soul. Similarly, if idol worshippers say, "Give us one of you and we shall kill him, or else we will kill you all," they must all allow themselves to be killed rather than hand over one Jewish soul.[6]

On the face of it, the law is illogical. The refusal to collaborate with tyranny by handing over a victim will not save the victim. She will be violated, or he killed, whatever the group chooses to do. Why then must they all allow themselves to be mistreated or killed? The key difference is between *active* and *passive*, between what a person does and what is done to him. An entire group must passively allow itself to be assaulted rather than actively sacrifice a single one of their number. Again, the rights of the individual take priority over the welfare of the group.

A third example is exemption from military service (in the case of a *milhemet reshut*, a non-obligatory war; the exemptions do not apply in the case of a war of self-defence):

> The officers shall say to the people: "Has anyone built a new house and not dedicated it? Let him go home, or he may die in battle and someone else may dedicate it. Has anyone planted a vineyard

---

6. Maimonides, *Mishneh Torah, Hilkhot Yesodei HaTorah* 5:5. On this, see David Daube, *Collaboration with Tyranny in Rabbinic Law* (London: Oxford University Press, 1965).

and not begun to enjoy it? Let him go home, or he may die in battle and someone else enjoy it. Has anyone become pledged to a woman and not married her? Let him go home, or he may die in battle and someone else marry her." (Deut. 20:5–7)

Wars are fought for the sake of the nation as a whole. The exempt categories refer to individuals who have not yet had the chance to enjoy a fundamental human good: marriage, a home, a vineyard. Again we have a case in which a private good overrides the public good.

At stake in these and many other examples is the supreme importance, in Judaism, of a single human life. This is how a famous mishna puts it:

> It was for this reason that man was created singly, to teach you that anyone who destroys a life is considered by Scripture to have destroyed an entire world, and anyone who saves a life is as if he saved an entire world. And also, to promote peace among the creations, that no man would say to his friend, "My ancestors are greater than yours...." And also, to express the grandeur of the Holy One, Blessed Be He: For a man strikes many coins from the same die, and all the coins are alike. But the supreme King of kings, the Holy One, Blessed Be He, strikes every man from the die of the first man, and yet no man is quite like his friend. Therefore, every person must say, "For my sake the world was created." (Mishna Sanhedrin 4:5)

In these words, we feel the full revolutionary significance of the first chapter of Genesis, with its momentous declaration that the human being is in the image and likeness of God – the single most radical consequence of monotheism. *The concept of God, singular and alone, gave rise to the concept of the human person, singular and alone.* This is the birth of the individual in Western civilisation.[7]

---

7. See Larry Siedentop, *Inventing the Individual: The Origins of Western Liberalism* (London: Allen Lane, 2014), who attributes it, wrongly I believe, to Christianity.

It goes without saying that this was unknown in the pagan world. More worthy of attention is the difference between biblical ethics and those of ancient Greece. In Greece the highest value was the polis, the city-state, the group. Ethics was a code of devotion to the city (Athens, Sparta). The supreme glory was heroism in the field of battle, or the willingness to die for the city's sake: *Dulce et decorum est pro patria mori* ("It is pleasant and proper to die for one's country"). The group takes precedence over the individual. That is a fundamental difference between Greek and Jewish ethics.

One thinker who reflected deeply on this was the late Rabbi Moshe Avigdor Amiel (1882–1945), Chief Rabbi of Antwerp and later of Tel Aviv. In his *HaTzedek HaSotziali VeHaTzedek HaMishpati Shelanu* (translated as *Ethics and Legality in Jewish Law*), he pointed out two consequences of the Jewish emphasis on the individual. On the one hand, it was vital to Jewish survival in exile. Jews were always a minority, and the minority usually conforms to the majority. Had this been the case among Jews, there would be no Judaism today. Jews, however, have had a long history of valuing the individual over the group. Jews did not bend to the majority. The one did not give way to the many.

But the very attribute that was a source of strength in exile could also be a source of weakness at times of Jewish national sovereignty:

> In order to enforce order, there must be some denial of the individual's rights in society, or sacrifice of the private to the public good. No government or political order in the world can always benefit every individual. Every form of government must strive for the public good, and if the individual must occasionally suffer, there is no great harm done. But the Jewish national character cannot bear this, for Jewish ethics preaches the absolute freedom of the individual, which cannot be abrogated on behalf of society.[8]

Nonetheless his analysis is insightful in showing the background against which this idea emerged.

8. Moshe Avigdor Amiel, *Ethics and Legality in Jewish Law* (Jerusalem: Rabbi Amiel Library, 1992), 1:71.

This gives rise to the fractious nature of Jews as a group:

> Everyone considers himself qualified to judge the judges, and sets
> up his own altar, not accepting any authority. If Jews are more
> prone to these faults than the rest of mankind, it is also the result
> of this outlook – that society exists for the sake of the individual.
> Thus every individual allows himself to separate from society,
> until there are an endless number of parties and splinter groups.
> This in turn generates much baseless hatred.[9]

This is one strand of Judaism, and it generates many of its most striking
characteristics, positive and negative: its diversity and argumentativeness,
its ability to generate iconoclasts and pioneers, its impact out of all proportion to its numbers, but also its fractions and factions, its perennial
tendency to split apart when unity is needed. Is there, within Judaism,
a counterweight to individualism? There is, and with great subtlety and
finesse, it is provided by the very next episode in Numbers, the one that
brings the book to its close. To this we now turn.

9.   Ibid., 1:79.

The Complexity of Human Rights

The book of Numbers ends in a way that is very strange indeed. In *Parashat Pinḥas* we read of how the five daughters of Tzlofhad came to Moses with a claim based on justice and human rights.[1] Their father had died without sons. Inheritance – in this case, a share in the land – passes through the male line, but here there was no male line. Surely their father was entitled to his share, and they were his only heirs. By rights, that share should come to them: "Why should our father's name be disadvantaged in his family merely because he did not have a son? Give us a portion of land along with our father's brothers" (Num. 27:4).

Moses had received no instruction about such an eventuality, so he asked God directly. God answered in favour of the women: "The daughters of Tzlofhad are right. You shall give them possession of an inheritance among their father's brothers and transfer the inheritance of their father to them" (Num. 27:7). He gave Moses further instructions

---

1. The word "rights" is, of course, an anachronism here. The concept was not born until the seventeenth century. Nonetheless it is not absurd to suggest that this is what is implied in the daughters' claim, "Why should our father's name be disadvantaged?" (Num. 27:4).

about the disposition of inheritance, and the narrative then passes on to other matters.

Only now, right at the end of the book, does the Torah report on an event that arose directly from that case. Leaders of Tzlofhad's tribe, Menashe son of Joseph, came and made the following complaint. If the land were to pass to Tzlofhad's daughters and they married men from another tribe, the land would eventually pass to their husbands, and thus to their husbands' tribes. Thus land that had initially been granted to the tribe of Menashe might be lost to it in perpetuity.

Again, Moses took the case to God, who offered a simple solution. The daughters of Tzlofhad were entitled to the land, but so too was the tribe. Therefore, if they wished to take possession of the land, they must marry men from within their own tribe. That way both claims could be honoured. The daughters did not lose their right to the land but they did lose some freedom in choosing a marriage partner.

The two passages are intimately related. They use the same terminology. Both Tzlofhad's daughters and the leaders of the clan "draw near." They use the same verb to describe their potential loss: *yigara*, "disadvantaged," "diminished." God replies in both cases with the same locution, "*ken... dovrot/dovrim*," rightly do they speak.[2] Why then are the two episodes separated in the text? Why does the book of Numbers end on this seemingly anticlimactic note? And does it have any relevance today?

Numbers as a book is about individuals. It begins with a census, whose purpose is less to tell us the actual number of Israelites than to "lift" their "heads," the unusual locution the Torah uses to convey the idea that when God orders a census it is to tell the people that they each count. The book also focuses on the psychology of individuals. We read of Moses' despair, of Aaron and Miriam's criticism of him, of the spies who lacked the courage to come back with a positive report, and of the malcontents, led by Korah, who challenged Moses' leadership. We read

---

2. These two passages may well be the source of the story of the rabbi who hears both sides of a marital dispute, and says to both husband and wife, "You are right." The rabbi's disciple asks, "How can they both be right?" to which the rabbi replies, "You too are right."

of Joshua and Caleb, Eldad and Medad, Datan and Aviram, Zimri and Pinhas, Balak and Balaam, and others. When Moses asked God to appoint a successor, he used an unusual locution: "God of the spirits of all flesh" – understood by the sages and Rashi to mean: appoint a leader who will deal with each individual as an individual, who will relate to people in their uniqueness and singularity. And as we saw in the previous essay, the laws of the city of refuge were understood by the sages and Maimonides to prioritise the rights of the individual over the claims of the community.

It is against this backdrop that we can understand the claim of Tzlofhad's daughters. They were invoking their rights as individuals. Justly so. As many of the commentators pointed out, the behaviour of the women throughout the wilderness years was exemplary while that of the men was the opposite. The men, not the women, gave gold for the Golden Calf. The spies were men; a famous comment by the *Kli Yakar* (Rabbi Shlomo Ephraim Luntschitz; Eastern Europe, 1550–1619) suggests that had Moses sent women instead, they would have come back with a positive report (commentary to Num. 13:2). Recognising the justice of the women's cause, God affirmed their rights as individuals.

But society is not built on individuals alone. As the book of Judges points out, individualism is another name for chaos: "In those days there was no king in Israel; everyone did what was right in his own eyes" (Judges 17:6; 21:25). Hence the insistence, throughout Numbers, on the central role of the tribes as the organising principle of Jewish life. The Israelites were numbered tribe by tribe. The Torah sets out their precise encampment around the Tabernacle and the order in which they were to journey. In *Parashat Naso*, at inordinate length, the Torah repeats the gifts of each tribe at the inauguration of the Tabernacle, despite the fact that they each gave exactly the same. The tribes were not accidental to the structure of Israel as a society. Like the United States of America, whose basic political structure is that of a federation of (originally thirteen, now fifty) states, so Israel was (until the appointment of a king) a federation of tribes.

The existence of something like tribes is fundamental to a free society.[3] The modern state of Israel is built on a vast panoply

---

3. See most recently Sebastian Junger, *Tribe: On Homecoming and Belonging* (London: Fourth Estate, 2016).

of ethnicities – Ashkenazi and Sephardi; Jews from Eastern, Central, and Western Europe, Spain and Portugal, Arab lands, Russia and Ethiopia, America, South Africa, Australia, and other places; some hasidic, some yeshivish, others "modern," others "traditional," yet others secular and cultural.

We each have a series of identities, based partly on family background, partly on occupation, partly on locality and community. These "mediating structures," larger than the individual but smaller than the state, are where we develop our complex, vivid, face to face interactions and identities. They are the domain of family, friends, neighbours, and colleagues, and they make up what is collectively known as civil society. A strong civil society is essential to freedom.[4]

That is why, alongside individual rights, a society must make space for group identities. The classic instance of the opposite came in the wake of the French Revolution. In the course of the debate in the French Revolutionary Assembly in 1789, the Count of Clermont-Tonnerre made his famous declaration, "To the Jews as individuals, everything. To the Jews as a nation, nothing." If they insisted on defining themselves as a nation, that is, as a distinct subgroup within the republic, said the Count, "we shall be compelled to expel them."

Initially, this sounded reasonable. Jews were being offered civil rights in the new secular nation-state. However, it was anything but. It meant that Jews would have to give up their identity as Jews in the public domain. Nothing – not religious or ethnic identity – should stand between the individual and the state. It was no accident that a century later, France became one of the epicentres of European anti-Semitism, beginning with Édouard Drumont's vicious *La France Juive* (1886), and culminating in the Dreyfus trial. Hearing the Parisian crowd shout "Mort aux Juifs," Theodor Herzl realised that Jews had still not been accepted as citizens of Europe, despite all the protestations to the contrary. Jews found themselves regarded as a tribe in a Europe that claimed to have abolished tribes. European emancipation recognised individual rights but not collective ones.

---

4. This is the argument made most powerfully by Edmund Burke and Alexis de Tocqueville.

The primatologist Frans de Waal makes the point powerfully. Almost the whole of modern Western culture, he says, was built on the idea of autonomous, choosing individuals. But that is not who we are. We are people with strong attachments to family, friends, neighbours, allies, coreligionists, and people of the same ethnicity. He continues:

> A morality exclusively concerned with individual rights tends to ignore the ties, needs, and interdependencies that have marked our existence from the very beginning. It is a cold morality that puts space between people, assigning each person to his or her own little corner of the universe. How this caricature of a society arose in the minds of eminent thinkers is a mystery.[5]

That is precisely the point the Torah is making when it divides the story of the daughters of Tzlofhad into two. The first part, in *Parashat Pinḥas*, is about individual rights, the rights of Tzlofhad's daughters to a share in the land. The second, at the end of the book, is about group rights, in this case the right of the tribe of Menashe to its territory. In the case of life, the most fundamental value of all, the Torah sets the individual above the group. But in the case of property – as here, the inheritance of land – the Torah affirms both, because both are necessary to a free society.

Many of the most seemingly intractable issues in contemporary Jewish life have appeared because Jews, especially in the West, are used to a culture in which individual rights are held to override all others. We should be free to live as we choose, worship as we choose, and identify as we choose. But a culture based solely on individual rights will undermine families, communities, traditions, loyalties, and shared codes of reverence and restraint.

Despite its enormous emphasis on the value of the individual, Judaism also insists on the value of those institutions that preserve and protect our identities as members of groups that make them up. We have rights as individuals but identities only as members of tribes. Honouring both is delicate, difficult, and necessary. Numbers ends by showing us how.

5. Frans de Waal, *Good Natured* (Cambridge, MA: Harvard University Press, 1996), 167.

The Religious Significance of Israel

The long journey is nearing its close. The Jordan is almost within sight. We have read the long itinerary of stops along the way. Finally the list draws to a close, and God tells Moses: "Take possession of the land and settle in it, for I have given you the land to possess" (Num. 33:53). This, according to Nahmanides (to Num. 33:53), is the source of the command to dwell in the land of Israel and inherit it.

With this we come to one of the central tensions in Judaism and Jewish history: the religious significance of the land of Israel. Its centrality cannot be doubted. Whatever the subplots and subsidiary themes of Tanakh, its overarching narrative is *the promise of and journey to the land.*[1] Jewish history begins with Abraham and Sarah's journey to it. Exodus to Deuteronomy are taken up with the second journey in the days of Moses. Tanakh as a whole ends with Cyrus king of Persia granting permission to Jews, exiled in Babylon, to return to their land – the third great journey (II Chr. 36:23).

The paradox of Jewish history is that though a specific territory, the holy land, is at its heart, Jews have spent more time in exile than in

1. See D. J. Clines, *The Theme of the Pentateuch* (Sheffield: JSOT, 1978).

Israel; more time longing for it than dwelling in it; more time travelling than arriving. Much of the Jewish story could be written in the language of *Parashat Masei*: "They journeyed from X and camped at Y."

Hence the tension. On the one hand, monotheism must understand God as non-territorial. The God of *every*where can be found *any*where. He is not confined to this people, that place – as pagans believed. He exercises His power even in Egypt. He sends a prophet, Jonah, to Nineveh in Assyria. He is with another prophet, Ezekiel, in Babylon. There is no place in the universe where He is not. On the other hand, it must be impossible to live fully as a Jew outside Israel, for if not, Jews would not have been commanded to go there initially, or to return subsequently. Why is the God beyond place to be found specifically in *this* place?

The sages formulated the tension in two striking propositions. On the one hand, "Wherever the Israelites went into exile, *the Divine Presence was exiled* with them."[2] On the other, "One who leaves Israel to live elsewhere is *as if he had no God*" (Ketubbot 110b). Can one find God, serve God, experience God, outside the holy land? Yes and no. If the answer were only yes, there would be no incentive to return. If the answer were only no, there would be no reason to stay Jewish in exile. On this tension, the Jewish existence is built.

What then is special about Israel? In *The Kuzari*, Judah Halevi says that different environments have different ecologies. Just as there are some countries, climates, and soils particularly suited to growing vines, so there is a country, Israel, particularly suited to growing prophets – indeed a whole divinely inspired people. "No other place shares the distinction of the divine influence, just as no other mountain produces such good wine."[3]

Nahmanides gives a different explanation. God, he says,

> created everything and placed the power over the ones below in the ones above and placed over each and every people in their lands according to their nations a star and a specific constellation.... But the land of Israel, in the middle of the inhabited earth, is the inherit-

2. *Mekhilta, Parashat Bo* 14.
3. *The Kuzari*, II:9–12.

ance of God…. He has set us apart from all the nations over whom He has appointed princes and other celestial powers, by giving us the land [of Israel] so that He, blessed be He, will be our God and we will be dedicated to His name. (Commentary to Lev. 18:25)

Though every land and nation is under the overarching sovereignty of God, only Israel is *directly* so. Others are ruled by intermediaries earthly and heavenly. Their fate is governed by other factors. Only in the land and People of Israel do we find a nation's fortunes and misfortunes directly attributable to their relationship with God.

Judah Halevi and Nahmanides both expound what we might call *mystical geography*. The difference between them is that Judah Halevi looks to earth, Nahmanides to heaven. For Judah Halevi, what is special about the land of Israel is its soil, landscape, and climate. For Nahmanides, it is its direct governance by God. For both of them, religious experience is possible outside Israel, but it is a pale shadow of what it is in the land. Is there a way of stating this *non-mystically*, in concepts and categories closer to ordinary experience? Here is one way of doing so.

The Torah is not merely a code of personal perfection. It is the framework for the construction of a society, a nation, a culture. It is about what Rabbi Aharon Lichtenstein called, in a memorable phrase, "societal beatitude." It contains welfare legislation, civil law, rules governing employer-employee relationships, environmental provisions, rules of animal welfare, public health, and governmental and judicial systems.

The Torah stands at the opposite end of the spectrum from Gnosticism and other world-denying philosophies that see religion as an ascent of the soul to ethereal realms of the spirit. For Judaism, God lives here, on earth, in human lives, interactions, and associations. The Torah is terrestrial because God seeks to dwell on earth. Thus the Jewish task is to create a society with the Divine Presence in its midst. Had Judaism been confined to matters of the spirit, it would have left vast areas of human concern – the entire realms of politics, economics, and sociology – outside the religious sphere.

What was and is unique about Israel is that it is the sole place on earth (barring short-lived exceptions like the Himyarites in the sixth century and Khazars in the eighth, whose kings converted to Judaism) where Jews have had the chance to create an entire society on Jewish lines. It is possible to live a Jewish life in Manchester or Monsey, Madrid or Minsk. But it is always a truncated experience. Only in Israel do Jews conduct their lives in the language of the Bible, within time defined by the Jewish calendar and space saturated in Jewish history. Only there do they form a majority. Only there are they able to construct a political system, an economy, and an environment on the template of Jewish values. There alone can Judaism be what it is meant to be – not just a code of conduct for individuals, but also and essentially the architectonics of a society.

Hence there must be some space on earth where Jews practise self-government under divine sovereignty. But why Israel, specifically? Because it was and is a key strategic location where three continents – Europe, Africa, and Asia – meet. Lacking the extended flat and fertile space of the Nile Delta or the Tigris-Euphrates valley (or today, the oil fields of Arabia), it could never be the base of an empire, but because of its location it was always sought after by empires. So it was politically vulnerable.

It was and is ecologically vulnerable, because its water resources are dependent on rain, which in that part of the world is never predictable (hence the frequent famines mentioned in Genesis). Its existence could never, therefore, be taken for granted. Time and again its people, surviving challenges, would experience this as a miracle. Small geographically and demographically, it would depend on outstanding achievement – political, military, and economic – on the part of its people. This would depend, in turn, on their morale and sense of mission. Thus the prophets knew, naturally as well as supernaturally, that without social justice and a sense of divine vocation, the nation would eventually fall and suffer exile again.

These are, as it were, the empirical foundations of the mysticism of Halevi and Nahmanides. They are as true today as they were in ancient times. There is a directness, a naturalness, of Jewish experience in Israel that can be found nowhere else. History tells us that the project of constructing a society under divine sovereignty in a vulnerable land is the highest of high-risk strategies. Yet, across forty centuries, Jews knew that the risk was worth taking. For only in Israel is God so close that you can feel Him in the sun and wind, sense Him just beyond the hills, hear Him in the inflections of everyday speech, breathe His presence in the early morning air and live, dangerously but confidently, under the shadow of His wings.

The Prophetic Voice

During the three weeks between *Shiva Asar BeTammuz* and Tisha B'Av, as we recall the destruction of the Temples, we read three of the most searing passages in the prophetic literature, the first two from the opening of the book of Jeremiah, the third from the first chapter of Isaiah.

At perhaps no other time of the year are we so acutely aware of the enduring force of ancient Israel's great visionaries. The prophets had no power. They were not kings or members of the royal court. They were (usually) not priests or members of the religious establishment. They held no office. They were not elected. Often they were deeply unpopular, none more so than the author of the *haftara* to *Parashat Masei*, Jeremiah, who was arrested, flogged, abused, put on trial, and only narrowly escaped with his life. Only rarely were the prophets heeded in their lifetimes; the one clear exception was Jonah, and he spoke to non-Jews, the citizens of Nineveh. Yet their words were recorded for posterity and became a major feature of Tanakh. They were the world's first social critics[1] and their message continues through the centuries.

---

1. See Michael Walzer, *Interpretation and Social Criticism* (Cambridge, MA: Harvard University Press, 1987).

As Kierkegaard almost said: When a king dies, his power ends; when a prophet dies, his influence begins.[2]

What was distinctive about the prophet was not that he foretold the future. The ancient world was full of such people: soothsayers, oracles, readers of runes, shamans, and other diviners, each of whom claimed inside track with the forces that govern fate and "shape our ends, rough-hew them how we will." Judaism has no time for such people. The Torah bans one "who practises divination or sorcery, interprets omens, engages in witchcraft, or casts spells, or who is a medium or spiritist or who consults the dead" (Deut. 18:10–11). It disbelieves such practices because it believes in human freedom. The future is not pre-scripted. It depends on us and the choices we make. *If a prediction comes true it has succeeded; if a prophecy comes true it has failed.* The prophet describes a future that will happen *unless* we heed the danger and mend our ways. He (or she – there were seven biblical prophetesses) does not predict; he (or she) warns.

Nor was the prophet distinctive in blessing or cursing the people. That was Balaam's gift, not Isaiah's or Jeremiah's. In Judaism, blessing comes through priests, not prophets.

Several things made the prophets unique. The first was his or her sense of history. The prophets were the first people to see God in history.[3] We tend to take our sense of time for granted. Time happens. Time flows. As the saying goes, time is God's way of keeping everything from happening at once. But actually there are several ways of relating to time and different civilisations have perceived it differently.

There is *cyclical* time – time as the slow turning of the seasons, or the cycle of birth, growth, decline, and death. Cyclical time is time as it occurs in nature. Some trees have long lives, fruit flies have short ones – but all that lives, dies. The species endures, individual members do not. Ecclesiastes contains the most famous expression of cyclical time in Judaism:

2. Kierkegaard actually said: "The tyrant dies and his rule is over; the martyr dies and his rule begins"; Kierkegaard, *Papers and Journals* (London: Penguin Books, 1996), 352.
3. See Yosef Hayim Yerushalmi, *Zakhor: Jewish History and Jewish Memory* (Seattle: University of Washington Press, 1982).

The sun rises and the sun sets, and hurries back to where it rises. The wind blows to the south and turns to the north; round and round it goes, ever returning on its course.... What has been done will be done again; there is nothing new under the sun. (Eccl. 1:5–9)

Then there is *linear* time, time as an inexorable sequence of cause and effect. The French astronomer Pierre-Simon Laplace gave this idea its most famous expression in 1814 when he said that if you "comprehend all the forces by which nature is animated and the respective situation of the beings that make it up," together with all the laws of physics and chemistry, then "nothing would be uncertain and the future just like the past would be open to its eyes."[4] Karl Marx applied this idea to society and history. It is known as "historical inevitability," and when transferred to the affairs of humankind it amounts to a massive denial of personal freedom.[5]

Finally, there is time as a mere *sequence of events* with no underlying plot or theme. This leads to the kind of historical writing pioneered by the scholars of ancient Greece, Herodotus and Thucydides.

Each of these has its place, the first in biology, the second in physics, the third in secular history, but none was time as the prophets understood it. The prophets saw time as the arena in which the great drama between God and humanity was played out, especially in the history of Israel. If Israel was faithful to its mission, its covenant, then it would flourish. If it was unfaithful it would fail. It would suffer defeat and exile. That is what Jeremiah never tired of telling his contemporaries.

The second prophetic insight was the unbreakable connection between monotheism and morality. Somehow the prophets sensed – it is implicit in all their words, though they do not explain it explicitly – that idolatry was not just false. It was also corrupting. It saw the universe as a multiplicity of powers that often clashed. The battle went to the strong. Might defeated right. The fittest survived while the weak perished. Nietzsche believed this, as did the social Darwinists.

4. Laplace, *Philosophical Essay on Probability* (New York: Springer New York, 1995), 2.
5. See Isaiah Berlin, *Historical Inevitability* (London: Oxford University Press, 1955).

The prophets opposed this with all their force. For them the power of God was secondary; what mattered was the righteousness of God. Precisely because God loved and had redeemed Israel, Israel owed Him loyalty as their sole ultimate sovereign. If they were unfaithful to God they would also be unfaithful to their fellow humans. They would lie, rob, cheat. Jeremiah doubts whether there was one honest person in the whole of Jerusalem (Jer. 5:1). They would become sexually adulterous and promiscuous: "I supplied all their needs, yet they committed adultery and thronged to the houses of prostitutes. They are well-fed, lusty stallions, each neighing for another man's wife" (5:7–8).

Their third great insight was the primacy of ethics over politics. The prophets have surprisingly little to say about politics.[6] Yes, Samuel was wary of monarchy but we find almost nothing in Isaiah or Jeremiah about the way Israel/Judah should be governed. Instead we hear a constant insistence that the strength of a nation – certainly of Israel/Judah – is not military or demographic but moral and spiritual. If the people keep faith with God and one another, no force on earth can defeat them. If they do not, no force can save them. As Jeremiah says in the *haftara* to *Parashat Masei*, they will discover too late that their false gods offered false comfort:

> They say to wood, "You are my father," and to stone, "You gave me birth." They have turned their backs to Me and not their faces; yet when they are in trouble, they say, "Come and save us!" Where then are the gods you made for yourselves? Let them come if they can save you when you are in trouble! For you have as many gods as you have towns, O Judah. (Jer. 2:27–28)

Jeremiah, the most passionate and tormented of all the prophets, has gone down in history as the prophet of doom. Yet this is unfair. He was also supremely a prophet of hope. He is the man who said that the People of Israel will be as eternal as the sun, moon, and stars (Jer. 31). He is the man who, while the Babylonians were laying siege to Jerusalem, bought a field as a public gesture of faith that Jews would return from exile: "For

---

6. See Michael Walzer, *In God's Shadow: Politics in the Hebrew Bible* (New Haven, CT: Yale University Press, 2012).

this is what the Lord Almighty, the God of Israel, says: Houses, fields, and vineyards will again be bought in this land" (Jer. 32:15).

Jeremiah's feelings of doom and hope were not in conflict; there were two sides to the same coin. The God who sentenced His people to exile would be the God who brought them back, for though His people might forsake Him, He would never forsake them. Jeremiah may have lost faith in people; he never lost faith in God.

Prophecy ceased in Israel with Haggai, Zechariah, and Malachi in the Second Temple era. But the prophetic truths have not ceased to be true. Only by being faithful to God do people stay faithful to one another. Only by being open to a power greater than themselves do people become greater than themselves. Only by understanding the deep forces that shape history can a people defeat the ravages of history. It took a long time for biblical Israel to learn these truths, and a very long time indeed before they returned to their land, re-entering the arena of history. We must never forget them again.

About the Author

An international religious leader, philosopher, award-winning author, and respected moral voice, Rabbi Lord Jonathan Sacks is the laureate of the 2016 Templeton Prize in recognition of his "exceptional contributions to affirming life's spiritual dimension." Described by HRH The Prince of Wales as "a light unto this nation" and by former British Prime Minister Tony Blair as "an intellectual giant," Rabbi Sacks is a frequent and sought-after contributor to radio, television, and the press, both in Britain and around the world.

He served as chief rabbi of the United Hebrew Congregations of the Commonwealth for twenty-two years, between 1991 and 2013. He holds seventeen honorary degrees, including a Doctor of Divinity conferred to mark his first ten years in office as chief rabbi, by the then-archbishop of Canterbury, Lord Carey.

In recognition of his work, Rabbi Sacks has won several international awards, including the Jerusalem Prize in 1995 for his contribution to Diaspora Jewish life, the Ladislaus Laszt Ecumenical and Social Concern Award from Ben-Gurion University in Israel in 2011, the Guardian of Zion Award from the Ingeborg Rennert Center for Jerusalem Studies at Bar-Ilan University, and the Katz Award in recognition of his contribution to the practical analysis and application of halakha in modern life in Israel in 2014. He was knighted by Her Majesty the Queen in 2005 and made a Life Peer, taking his seat in the House of Lords in October 2009.

The author of more than thirty books, Rabbi Sacks has published a new English translation and commentary for the *Koren Sacks Siddur*, the first new Orthodox siddur in a generation, as well as powerful commentaries for the *Rosh HaShana, Yom Kippur, Pesaḥ, Shavuot,* and *Sukkot Maḥzorim*. A number of his books have won literary awards. His most recent work, *Not in God's Name*, was awarded a 2015 National Jewish Book Award in America and was a top ten Sunday Times bestseller in the UK. Others include *The Dignity of Difference*, winner of the Grawemeyer Award in Religion in 2004 for its success in defining a framework for interfaith dialogue between people of all faiths and of none, and National Jewish Book Awards for *A Letter in the Scroll* in 2000, *Covenant & Conversation: Genesis* in 2009, and the *Koren Sacks Pesaḥ Maḥzor* in 2013. His Covenant & Conversation commentaries on the weekly Torah portion, which are translated into Hebrew, Spanish, Portuguese, and Turkish, are read in Jewish communities around the world.

After achieving first-class honours in philosophy at Gonville and Caius College, Cambridge, he pursued post-graduate studies in Oxford and London, gaining his doctorate in 1981 and receiving rabbinic ordination from Jews' College and Yeshivat Etz Chaim. He served as the rabbi for Golders Green Synagogue and Marble Arch Synagogue in London before becoming principal of Jews' College.

Born in 1948 in London, he has been married to Elaine since 1970. They have three children and several grandchildren.

www.rabbisacks.org / @RabbiSacks

The fonts used in this book are from the Arno family

The Covenant & Conversation Series:

Genesis: The Book of Beginnings
Exodus: The Book of Redemption
Leviticus: The Book of Holiness
Numbers: The Wilderness Years
Deuteronomy: Renewal of the Sinai Covenant

Ceremony and Celebration
Lessons in Leadership
Essays on Ethics

Maggid Books
The best of contemporary Jewish thought from
Koren Publishers Jerusalem Ltd.